Understanding
MICROECONOMICS

Ninth Edition

Robert L. Heilbroner
The New School for Social Research

James K. Galbraith
University of Texas—Austin
Lyndon B. Johnson School of Public Affairs

PRENTICE HALL, ENGLEWOOD CLIFFS, NJ 07632

Library of Congress Cataloging-in-Publication Data

Heilbroner, Robert L.
Understanding microeconomics / Robert L. Heilbroner, James K. Galbraith. -
- 9th [ed.]
   p.   cm.
Includes index.
ISBN 0-13-933367-3
1. Microeconomics. I. Galbraith, James K. II. Title.
HB172.H44 1990
338.5--dc20   89-15936
                                                               CIP

Editorial/production supervision: Susan Fisher and Anne Pietropinto
Interior design: Natasha Sylvester, Maureen Eide, and Janet Schmid
Cover design: Bruce Kenselaar
Manufacturing buyer: Laura Crossland and Peter Havens

©1990, 1987, 1984, 1978, 1975 by Prentice-Hall Inc.
A Division of Simon & Schuster
Englewood Cliffs, New Jersey 07632
©1972, 1968 by Robert L. Heilbroner

Printed in the United States of America

10 9 8 7 6 5 4 3 2 1

ISBN 0-13-933367-3

Prentice-Hall International (UK) Limited, *London*
Prentice-Hall of Australia Pty. Limited, *Sydney*
Prentice-Hall Canada Inc., *Toronto*
Prentice-Hall Hispanoamericana, S.A., *Mexico*
Prentice-Hall of India Private Limited, *New Delhi*
Prentice-Hall of Japan, Inc., *Tokyo*
Simon & Schuster Asia Pte. Ltd., *Singapore*
Editora Prentice-Hall do Brasil, Ltda., *Rio de Janeiro*

Contents

PART ⅠⅠ   *SOME BASIC ECONOMICS*

Supply and Demand   The Market Clears   Characteristics of Equilibrium
Prices   Does "Demand" Equal "Supply"?   The Role of Competition   **Shifts in
Demand and Supply**   Shifts in Curves vs. Movements along Curves   Price
Changes   Long and Short Run   A Last Word on Maximizing

Instead of Buying   Privatizing Public Goods?   **Externalities**   Pollution
"Bads" Escape the Market   Marginal Private and Social Costs   **Controlling
Externalities**   1. Regulation   2. Taxation   3. Subsidies   Externalities in
Review   Market Strengths and Weaknesses

Taxes   Total Incidence   Tax Reform   **Public Spending**   Voting vs. Spending—The Public Choice Perspective   Is Spending Rational?   **Cost-Benefit Analysis**   Calculating Costs and Benefits   Cost Effectiveness   Sunk Costs "Throwing Good Money After Bad"   **The Market in Final Retrospect   An Extra Word About Fair Taxation**

Section Three: *Microeconomic Challenges*

PART IV *THE REST OF THE WORLD*

Preface

Here is the ninth edition of *Understanding Microeconomics.* That makes this book slightly older than some of its readers. It clearly labels us as belonging to the generation of Methuselah.

How can microeconomics have changed so much over the year to warrant all these editions? Partly, books simply get out of date. Statistics have to be brought up to the moment, or as close as we can get. History has to be unrolled a little further. New problems suddenly rise up and demand a whole chapter to themselves.

As before we have tried to combine a concern for contemporary problems, such as the impact of market processes on the environment, with the clearest possible presentation of the central issues of price theory and resource allocation. Microeconomics, for all the allure of its big brother macro-theory, is where the deep core of modern eonomic analysis is concentrated. It is the indispensable tool for anyone who wants to be an economist.

As before we have tried to combine a concern for contemporary problems, such as the impact of market processes on the environment, with the clearest possible presentation of the central issues of price theory and resource allocation. Microeconomics, for all the allure of its big brother macro-theory is where the deep core of modern economic analysis is concentrated. It is the indispensable tool for anyone who wants to be an economist.

It is a great satisfaction for us that our text has been used for so many years. May this new edition have a very long life! That would mean that no new issues will come to the fore, and that everything we say remains as cogent three or four years hence as we hope it is now. Judging by the past, there's little chance of that!

About the Authors

Photo by Waring Abbott

Photo by Maria de la Luz Martinez

Robert L. Heilbroner began his studies in economics at Harvard University, from which he graduated, summa cum laude, in 1940; and went on to complete his graduate work at the New School for Social Research in New York City. While still a graduate student, he published his first book, *The Worldly Philosophers,* which quickly became a standard introduction to economics in hundreds of colleges. Later books, including *The Making of Economic Society* and *An Inquiry into the Human Prospect,* together with a wide variety of articles in both scholarly and popular journals, won for him a wide audience as both economic historian and social philosopher. Dr. Heilbroner has been the recipient of numerous awards and honors, including election as vice president of the American Economic Association. He teaches at his graduate alma mater as Normal Thomas Professor, specializing in the history of economic thought. He is married and lives in New York City.

James K. Galbraith is Associate Professor at the Lyndon B. Johnson School of Public Affairs, University of Texas at Austin. Before becoming a Texan, he served on the staff of the U.S. Congress, including as executive director of the Joint Economic Committee, where he was responsible for congressional oversight of monetary policy and of the Reagan economic program. He has been a Visiting Scholar at the Brookings Institution and a Marshall Scholar at King's College, University of Cambridge. He holds an A.B. from Harvard College and a Ph.D. in economics from Yale University. He is married to Lucy Ferguson Galbraith, a microeconomist. They have a son, Douglas, and daughter, Margaret, who shares her birthday (June 5) with Adam Smith and John Maynard Keynes. A prolific writer, Dr. Galbraith's most recent book is *Balancing Acts: Technology, Finance and the American Future.*

PART I

THE ECONOMIC BACKGROUND

CHAPTER 1

What This Book Is All About

A LOOK AHEAD

This is the chapter in which to get your bearings. As you read, keep in mind these objectives:

1 To get a feel for what is to come.
2 To learn how the book is organized.
3 Most important of all, to pick up a few study hints—you really want to pay attention to these.

THE ECONOMIC MYSTIQUE

*L*ike most students who begin a first course in economics, you probably realize that economics is terribly important. You also probably have the uneasy feeling that it is terribly difficult. It may reassure you to learn that you are not alone in this frame of mind. Every year national pollsters report that economic problems, such as inflation or unemployment or taxes, rank high among the public's worries. But every year the pollsters also discover that the economics and business pages of newspapers and magazines are those that are *least* read. It seems that we all worry about economic matters, but throw up our hands at the idea of trying to understand what they are all about.

Why does economics have this curious mystique? Three reasons suggest themselves.

1. Mystery of Money

The first is that economics is intrinsically involved with money, and money is, well, perplexing. Why is a piece of paper worth anything at all? What do banks do with the money we put into them? Why isn't there enough money to go around at some times, "too much" money at others—to repeat the baffling opinions we hear?

Money is surely one reason for the economic mystique. But the problem with money is not just its inherent complexity. It is that we all use money, talk about money, worry about money, without ever having been educated about it. One purpose of learning economics is to repair that serious omission in our knowledge.

2. Language of Economics

A second reason is that economics speaks in a tongue we don't quite understand. "Prices are up because of rising demand," says the TV commentator, and we nod our heads. But exactly what is "demand"? What makes it "rise"? And those other words that the commentators use with such assurance—gross national product, consumption, investment—what do they really mean? Because we do not "speak" economics, we wonder whether we are being bamboozled; and when we ourselves use the words of economics, we often know that we are partly bluffing.

Therefore another purpose of this book is to introduce you to the language of economics. This language, like that of all disciplines, has a fair number of specialized terms, but it is certainly no more difficult to speak or to understand than the language of any of a dozen familiar subjects. By the end of the course, you should speak it pretty fluently.

3. The "Difficulty" of Economics

Last, there is the matter of the mystique itself, the reputation for difficulty that economics has acquired. It may come as a surprise to learn that in the 1830s economics was reputed to be a rather easy subject, especially suited to the education of proper young ladies. Later—indeed, up to the Great Crash of 1929— economics was still widely regarded as little more than common sense, instantly comprehensible by all right-thinking persons, especially if they thought along Solid Business Principles.

The aura of mystery that clings to economics today is mainly a product of the past generation or so, when economics itself came into national prominence. The aura is undoubtedly mixed up with the increased use of government powers in the economy, especially the use of spending and taxing to affect the level of national well-being. Here *is* something to be learned that is different from Solid Business Principles. But as you will discover, it is still nothing but logical thought, although applied from a national perspective, rather than from that of an individual enterprise.

Thus the overriding aim of our book is to demystify economics. Of course this does not mean that we can give you answers to all the problems of the economy. We don't know them. But we hope that when you finish the book, you will never again throw up your hands at the idea of *thinking* about economic problems. Once and for all, that should have lost its terror.

ORGANIZING THE SUBJECT

Economics is a very large subject with many aspects—economic history, economic statistics, economic theory, economic policy, and still others. We cannot study all these aspects in an introductory text, but it will help you grasp the larger subject of economics if we outline very generally what lies ahead.

We have organized our book into five major *parts,* each one of which has groups of related chapters or *sections.* The five major parts are these:

1. Economic history and background
2. Economic science
3. The study of the macro system of economic growth
4. The market mechanism, or microeconomics
5. International economics

Different instructors will have different inclinations about what parts to stress, and we have written the text to allow as much flexibility as possible in planning a coherent course. Even if there is no time to study all the parts of the text, you ought to glance at them to round out your understanding of what the dimensions of the subject embrace.

THE FIRST PART: ECONOMIC BACKGROUND

Many students would like to jump right into the midst of our current economic problems, and some instructors like to teach their courses that way. In fact, our book is organized so that a direct approach to major issues is possible by starting in macroeconomics or microeconomics.

But ideally we ought to acquire some perspective on our subject before getting embroiled in how things work. We ought, for example, to have a good working idea of economic history—of how our economy got where it is. We should know at least the rudiments of what some great economists of the past have said about how the economic system works. And we should be familiar with the economy in the same sense that we are familiar with the size and shape of the United States and where its great rivers and mountain ranges are.

That is what Part One is about. Chapter 2 gives you a jet-speed voyage through economic history. Chapter 3 takes you rapidly down the gallery of the world's great economists—the "worldly philosophers." Then, in three successive chapters, we fly you over the economic continent and then over the economic planet. *Try to read these chapters as background, even if your instructor doesn't assign them as classwork.*

NEXT: FROM FACT TO THEORY

In Part Two we turn to a very different subject—the core elements of economic "science." We put the word in quotes because, as you will discover, our subject both is and is not a science like the natural sciences. It has aspects that very much resemble sciences like physics, and aspects that are much more akin to studies like government or morality.

The science-like aspect has to do with the fact that the economic world, for all its variety and complexity, can often be understood in a highly generalized, abstract way. As a result, economists do not consider their task to be only that of describing phenomena, such as we have done in Part One. They also seek to find similar characteristics hidden within seemingly different problems or institutions, much as a doctor first takes a patient's life history and then examines him or her for signs of a general condition called a "disease."

In Chapter 7 we tell you something about the basis on which this capacity for generalization and abstraction rests. It is our introduction to the idea of *economic theory.* Then in Chapter 8 we go on to apply theory to the single most widely used generalization about economic life—supply and demand. Thereafter, to balance the picture, we look at another side of economics in a chapter whose subject matter you must surely have wondered about: "Why Economists Disagree." Finally, in Chapter 10 we add a kind of appendix to Part Two in a "Kit of Tools." Here is a brief introduction to the basic technical elements you will have to know, from how to read a chart to how to say some easy but powerful things in mathematical sentences. Many students will not need this chapter at all; others may find it a lifesaver.

THE MICROECONOMIC SIDE: PART THREE

Microeconomics is every bit as interesting and important as its well-known brother, macroeconomics—some economists would say more interesting and more important. It certainly offers a clearer perspective on some kinds of issues than can be gained from the macroeconomic vantage point.

As with macro, we have organized the micro portion of our text into a series of sections—chapters that fit together to make a unit of study. The first of these, Chapters 11 through 13, takes us through the workings of the market system itself, just as the first part of macro took us through the basic mechanisms of growth. The next section, Chapters 14 to 17, brings a new subject to our attention—the unit of business enterprise that economists call "the firm." Unless we understand how the firm operates, we can't really understand how the market system works.

The third micro section, Chapters 18 through 21, brings us to the counterpart of the challenges confronting macroeconomics. Here we look into poverty, welfare, regulation, and other questions, all as unsettled as their macro sisters. Once again, we have tried to show both sides of these issues, as well as our own diagnosis.

THE REST OF THE WORLD: PART FOUR

Traditionally, there has been a terrible parochialism to American economics. It has tended to assume that learning about domestic issues, macro and micro, was really all a student—especially a beginning student—had to do. The rest of the world was relegated to the back pages of texts, and to the second and third years of economic studies.

As our text illustrates, this indifference to international economic problems is no longer the rule. Already in Chapter 6 we have looked into the ways in which the American economy is entangled with the economics of other nations, and an international theme has surfaced again and again in our studies of both macro- and microeconomics.

Nevertheless, there are aspects and elements of international economics that do have to be postponed until a student has some working grasp of the fundamentals. These are the matters we take up in this part, where the mysteries of the exchange rate and of international competition are examined.

HOW SHOULD YOU STUDY ECONOMICS?

Vocabulary

We have already stressed the importance of acquiring a new economic vocabulary. **To become economists, you will have to learn several dozen words and phrases that have meanings somewhat different from those of everyday usage:** *capital, investment, demand,* **for example.** You will have to master another dozen or so phrases that come awkwardly to the tongue (and sometimes not at all to the mind): *marginal propensity to consume* is a good example.

In economics, as in French, some people acquire new words and phrases easily, some do not; and in economics, as in French, until you can say things correctly, you are apt to say them very wrongly. So when the text says *gross private domestic investment* those are the words to be learned, not just any combination of three of them because they seem to mean the same thing. Fortunately, the necessary economic vocabulary has far fewer words than French has, and the long and awkward phrases seem shorter and easier after you've said them a few times.

Diagrams

Associated with learning the vocabulary of economics is learning how to draw a few diagrams. Diagrams are an immensely powerful way of presenting many economic ideas. Far from complicating things, they simplify them enormously. A supply and demand diagram makes things immediately clear in a way that a dozen pages could not.

So you must learn to draw a few diagrams. There is a great temptation to do so hastily, without thinking about the problem that the diagram is trying to make clear. A little care in labeling your axes (how else can anyone know what the diagram is about?) or in making lines tangent where they are supposed to touch, or cross where they are supposed to intersect, will not only make the difference between a poor grade and a better one, but will demonstrate that you truly understand the matter being illustrated.

You will also note that throughout the book, with each figure and most tables, a sentence or a paragraph highlights the point being made. This should help you in reviewing the material.

Key Ideas

Studying a vast subject requires organization. This means putting first things first and keeping details and secondary material in the background.

We've tried to simplify the task of learning by putting a highly abbreviated and goal-oriented "A Look Ahead" and "Looking Back" at the beginning and at the end of each chapter. These sections do not necessarily embrace all the vocabulary or ideas in each chapter; instead, they try to give you objectives to bear in mind before starting, and summaries to collect your thoughts when you're done.

At the end of each chapter, first read the general review. Then look only at Key Concepts to see if you can reproduce that review. Last, a glance at Economic Vocabulary will serve as a final test. Page numbers follow each word for easy reference.

Questions and Extra Words

Next, take time to answer all the questions at the ends of chapters. We have tried to make them few and central. If your instructor assigns the Student Guide that accompanies this text, do those problems too. There is no substitute for working out an example or for jotting down three reasons for this, four reasons for that. Learning is a process about which we know very little, but we do know that the physical and intellectual act of writing (or mumbling to yourself) is much more effective than merely thinking. Practice, as they say, makes perfect. You might reflect on the story of the sailor on a sinking ship. When asked if he knew how to swim, he answered, "Well, I understand the theory of it . . ."

Economics has to be learned by arguing about it. Therefore after many chapters you will find a few additional pages—sometimes to add to your historical, statistical, or analytic knowledge, more often to open for your consideration problems of public policy that are related to the issues we have studied. The policy issues are often controversial. We hope you will worry about them—not just read them. They are there to open debate, not close it.

Analysis and Abstraction

The idea of arguing brings us to our last word of counsel. Economics, as we have been at pains to say, is really not a hard language to learn. The key words and concepts are not too many or too demanding; the diagrams are no more difficult than those of elementary geometry. It is economic *thinking* that is hard, in a way that may have something to do with the aura of mystery we are out to dispel.

The hardness is not the sheer mental ability that is required. The reason lies, rather, in **a special attribute of economic thought:** *its abstract, analytic character.* Abstractness does not imply indifference to the problems of the real world. Economics is about things as real as being without work. Nevertheless, as economists we do not study unemployment to learn firsthand about the miseries and sufferings that joblessness inflicts. We study unemployment to understand and analyze the causes of this malfunction of the economic system. Similarly, we do not study monopoly to fulminate against the profiteering of greedy capitalists, or labor unions to deplore the abuse of power by labor leaders, or government spending to declaim against politicians. We study these matters to shed light on their mechanisms, their reasons for being, their consequences.

There is nothing unusual in this abstract, analytic approach. All disciplines necessarily abstract from the immediate realities of their subject matters so that they may make broader generalizations or develop theories. What makes abstraction so difficult in economics is that the problems of the discipline are things that affect us deeply in our lives. It is difficult, even unnatural, to suppress our feelings of approval or anger when we study the operations of the economic system and the main actors in it. The necessary act of analysis thus becomes mixed up with feelings of economic concern or even partisanship. **Yet, unless we make an effort to think analytically and abstractly in a detached way, we can be no more than slaves to our unexamined emotions.** Someone who *knows* that corporations or labor unions or governments are "good" or "bad" does not have to study economics, for the subject has nothing to teach such a person.

You must therefore make an effort to put aside your natural partisanship and prejudice while you study the problems of economics from its abstract, analytic, detached perspective. After you are done, your feelings will assuredly come back to you. No one has ever lost a sense of social outrage or social justice by taking a course in economics. But many students have changed or modified their preconceived judgments in one way or another. There is no escape, after all, from living in the world as economic citizens. But there is the option of living in it as intelligent and effective economic citizens. That is the prize we hope you carry away from this course.

CHAPTER 2

The Evolution of Capitalism

A LOOK AHEAD

There is one central idea this chapter will present—a very simple but exceedingly important idea. It is that capitalism—our Western economic society—represents a dramatic change in the way that humankind has grappled with its economic problems. In this chapter we will trace three main aspects of this change:

1 The emergence of a market system.
2 The development of a powerful industrial technology.
3 The assertion of political limits on the economic machinery.

The purpose of this chapter is not only to review these critical elements of economic history, but also to make you think about the subject of economics itself in a historical, evolutionary way.

WHERE DID CAPITALISM COME FROM?

*T*he economic system we are going to study in this book is called **capitalism,** or sometimes the *free enterprise system.* In a way, we all know about capitalism because it surrounds us. It is the world we live in. But the question we are going to start with is far removed from our daily experience: Where did capitalism come from? How did the free enterprise system come to be?

People sometimes talk about capitalism as if it were as old as the hills, as ancient as the Bible. Yet this is clearly not the case. Nobody ever called the Egyptian pharaohs "capitalists." The Greeks about whom Homer wrote were not a business society, even though there were merchants and traders in Greece; neither was imperial Rome a capitalist system. Medieval Europe was certainly not capitalist. Nor would anyone use the word *capitalist* to describe the brilliant civilizations of India and China, about which Marco Polo wrote, or the great empires of ancient Africa or the Islamic economies of which we catch glimpses in *The Arabian Nights.*

We will make explicit why these were not capitalist economies in a moment. But we must begin by realizing that capitalism is a modern economic system—and furthermore, a geographically limited one. **Most of the people in the world's history never had any direct contact with it. Even today, less than half of the world's population lives in a system that we would call capitalist—though events could change that picture over the next few decades.**

The Elements of Capitalism

What is capitalism? The fact that the system appears in history only after many thousands of years suggests that we would do well to search for its identifying characteristics in historic changes rather than in specific institutions that exist today. Here are three of the changes that help us recognize capitalism as a unique development in the organization of human affairs.

1. CAPITALISM BECOMES VISIBLE WHEN ECONOMIC ACTIVITY BECOMES DE-TACHED FROM THE ACTIVITY OF THE STATE. Economic activity refers to all the tasks carried on in society to produce and distribute wealth. Before capitalism, those activities were bound up with the exercise of rulership itself. Precapitalist societies were large, imperial kingdoms in some cases and small domains ruled by local lords in others. Yet in all these societies, large or small, production and distribution were carried on under the supervision of the ruler. The peasant working in the field and the artisan in his workshop were not working for their own account. They were directly or indirectly carrying out orders from overlords, for whose power and glory their labors would be used. Such societies have been described as "tributary" systems—a telling phrase that emphasizes the subordination of economic activity to the benefit of political elites.

Merchants, who *did* carry on economic activity for their own account, also existed in these societies. But they were at the fringes of society, not at its center. The provision of the essentials of state power and continuity—basic foodstuffs, for example, or weapons—was not entrusted to the pull and tug of mercantile activity.

So a decisive change that marks the emergence of capitalism as a new mode of social organization was the spread of market activity into every area of economic life.

Shortly we shall see how this took place. But here we need to note an important consequence of that spread. As buying and selling expanded, the authority of the state shrank. Within the state a new entity appeared—an *economy* whose function was to carry on the production and distribution of wealth. The economy thus appears as a kind of state within a state, a realm of society containing the vital activities formerly carried on as part of the overall exercise of authority from above. **Thus capitalism brings into being a new sphere of private economic activity —activity conducted for the self-interest of its actors.**

This new private sphere is the root of one of the most important political accomplishments of capitalism, the establishment of economic freedom, a theme to which we will often revert. But it is crucial not to think of capitalism as consisting only of private economic activity. The state persists under capitalism, not merely to carry on its traditional functions of waging war and maintaining peace and internal order, but also to provide essential services to the private sphere of activity—roads and ports, public works needed for health and safety, courts and coinage, to name only a few. Thus the public sphere shrinks as capitalism emerges, but it does not disappear. The state is indispensable for the operation of a market economy, in ways we will talk about many times in the pages to follow.

It is also clear, however, that there is a deep tension between the economic and political activities of a capitalist state. This tension is not just a passing "political" issue, but comes from the very nature of the system, which creates two realms of authority where formerly there was only one.

2. CAPITALISM IS MARKED BY ITS DYNAMIC SEARCH FOR THE ACCUMULATION OF MATERIAL WEALTH. The next historic change follows from the first. It is the extraordinary dynamism developed by capitalism, a dynamism that takes the form of an unprecedented piling up of wealth in a new form—not for consumption and display, but as capital.

Here a glance backward serves to illustrate the point. Precapitalist societies were certainly capable of accumulating staggering displays of wealth. No single creation of capitalism is likely to endure as long as the pyramids of Egypt, the Great Wall of China, the monuments of the Incas, or the stupendous cathedrals of medieval Europe.

Yet when we look back over the empires that built these monuments, what strikes us is how changeless was the tenor of most people's daily lives. The boundaries of empires might expand or contract, great works might take shape over a ruler's lifetime, but the level of mass existence varied little for generations. The diet, the housing, the clothing and material possessions of the Egyptian peasants at the time of Napoleon's invasion of Egypt differed little from those of the time of Cheops, builder of pyramids. The level of material life of the French craftspeople who labored on the cathedral of Chartres was not substantially different from that of their ancestors who helped the Roman legions construct the aqueducts through Gaul.

It is this basically static quality of life that capitalism removes. Economic historian W.W. Rostow has estimated that between the age of the American

Revolution and our own times, the volume of manufactured goods increased by *seventeen hundred times.** This is a display of expansion and accumulation beside which the achievements of prior civilizations pale into insignificance. Nothing resembling such a force for the creation of material wealth had ever existed before.

What was the source of this accumulative thrust? Essentially it was the very change we have just noted—namely, the emergence of a realm of economic life separated from the state itself. In the previous "tributary" mode of organizing economic life, the surplus of society's production was devoted to the construction of monuments to glorify its rulers or affirm its religious faith, or was used for arms to protect the kingdom or for the luxury goods through which imperial majesty displayed itself to the world.

For the new mercantile groups economic activity had a different aim—not to display wealth, but to accumulate it as a route to power and prestige. This required that wealth take the form of capital. What is capital? It is wealth that can be used to create still more wealth. The humblest commodities can be capital as well as the most dazzling jewels, as long as they are sold to gain still more wealth. **This use of wealth as capital rather than as a means of display or of luxury consumption was the vital difference brought about by the detachment of the economic sphere of life from the state.**

The consequences of the drive for the accumulation of capital are immense—indeed, capitalism derives its name from a recognition of the central importance of this propulsive force. One of these consequences is instability: The system is bursting with energy when the accumulation of wealth goes smoothly, wracked with economic and social troubles when it does not. A major theme of economics is to investigate this sequence of fast and slow accumulation—of growth and stagnation, boom and bust, prosperity and depression—that capitalism brings.

But another consequence deserves special attention at this initial stage of our inquiry: It is the encouragement given by capitalism to the development of technology as a principal means from which the expansive tendency of the system gains its momentum and through which it exerts its impact on daily life. At the end of this chapter we will look more closely into technology and its special significance for capitalism.

3. Capitalism Develops a New Mechanism for Its Internal Guidance.
The mechanism was the market system—not just individual markets, but a network of interconnected markets that would guide the production and distribution of economic activity as a whole. We will spend much of this book learning how such a market system serves as a guidance mechanism for capitalism. Here we want once again to see the rise of such a system in a manner that helps us identify, and therefore understand, the larger historic change itself.

How did the market system come into being? The answer is that a vast revolution undermined an older world of tradition and command, and brought into existence a world in which not only goods, but also the services of labor, land, and capital were offered for sale. We have a name for the services of labor, land, and capital that are hired or fired in a market society. They are called the **factors of production,** and a great deal of economics is about how the market combines their

*W. W. Rostow, *The World Economy* (Austin, TX: University of Texas Press, 1978), p. 48.

essential contributions to production. But just because they *are* essential, a question must be answered. How were the factors of production put to use prior to the market system? The answer tells us a great deal.

There were no factors of production before capitalism. Of course, human labor, nature's gift of land and natural resources, and the artifacts of society have always existed. But labor, land, and capital were not commodities for sale. Labor was part of the social duties of a slave or a serf, a peasant bound to his lord and master, who was not paid "wages" for doing his work. Indeed, the serf paid fees to his lord for the use of the lord's equipment, and he never expected to be remunerated when he turned over a portion of his crop as the lord's due. Land was regarded as the basis for military power or civil administration, just as a state is regarded today—not as real estate to be bought and sold. And capital was thought of as "treasure" or as the necessary equipment of an artisan, not as an abstract sum of wealth with a market value. The idea of liquid, fluid capital would have been as strange in medieval life as we would find it strange to think of stocks and bonds as heirlooms never to be sold.

The Economic Revolution

How did wageless labor, unrentable land, and private treasures become "factors of production"; that is, homogeneous commodities to be bought and sold like so many yards of cloth or bushels of wheat? Beginning roughly in the sixteenth century—although with roots that can be traced much further back—a process of change, sometimes gradual, sometimes violent, broke the bonds and customs of the medieval world of Europe and ushered in the market society we know.

We can only touch on that long, tortuous, and sometimes bloody revolution here. In England the process bore with particular severity on the peasants, who were expelled from the common grazing lands, which were then "enclosed" to make private pasturage for the lord's sheep, whose wool had become a profitable commodity. As late as 1820, the Duchess of Sutherland evicted 15,000 tenants from 794,000 acres, replacing them with 131,000 sheep. The tenants, deprived of their traditional access to the fields, drifted into the towns, where they were forced, for the first time, to sell their services as a factor of production: *labor*.

In France the creation of factors of production bore painfully on the traditional landowners, less so on the peasants. When prices began to rise in sixteenth-century Europe as gold from the New World flowed in, feudal lords found themselves in a terrible squeeze. While the rents and dues they received from their serfs were fixed and unchangeable, the prices of merchandise they needed to buy were not fixed. Although more and more of the serfs' obligations were converted from "kind" to cash, and from physical duties to money dues, prices kept rising so fast that the feudal lords found it impossible to meet their bills.

Hence we begin to find a new economic individual, the *impoverished aristocrat*. In the year 1530, in the Gévaudan region of France, the richest manorial lord had an income of 5,000 livres; but in towns some merchants had incomes of 65,000 livres. Thus the balance of power turned against the landed aristocracy, reducing many to shabby gentility. The upstart merchants lost no time in acquiring lands that they soon came to regard not as ancestral estates, but as potential capital.

This brief glance at economic history brings home an important point. **The factors of production, without which a market society could not exist, are not eternal attributes of a natural order. They are the creations of a process of historic change, a change that divorced labor from social life, that created real estate out of ancestral land, and that made treasure into capital. Capitalism is the outcome of a revolutionary change—a change in laws, attitudes, and social relationships as deep and far-reaching as any in history.***

Freedom and Necessity

The revolutionary aspect of capitalism lies in the fact that an older, feudal way of life had to be dismantled before the market system could come into being. This brings us to think again about the economic freedom that accompanies the rise of a private sector of economic life, detached from the state. For we can now see that economic freedom did not arise just because men and women directly sought to shake off the bonds of custom and command. It was also thrust upon them, often as a very painful and unwelcome change.

For feudalism, with all its cruelties and injustices, did provide a modicum of economic security. However mean a serf's life, he could not be arbitrarily thrown off the lord's land, and in bad times he was guaranteed a small dole from his lord's granary. However exploited a medieval journeyman, at least he knew that he could not be summarily thrown out of work under the rules of his master's guild. And however squeezed a lord, he too knew that his rents and dues were secured by law and custom and would be coming in, weather permitting.

The eruption of the market system destroyed all of that. The creation of factors of production meant the end of assured livelihoods. If a landless laborer could not find work, his unemployment was not the responsibility of his lord, for he no longer *had* a lord. Nor was it the lookout of his former employer, who had no obligation to pay anyone who was no longer an employee. If a worker in the market system was fired, he or she could not complain to the guild, because there *was* no guild. For that matter, neither could an employer protest to the guild about some intruder who was "stealing" trade. And if a landlord's rents declined in a bad year, that was no one's worry but his own; there were no more "customary" rents to rely on.

Economic freedom therefore meant that each person was thrown into the marketplace to sink or swim. This freedom could be a precious achievement for individuals who had formerly been deprived of the right to enter into legal contracts. For many, it meant the chance to rise out of a station in life from which, in earlier times, there was no exit. But economic freedom had another equally important aspect. This was the necessity to stay afloat by one's own efforts in rough waters where all were struggling to survive, and where no one much cared when a

---

*One of the many fascinating questions that surround the origins of capitalism is why it arose only in Europe, and never in any other part of the world. The probable explanation is that the collapse of the Roman Empire left many towns without an allegiance to anyone. In time, these towns, which were naturally centers of trading and artisan work, grew powerful and managed to bargain for privileges with kings and lords. Capitalism thus grew up in the chinks and crevices of the medieval system. A similar opportunity and stimulus did not present itself elsewhere. Is it possible that capitalism is now appearing in the Soviet Union, Eastern Europe, and China? We will turn to this momentous question at the end of our book.

laborer, a landowner, or a capitalist disappeared from view.

The market system was thus the cause of unrest, insecurity, and individual suffering, just as it was also the source of progress, opportunity, and fulfillment. In this contest between the costs and benefits of economic freedom lies a theme that is still a crucial issue for capitalism.

THE UNLEASHING OF TECHNOLOGY

As we have already noted, the creation of a market society paved the way for a change of profound significance. This was the incorporation of science and technology into the very midst of daily life.

Precapitalist Technology

Technology is not, of course, a modern phenomenon. The arrangement of the gigantic stones that form prehistoric Stonehenge, the precision and delicacy of the monumental Egyptian pyramids, the Incan stone walls fitted so exactly that a knife blade cannot be put between adjoining blocks, the Chinese Great Wall, and the Mayan observatories attest to mankind's long possession of the ability to transport and hoist staggering weights, to cut and shape hard surfaces, and to calculate complex problems. Indeed, many of these works would challenge our present-day engineering capabilities.

Nonetheless, although precapitalist technology reached great heights, it had a very restricted base. The basic tools of agriculture and artisan crafts remained little changed over millennia. So "simple" an invention as a horse collar shaped to prevent a straining animal from pressing against its windpipe did not appear during all the glories of Greece and triumphs of Rome. Not until the Middle Ages was there a switch from the ox to the draft horse as a ploughing animal (a change that improved efficiency by an estimated 30 percent), or was the traditional two-field system of crop rotation improved by adopting a three-field system (see box).

Thus precapitalist technology was lavished on the needs of rulers, priests, and warriors; its potential application to the everyday work of ordinary people was virtually ignored.

THE DIFFERENCE TECHNOLOGY MAKES: THREE FIELDS VS. TWO

Until the Middle Ages, the prevailing system of cultivation was to plant half of a lord's arable land in a winter crop, leaving the other half fallow. The second year, the two fields simply changed functions.

Under the three-field plan, the arable land was divided into thirds. One section was planted with a winter crop, one section with a summer crop, and one was left fallow. The second year, the first section was put into summer crops, the second left fallow, and the third put into winter grains. In the third year, the first field was left fallow, the second used for winter crops, the third for spring planting.

Therefore, under the three-field system only one-third, not one-half, of the arable land was fallow in any year. Suppose that the field as a whole yielded 600 bushels of output. Under the two-field system, it would give an annual crop of 300 bushels. Under the three-field system, the annual crop would be two-thirds of the area, or 400 bushels—an increase of one-third. Further, in those days it was customary to plough fallow land twice and cultivated land only once. By cutting down the ratio of fallow to cultivated land, plowing time was greatly reduced, and peasant productivity even more significantly improved. For more on this and other fascinating advances in precapitalist technology, see Lynn White, *Medieval Technology and Social Change* (Oxford: Clarendon Press, 1962).

Why Technology Slumbered

There were, of course, good reasons why the technology of daily life was ignored. The primary effect of technological change in daily activity is to increase output, to enhance the productivity of the working person. But in a society still regulated by tradition and command, where production was mainly carried on by serfs and slaves and custom-bound artisans, there was little incentive to look for increases in output. The bulk of any increase in agricultural yields would only go to the lord, the king, or the church, not to the serf or the slave who produced them. Indeed, what would happen to the serfs if means were found to work the lands with fewer of them?

So, too, any artisan who altered the techniques of his trade would be expected, as a matter of course, to share these advances with his brethren. And how could his brethren, accustomed over the years to disposing of a certain quantity of pots or pans or cloth in the village market, expect to find buyers for more output? Would not the extra production—and the artisans responsible for it—simply go begging?

Thus productive technology in precapitalist societies slumbered because there was no incentive to search for change. Indeed, because technological change could only introduce an unsettling element into the world, powerful social forces were ranged against it. A society whose whole way of life rested on the reproduction of established patterns of existence could not even imagine a world where the technology of production was constantly in flux and where limits were no longer recognized in any endeavor.

Economic Life in the Middle Ages, Illustrated in the Breviarium Grimani
(The Bettmann Archive, Inc.)

The Incentive of Capitalism

These inhibiting forces were ruthlessly swept away by the emerging markets for labor, land, and capital. Serfs were uprooted to become workers forced to sell their labor power for wages; landlords were rudely shouldered aside by money-minded parvenus; guild masters and artisans watched commercial enterprises take away their accustomed livelihood; a new sense of necessity, of urgency, altered economic life. What had been a more or less unchanging routine of life became increasingly a scramble for existence.

The growing importance of the market, where a producer had to win a place for himself every day, radically altered the place of technology, especially in the small workshops and miniscule factories that were the staging areas of the capitalist revolution. Here the economic free-for-all forced people to look for toeholds in the struggle for a livelihood. And one toehold available to any aspiring capitalist with an inquiring mind and a knowledge of the actual processes of production was technology itself—some invention or improvement that would lower costs or change a product to give it an edge on its competitors.

This is where the appearance of wealth as *capital* made an enormous difference. It brought into being a wholly new personage in economic history—the *industrial capitalist* who made his wealth in pursuits that would never have led to riches in another age.*

For example, there was John Wilkinson, son of an iron producer who became a driving force for technical change in his trade. Wilkinson insisted that everything be built of iron—pipes and bridges, bellows and cylinders (one of which powered the newfangled steam engine of James Watt). He even constructed a much derided iron ship—later much admired. There was Richard Arkwright, barber by trade, who made his fortune by inventing (or perhaps by stealing) the first effective spinning machine, becoming in time a great mill owner. There were Peter Onions, an obscure foreman who originated the puddling process for making wrought iron; Benjamin Huntsman, a clockmaker who improved the method of making steel; and a score more. "A wave of gadgets swept over England," in the copybook phrase of an English schoolboy. A few of the "gadgeteers," like Sir Jethro Tull, a pioneer in the technology of agriculture, were great gentlemen, but most of the technological leaders in industry were men of humble origin.

---

*This is not a text in economic history, and therefore we must pass too quickly over a change of great importance in the evolution of the system. It is the leap from the earliest form of *merchant capitalism* into *industrial capitalism,* the form of the system on which we will henceforth concentrate our attention.

The crucial change is the rise of industrial activity, with its key institution of labor working for wages in factories. As a consequence of that new institution, the focus of profit-seeking shifted from mercantile trading to the production process itself. That is, the main source of profits was no longer sought in profitable exchange but in profitable production, brought about by driving and disciplining labor and developing its productivity through machinery.

That change did not occur everywhere. For instance, the shift from mercantile to industrial capitalism was not made in early-eighteenth-century Holland, so that the Dutch—formidable rivals of the English in the seventeenth century—were bypassed when England became an industrial society and Holland remained a trading one. Anyone interested in this chapter of the history of capitalism should look into Jan de Vries' marvellously interesting book, *The Economy of Europe in an Age of Crisis: 1600–1750* (New York: Cambridge University Press, 1976).

The Industrial Revolutions

The new dynamism revealed itself in a series of technological "revolutions" —periods in which the basic ways of making things suddenly underwent startling changes, and in which new kinds of goods and services entered, and radically changed, daily life.

The first of these periods is often called *the* Industrial Revolution, although actually it was only the initial rush of a long, multiphase process. Beginning in the late eighteenth century and continuing for over 25 years, the first industrial revolution mechanized spinning and weaving, enormously improved and expanded iron production, brought the all-important gift of power in the form of the steam engine, and introduced a crucial change in the application of technology to production—the large, controlled workplace we call the factory.

The second industrial revolution followed in the mid-nineteenth century, bringing railroads and steamships, cheap steel, agricultural machinery, and the first mass-produced chemicals. Then in the early years of the twentieth century, a third burst came with the development of the automobile, electrical power, and consumer durable goods; and in our own day we are witnessing a fourth—the revolution of computers, air transportation, medical science, perhaps genetic engineering.

The Effects of Technology

Many profound changes have followed in the wake of capitalism—no other socioeconomic upheaval has so fundamentally altered life in its every aspect. But of the changes wrought, none was more dramatic than the industrial revolutions. The new technology literally remade life, and we should take a few moments to clarify some of the ways in which it did so.

1. OUTPUT INCREASED ENORMOUSLY, RAISING LIVING STANDARDS. First a few figures. Between 1701 and 1802, as the technology of spinning and weaving was gradually perfected, the use of cotton in England expanded by 6,000 percent. Between 1788 and 1839, when the process of iron manufacture passed through its first technological upheaval, the output of pig iron jumped from 68,000 to 1,347,000 tons. In France, in the 30 years after 1815, iron output quintupled, coal output grew sevenfold, and transportation tonnage mounted ten times.

But these figures do not convey a sense of the effect of technology on daily life. *Things* became more common—and more commonplace. As late as the seventeenth century, what we would consider the most ordinary possessions were scarce. A peasant counted his worldly wealth in terms of a few utensils, a table, perhaps one complete change of clothes. Shakespeare left Anne Hathaway his "second best bed." Iron nails were so scarce that pioneers in America burned down their cottages to retrieve them. In the wilder parts of Scotland in Adam Smith's time, nails even served as money.

Technology brought a widening and deepening and ever faster flowing river of things. Shoes, coats, paper, window glass, chairs, buckles—objects of solicitous respect in precapitalist times for all but the privileged few—became everyday articles. **Gradually, capitalism gave rise to what we call a "rising standard of living"—a steady, regular, systematic increase in the number, variety, and quality of material goods enjoyed by the great bulk of society. No such process had ever occurred before.**

2. THE SCALE OF ECONOMIC ORGANIZATION GREW VASTLY LARGER. A second change wrought by technology was a striking increase in the size of society's productive apparatus.

The increase began with the enlargement of the equipment used in production —an enlargement that stemmed mostly from advances in the technology of iron and later steel. The typical furnace used in extracting iron ore increased from 10 feet in height in the 1770s to over 100 feet a century later; during the same period the crucibles in which steel was made grew from cauldrons hardly larger than an oversized jug to converters literally as big as a house. The looms used by weavers expanded from small machines that fitted into the cottages of artisan-weavers to monstrous mechanisms housed in mills that still impress us by their size. Perhaps the thrust to bigness in machinery was best symbolized in the great Corliss engine (see illustration) that dominated the Philadelphia Exposition of 1876, perfectly illustrating the technological imperative for power and strength.

Equally remarkable was the expansion in the social scale of production. The new technology quickly outstripped the administrative capability of the small-sized business establishment. As the apparatus of production increased in size, it also increased in speed. As outputs grew from rivulets to rivers, a much larger organization was needed to manage production—to arrange for the steady arrival of raw materials, to supervise the work process, and to find a market for its end product.

Thus we find the size of the typical business enterprise steadily increasing as its technological basis became more complex. In the last quarter of the eighteenth century, a factory of ten persons was worthy of note by Adam Smith, as we shall see in the next chapter. By the first quarter of the nineteenth century, an ordinary textile mill employed several hundred men and women. Fifty years later, some railways employed as many individuals as constituted the armies of respectable monarchs in Adam Smith's time. And in still another 50 years, by the 1920s, many large manufacturing companies had as many employees as respectable eighteenth-century cities had people. The Ford Motor Company, for example, had 174,000 employees in 1929.

3. THE DIVISION OF LABOR CHANGED THE NATURE OF WORK. Technology also played a decisive role in changing the nature of that most basic of all human activities, work. **It did so by breaking down the complicated tasks of productive activity into much smaller subtasks, many of which could then be duplicated, or at least greatly assisted, by mechanical contrivances. This process was called the division of labor.** Adam Smith was soon to explain that the division of labor was mainly responsible for the increase in productivity of the average worker.

The division of labor altered social life in other ways as well. Work became more fragmented, monotonous, tedious, "alienated." And the self-sufficiency of individuals was greatly curtailed. In precapitalist days most people produced their own

The Corliss Engine

subsistence or made some article that could be exchanged for subsistence: Peasants grew crops; artisans produced cloth, shoes, implements. But as work became more and more finely divided, the products of work became ever-smaller pieces in an ever-larger puzzle. Individuals did not spin thread or weave cloth, but manipulated levers and fed the machinery that did the actual spinning or weaving. A worker in a shoe plant made uppers or lowers or heels, but not shoes. No one of these products, by itself, would have sustained its performer for a single day; and no one of these products could have been exchanged for another product except through a complicated network of exchange. **Technology freed men and women from much material want, but it bound them to the workings of the market.**

4. A NEW FORM OF ECONOMIC INSECURITY AROSE. Not least of the mighty effects of technology was its exposure of men and women to unprecedented change. Some of this was welcome, for change opened new horizons of material life. Travel, for instance, once the prerogative of the wealthy, became a possibility for the masses.

Yet the changes introduced by technology had their negative side as well. Already buffeted by market forces that could mysteriously dry up the need for work or just as mysteriously create it, society now discovered that entire occupations, skills acquired over a lifetime, companies laboriously built up over generations, even age-old industries, could be threatened by technological change. **For the first time in history, machinery appeared as the enemy, as well as the ally, of humankind.** No wonder that the textile weavers, whose cottage industry was destroyed by competition from the mills, banded together as Luddites to burn down the hated buildings.*

These aspects of change do not begin to exhaust the ways in which technology, coupled with the market system, altered the very meaning of human existence. But in considering them, we begin to see how profound and how wrenching was the revolution capitalism introduced. Technology was a genie that capitalism let out of the bottle; it has ever since refused to go back in.

THE POLITICAL DIMENSION

The disturbing, upsetting, revolutionary nature of the market and of technology sets the stage for one last aspect of capitalism that we want to note. This is the political currents of change that capitalism brought—political currents that are as much a part of the history of capitalism as the emergence of the market or the dismantling of the barriers against technical change.

Political Freedom

One of these political currents was the rise of democratic, or parliamentary, institutions. Democratic political institutions far predate capitalism, as the history of ancient Athens or the Icelandic medieval parliamentary system shows. Nonetheless, the rise of the mercantile classes was closely tied to the struggle against the privileges and legal institutions of medieval European feudalism. The historic movement that eventually swept aside the precapitalist economic order also swept aside its political order. **Along with the emergence of the market system we find a parallel and supporting emergence of more open, libertarian political ways of life.**

We should be cautious, however, in maintaining that capitalism either guarantees or is necessary for political freedom. We have seen some capitalist nations, such as pre-Hitler Germany and, more recently, Argentina and Chile, descend into nightmarish dictatorship. We have seen other capitalisms, such as Sweden, move toward a kind of socialism without impairing their democratic liberties. Moreover, the exercise of political democracy was very limited in early capitalism. Adam Smith, for example, although comfortably off, did not possess enough property to allow him to vote!

Therefore we cannot claim a hard-and-fast tie between capitalism and political freedom. It is true nonetheless that political liberties do not exist, or scarcely exist, in most nations that have deliberately sought to remove the market system. And today we see that even in the Soviet Union efforts to expand political liberty

---

*The word *Luddite* comes from a mythical General Ludd who supposedly led these raids of anger and desperation. The term has come to mean an "antimachine" attitude.

(*glasnost*) go hand-in-hand with the expansion of the market (*perestroika*). This suggests, although it does not prove, that some vital connection exists between democratic privileges as we know them and an open society of economic contract, whether it be formally capitalist or not.

Laissez-Faire vs. Political Intervention

Because of the economic freedom on which the market system rested, the basic philosophy of capitalism from Adam Smith's day forward has been laissez-faire—a French phrase, difficult to translate exactly, that means "leaving things alone."* But within a few years of Adam Smith's time, the idea of leaving things alone was already being breached. In England the Factory Act of 1833 established a system of inspectors to prevent child and female labor from being abused. The Ten Hour Act (1847) set limits to the number of hours an employer might demand of his work force. In the United States the Sherman Antitrust Act (1890) made illegal the banding together of large companies to create "trusts." In the 1930s the Social Security Act established a system of old-age pensions; unemployment insurance assured unemployed workers of incomes; the Securities and Exchange Act imposed restrictions on the issuance of new securities. And in our time a long roster of legislation imposes government regulations with respect to the environment, occupational safety, and nuclear power, to mention only a very few instances.

The effects of these interventions into the market process have become central questions for economics itself. As we study micro- and macroeconomics, we will be studying not only how the market system works, but also how various efforts to interfere with the market system exert their influence. Needless to say, government intervention in the market is one of the most controversial aspects of economics. But we are not interested at this juncture in taking sides, pro or con. Rather, we should understand that from the first Factory Acts, intervention has largely arisen out of a desire to impose corrective limits on the way in which the market system works or on the unwanted effects produced by technology.

Thus, if capitalism has brought a strong impetus for laissez-faire, it has also brought a strong impetus for political intervention. **Indeed, the very democratic liberties that capitalism has encouraged have been a main source of demands for political action to curb or change the manner in which the economic system works. The political economy of capitalism has always revealed a tension between laissez-faire and intervention—a tension rooted in the tug of war between the equal distribution of voting power and the unequal distribution of buying power.** That tension continues today, a deeply embedded part of the historic momentum of the capitalist system.

---

*It is said that a group of merchants called on the great Colbert, French finance minister from 1661 to 1683, who congratulated them on their contribution to the French economy and asked what he could do for them. The answer was *Laissez-nous faire*—"Leave us alone." Since Colbert was a strong proponent of the complex regulations and red tape that tied up industry in France at this time—a system we call *mercantilism*—we can imagine how gladly he received this advice.

▬▬ LOOKING BACK ▬▬

KEY CONCEPTS

The purpose of this chapter is to set our economic system into historic perspective. We have highlighted a few central ideas to give structure to this perspective.

Capitalism brings three historic changes:
- **a private sphere**
- **accumulation of wealth as capital**
- **a market system**

1 Capitalism is a complex system. We have sought to emphasize three striking changes that it introduces into economic history. First, it creates a realm of production and distribution that is no longer under state authority. This is the genesis of economic freedom. Second, the new economic sphere accumulates capital—wealth used to create more wealth, not luxurious consumption or public monuments. Third, the new manner of organizing economic life develops a new internal guidance mechanism—the market.

The market creates factors of production.

2 The market creates "factors of production"—workers who own and sell their laboring power, landlords who own and freely sell land, capitalists who own and sell capital. This means that labor, land, and capital have become commodities offered for hire in a vast market system where their owners are paid wages, salaries, rents, or interest. This way of bringing the services of these forces of production into social use contrasts sharply with the older means of tradition or command. Capitalism relies on economic freedom and its linked aspect, economic necessity.

The market contrasts with tradition and command. Capitalism encourages technology, which has come in waves—industrial revolutions.

3 Capitalism is closely entwined with technology. The market system encouraged the introduction of technology into everyday productive use by removing the inhibitions of serf- and slave-based modes of production and by thrusting responsibility for economic success or failure on the shoulders of each person. Technological advance has come in a series of great bursts or waves called industrial revolutions, beginning with *the* Industrial Revolution (spinning, ironmaking, steam power) of the late eighteenth and early nineteenth centuries.

Technology affects output, scale, and the division of labor.

4 Technology has profoundly affected economic and social life. It is responsible for the beginning of the rise in standard of living associated with capitalism. It is the main factor in the vast growth in size of business organizations. It is the source of a much greater division of labor and of a highly intensified interdependence of individuals.

The rise of capitalism is associated with political liberty; this has created tension between laissez-faire and intervention.

5 Capitalism is closely connected with political movements. One of these is parliamentary democracy, which arose out of the struggle to break the hold of feudalism. Another is an underlying belief in laissez-faire as a main principle of economic policy. A third is the effort to intervene against the workings of the market and technology whenever these powerful forces disrupt or endanger social life.

ECONOMIC VOCABULARY

Capitalism 12	Technology 21
Factors of production 14	Division of labor 22
Industrial Revolution 21	Laissez-faire 25

QUESTIONS

1. Are there elements of tradition and command still visible in our market system? How important do you think they are? Can you imagine a system in which there was *no* guiding force of tradition and *no* exercise of command (government) at all?

2. What reasons do you think are plausible in explaining why it took so long for capitalism to burst on the scene; and how do you explain the fact that it emerged only in Europe, not in Africa, Asia, or South America? *Note:* The question is far from settled. If you devise a really persuasive answer, you will be well on your way to becoming a world-famous historian.

3. Profit-making is certainly as old as biblical man. Why are the institutions of capitalism not equally old?

4. Describe the social, political, and economic repercussions of the following: the typewriter, the jet plane, TV, antibiotics. Is the economic impact always greater than the social or political impact? Is the economic impact always favorable?

5. Do you think capitalism is necessary for political freedom? First frame your answer, and then test it against these facts: (a) There has been little political freedom in any modern nation that has decisively rejected capitalism (that lets out Sweden, which does not actively oppose capitalism). (b) The Republic of South Africa is certainly capitalist, and is not a politically free nation, especially for those who are not white. *Note:* These facts suggest that there are *no* open-and-shut answers to this question. The issue is a complicated one—more complicated than many people suspect.

The Great Economists

The rise of the market system brought with it a great puzzle: How did such a system "work"—what kept it together and in what direction was it headed? The name of this puzzle is economics.

In this chapter we learn more about the background of economics by looking into the ideas of three great economists whose thoughts still dominate our understanding of capitalism: Adam Smith, Karl Marx, and John Maynard Keynes.

As we study them, a few central questions come to the fore:

1 What holds the system together and gives it "micro" order?

2 Where is the system headed, giving it "macro" motion?

3 What should we do to improve the system's operations, or what policies should we pursue?

THE INVENTION OF ECONOMICS

*T*he emergence of capitalism brought an extraordinary puzzle into being. The puzzle was to explain how a society could hang together when the time-honored mechanisms of tradition and command no longer played their accustomed roles. How could economic life unfold in an orderly and reliable fashion when each actor on the marketplace was out for himself, devil take the hindmost; and when it was already clear that change, not inertia, was to be the order of the day?

Mercantilism

Capitalism needed a philosophy—a reasoned explanation of how it worked. But the philosophy was a long time in emerging. All during the seventeenth and eighteenth centuries, for example, the understanding of market society was very imperfect. One group of British pamphleteers, whom we call the Mercantilists, tried to explain its workings in terms of a struggle among nations to gather "treasure"—gold and silver bullion. In this struggle, the Mercantilists saw merchants (hence *Mercant*—ilism) playing a central role because they exported goods that were paid for in treasure.

Early mercantilist policy was very simple: Let England sell as much and buy as little abroad as possible. In that way, its national wealth would steadily pile up. Later mercantilist theory was a good deal more sophisticated. Can you see why the earlier idea of amassing treasure could not successfully serve as a policy for *all* nations?

Physiocracy. In France during the eighteenth century an entirely different and equally inadequate explanation was called physiocracy. In many ways the French school of ideas was the opposite of the British school. Physiocracy taught that the real wealth of economic life lay in production, not in exchange—an important step in the right direction. But the Physiocrats believed that production was essentially a gift of nature (*physiocracy* means the order of nature), and that therefore only labor working with nature was truly productive. Thus, whereas the Mercantilists extolled the merchants as active agents in creating national wealth, the Physiocrats regarded them as a "sterile" class that did no more than handle the wealth produced by the agriculturalists.

Mercantilism and physiocracy are both indispensable steppingstones on the road to modern economics. Each yielded useful insights into the still unfinished economic revolution. But neither made the crucial breakthrough of seeing that the market was a *system*. That is, neither Mercantilists nor Physiocrats saw that the market network possessed an internal guidance mechanism to keep it on a steady course and that a society powered by the market was headed toward a visible destination.

These crucial insights came with Adam Smith, patron saint of our discipline and a figure of towering intellectual stature.

ADAM SMITH (1723–1790)

Adam Smith's fame resides in his masterpiece, *The Wealth of Nations,* published in 1776, the year of the Declaration of Independence. All things considered, it is not easy to say which document is of greater historic importance. The Declaration sounded a new call for a society dedicated to "Life, Liberty, and the pursuit of Happiness." The *Wealth* explained how such a society worked.

The Role of Competition

Smith set himself two main problems, one on the micro and the other on the macro level (although you will not find these terms used in his great, rambling, discursive tract). The first problem was to elucidate how a market-run economic system was articulated, how it achieved what we would call micro order.

Here Smith begins by resolving a perplexing question. The actors in the market, as we know, are all driven by the desire to make money for themselves—to "better their condition," as Smith puts it. The question is obvious: How does a market society prevent self-interested, profit-hungry individuals from holding up their fellow citizens for ransom? How can a socially workable arrangement arise from such a dangerously unsocial motivation as self-betterment?

PORTRAIT OF AN ABSENTMINDED PROFESSOR

"I am a beau in nothing but my books" was the way that Adam Smith once described himself. Indeed, the famous medallion profile shows us a homely face. In addition, Smith had a curious stumbling gait that one friend called "vermicular," and was given to notorious fits of absentmindedness. On one occasion, absorbed in discussion, he fell into a tanning pit.

Few other adventures befell Smith in the course of his scholarly, rather retiring life. Perhaps the high point was reached at age four when he was kidnaped by a band of gypsies passing near Kirkaldy, his native hamlet in Scotland. "His captors held him only a few hours; they may have sensed what a biographer later wrote: "He would have made, I fear, a poor gypsy."

Marked out early as a student of promise, at 16 Smith won a scholarship that sent him to Oxford. But Oxford was not then the center of learning that it is today. Little or no systematic teaching took place, the students being free to educate themselves, provided they did not read dangerous books. Smith was nearly expelled for owning a copy of David Hume's *Treatise of Human Nature,* a work we now regard as one of the philosophic masterpieces of the eighteenth century.

After Oxford, Smith returned to Scotland, where he obtained an appointment as Professor of Moral Philosophy at the University of Glasgow. Moral philosophy covered a large territory in Smith's time: We have notes of his lectures in which he talked about jurisprudence, military organization, taxation, and "police"—the last word meaning the administration of domestic affairs that we would call economic policy.

In 1759 Smith published *The Theory of Moral Sentiments,* a remarkable inquiry into morality and psychology. The book attracted widespread attention and brought Smith to the notice of Lord Townshend, one day to be the Chancellor of the Exchequer responsible for the notorious tax on American tea. Townshend engaged Smith to serve as tutor to his stepson, and Smith resigned his professional post to set off on the Grand Tour with his charge. In France he met Voltaire, Rousseau, and François Quesnay, the brilliant doctor who had originated the ideas of physiocracy. Smith would have dedicated *The Wealth of Nations* to him had Quesnay not died.

Returning to Scotland in 1766, Smith lived out the remainder of his life largely in scholarly retirement. It was during these years that the *Wealth* was slowly and carefully composed. When it was done, Smith sent a copy to David Hume, by then his dear friend. Hume wrote: "Euge!* Belle! Dear Mr. Smith: I am much pleased with your Performance . . ." Hume knew, as did virtually everyone who read the book, that Smith had written a work that would permanently change society's understanding of itself.

*Greek for "Well done!"

The answer introduces us to a central mechanism of a market system, the mechanism of competition. For each person, out for self-betterment, with no thought of others, is faced with a host of similarly motivated persons. As a result, each market actor is forced to meet the prices offered by competitors.

In the kind of competition that Smith assumes, a manufacturer who tries to charge more than other manufacturers will not be able to find any buyers. A job seeker who asks more than the going wage will not be able to find work. And an employer who tries to pay *less* than competitors pay will not find anyone to fill the jobs.

In this way, the market mechanism imposes a discipline on its participants: Buyers must bid against other buyers, and therefore cannot gang up against sellers. Sellers must contend against other sellers, and therefore cannot impose their will on buyers.

The Invisible Hand

But the market has a second, equally important function. Smith shows that the market will arrange for the production of the goods that society wants, in the quantities society wants—without anyone ever issuing an order of any kind! Suppose that consumers want more pots and fewer pans than are being turned out. The public will buy up the existing stock of pots, and as a result the price of pots will rise. Contrariwise, the pan business will be dull; as panmakers try to get rid of their inventories, pan prices will fall.

Now a restorative force comes into play. As pot prices rise, so will profits in the business of pot making; and as pan prices fall, so will profits in that business. Once again, the drive for self-betterment will go to work. Employers in the favored pot business will seek to expand, hiring more factors of production—more workers, more space, more capital equipment; and employers in the disfavored pan business will reduce their use of the factors of production, letting workers go, giving up leases on space, cutting down on capital investment.

Hence the output of pots will rise and that of pans will fall. And this is what the public wanted in the first place. **Thus the pressures of the marketplace direct the selfish activities of individuals as if by an Invisible Hand (to use Smith's wonderful phrase) into socially responsible paths. The Invisible Hand transmutes private, self-regarding motives into public, socially oriented behavior. The market becomes a mechanism for the allocation of resources into the channels desired by society.**

The Self-Regulating System

Smith's demonstration of how a market performs its social functions has never ceased to be of interest. Much of microeconomics, as we shall see, consists of learning again, or of examining more closely, how the Invisible Hand works. Not that it does always work. There are areas of economic life where the Invisible Hand does not exert its influence at all. In every market system, for instance, tradition continues to play a role in nonmarket methods of remuneration such as tipping or the sharing of incomes within a family. So, too, command is always in evidence within organizations or in the exercise of government powers such as taxation. Further, the market system has no way of providing certain public goods—goods that cannot be privately marketed, such as national defense or public law and order. Smith knew about these areas and recognized that such goods would have to be supplied by the government, not by the market.

Then, too, the market does not always meet the ethical or aesthetic criteria of society, or it may produce goods that are profitable to make, but harmful to consume. We shall look into these problems in due course. At this juncture, however, we had better stand in considerable awe of Smith's basic insight, for he showed his generation and all succeeding ones that a market system is a responsive and reliable force for basic social provisioning.

He also showed that it was self-regulating. The beautiful consequence of the market is that it is its own guardian. If anyone's prices, wages, or profits stray from levels that are set for everyone, the force of competition will drive them back. Thus a curious paradox exists. The market, which is the acme of economic freedom, turns out also to be the strictest of economic taskmasters.

Smith's Philosophy

Because the market is its own regulator, Smith vehemently opposed government intervention that would interfere with the workings of self-interest and competition. Therefore laissez-faire became his fundamental philosophy—not because Smith opposed the idea of social responsibility, but rather because he thought it would be most effectively provided by the Invisible Hand, not by the efforts of government.

His commitment to laissez-faire does not make Smith a conventional conservative. The *Wealth of Nations* is shot through with biting remarks about the "mean and rapacious" ways of the manufacturing class (Smith does not use the word *capitalist*), and the book is openly sympathetic with, and concerned about, the lot of the workingman, hardly a popular position in Smith's day. If Smith was passionately in favor of the "system of natural liberty"—the system founded on economic freedom—the reason is that he believed it would benefit the general public, not the interests of any single class.

Economic Growth

Smith's discovery of the self-regulating properties of a market system was his great "micro" insight (remember that is our phrase, not his). But his vision of an internally coherent market system was matched in importance by a second, "macro" vision. **Smith saw that the market system, left entirely to its own devices, would grow, that the wealth of a nation under a system of "natural liberty" would steadily increase.**

What brought about this growth? As before, the motive force was the drive for self-betterment, the thirst for profits, the wish to make money. This meant that every employer was constantly seeking to accumulate more capital, to expand the wealth of the enterprise. In turn, this led each employer to seek to increase sales in the hope of gaining a larger profit.

The Division of Labor Again

But how to enlarge sales at a time long before advertising existed as we know it? Smith's answer was to improve productivity: Increase the output of the work force. And the road to increasing productivity was very clear: **Increase the division of labor.**

In Smith's conception of the growing *wealth* (we would say the growing *production*) *of nations,* the division of labor therefore plays a central role, as this famous description of a pin factory makes unforgettably clear:

> *One man draws out the wire, another straits it, a third cuts it, a fourth points it, a fifth grinds it at the top for receiving the head; to make the head requires two or three distinct operations; to put it on is a peculiar business; to whiten it another; it is even a trade by itself to put them into paper.*

. . . I have seen a small manufactory of this kind where ten men only were employed and where some of them consequently performed two or three distinct operations. But though they were poor, and therefore but indifferently accommodated with the necessary machinery, they could when they exerted themselves make among them about twelve pounds of pins in a day. There are in a pound upwards of four thousand pins of middling size. These ten persons, therefore, could make among them upward of forty-eight thousand pins in a day . . . But if they had all wrought separately and independently . . . they could certainly not each of them make twenty, perhaps not one pin in a day.*

Capital and Growth

But how is the division of labor to be enhanced? Smith places principal importance on the manner already announced in his description of the process of making pins: *Machinery is the key.* The division of labor—and therefore the productivity of labor—is increased when the tasks of production can be taken over, or aided and assisted, by the capacities of machinery. In this way, each firm seeking to expand is naturally led to introduce more machinery as a way of improving the productivity of its workers. **The market system thus becomes an immense force for the accumulation of capital, mainly in the form of machinery and equipment.** Moreover, Smith showed something remarkable about the self-regulating properties of the market system as a growth-producing institution. We recall that growth occurred because employers installed machinery that improved the division of labor. But as they added to their work force, would not wages rise as all employers competed to hire labor? And would that not squeeze profits and dry up the funds by which machinery could be bought?

Once again, however, the market was its own regulator. For Smith showed that the increased demand for labor would be matched by an increased supply of labor, so that wages would not rise or would rise only moderately. The reason was plausible. In Smith's day, infant and child mortality rates were horrendous: "It is not uncommon," wrote Smith, ". . . in the Highlands of Scotland for a mother who has borne twenty children not to have two alive." As wages rose and better food was provided for the household, infant and child mortality would decline. Soon there would be a larger work force available for hire: Ten was the working age in Smith's day. The larger work force would hold back the rise in wages—and so the accumulation of capital could go on. Just as the system assured internal micro order, so did it provide an overall macro dependability.

Smith Today

Of course, Smith wrote about a world that is long since vanished—a world in which a factory of ten people, although small, was still significant enough to play a central

---

*Adam Smith, *The Wealth of Nations* (New York: Modern Library, 1937), pp. 4, 5.

illustrative role; in which remnants of mercantilist, and even feudal, restrictions determined how many apprentices an employer could hire in many trades; in which labor unions were largely illegal; in which almost no social legislation existed; and above all, in which the great majority of people were very poor.

Yet Smith saw two essential attributes of the economic system that was not yet fully born in his time:

1. **A society of competitive profit-seeking individuals can assure its orderly material provisioning through the self-regulating market mechanism.**
2. **Such a society tends to accumulate capital, and in so doing enhances its productivity and wealth.**

These insights are not the last word. We have already mentioned that the market mechanism does not always work successfully, and our next two economists will demonstrate that the growth process is not without serious defects. But the insights themselves are still germane. Micro- and macroeconomics are about internal order and growth, even though we may come to different conclusions than those of Smith. What is surprising after two centuries is not how mistaken Smith was, but how deeply he saw. In a real sense, as economists we are still his pupils.

KARL MARX (1818–1883)

Every economist is roughly familiar with the ideas and influence of Adam Smith. Not so many recognize the degree to which economics also owes a debt to Karl Marx—not as the founder of a political movement that has troubled the world ever since, but as an economist whose dissection of capitalism has much to teach us.

Class Struggle

Adam Smith was the architect of capitalism's orderliness and progress; Marx, the diagnostician of its disorders and eventual demise. Their differences are rooted in the fundamentally opposite way each saw history. In Smith's view, history was a succession of stages through which humankind traveled, climbing from the "early and rude" society of hunters and fisherfolk to the final stage of commercial society. **Marx saw history as a continuing struggle among social classes, ruling classes contending with ruled classes in every era.**

Moreover, Smith believed that commercial society would bring about a harmonious, mutually acceptable solution to the problem of individual interest in a social setting that would go on forever—or at least for a very long time. Marx saw tension and antagonism as the outcome of the class struggle, and the setting of capitalist society as anything but permanent. Indeed, the class struggle itself, expressed as the contest over wages and profits, would be the main force for changing capitalism and eventually undoing it.

PROFILE OF A REVOLUTIONARY

A great, bearded, dark-skinned man, Karl Marx was the picture of a revolutionary. And he was one—engaged, mind and heart, in the effort to overthrow the system of capitalism that he spent his whole life studying. As a political revolutionary, Marx was not very successful, although with his lifelong friend Friedrich Engels he formed an international working-class "movement" that frightened a good many conservative governments. But as an intellectual revolutionary, Marx was probably the most successful disturber of thought who ever lived. The only persons who rival his influence are the great religious leaders, Christ, Mohammed, and Buddha.

Marx led as turbulent and active a life as Smith's was secluded and academic. Born to middle-class parents in Trier, Germany, he was early marked as a student of prodigious abilities, but not temperamentally cut out to be a professor. Soon after getting his doctoral degree (in philosophy), Marx became editor of a crusading newspaper, which rapidly earned the distrust of the reactionary Prussian government. It closed down the paper. Typically, Marx printed the last edition in red. With his wife Jenny (and Jenny's family maid, Lenchen, who remained with them, unpaid, all her life), Marx thereupon began life as a political exile in Paris, Brussels, and finally in London. There, in 1848, together with Engels, he published the pamphlet that was to become his best known, but certainly not most important, work: *The Communist Manifesto.*

The remainder of Marx's life was lived in London. Terribly poor, largely as a consequence of his hopeless inability to manage his own finances, Marx's life was spent in the reading room of the British Museum, laboriously composing the great, never-finished opus *Capital.* No economist has ever read so widely or so deeply as Marx. Before even beginning *Capital,* he wrote a profound three-volume commentary on all the existing economists, eventually published as *Theories of Surplus Value,* and filled 37 notebooks on subjects that would be included in *Capital*—these notes, published as the *Grundrisse* (Foundations), did not appear in print until 1953! *Capital* itself was written "backwards"—first Volumes II and III, in very rough draft form, then Volume I, the only part of the great opus that appeared in Marx's lifetime, in 1867.

Marx was assuredly a genius, a man who altered every aspect of thinking about society—historical and sociological as well as economic—as decisively as Plato altered the cast of philosophic thought and Freud that of psychology. Very few economists today work their way through the immense body of Marx's work; but in one way or another, his influence affects most of us, even if we are unaware of it. We owe to Marx the basic idea that capitalism is an *evolving* system, deriving from a specific historic past and moving slowly and irregularly toward a dimly discernible, different form of society. That is an idea accepted by many social scientists who may or may not approve of socialism, and who are on the whole vehemently "anti-Marxist"!

Capitalist Growth: Using M

A great deal of interest in Marx's work focuses on that revolutionary perspective and purpose. But Marx the economist interests us for a different reason: Marx also saw the market as a powerful force in the accumulation of capital and wealth. From his conflict-laden point of view, however, he traces out the process—mainly in Volume II of *Capital*—quite differently than Smith does. As we have seen, Smith's conception of the growth process stressed its self-regulatory nature, its steady, hitch-free path. Marx's conception is just the opposite. To him, growth is a process full of pitfalls, a process in which crisis or malfunction lurks at every turn.

Marx starts with a view of the accumulation process that is much like that of a businessman. The problem is how to make a given sum of capital—money sitting in a bank or invested in a firm—yield a profit. **As Marx puts it, how does M (a sum of money) become M', a *larger* sum?**

Marx's answer begins with capitalists using their money to buy commodities and labor power. Thereby they ready the process of production, obtaining needed raw or semifinished materials and hiring the work capabilities of a labor force. Here the possibility for crisis lies in the difficulty that capitalists may have in getting their materials or their labor force at the right price. If that should happen—if labor is too expensive, for instance—M stays put, and the accumulation process never gets started at all.

Karl Marx
(Courtesy of the Library of Congress)

The Labor Process

But suppose the first stage of accumulation takes place smoothly. Now money capital, *M,* has been transformed into a hired work force and a stock of physical goods. These have next to be combined in the labor process; that is, actual work must be expended on the materials and the raw or semifinished goods transformed into their next stage of production.

It is here, on the factory floor, that Marx sees the genesis of profit. **In his view, profit lies in the ability of capitalists to pay less for labor power—for the working abilities of their work force—than the actual value workers will impart to the commodities they help to produce.** This theory of *surplus value* as the source of profit is very important in Marx's analysis of capitalism. But it is not central to our purpose here. Instead, we stop only to note that the labor process is another place where accumulation can be disrupted. If there is a strike, or if production encounters resistances, the *M* that is invested in goods and labor power will not move along toward its objective, *M'*.

Completing the Circuit

But once again, suppose that all goes well and workers transform steel sheets, rubber casings, and bolts of cloth into automobiles. The automobiles are not yet money. They have to be sold—and here, of course, lie the familiar problems of the marketplace: bad guesses as to the public's taste; mismatches between supply and demand; recessions that diminish the spending power of society.

If all goes well, the commodities *will* be sold—and sold for *M'*, which is bigger than *M*. In that case, the circuit of accumulation is complete, and the capitalists will have a new sum *M'*, which they will want to send on another round, hoping to win *M''*. But unlike Adam Smith's smooth growth model, we can see that Marx's conception of accumulation is riddled with pitfalls and dangers. **Crisis is possible at every stage. Indeed, in the complex theory Marx unfolds in *Capital*, the inherent tendency of the system is to generate crisis, not to avoid it.**

We will not trace Marx's theory of capitalism further except to note that at its core lies a complicated analysis of the manner in which surplus value (the unpaid labor that is the source of profit) is squeezed out through mechanization. A student who wants to learn about Marx's analysis must turn to other books, of which there are many.*

Instability and Breakdown

Our interest in Marx lies in his being the first theorist to stress the *instability* of capitalism. Adam Smith originated the idea that growth is an inherent characteristic of capitalism, but to Marx we owe the idea that that growth is wavering and uncertain, far from the assured process Smith described. Marx makes it clear that

---

*At the risk of appearing self-serving, a good first reader is R. L. Heilbroner, *Marxism: For and Against* (New York: Norton, 1980).

capital accumulation must overcome the uncertainty inherent in the market system and the tension of the opposing demands of labor and capital. The accumulation of wealth, although certainly the objective of business, may not always be within its power to achieve.

In *Capital* Marx sees instability increasing until finally the system comes tumbling down. His reasoning involves two further, very important prognoses for the system. **The first is that the size of business firms will steadily increase as the consequence of the recurrent crises that wrack the economy.** With each crisis, small firms go bankrupt and their assets are bought up by surviving firms. A trend toward big business is therefore an integral part of capitalism.

Second, Marx expects an intensification of the class struggle as the result of the "proletarianization" of the labor force. More and more small businesspeople and independent artisans will be squeezed out in the crisis-ridden process of growth. Thus the social structure will be reduced to two classes—a small group of capitalist magnates and a large mass of proletarianized, embittered workers.

In the end, this situation will prove impossible to maintain. In Marx's words:

Along with the constant decrease in the number of capitalist magnates, who usurp and monopolize all the advantages of this process of transformation, the mass of misery, oppression, slavery, degradation and exploitation grows; but with this there also grows the revolt of the working class, a class constantly increasing in numbers, and trained, united and organized by the very mechanism of the capitalist process of production. The monopoly of capital becomes a fetter upon the mode of production which has flourished alongside and under it. The centralization of the means of production and the socialization of labour reach a point at which they become incompatible with their capitalist integument. This integument is burst asunder. The knell of capitalist private property sounds. The expropriators are expropriated. *

Was Marx Right?

Much of the economic controversy Marx generated has been focused on the questions: Will capitalism ultimately undo itself? Will its internal tensions, its "contradictions," as Marx calls them, finally become too much for its market mechanism to handle?

There are no simple answers to these questions. Critics of Marx insist that capitalism has *not* collapsed, that the working class has *not* become more and more "miserable," and that a number of predictions that Marx made, such as that the rate of profit would tend to decline, have not been verified.

Supporters of Marx argue the opposite case. They stress that capitalism almost did collapse in the 1930s. They note that more and more people have been reduced to "proletarian" status, working for a capitalist firm rather than for themselves: In 1800, for example, 80 percent of Americans were self-employed; today the figure is 10 percent. They stress that the size of businesses has constantly grown, and that Marx did correctly foresee that the capitalist system itself would expand, pushing into noncapitalist areas such as Asia, South America, and Africa.

*Karl Marx, *Capital,* Vol. I (New York: Vintage, 1977), p. 929.

Marx's Socioanalysis

There is much more to Marx than the few economic ideas sketched here suggest. Indeed, Marx should not be thought of primarily as an economist, but as a pioneer in a new kind of critical social thought: It is significant that the subtitle of *Capital* is *A Critique of Political Economy.*

In the gallery of the world's great thinkers, where Marx certainly belongs, his statue would be centrally placed, overlooking many corridors of thought—sociological analysis, philosophic inquiry, and of course, economics. For Marx's lasting contribution was a penetration of the *appearances* of our social system, and of the ways in which we think about that system, in an effort to arrive at buried essences deep below the surface. That most searching aspect of Marx's work is not one that we will pursue here; but bear in mind, because it accounts for the persisting interest of Marx's thought.*

JOHN MAYNARD KEYNES (1883–1946)

Marx was the intellectual prophet of capitalism as a self-destructive system; John Maynard Keynes (the name should be pronounced "canes," not "keens") was the engineer of capitalism repaired. Today that is not an uncontested statement. To some people, Keynes's doctrines are as dangerous and subversive as those of Marx—a curious irony, since Keynes himself was totally opposed to Marxist thought and wholly in favor of sustaining and improving the capitalist system.

The reason for the present distrust of Keynes is that more than any other economist he is the father of the idea of a "mixed economy" in which the government plays a crucial role. To many people these days, all government activities are suspicious at best and downright injurious at worst. Thus in some quarters Keynes's name is under a cloud. Nonetheless, he remains one of the great innovators of our discipline, a mind to be ranked with Smith and Marx as one of the most influential our profession has brought forth. As Nobelist Milton Friedman, a famous conservative economist, once declared: "We are all Keynesians now."

The Great Depression

The great economists were all products of their times: Smith, the voice of optimistic, nascent capitalism; Marx, the spokesman for the victims of its bleakest industrial period; Keynes, the product of a still later time, the Great Depression.

---

*What about the relation of Marx to present-day communism? That is a subject for a book about the politics, not the economics, of Marxism. Marx himself was a fervid democrat—but also a very intolerant man. Perhaps his system of ideas has encouraged intolerance in revolutionary parties that have based their ideas on his thought. Marx himself died long before present-day communism came into being, so we cannot know what he would have made of it.

PORTRAIT OF A MANY-SIDED MAN

Keynes was a man of many talents. Unlike Smith or Marx, he was at home in the world of business affairs, a shrewd dealer and financier. Every morning, abed, he would scan the newspaper and make his commitments for the day on the most treacherous of all markets, foreign exchange. An hour or so a day sufficed to make him a very rich man; among economists, only the great David Ricardo (1772–1823) could match him in financial acumen. Like Ricardo, Keynes was a speculator by temperament. During World War I, when he was at the Treasury office running England's foreign currency operations, he reported with glee to his chief that he had got together a fair amount of Spanish pesetas. The chief was relieved that England had a supply of *that* currency for a while. "Oh no," said Keynes. "I've sold them all. I'm going to break the market." And he did. Later during the war, when the Germans were shelling Paris, he went to France to negotiate for the English government; on the side, he bought some marvelous French masterpieces at much reduced prices for the National Gallery—along with a Cézanne for himself!

More than an economist and a speculator, Keynes was a brilliant mathematician; a businessman who successfully ran a great investment trust; a ballet lover who married a famous ballerina; a superb stylist and an editor of consummate skill; a man of huge kindness when he wanted to exert it, and of ferocious wit when (more often) he chose to exert that. On one occasion, banker Sir Harry Goshen criticized Keynes for not "letting things take their natural course." "Is it more appropriate to smile or rage at these artless sentiments?" wrote Keynes. "Best, perhaps, to let Sir Harry take *his* natural course."

Keynes's greatest fame lay in his economic inventiveness. He came by this talent naturally enough as the son of a distinguished economist, John Neville Keynes. As an undergraduate, Keynes had already attracted the attention of Alfred Marshall, the commanding figure at Cambridge University for three decades. After graduation, Keynes soon won notice with a brilliant little book on Indian finance; he then became an adviser to the English government in the negotiations at the end of World War I. Dismayed and disheartened by the vengeful terms of the Versailles Treaty, Keynes wrote a polemic, *The Economic Consequences of the Peace,* that won him international renown.

Almost 30 years later, Keynes would himself be a chief negotiator for the English government, first in securing the necessary loans during World War II, then as one of the architects of the Bretton Woods agreement that opened a new system of international currency relations after that war. On his return from one trip to Washington, reporters crowded around to ask if England had been sold out and would soon be another American state. Keynes's reply was succinct: "No such luck."

The Great Depression hit the world like a typhoon. In America one-half the value of all production simply disappeared. One-quarter of the working force lost their jobs. Over a million urban families found their mortgages foreclosed, their houses taken from them. Nine million savings accounts went down the drain when banks closed, never to reopen.

Against this terrible reality of joblessness and loss of income, the economics profession, like the business world or government advisers, had nothing to offer. Economists were as perplexed at the behavior of the economy as were the American people themselves. In many ways, the situation reminds us of the uncertainty that the public and the economics profession share in the face of inflation or international competition today.

The General Theory

It was against this setting of dismay and near-panic that Keynes's great book appeared: *The General Theory of Employment Interest and Money.* A complicated book—much more technical than the *Wealth of Nations* or *Capital*—the *General Theory* nevertheless had a central message that was simple enough to grasp. The overall level of economic activity in a capitalist system, said Keynes (and both Marx and Adam Smith would have agreed with him), was determined by the willingness of its entrepreneurs to make capital investments. From time to time, this willingness was blocked by considerations that made capital accumulation difficult or impossible: In Smith's model, we saw the possibility of wages rising too fast, and Marx's theory pointed out difficulties at every stage of the process.

But all the previous economists, even Marx to a certain extent, believed that a failure to accumulate capital would be a temporary, self-curing setback. In Smith's scheme, the rising supply of young workers would keep wages in check. In Marx's conception, each crisis (up to the last) would present the surviving entrepreneurs with fresh opportunities to resume their quest for profits. For Keynes, however, the diagnosis was more severe. **He showed that a market system could reach a position of "underemployment equilibrium"—a kind of steady, stagnant state—despite the presence of unemployed workers and unused industrial equipment. The revolutionary implication of Keynes's theory was that there was no self-righting property in the market system to keep capitalism growing.**

The Role of Government

We will not understand the nature of Keynes's diagnosis until we get into our study of macroeconomics, but we can easily see the conclusion to which his diagnosis drove him. If there was nothing that would automatically provide for capital accumulation, a badly depressed economy could remain in the doldrums—unless some substitute were found for business spending. And there was only one such possible source of stimulation: the government. **The crux of Keynes's message was therefore that government spending might be an essential economic policy for a depressed capitalism trying to recover its vitality.**

Whether or not Keynes's remedy works and what consequences government spending may have for a market system have become major topics in contemporary economics—topics we will deal with later at length. But we can see the significance of his work in changing the very conception of the economic system in which we live. Adam Smith's view of the market system led to the philosophy of laissez-faire, allowing the system to generate its own natural propensity for growth and internal order. Marx had stressed a very different view in which instability and crisis lurked at every stage, but of course Marx was not interested in policies to maintain capitalism. Keynes propounded a philosophy as far removed from Marx as from Smith. For if Keynes was right, laissez-faire was not the appropriate policy for capitalism—certainly not for capitalism in depression. And if Keynes was right about his remedy, the gloomy prognostications of Marx were also incorrect—or at least could be rendered incorrect.

John Maynard Keynes
(The Bettmann Archive, Inc.)

Was Keynes Right?

But was Keynes right? Was Smith right? Was Marx right? To a very large degree these questions frame the subject matter of economics today. That is why, even if their theories are part of our history, the "worldly philosophers" are also contemporary. A young writer once remarked impatiently to T. S. Eliot that it seemed so pointless to study the thinkers of the past, because we knew so much more than they. "Yes," replied Eliot. "They are what we know."

LOOKING BACK

KEY CONCEPTS

This chapter has tried to give us a conception of capitalism as seen by the three greatest economists—whose ideas still powerfully affect our understanding of the system. Let us go over the main ideas that have emerged from this survey:

Mercantilists and Physiocrats extolled treasure and land.

1 Economics itself is a modern intellectual invention that awaited the advent of market society. Prior to Adam Smith, the main attempts to understand and explain the system were those of the Mercantilists, who stressed the importance of foreign trade as a means of gaining gold or treasure; and those of the French Physiocrats, who extolled the wealth-generating powers of the land and who dismissed the merchant class as sterile.

Adam Smith's Invisible Hand—competition plus self-interest

2 Adam Smith contributed two immensely important ideas to economic understanding. The first was the idea of an Invisible Hand by which the market system converted the selfish drives of individuals to a coordinated mechanism for social provisioning. Smith showed how this fortunate outcome arose from the workings of competition, which prevented the drive for profits or selfish interest from simply gouging the consumer or the worker.

Capital accumulation and division of labor bring growth.

3 Smith was also the first economist to explain how the market provided a powerful mechanism for accumulating capital. Smith's theory of economic growth hinged on the steady improvement in productivity that occurred when machinery was added to production, making possible a finer division of labor.

Class struggle

4 Marx was the great prophet of capitalism's doom. The essential cause of its demise would be the class struggle between workers and capitalists.

The unstable process of production

5 Marx also saw the market mechanism as inherently unstable—as tending toward crisis or disruption in the accumulation of capital. He analyzed this instability by tracing the obstacles faced by a firm as it sought to convert *M*, a sum of capital, into *M*, *a larger sum. This was done in three stages: first by using M to buy labor power and materials, then by combining labor power with materials, and finally by selling the finished goods.* At each stage the accumulation process was subject to disruption of various sorts.

Growth of monopolies and impoverished proletariat leads to revolution.

6 In Marx's view, the process of capitalist accumulation leads to the growth of big business and an "immiserated" proletariat. As successive crises wracked the system, the working class would eventually revolt, and a transition would be made from capitalism to socialism.

Marxism as a system of thought

7 Marx's system of thought was much larger than an analysis of the economic tensions of capitalism. Essentially it embraced a mixture of philosophy, historical analysis, and a critique of economic beliefs and forms.

Keynes's *General Theory* with its idea of underemployment equilibrium, ushered in the mixed economy.

8 John Maynard Keynes's *General Theory* (as it is widely called) was an attempt to explain how capitalism could have a *lasting* depression. In technical terms, Keynes's breakthrough was the explanation of underemployment equilibrium.

9 Equally important was Keynes's work in paving the way for the mixed economy in which government plays a crucial role in maintaining the economic growth of capitalism. Mixed economies are found in every capitalist system today; we will be studying them in depth in the pages to come.

ECONOMIC VOCABULARY

Mercantilism   30
Physiocracy   30
Invisible Hand   32
Self-regulation   33

Division of labor   34
Marx's circuit of production:
  M-into-M' 38
Underemployment equilibrium   43

QUESTIONS

1. Why does Smith's model of the economy require *two* elements—the motivation of self-betterment and the restraining institution of competition? Explain why the system would not work with only one of the two.

2. Think of how the division of labor can increase productivity. Choose one example from agriculture, one from manufacturing, and one from a service industry, such as hotel management, transportation, or retailing.

3. Is the accumulation of capital needed for the improvement of productivity today? In what ways could additional capital—more machines, buildings, roads, etc.—improve the amount of production a typical farmer or worker could create?

4. Take any business you know about and see if you think that Marx's description of the circuit *M*-into-*M'* describes the way in which that business tries to accumulate capital. Which of Marx's three phases of the accumulation process is most likely to lead to trouble, in your opinion?

5. How do you feel about the idea of a mixed economy? Do you think it means an economy in which the government does a lot of interfering? Could a government simply spend money—for example, for social security—and not interfere in the market system at all? Could it interfere extensively, but not spend much money? Which of the two functions—interfering (regulating) or spending—is basic to Keynes's theory? Is it possible, do you think, to have a basically laissez-faire policy with respect to the market and yet use government spending to cure a depression?

AN EXTRA WORD ABOUT

Paradigms

How does science advance? The prevailing view used to be that it grew by accretion, gradually adding new knowledge and better-established hypotheses while shedding error and disproved hypotheses. That view has been seriously challenged by an influential book, *The Structure of Scientific Revolutions* by Thomas Kuhn, published in 1962.

Kuhn's view is that the growth of science is not a continuous, seamless extension of knowledge. Rather, science grows in discontinuous leaps, in which one prevailing paradigm is displaced by another. *A paradigm is a set of premises, views, rules, conventions, and beliefs that form the kinds of questions that a science asks.* For example, the Ptolemaic paradigm, with its view of the earth as the center of the universe, was replaced by the Copernican paradigm, which based its questions on the premise that the planets revolve around the sun. In cosmology the Newtonian paradigm was displaced by the Einsteinian, in biology the biblical paradigm by the Darwinian.

Paradigms change, says Kuhn, when the puzzles encountered by scientists become more and more difficult to answer within the existing set of ground rules. Then, usually in a short space of time, a new view of things comes to the fore, explaining the puzzles of the earlier paradigm and reorienting the questions for scientists, who then work within the new rules.

PRE-CLASSICAL AND CLASSICAL ECONOMICS

Kuhn's short, provocative book is worth reading by anyone interested in science or social science. The question it raises for us is whether economics also has paradigms. The answer seems to be both "yes" and "no."

First the "yes" answer. We can easily separate the history of economic thought into paradigm-like divisions that resemble the bounded inquiries of science. *One of the first such paradigms was the economics of the medieval schoolmen who argued and worried about the moral problems raised by the emerging market process.* For example, one of their main concerns was whether lending money at interest (usury) was in fact a sin (remember, in the early Middle Ages it had been considered a *mortal* sin); and they endlessly discussed the criteria for the "just" prices at which commodities should sell.

That view of the economic world was displaced by the Classical economists, whose most brilliant achievements were expressed in the works of Adam Smith and David Ricardo (1772–1823). The Classical economists had no interest whatever in just prices or in the sinfulness of usury. For them the great question was *how to understand, not evaluate, economic processes, in particular the accumulation and distribution of national wealth.* Smith, as we have seen, wrote an extraordinary exposition of how the members of society, although engaged in a search for their individual betterment, were nonetheless guided by an Invisible Hand (the market) to expand the wealth of nations. Ricardo wrote with equal force about the course of national economic growth, arguing that a growing population, pressing against limited fertile acreage, would drive up crop prices and divert the wealth of the country into the hands of the landlords.

MARGINALIST ECONOMICS

The Classical paradigm concerned large issues of national growth and dealt boldly with the fate of social classes. The Marxian paradigm, in turn, grew out of the Classical, differing from it in its much more critical approach to society and to thinking about society. Then, around the 1870s, a new angle of vision abruptly displaced the older one. The new view had numerous European originators, preeminent among them W. Stanley Jevons and Leon Walras. As a group they are referred to as the Marginalists, for *they turned the focus of economic inquiry away from growth and class conflict into a study of the interactions of individuals.*

The new paradigm explained many things that the older one did not—above all, the finer workings of the price system. But just as the Classical and Marxian paradigms had dropped all interest in the just prices that had so obsessed the medievalists, so the Marginalists paid little attention to the questions of growth and class fortune that had preoccupied the Classicists and Marxists.

KEYNESIAN ECONOMICS

Inherent in the Marginalist view of the world, with its extreme emphasis on interacting individuals rather than on classes, was a micro approach to economic problems. The next radical shift in view came from the work of John Maynard Keynes, whose perception of the economic system brought into focus a macro perspective on *total* income, *total* employment, *total* output. *The most striking result of Keynes's shift from a micro to a macro perspective was his discovery that an economy that worked well at the micro level did not necessarily work well at the macro level.* From the perspective of the Marginalists, such an economic state of affairs could hardly be envisioned.

PARADIGMS OR NOT?

Hence we can certainly discern sharp changes in the views and visions of economics.

The very definition of the economic problem alters as we go from the medieval schoolmen to the Keynesians. Classical economists, as we have said, forgot about economic justice; Marginalist economists, about growth or classes; Keynesian economists, about the inner working of the market.

These shifts in economic concerns resemble those of natural science. According to Kuhn, new paradigms bring new problems into focus, rather than resolving old ones within a new encompassing view. The camera of science is aimed, as it were, at a new subject and the former subject is relegated to the background, or drops out of the picture entirely.

Now the "no" part of the answer. Where economics differs from science in these paradigmatic jumps is that in economics we can relate changes in focus to a changing backdrop of social organization. Each "school" of economic thought reflects to some degree the historical characteristics and problems of its time; whereas a change in social structures generally plays a small role in causing one scientific perspective to replace another.

What "paradigm" rules economics today? A mixture of Marginalist and Keynesian thought lies behind most contemporary micro- and macroeconomics. A Marxian view underlies much of the radical critique of our time. Perhaps it is fair to say that no paradigm is firmly ensconced today. We live in a period in which much of the conventional wisdom of the past has been tried and found wanting. Economics is in a state of self-scrutiny, dissatisfied with its established premises, not yet ready to formulate new ones. Indeed, perhaps the search for a new vision of economics, a vision that will highlight new elements of reality and suggest new modes of analysis, is the most pressing economic task of our time.

CHAPTER 4

A Bird's-Eye View of the Economy

A LOOK AHEAD

Before we begin our study of economics as a subject, we ought to know something about the economy. In this chapter we take a high-altitude pass over the terrain.

Things to watch for are:

1 The general dimensions of the two worlds of business—big business and small business.

2 The way in which income is divided up among households.

3 The size of the various government sectors. Note the plural—there is more than one meaning to "the government."

W e can't begin to study economics without knowing something about the economy. But what is "the economy"? When we turn to the economics section of *Time* or *Newsweek* or pick up a business magazine, a jumble of things meets the eye: stock market ups and downs, reports on company fortunes and mishaps, accounts of incomprehensible "fluctuations in the exchange market," columns by business pundits, stories about unemployment or inflation.

How much of this is relevant? How are we to make our way through this barrage of reporting to something that we can identify as the economy?

BUSINESS

Of course we know where to start. Business enterprise is the very heart of an economic system of private property and market relationships. Let us begin, then, with a look at the world of business.

The first thing we notice is the enormous number of business enterprises—over 16 million in all. If we divide them into proprietorships (businesses owned by a single person), partnerships, and corporations, the world of business is classified in Table 1.

Small Business

Just looking at Table 1 makes one conclusion immediately clear: **There are at least two worlds of business.** One of them is the world of small business. It embraces nearly all proprietorships and partnerships, as well as a large percentage of corporations. Here are the vast bulk of the firms we find in the Yellow Pages of the phone book, the great preponderance of the country's farms, myriad mom-and-pop stores, restaurants, motels, movie houses, dry cleaners, druggists, retailers—in short, perhaps 95 percent of all the business firms in the nation.

Small business is the part of the business world with which we are all most familiar. We understand how a hardware store operates, whereas we have only vague ideas about how General Motors operates. But the world of small business

TABLE 1
Dimensions of Business, 1984
Note that corporations are overwhelmingly the most important, but by no means the most numerous, form of business organization.

	Total Number of Firms (000s)	Total Sales (Billions)	Average Sales per Firm
Proprietorships	11,262	$ 516	$ 45,817
Partnerships	1,644	318	193,430
Corporations	3,171	6,948	2,191,106

Sources: *Statistical Abstract of the United States;* Bureau of the Census, Washington, D.C., 1988.

warrants our attention for two other reasons.

First, small business is the employer of a substantial fraction—about half—of the nation's labor force. Second, the world of small business is the source of much "middle-class" opinion. As we can tell from Table 1, the 11 million proprietorships in the country have average sales (not profits) of less than $50,000 a year. These are tiny enterprises, but they certainly give a small-business point of view to over 11 million households—one out of every seven.

We should know something about what life is like in this world, and indeed, a considerable amount of economics is concerned with the problems of operating a small business. Later, when we reach microeconomics, we will study how small business fits into the economic picture.

Big Business

We have already glimpsed another business world, mainly to be found in the corporate enterprises of the nation. Compare the average size of the sales of corporations (Table 1) with those of proprietorships and partnerships. But even these figures hide the extraordinary difference between very big business and small business. Within the world of corporations, for example, 84 percent do less than $1 million worth of business a year. But the 16 percent that do more than $1 million worth of sales a year take in 92 percent of the receipts of all corporations.

Thus counterposed to a world of very numerous small businesses is a world of much less numerous big businesses. How large a world is it? Suppose we count as a big business any corporation with assets of $250 million or more. There are roughly 3,600 such businesses in America. More than half of them are in finance, insurance, and real estate. A fifth are in manufacturing. The rest are to be found in transportation, utilities, communication, trade. Just to get an idea of scale, the largest enterprise in the nation in 1987 was General Motors, with assets of $87 billion and sales of $101 billion.

Big business is to be found in all sectors; but its special place is the industrial sector, where manufacturing plays the predominant role.

The figures in Table 2 show once again the twofold division of the business world. If we subtract the 500 biggest industrial corporations and their sales from the total of all manufacturing firms and their sales, we find that the top 500 firms—not even one-tenth of one percent of the total number—accounted for more than three-quarters of all sales. **Indeed, if we take only the biggest 100 firms, we find that they are the source of just over half the sales of the entire industrial sector.**

TABLE 2
Industrial Sector, 1987
The 500 biggest firms—about .003 percent of all firms—account for three-fourths of all manufacturing sales.

	$ Billion
Total manufacturing sales	$2,268
Total sales of the 500 biggest industrial corporations	1,879

Sources: *Economic Report of the President,* 1988; Fortune 500.

A PARADE OF BUSINESS FIRMS

We shall have a good deal to investigate in later chapters about the world of big business. But it might be useful to end this initial survey with a dramatization of the problem. Suppose that we lined up our roughly 16 million businesses in order of size, starting with the smallest, along an imaginary road from San Francisco to New York. There will be 4,000 businesses to the mile, or a little less than one per foot. Suppose further that we planted a flag for each business. The height of the flagpole represents the volume of sales: each $10,000 in sales is shown by one foot of pole.

The line of flagpoles is a very interesting sight. From San Francisco to about Reno, Nevada, it is almost unnoticeable, a row of poles about a foot high. From Reno eastward the poles increase in height until, near Columbus, Ohio—about four-fifths of the way across the nation—flags fly about 10 feet in the air, symbolizing $100,000 in sales. Looking backward from Columbus, we can see that 12 million out of 16 million firms have sales of less than that amount.

But as we approach the eastern terminus, the poles suddenly begin to mount. There are about 850,000 firms in the country with sales over $500,000. These corporations occupy the last 71 miles of the 3,000-mile road. There are 505,000 firms with sales of over $1 million. They occupy the last 50 miles of the road, with poles at least 100 feet high. Then there are 1,500 firms with sales of $50 million or more. They take up the last quarter mile before the city limits, flags flying at skyscraper heights, 500 feet up.

But this is still not the climax. At the very gates of New York, on the last 100 feet of the last mile, we find the 100 largest industrial firms. They have sales of at least $11 billion, so that their flags are already miles high, far above the clouds. Along the last 10 feet of the road, there are the ten largest companies. Their sales are roughly $26 billion and up: Astronauts are the only ones who ever get a chance to see these flags.

HOUSEHOLDS

Business is not the only institutional feature we need to inspect in this introduction to the economy. How could business operate without a work force? Let us look at this work force as a collection of "households," as shown in Table 4.

The Work Force

Our table shows us an interesting fact about the household "sector." There are more individual workers than there are households. This means that a typical household must have more than one member in the labor market.

SECTORS

Economists are always talking about sectors. Sometimes, as is frequently the case in this book, they mean a part of the economy in which *motivations* are similar. For example, we talk of a private sector, made up of households and firms, and a public sector comprised of local, state, and federal agencies. The key difference here is motive. The private sector is driven by the desire for income or wealth. The public sector is directed by the aims and ambitions of people in political life. Private enhancement may be among these aims and ambitions, but usually much larger and more "public" issues motivate the lawmakers and administrators.

Sometimes, however, economists mean a *functional* division of the economy's activities. Then they typically speak of three sectors: (1) an agricultural sector that grows and harvests natural products; (2) an industrial sector that extracts and alters and assembles raw materials; and (3) a service sector that performs a miscellany of tasks: providing power and transportation, performing the tasks of storage and selling, and furnishing the thousand ministrations of personal service—legal services, maids' services, doctors' services, various governmental services.

Table 3 gives a general idea of the way in which employment and output are distributed among the three main functional sectors.

TABLE 3
Employment and GNP by Sectors, 1988
Most of the labor force works in stores or offices. Note how this ties into occupations, shown in Table 6.

	Employment	*GNP*
Agriculture	2%	2%
Industry	24	47
Services	74	51

Sources: *Survey of Current Business;* Bureau of Labor Statistics, *Employment and Earnings.*

Notice that roughly three-fourths of all employment and half of all output take place in the service sector. This does *not* mean that industry and agriculture are therefore unimportant. Try to imagine the consequences of one summer's shutdown in our smallest sector, farming!

TABLE 4
Household Characteristics, 1987
There are more workers than households.

	Millions
Total population	240
Number of households	89.5
Families	64
Nonfamily households	25.5
Individuals in work force	114

Sources: Census Bureau Reports *P-20* (March 1987); Bureau of Labor Statistics, *Employment and Earnings,* June 1988.

But what is a typical household? The answer is not easy, because there are many kinds of households: young or elderly households with only one individual in them; young married households without children; families with young children; families with offspring who are no longer young.

Economists look at the relation between households and work in terms of a **participation rate,** which shows the percentage of various groups who are working or looking for work. In the formal language of the statistician, they are "in the labor market." Table 5 shows how considerable is the variation of these rates.

Occupations

The table also shows us that sex is still a decisive element in determining the characteristics of the labor force. This has changed significantly and will probably change still further in the years to come: Women were only 31 percent of all workers in 1950; today they are roughly 50 percent.

What sort of work does our labor force perform? Table 6 tells us.

Later we will be looking more carefully into problems of occupations. Here we might note in passing that "white-collar" jobs—professional, managerial, sales, and clerical—employ over half the working force. Here is another strong root of the American middle class.

Distribution of Income

Households interest us not only because they are the source of our labor power, but also because they are the focus of our income and our wealth. Much of the buying

TABLE 5
Participation Rates, 1988
Participation rates vary greatly.

	Percent of Group in Labor Market
Males, 20 years and older	78.0
Females, 20 years and older	56.4
Both sexes, 16–19	52.4
Males, 65 and older	16.5
Females, 65 and older	9.3

Source: Bureau of Labor Statistics, *Employment and Earnings.*

TABLE 6
Occupational Distribution of the Labor Force, 1986
Over half the work force is white-collar.

		Percent	
Professional		13	
Managerial	White-	11	
Sales	collar	12	54
Clerical		16	
Craftsmen		12	
Operatives	Blue-	11	30
Nonfarm laborers	collar	4	
Farm workers		3	
Other service workers	Both	18	

Source: Statistical Abstract of the United States.

that powers the economic machine is cycled through the household, where purchasing power is collected as wages, salaries, dividends, interest, and rents, to be pumped out again as a flow of spending for consumer goods. Consumer buying, as we will see later, is a strong force for growth in our economy, although we should emphasize right away that it is not the only force. Business and government are also buyers in their own right and strongly influence the flow of purchasing power.

We focus on households at this stage of our inquiry because their function as buyers leads us naturally to inquire into the distribution of purchasing power among families. There are many ways of describing income distribution. We will use a method that will divide the country, like a great cake, into "quintiles"—five layers of equal size. The layers will help us give dollars-and-cents definitions of what we usually have in mind when we speak of the poor, the working class, the middle class, and so on. As we will see, the amounts are not at all what most of us imagine.

The Poor

We will begin with the bottom layer, the poor. Our definition will include as "poor" all the households in the bottom 20 percent of the income distribution. From data gathered by the Census Bureau, we know that the highest income of a family in this bottom slice of the five-layered cake was $13,886 in 1986. This way of defining and measuring income distribution gives us a picture of *relative* poverty, since the bottom quintile will always be considered "poor," no matter what its income. Government statistics often stress *absolute* poverty levels, calculated according to the cost of a minimal basket of consumption goods. The income figure calculated on an absolute basis is somewhat lower than the one done on a relative basis, and the number of households living in "absolute" poverty is lower than the number existing in relative poverty: In 1986 the Census Bureau calculated that 13.6 percent of the total population was below its absolute poverty level of $11,203 for a family of four.

The box titled "Who Are the Poor?" on page 58 shows us some of the characteristics of poor families, but there are two additional facts that we should note.

First, not all families below the poverty line in any given census are still

WHO ARE THE POOR?

Work and Welfare. In 1986 there were 32.4 million people living in "absolute" poverty in the United States, an increase from 24.7 million in 1977. Of these, many were poor *despite* holding a job: 41.7 percent of poor people over the age of 14 worked, and these "working poor" constituted the most rapidly growing part of the poverty population. Only one-third of poor people in the United States receive "welfare" (Aid to Families with Dependent Children) payments. Medicaid, the program that provides health insurance for poor people, reaches only 42 percent of the poor.

Age and Race. Until recently, the elderly were disproportionately poor. Today, however, the burden of poverty falls most heavily on children: 20.5 percent of all children were poor in 1986. Race is a major factor: Poverty afflicted 43.1 percent of black children and 37.7 percent of Hispanic children in that year. Still, the overwhelming majority of the poor are (and always have been) white: 69 percent, compared with 28 percent who are black and 3 percent of other races.

Homelessness and Hunger. A recent task force on hunger reported that 20 million Americans, including 12 million children, went hungry at some point each month. And then there were the homeless—in 1986, 28 percent of them with children.

Adapted from *Who Are the Poor?* by Michael Harrington, published by Justice for All; reprinted in *Dissent*, Spring 1988, 148.

there in the next. About one-fifth of all poor households are young people just starting their careers. Some of these low-income beginners will escape from poverty. In addition, about an eighth of the members of the poverty class are older people. Many of these were not poor in an earlier, more productive stage of their economic lives. At the same time, some families that are not poor when a census is taken will fall into poverty at a later stage of their lives. The moral is that poverty is not entirely static. At any moment, some families are escaping from poverty, some entering it. What counts, of course, is whether the net movement is in or out. This is important with regard to welfare, a problem we will take up in Chapter 35.

A second characteristic is that 60 percent of the families below the poverty line have at least one wage earner in the labor force. Thus their poverty reflects inadequate earnings. A considerable amount of poverty, in other words, stems from the fact that some jobs do not pay enough to lift a jobholder above the low-income level. In some regions certain jobs pay so little that even families with two jobholders (especially if one works only seasonally) cannot pull themselves out of poverty. This is often the case, for example, with migrant farm workers or with immigrants who must take the least desirable jobs.

The Working Class

We usually define the working class in terms of certain occupations. We may call a factory operative—but not a salesclerk—working class, even though the factory employee may make more than the salesclerk.

For present purposes, however, we will just add together the next two layers of the income cake and call them working class. This will include the 40 percent of the population that is above the poor. We choose this method to find out how large an income a family can make and still remain in the working class, as we have defined it. The answer for 1987 is just under $35,015. To put it differently, 40 percent of the families in the country earned more than $13,886 but less than $35,015 that year.

UNIONS

How many members of the labor force offer their services through labor unions? In 1987 there were 17 million. That was 18 percent of the work force.

These figures do not convey the power of labor unions because they do not point out the strengths of unions in the industrial sector. The table shows more accurately how labor unions fit into the overall work picture.

Like corporations, unions show great disparity of size and strength. In the mid-1980s there were some 50,000 local unions. Many of these small locals had memberships of 50 persons or fewer and were confined to a single enterprise. At the other end of the scale we find 210 large "national" unions, including such giants as the Teamsters or the United Auto Workers. In fact, the 10 biggest unions in the country account for over half of all union membership. Thus unions, like corporations, divide into a world of small and large operations, although the contrast in the unions is not quite so dramatic as in the corporations.

TABLE 7
Percent of Unionization, 1986
Unionization is very unevenly distributed by sectors.

Sector	Employment (Millions)	Unionized (percent)
Agriculture	1.4	2.4
Industry (manufacturing and mining)	21.1	23.7
Services and other	75.2	14.0
Government (federal, state, and local)	16.3	36.0

Source: Statistical Abstract of the United States, 1988.

The Rich and the Upper Class

With the bottom three-fifths of the nation located on the income scale, we are ready to look into the income levels of the upper echelons.

First, the rich. Where do riches begin? A realistic answer is probably around $200,000 a year, an income that usually means significant corporate responsibility. There are at least 500,000 such rich families in America, or a little under 1 percent of the total. They are the icing on the cake.

But under the truly rich is a considerably larger group that we call the upper class. This is the top 5 percent of the nation, its average doctors, airline pilots, managers, lawyers—even some economists. Some 4.5 million families are in this top 5 percent.

How much income does it take to get there? In 1987 a family made it into the 95th percentile with an income of $82,273. These numbers have a certain shock value. **It takes more money to be rich, but less to be upper class, than many of us ordinarily think.**

The Middle Class

This leaves us with the middle class—the class to which we all think we belong. By our method of cutting the cake, the middle class includes 35 percent of the nation—everyone above the $35,015 top working-class income and below the $82,273 threshold of upper-class income. In 1987 an average white married couple, both working, earned about $40,000, enough to enter middle class economic territory. No wonder that a middle-class feeling pervades American society, regardless of the occupation or social milieu from which families come.*

WEALTH

It is obvious that there are great extremes of income distribution in the United States. The famous economist Paul Samuelson has made the observation that if we built an income pyramid out of children's blocks, with each layer representing $1,000 of income, the peak would be far higher than the Eiffel Tower—but most of us would be within a yard of the ground.

Even more striking than the inequality of income, however, is the inequality of wealth—that is, the ownership of assets of all kinds. The latest survey by the Federal Reserve Board gives us the overall distribution of wealth, which we show in Table 8. It tells us that four out of ten American families in 1983 had little or no wealth. Their average holdings probably include a small bank account, a mortgaged home, perhaps some life insurance or pension rights. The next third of all

---

*Maybe you wonder how an "average white married couple" could enter an income group that we have defined as being not average. The answer is that not every household in our national layer cake is white or married, with both husband and wife working. Moreover, don't forget that these figures apply to 1987. To bring them up to date, increase them by the change in average prices since 1987. That won't be precisely accurate, but close enough.

TABLE 8
The Distribution of Wealth, 1983
We can see that wealth is much more unevenly distributed than income

Net Worth	Percentage of All Families
Less than $16,000	40
16,001 to 82,000	33
82,001 to 327,000	21
327,001 to 655,000	4
655,000 or more	3

Source: *Federal Reserve Bulletin*, March 1986, p. 167. All figures have been rounded for convenience sake.

families have modest assets—a larger bank account, a better home less encumbered with a mortgage, more insurance coverage. It is not until we reach the upper quarter (actually the upper twenty-eight percent) that we begin to find considerable personal assets, and not until we enter the top group that we encounter substantial holdings. Here is where the millionaire category begins.

A PARADE OF INCOMES

Suppose that like our parade of flags across the nation representing the sales of business firms, we lined up the population in order of its income. Assume the height of the middle family to be 6 feet, representing a median income of $29,458 in 1987. This will be our height, as observers. What would our parade look like?*

It would begin with a few families *below* the ground, for there are some households with negative incomes; that is, they report losses for the year. Mainly these are families with business losses, and their negative incomes are not matched by general poverty. Following close on their heels comes a long line of economic dwarfs who make up about one-fifth of all families. These are people less than 3 feet tall; some are shorter than 1 foot.

Only after the parade is half over do we reach people whose faces are at our level. Then come the giants. When we reach the last 5 percent of the parade—incomes around $82,000—people are at least 17 feet tall. At the very end of the parade are people towering 600 to 6,000 feet into the air—100 to 1,000 times taller than the middle height. What is the largest income in the country? We do not know: Probably our 15 or so billionaires have *incomes* of over $100 million.

*Adapted from the description of an "income parade" by Jan Pen, *Income Distribution*, trans. Trevor S. Preston (New York: Praeger, 1971), pp. 48–59.

Millionaires

How many U.S. families are millionaires—that is, own net assets worth $1 million or more? The Federal Reserve study shows that the number is considerably larger than was the case 20 years ago (allowing for inflation, of course) Four percent of all American families were estimated to be worth $500,000, and 2 percent (an estimated 1,310,000) had a net worth of $1 million in 1983. If we exclude the direct ownership of a home or personal business, about 376,000 families (one-half of one percent of all families) were worth $1 million or more in financial assets alone— stocks and bonds of publicly owned companies, mutual funds, insurance, bank deposits, and the like. This is about twice as large as a percentage of all families as in 1962—once again, taking inflation into account.*

America's millionaires own a very large proportion of the nation's financial assets. The Federal Reserve study showed that in 1983 the top one-half of one percent of families owned 56 percent of the nation's municipal (tax-exempt) bonds, 43 percent of all publicly traded stock, 69 percent of all trust accounts. The top *10* percent of all families owned 92 percent of all municipal bonds, 85 percent of all traded stock, and 88 percent of all trust funds, as well as about 40 percent of all checking accounts, almost three-quarters of all money market mutual funds, and almost two-thirds of all retirement or Keogh accounts.

How Millionaires Have Fared

There is no doubt, in other words, that the ownership of wealth is heavily concentrated. The *value* of this wealth can fluctuate considerably, however. Take a man who was a millionaire in 1970, and who invested his wealth in common stocks. He would have lost about one-half the value of this wealth by early 1982 because the cost of living doubled but the stock market stubbornly refused to budge.

Then came a great stock market boom in 1982 and a second, even more dramatic one from late 1985 through the summer of 1987. This was followed by the biggest selloff in history, when the market plunged by about a third in October 1987. At the end of this roller-coaster ride, our millionaire would have been worth approximately two and a half times as many dollars as he started with in 1982. Even after inflation, he would still have more or less doubled his real wealth. Of course, if our investor had had 20-20 foresight (there are not so many of those), he would have stepped off the train at the end of August in 1987. By then, he would have tripled his real wealth—always assuming that he had bought stocks that reflected how the market performed on the average. At any rate, we can see that the value of the wealth held by the top wealth-holders can change dramatically, even though the actual holdings of assets hardly changes at all.

*Financial Characteristics of High-Income Families," *Federal Reserve Bulletin,* March 1986, pp. 163–177.

TABLE 9
Size of Government Sector, 1986
Note that the size of the sector varies, depending on what function of government we emphasize.

	Percent of Total
Employment by government	15%
GNP bought by government	20
Personal income paid by government	26

Source: *Economic Report of the President.*

GOVERNMENT

We have almost completed our first overview of the economy, but there remains one institution with which we must gain an acquaintance: the government. How shall we size up so vast and complex an institution? Let us begin with the question of size: How big is the government within the overall economy?

The Size of the Public Sector

The question can be answered in at least three different ways, as Table 9 shows. **In round numbers government employs about one-sixth of the labor force; it buys about one-fifth of our total output (GNP); and it pays out about one-quarter of all personal incomes.** This is obviously big government. Is it too big? That is not a question that can easily be answered "yes" or "no." The following facts bear on our answer.

Government as Employer

When economists speak of "government" or the "public sector," they refer to *all* government activities, not just those of the federal government. For example, as Table 10 shows, state and local government play a considerably larger role than federal government when it comes to our first measure—public employment. Indeed, if we take away national defense, as a special kind of activity, state and local government becomes about *seven times larger* than the federal government as an employer.

Government as a Buyer of GNP

Next let us consider the size of government as a buyer of GNP—that is, as a direct purchaser of the goods and services counted within GNP. Here two considerations should be borne in mind. First, about 44 percent of the GNP bought by the public sector is purchased by the federal government. Three-quarters of this is for defense. Fifty-six percent of GNP purchases are bought by state and local

TABLE 10
Kinds of Public Employment, 1985
Most public employees work for states and localities, not for the federal government. The figure for national defense includes civilian employment only. It does not cover some 2 million in the armed forces.

	Federal	State	Local
		(Number of Employees in Thousands)	
National defense	1,101	—	—
Postal service	754	—	—
Education	15	1,764	5,340
Highways	4	252	296
Health	263	678	712
Public Welfare	12	186	282
Police	66	81	613
Fire protection	—	—	317
Sanitation	—	1	220
Resources and recreation	241	196	269
Financial administration	118	131	190
Other	447	695	1,496
Totals	2,638	3,984	9,685

Source: Statistical Abstract of the United States.

governments for the kinds of purposes outlined in Table 8. Second, the fraction of GNP bought by the total government sector is roughly the same in this country as in European capitalisms, as Table 11 shows. Japan's percentage is smaller, mainly because it has so small a defense establishment.

Government as an Income Source

Finally, we have to consider the size of government measured by its contribution to income. As we have seen, the contribution of government to total incomes is larger than the value of public output. The reason is that government pays out some money to households other than the wages and salaries earned by public employees. The additional incomes are called *transfer payments* because they transfer incomes from some members of the community (usually taxpayers) to others—retirees, handicapped persons, disadvantaged citizens.

Transfers are almost entirely paid by the federal government. Of the many kinds

TABLE 11
Size of the Public Sector in Western Capitalisms, 1983
Measured by employment or expenditure, the United States public sector is well within the range of the public sectors in other major capitalist countries.

Country	Gov't Employment as Percent of Total Employment	Gov't Outlays as Percent of Total GDP*
United States	16.5	38.1
Japan	6.5	34.8
West Germany	15.9	48.6
United Kingdom	22.0	47.2

*GDP is gross domestic product (GNP less net factor payments to foreigners).
Source: OECD Historical Statistics (OECD, 1985).

of transfer payments, social security is by far the most important. Together with Medicare, this absorbs about a third of all expenditures made by the public sector. A quite different form of transfer is interest payments on the national debt or subsidies to farmers or businesses. Still another form of transfers is unemployment benefits or out-and-out welfare programs of one kind or another.

Welfare programs are a bone of contention among economists, as they are among politicians. We will just note here that the share of all transfer payments in GNP tends to be smaller in the United States than in other advanced capitalisms. We are not carrying a transfer burden that is heavier than that of, say Canada or West Germany or Italy.

Government Waste

Finally, in examining the size of the public sector, we have to consider its weight on our backs. Does government spending retard economic growth? Is it wasteful? That is a question we will meet many times as we go along. But in view of the heat it generates, we ought to state our own position now. **We believe that government can be a source of vitality and growth to the economy as well as a drag and a drain.** Everyone is acutely aware of the wasteful nature of many public projects, local as well as federal, civilian as well as military. On the other side of the coin, anyone who has ever gone to a public school, been treated in a public hospital, traveled on a public road, or flown in a plane guided by a public beacon system knows how useful public output can be. No simple judgment about the public sector can be an intelligent one.

LOOKING BACK

KEY CONCEPTS

The purpose of this chapter is not to load you with facts and figures, but to give you a sense of economic geography—a feeling for the terrain we call The Economy. The central ideas that we ought to have clearly in mind are these:

Business institutions:
• corporations
• partnerships
• proprietorships

1 Business is the most distinctive and important institution in a capitalist system. There are a very large number of private business organizations, but by far the most important of them are corporations, not partnerships or proprietorships. If you are not sure of the difference, read the important extra word following this.

Big business accounts for the preponderance of sales; small business is a substantial source of employment.

2 In the world of corporations there are clearly visible two subworlds of business—big business and little business. There is no official dividing line between the two. But if we take the top 500 corporations, we find that we account for 74 percent of all industrial sales, 60 percent of all industrial employment, and about 11 percent of all employment. Small business is also important because it is a big employer of nonindustrial workers, particularly retail or service workers.

Households are the source of labor.

3 Households are the source of the nation's labor force. Most households supply more than one worker, but participation rates vary widely among age and sex groups.

Income distribution: about one-fifth poor; about one-third middle class; about 5 percent affluent

4 For illustrative purposes we can classify one-fifth of all families and individuals as poor; two-fifths as working class; one-third as middle class; and 5 percent as upper class. While this classification gives us some idea of the ranges of family incomes in the different layers of the national income cake, we should note that the distribution of wealth is much more lopsided than the distribution of income.

The government sector varies in size, depending on what you measure.

5 Government is a very important but confusing institution to study. Its size depends on whether we assess its contribution to employment (roughly one-sixth); to GNP (about one-fifth); or to total household incomes (about one-quarter). Facts to remember: (a) State and local government is the main source of government employment and buys more of GNP than the federal government, whose purchases are mainly for defense; (b) transfer payments, largely for social security, swell the total of income payments above that of purchases of goods and services; and (c) the overall size of U.S. government in GNP, on any measure, is much like that of other advanced Western capitalist systems.

ECONOMIC VOCABULARY

Corporations   53
Sector   55
Poverty, relative and absolute   57

Participation rate   56
Quintiles   57

QUESTIONS

1. How would you explain the fact that big business has made so much headway in industrial production, but not in farming or retailing?

2. Do the facts of income and wealth distribution surprise you? Please you? Shock you? With what arguments would you defend the existing distribution: Fairness and equity? Efficiency? Natural differences among individuals?

3. When we say that the government is "too big" in this country, do we mean as a producer, an employer, or a payer of incomes? Is it possible to argue that the government is too *small* a producer, employer, or income payer? Suppose you wanted to increase our defense budget. Would you not be arguing just that?

AN EXTRA WORD ABOUT

Business Organization

Business is a central institution in our economic system, and all of us ought to know something about how business, especially the corporation, is legally organized. Although corporations are the dominant form of business property, too few people are well informed about them. Here is a brief introduction to the main forms of business organization.

PROPRIETORSHIPS

A proprietorship is the simplest kind of business organization. Usually it can be set up without any legal fuss at all, simply by opening a place of business. Sometimes one has to register or get a license, for instance, to open a liquor store or to set up practice as a physician or lawyer. But proprietorships are the easiest to understand of all forms of business.

They are also, as we have seen, the most widespread form (see Table 1). Why are not all businesses proprietorships? The answer lies in certain problems that proprietorships have.

1. A proprietorship has difficulty growing because its ability to borrow money is limited to the amount of credit its owner-proprietor can raise. Only a very rich man can borrow very much.

2. A proprietor is personally liable for all losses that his business may incur (he also gets all its profits). A rich man is not likely to open a proprietary business because if an unexpected loss is incurred—if his business is sued by an irate customer and loses the case—*the proprietor must pay from his own funds any obligations that the business cannot pay from its funds.* In fact, there is really no division between the property of the owner and that of the business.

3. When a proprietor dies, the business legally comes to an end. All debts must be paid, and a new business established to take over the old. This is hard on the spouse of the proprietor, the employees, and the creditors.

PARTNERSHIPS

Partnerships remedy many of these difficulties. Basically, a partnership is a combination of proprietors who have agreed, usually by legal formalities, to share a certain proportion of the profits and the losses of their business. The fact that there are now several people associated in the business obviously makes it easier to raise additional capital. Some very large businesses have been partnerships, at least until recent days.

Nonetheless, there are still problems for partnerships.

1. Partners are together responsible for all the losses or debts of the business. Like proprietors, partners jointly have "unlimited" liability, although some individual partners may have only limited liability.

2. The death of any partner requires that the business be legally reconstituted. When a partner of a firm dies, the firm usually has to undergo a reorganization.

CORPORATIONS

The corporation, as we have seen, is the most powerful, although not the most prevalent, form of business organization. Let us be sure that we understand exactly what a corporation is.

1. A corporation is a legal entity created by the state. Unlike a proprietorship or a partnership, all corporations must apply to their states for a charter allowing them to carry on business. The charter specifies in general terms the kinds of business they will carry on and the general financial structures they will have. Charters cost money, which is one reason that all proprietorships are not corporations. Another reason is that corporations pay income taxes on their income before it goes to stockholders.

2. Once a corporation is chartered, it exists as a "person." That is, the corporation itself—not the individuals who own it or work for it—can bring suit, be sued, or own property. This has the immediate advantage of limiting the liability of an owner of a corporation to the money he has put into the corporation. If the corporation is sued for more funds than the business possesses, the corporation will declare bankruptcy and the suer has no recourse to the private funds of the persons who own it.

3. Because the corporation is a "person," it does not go out of business when its owners die. The corporation is "immortal." It goes on until it fails as a business organization or voluntarily goes out of business, or until its charter is revoked by the state.

CORPORATE ORGANIZATION

Clearly, the corporation has substantial advantages over proprietorships and partnerships. But how does it run? Who owns it?

A corporation is owned by the individuals who buy shares in it. Suppose that a corporation is granted a charter to carry on a business in retail trade. The charter also specifies how many shares of stock this business enterprise is allowed to issue. For example, a corporation may be formed with the right to issue 100,000 shares. If these shares are sold to individuals at a price of $10 each, the original shareholders (also called stockholders) will have put $1 million into the corporation. In return, each will receive stock certificates indicating how many shares that person has bought.

These stock certificates are somewhat like a partnership agreement, although there are noteworthy differences. If you buy 1,000 shares in our imaginary corporation, you will own 1 percent of the corporation. You will have the right to receive 1 percent of all income that it pays out as dividends on its stock. You will also be entitled to cast

1,000 votes—one vote per share—at the meetings of shareholders that all corporations must hold. In this way, a shareholder is very much like a junior partner who was given a 1 percent interest in a business.

ADVANTAGES OF SHARE OWNERSHIP

But here are the critical differences between corporations and partnerships:

1. As we have already said, a stockholder is not personally liable for any debts that the corporation cannot pay.   If the company goes bankrupt, the shareholder will lose his investment of $10,000 (1,000 shares at $10 a share) but cannot be sued for any further money. *Liability is thereby limited to the amount the shareholder has invested.*

2. Unlike partnership shares, which are usually very difficult to sell, corporation shares are generally easy to sell if one owns the stock of a company that is listed (bought and sold) on one of the nation's several stock markets.   (The shares of a very small corporation are not as easy to sell, although they are less difficult to dispose of than a partnership.) Moreover, a stockholder may sell shares to anyone, at any price. If our imaginary corporation prospers, its shares may sell for $20 each. A stockholder is perfectly free to sell his or her shares at that price. As we have just mentioned, marketplaces for stocks and bonds have developed along with the corporation, to facilitate such sales of stock. The most important of these markets, the New York Stock Exchange, was organized in 1817. Today some 40 billion shares a year are bought and sold on the stock exchange. Thus, with the corporation comes the advantage of a much greater "liquidity" of personal wealth—that is, greater ease of turning assets into cash.

3. Shares of stock entitle the stockholder to the dividends that the directors of the corporation (see below) may decide to pay out for each share.   But a shareholder is not entitled to any fixed amount of profit. If the corporation prospers, the directors may vote to pay a large dividend. But they are under no obligation to do so. They may wish to use the earnings of the corporation for other purposes, such as the purchase of new equipment or land. If the corporation suffers losses, ordinarily the directors will vote to pay no dividend or only a small one out of past earnings. Thus, as an owner of ordinary common stock, the stockholder takes the risk of having dividends rise or fall.

4. Corporations are also allowed to issue bonds.   A bond is different from a share of stock in two ways. First, a bond has a *stated value* printed on its face, whereas a share of stock does not. A $1,000 bond issued by a corporation is a certificate for a debt of $1,000. The bondholder is not a sharer in the profits of the company but a creditor of the corporation—someone to whom the corporation is in debt for $1,000. In case of corporate bankruptcy, the claims of bondholders take precedence over those of shareholders.

Second, a bond also states on its face the *amount of income* it will pay to bondholders. A $1,000 bond may declare that it will pay $80 a year as interest. Unlike dividends, this interest payment will not rise if the corporation makes money, nor will it fall if it does not. Thus there is no element of profit-sharing in bonds, as there is in stocks. Like stocks, bonds can rise and fall in price when they are bought and sold, but bond interest does not change the way that stock dividends can. A bond's *coupon*—its stated interest payment—always remains the same; it is the *yield* on bonds—the ratio between the coupon and the market price—that varies.

Bondholders are compensated for not sharing in profits. The risk of owning a bond is usually less than that of owning a stock. A bond is a legal obligation of the corporation, which *must* pay interest, and which *must* buy back the bond itself when a fixed term of years has expired and the bond becomes "due." If it fails to meet either of these obligations, the courts will declare the firm bankrupt, and all its assets will be turned over to the bondholders to satisfy their debts. If the firm's assets are not enough to repay the bondholders, they will suffer a degree of loss; but the shareholders will lose *all* of their equity, for a share of stock has no such obligations attached to it and never becomes due. No shareholder can sue a corporation if it fails to pay a dividend.

OWNERSHIP AND CONTROL

One last matter is of significance in discussing the organization of the corporation. This mode of structuring enterprise has made possible a development of great importance: the separation of ownership and control.

As we have seen, stockholders are the actual owners of a corporation, but it is obviously impossible for large numbers of stockholders to meet regularly and run a company. A.T.&T. has well over a million stockholders. Where could they meet? And how could they possibly decide what the company should do?

All corporations, small or large, therefore, are run by boards of directors (who may or may not own stock in the company) who are elected by the stockholders. At regular intervals, all stockholders are asked to elect or reelect members of the board, each casting as many votes as the number of shares that he or she owns. In turn, the board of directors appoints the "management"—main officials of the corporation; for example, its chief executive officer. Management hires the rest of the employees. As the number of shareowners grows, it is not surprising that power drifts into the hands of the management. (The extent to which managers can operate independently of, or even contrary to, the interests of stockholders is one of the hotly debated questions in economics.)

STOCK EXCHANGES

We have mentioned stock exchanges as the organized markets in which shares are traded. *An important thing to realize is that buying a share of stock does not put money into a corporation, unless the stock is newly issued by the company.*

Most of the shares bought and sold on the stock exchanges are old shares, issued years ago. When you buy a share of General Motors, the money you pay does *not* go to General Motors. It goes to the individual who sold you the shares. If you own shares in a company that produces cigarettes, and you want to get out of this business because you disapprove of smoking, you sell your shares. *But doing so does not take any money out of the cigarette business.* It simply transfers your shares to another person who will pay you for your stock certificates.

Does it then make no difference to a cigarette company whether you buy its shares or not? Not quite. Corporations like to have their shares well regarded by the public because from time to time they *do* issue new shares, and they want an eager market for these shares. If their shares are in general disfavor, they will sell for lower prices, and at a lower price a company is easier to "take over" than at a higher price.* Finally, managers usually own shares in their own companies. As the shares go up, they become richer. So companies are far from indifferent to the fate of their shares. Nonetheless, we should clearly understand that we do not put money into businesses when we buy their outstanding shares.

*A "takeover" is a concerted effort, usually by a small group of individuals who own a considerable amount of the company's stock, to round up enough proxies (votes) to oust an incumbent management and to install a management of its own. Takeovers are dramatic when they occur. They are not frequent, but they happen often enough so that corporations keep an eye out for "raiding" interests. If the price of the stock falls, it is often an invitation to be taken over, simply because it is cheaper to buy the votes (shares) when the price is depressed.

CHAPTER 5

The Trend of Things

A LOOK AHEAD

The last chapter was an aerial photo of the economy, giving us the lay of the land. Now we want to take a series of pictures over time to give us a sense of change in the economic landscape. This will fit into our first historic conception of capitalism, gained in Chapter 2, and will also give us a chance to test some of the theories about capitalism we covered in Chapter 3.

In particular, we are going to examine four major trends of modern times:

1 The growth of production measured by GNP—gross national product.
2 Trends in income distribution.
3 The drift toward big business.
4 The rise in government.

Warning before you begin: Don't get bogged down in facts and figures. Keep your eye out for trends and for explanations of trends. The facts are there to illustrate these trends and to test explanations, not to be learned for themselves.

THE PROCESS OF GROWTH

*I*magine that we have had a camera trained on the U.S. economy over the last 60 years. What would be the most striking changes to meet our eye?

There is no doubt about the first impression: It would be a sense of growth. Everything would be getting larger. Business firms would be growing in size. Labor unions would be bigger. There would be many more households, and each household would be richer. Government would be much larger. And underlying all of this, the extent of the market system itself—the great ongoing flow of inputs and outputs—would be steadily increasing in size.

Growth is not, of course, the only thing we would notice. Businesses are different as well as bigger when we compare 1988 and 1929: There are far more corporations now than in the old days, far more diversified businesses, fewer family firms. Households are different because more women work outside the home. Labor unions today are no longer mainly craft unions, limited to one occupation. Government is not only bigger but has a different philosophy.

Total Output

Nonetheless, it is growth that first commands our attention. The camera vision of the economy gives us a picture that keeps widening. It *has* to widen to encompass the increase in the sheer mass of output. Hence the first institution whose growth we must examine is that of the market system itself.

More specifically, we must trace the tremendous growth in our total output. The technical name for this flow of output is gross national product (GNP), a term we will use many times in the future and will later define more carefully. Here we only note that it is the dollar value of our annual flow of final output. Figure 1 gives us a graphic representation of this increase in yearly output.

Correcting for Inflation

As we can see, the dollar value of all output from 1929 to 1988 has grown enormously. But perhaps a cautionary thought will have already struck you. If we measure the growth of output by comparing the dollar value of production over time, what seems to be growth in actual economic activity may be no more than a rise in prices. If the economy in 1988 produced no more actual tons of grain than the economy in 1929 but grain prices were double those of 1929, our GNP figures would show growth where there was really nothing but inflation.

To arrive at a measure of real growth, we have to correct for changes in prices. To do so, we take one year as a *base* and use the prices of that year to evaluate output in all succeeding years.

Here is an elementary example. Suppose our grain economy produced 1 million tons in 1929 and 2 million in 1988, but wheat sold for $1 in 1929 and $4 in 1988. Our GNP in the current prices of 1929 and 1988 is $1 million for 1929 and $8 million 59 years later. But if we evaluate the GNP *using only the 1929 prices* (i.e., $1

FIGURE 1
Value of GNP 1929–1988
Gross national product (GNP) increased 44-fold in 59 years, as measured in the prices of each year's production. In this graph we use a semilog scale because it shows more clearly the rate of growth rather than the absolute dollar growth of GNP. Note how the rate of growth of nominal GNP has accelerated since 1940. From 1940 to 1965 the speedup reflects mainly an acceleration of real GNP growth. After 1965 the further acceleration mainly reflects inflation.

per bushel), our GNP is reduced to $2 million in 1988. This constant-dollar GNP is often referred to as the *real GNP,* while the current-dollar GNP is called the *nominal GNP.* We can use the prices of any year as the base. The important thing is that all outputs must be evaluated with only one set of prices.

Figure 2 shows us the much-reduced growth of output when output is measured in 1982 dollars, the year now most frequently used as a base.

As we can see, growth in real (or constant-dollar) terms is much less dramatic than growth in current dollars that make no allowance for rising prices. Nonetheless, the value of 1988 output, compared to that of 1929, with price changes eliminated as best we can, still shows a growth factor of almost 5½.

FIGURE 2
GNP in Constant (1982) Dollars
Measured in real terms, GNP increased only about 5½ times, not 44 times, between 1929
and 1988. Note that, except for the major interruption of the Depression and World War
II, real economic growth has followed a nearly constant trend in history.
Source: *Economic Report of the President, 1986.*

Per Capita Growth

But there still remains one last adjustment to be made. The growth of output is a
massive assemblage of goods and services to be distributed among the nation's
households, and the number of those households has increased. In 1929 the United
States population was 122 million; in 1988 it was about 243 million. To bring our
constant GNP down to life size, we have to divide it by population to get GNP per
person, or per capita.

Historical Record

In Figure 3 we see the American experience from the middle of the nineteenth
century in terms of real per capita GNP, this time in 1929 prices.* Viewed from the
long perspective of history, our average rate of growth has been astonishingly
consistent. This holds true for an average over the past half century since the Great

*Why do we use 1929 as a base here and 1982 as a base in Figure 2? We do it to accustom you to the
idea that different years can serve as the basis for comparison. Note, too, that our 10% bands are
approximate—they should be wider in the later years, and narrower in the earlier, than they are
drawn.

VOLUME AND VALUE

You should be warned that there is no entirely satisfactory way of wringing price increases out of the hodgepodge of goods and services called GNP, and so of measuring precisely the increase in the "real" volume of goods and services. That is because there is an unavoidable element of arbitrariness in grouping or adding together the various price changes that occur in different goods when the relative proportions of these goods in total output are also changing. This class of difficulties is known as "index number problems."

For example, consider an economy that produces two goods, wheat and steel, in two periods, 1900 and 1990. Suppose in 1900 the price of wheat is $1 per bushel and 100 bushels are produced, while the price of steel is $5 per ton and 100 tons are produced: 1900's GNP is thus $600. In 1990 the price of wheat is still $2 per bushel and 200 bushels are produced, while the price of steel is $8 per ton and 1,000 tons are produced: 1990's GNP is therefore $8,400 *current* dollars. But the *real* GNP in 1990 depends on whether you use the wheat-to-steel proportions of 1900 or those of 1990 as the "base" for your calculations of the price index. With 1900 proportions of 50 percent by value for each commodity, the price level has increased from 100 to 180, and the real value of GNP in 1990 is $8400/1.8 = $4666.67 1900 dollars. But using 1990 proportions (20 to 1), the price level change is calculated as approximately 1.6 times, since the smaller proportionate price increase (in steel) is given a greater weight. The result: Real GNP growth in one case is measured as [(8400/1.8)/600] = 7.77 times over nine decades, and as [(8400/1.6)/600] = 8.75 times in the other. A difference!

Index number problems arise *whenever* we try to group together commodities whose relative volumes of output are changing. So we cannot just add up tonnages of wheat and steel and rice and coal to arrive at approximations of real GNP. The best we can do is agree that we will use a *common* base year for calculations of price indices (usually the earlier year, or 1900 in the above example). That way at least our calculations will be consistent.

What about adding up, not the goods themselves, but the *labor time,* the millions of hours of work embodied in the production of those goods? By this means we might get a measure of the "pure volume" of output, independent of prices. But the problem is that we want our measure of GNP to reflect some measure of value—and not all hours of labor are valued equally. We would have to boil down all kinds of labor, skilled and unskilled, trained and untrained, manual and intellectual, to multiples of some "basic" kind of labor, representing an elemental amount of "economic effort." And how would we do that? By looking at the value, *measured in prices,* of the resulting output! Thus there is no way to escape the index number problem.

In the end, the task of measuring an aggregate of different things can never be solved to our complete satisfaction. Growth is a concept we constantly use, but it remains beyond precise definition.

FIGURE 3
Real GNP Per Capita (1929 Dollars)
Real GNP per capita has shown a long, irregular, but fairly steady upward trend.

Depression or back to the 1870s (or even 1830s). As the chart shows, the swings are almost all contained within a range of 10 percent above or below the trend. The trend itself comes to about 3.5 percent a year in real terms, or a little over 1.5 percent a year per capita. Although 1.5 percent a year may not sound like much, remember that this figure allows us to double our real per capita living standards every 47 years. This is Adam Smith's growth model come to life!

Sources of Growth

How do we explain this long upward trend? Here we can give only a brief summary of the causes we will study more systematically later. Essentially, we grew for two reasons:

1. THE QUANTITY OF INPUTS GOING INTO THE ECONOMIC PROCESS INCREASED. In 1929 our civilian labor force was 53 million. In 1987 it was about 122 million. Obviously, larger inputs of labor produce larger outputs of goods and services. (Whether they may even produce *proportionally* larger outputs—i.e., larger outputs *per man or woman who works*—is another question we will investigate later.)

2. THE QUALITY OF INPUTS IMPROVED. The population working in 1987 was not only greater than in 1900, it was better fed, healthier, and above all better schooled. The best overall gauge of this is the amount of education stored up in the work force. In 1900, when only 6.4 percent of the working population had gone beyond grade school, there were only 223 million person-years of schooling embodied in the population. In 1986, when over three-fourths of the population had finished high school, the stock of education embodied in the population had grown to over a billion person-years.

The quality of capital has also increased, along with its quantity. Consider, for example, the contribution made to our output by the availability of surfaced roads. In 1900 there were about 150,000 miles of such roads. In 1988 there were almost 4 million miles. That is an increase in the quantity of roads of over 25 times. But that increase does not begin to measure the difference in the transport capability of the two road systems, one of them graveled, narrow, built for traffic that averaged 10 to 20 miles per hour; the other, concrete or asphalt, multilane, capable of supporting heavy trucks at 65 miles per hour.

Productivity

Improvements in the quality of inputs—in human skills, in improved designs of capital equipment—have been far more important than mere increases in quantity. Better skills and technology enable the labor force to increase the amount of goods and services it can turn out in a given time.

Figure 4 shows the trend in productivity since 1950. As you can see, the growth has been fairly steady up to the early 1970s, despite occasional dips. After 1972 the trend seems to shift downward, and in 1979 and 1980 it actually turns negative—we grew less productive! This may have been a short-lived phenomenon, having to do with the inefficient (unproductive) use of labor in a recession.

GNP AND QUALITY CHANGE: THE CASE OF COMPUTERS

One of the most difficult practical issues in measuring GNP concerns products whose quality changes rapidly from one year to the next. In principle, such quality changes are equivalent to a *decline* in the price of a "standard" or unchanged version of the product. But in real life it is very hard for national income accountants to estimate just how quickly such quality-adjusted prices are really declining.

In the case of computers, the Commerce Department's Bureau of Economic Analysis worked from 1969 through 1984 on the assumption that the price of a computer was unchanged, so that the nominal and the real measures of output in the computer industry were the same. Then, in 1985, the Bureau introduced new figures which showed that the price of computers (in terms of units of computing power embodied in the machines) had in fact fallen by *a factor of nine* over this period because of enormously improved productivity. The result: In 1972 dollars the real output of computers was reestimated to be *over $100 billion higher* than originally thought.

Such corrections are large enough to make a difference to measures of total output growth and of total productivity growth in the 1970s. Indeed, a significant part of the measured slowdown of productivity growth may be simply a failure to measure the effects of technological progress in a timely way.

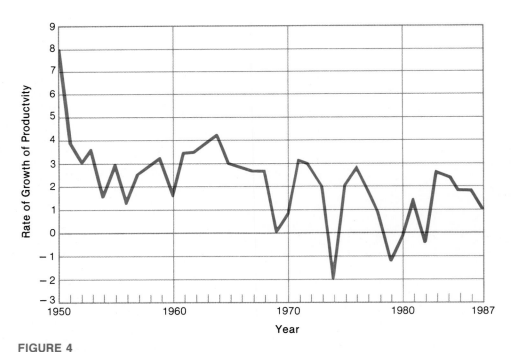

FIGURE 4
The Productivity Picture
These data show that measured increases in productivity have fallen precipitously in some recent years, especially in recession years, when the rate of output was also low (or negative).
Source: *Economic Indicators.*

Here we want to emphasize the contribution made to long-term growth by our normal steady improvement in our ability to grow and extract and handle and shape and transport goods.

CHANGES IN DISTRIBUTION

We have seen how striking was the increase in output in the twentieth century. But what happened to the division of this output? Have the rich gotten richer and the poor poorer, as Marx predicted? Or has the trend been in the direction of greater equality?

Changes in Dollar Incomes vs. Changes in Shares

The question is not easy to answer. Remember, we are interested in the changes in *shares* going to different groups, not just in absolute amounts. There has certainly

THE DIFFERENCE GROWTH RATES MAKE

The normal range in growth rates for capitalist economies does not seem to be very great. How much difference does it make, after all, if output grows at 1.7 or 2.7 percent?

The answer is: an amazing difference. This is because growth is an *exponential* phenomenon involving a percentage rate of growth on a steadily rising base. At 1.7 percent, per capita real income will double in about 40 years. At 2.7 percent, it will double in 26 years.

Professor Kenneth Boulding has pointed out that before World War II no country sustained more than 2.3 percent per capita growth of GNP. From World War II until 1973, Japan achieved a per capita growth rate of about 8 percent. Boulding writes: "The difference between 2.3 and 8 percent may be dramatically illustrated by pointing out that [at 2.3 percent] children are twice as rich as their parents—i.e., per capita income approximately doubles every generation—while at 8 percent per annum, children are six times as rich as their parents."

been a tremendous change in the dollar amounts that we have used to define different social classes, as Figure 5 demonstrates.

The figures show that growth has helped boost all income classes. But has the *proportion* of income going to the various classes also changed? That is not what we find. Figure 6 shows that the sharing out of incomes among social groups has been remarkably steady, at least until the beginning of this decade. Only if we go back to the 1920s do we find a marked change. In those days the share of the top 5 percent was perhaps twice as large as it is today, and, of course, such programs as Medicaid, food stamps, and public housing, which have significantly improved the real living standards of the poor in our own time, did not exist.*

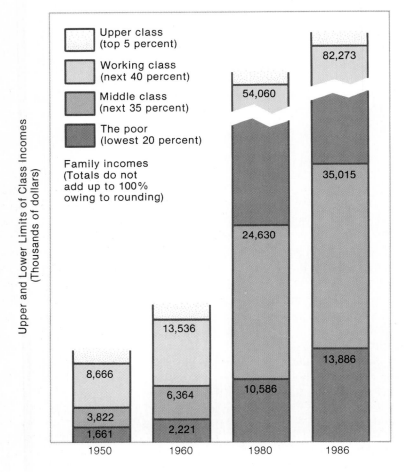

FIGURE 5
Upper and Lower Dollar Limits of Social Classes
The dollar incomes of all social classes have increased markedly. (Notice there is no upper hand in the topmost class. Do you understand why?)
Source: *Census Bureau P–60, 149.*

*A more detailed study of changes in income distribution would have to take into account some facts that are not included in the figures above. For technical reasons, the Census Bureau does not include most forms of capital income (such as capital gains on stocks or real estate) in its computation of incomes. If it did, the share of the top 1 percent would be larger. The Census Bureau also does not fully take into account cash and noncash payments to the poor, such as food stamps or welfare aid. This would add to the share of the poor. In other words, the Census figures are mainly derived from earnings, not returns on capital or "in-kind transfers" that may benefit high- or low-income groups.

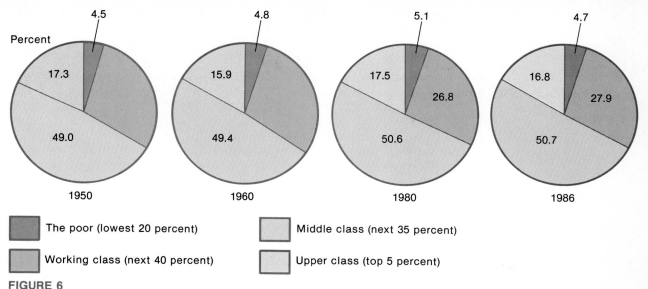

The poor (lowest 20 percent)

Middle class (next 35 percent)

Working class (next 40 percent)

Upper class (top 5 percent)

FIGURE 6
Shares of Total Income Going to Different Social Classes
The distribution of income among different social classes has shown very little change.
Source: *Census Bureau P-69.*

What has happened to the distribution of income since 1980 is not so encouraging. The deep recession of 1981 put a halt to further improvements in income equality, as large numbers of the newly unemployed slipped to the bottom of the income pile. Cuts in social programs further reduced the share of the poorest, while cuts in progressive tax rates and in capital gains and inheritance taxes raised the after-tax income shares of those in upper-income brackets. Economic recovery after 1982 restored some of the income share of the middle classes, but we remain today a less equal nation than we were a decade or two ago.

The Elimination of Poverty?

What about poverty? For many years the number of persons below the government's designated low-income level was dropping, both absolutely and in relation to the larger population. We can see this gradual shrinkage in Table 1, where poverty declines markedly from 1959 through 1969. By 1975 the decline has stopped owing to two recessions, in 1970 and 1974–1975. Thereafter poverty rises and falls with economic conditions: down in the recovery of 1976–1980, up sharply with the deep recession and cutbacks in antipoverty programs of 1981–1982. In the recovery since 1982 the *proportion* of the population defined as poor has fallen, in large measure because of the rise of the multi-income family unit as many more women entered the labor force. However, the *absolute number* of poor people was still higher in 1986 than in 1981. Thus social stagnation afflicting millions of poor people coincided with economic recovery; the rising tide did not "lift all boats."

TABLE 1
Persons Below Low-Income Level

	1959	1969	1975	1981	1986
All persons (millions)	39.5	24.1	25.9	31.8	32.4
Percent of population	22.4	12.1	12.3	14.0	13.6

Source: Census Bureau *P-60*.

What caused the decline in poverty up to 1975? The progress against poverty was heavily concentrated in one section of the population—the elderly. This was due primarily to a rise in the coverage and real value of social security benefits. By the mid-1980s, poverty among older people had fallen to historically low levels. On the other hand, conditions for single women with children and for minorities had not gotten better, and had perhaps even deteriorated. The advent of the homeless in the 1980s has been a new and shocking experience, showing that dramatic poverty persists among a small part of our population.

TRENDS IN BUSINESS

We have examined the main trends in personal income. Now let us turn to business. Here one change immediately strikes the eye. There is a marked decline of the independent small business—with its self-employed worker—as a main form of enterprise.

Decline in Small Business

In 1900 there were about 8 million independent enterprises, including 5.7 million farms. By 1986, as we saw in the last chapter, the number of proprietorships had grown to over 12 million, a figure that included some 2.1 million farms. Meanwhile the labor force itself more than tripled. Thus as a percentage of all persons working, the proportion of self-employed has fallen from about 30 percent in 1900 to under 10 percent today.

Rise of Big Business

With the decline of the self-employed worker has come the rise of the giant firm. Back in 1900, the giant corporation was just arriving on the scene. In 1901 financier J.P. Morgan created the first billion-dollar company when he formed the United States Steel Corporation out of a dozen smaller enterprises. In that year the total capitalization of all corporations valued at more than $1 million was $5 billion. By 1904 it was $20 billion. In 1986 it was over $7 trillion.

CAUSES OF POVERTY

In a box on page 58 we took a quick look at some of the characteristics of the poor. Here is a second, more systematic glance. It puts all households—families and individuals—into various categories and shows us the chance that someone in a given category will be a member of a low-income (poor) household (once again using the official definition).

TABLE 2
Chances of Being Poor, 1986

	%
All families	12.0
Single persons	21.6
White families	9.4
Black families	29.7
Families headed by females	
White	30.6
Black	53.8
Children	20.5
Elderly	12.4

Source: Census Bureau *P-60.*

But we must always be very careful before we impute poverty to any single source. One of the authors, sitting in a Ph.D. exam, was questioning a candidate about a dissertation on poverty. It seemed there were many causes for poverty, all impressively substantiated with evidence.

"But if you had to single out one cause as the *most* important," asked the examiner, "which would it be?"

The candidate hemmed and hawed. There was skill. There was health. There was culture. There was native ability. But if he *had* to choose, he would say that education—or rather, the lack of it—was the greatest contributory factor in poverty. Most poor people simply didn't have the knowledge to enable them to get high-paying jobs.

"And why didn't they have the education?" asked the examiner.

That was easy. Education was expensive. Poor people couldn't afford private schools. Their need for income was so great that they even dropped out of public school early to earn money.

"I see," said the examiner. "People are poor because they are uneducated. They are uneducated because they haven't the money to buy education. So *poverty causes poverty.*"

TABLE 3
Largest Manufacturers' Share of Assets (%)
The share of the biggest corporations grew rapidly during the 1950s and 1960s and stabilized in the 1970s. It may have risen since then.

	1948	*1960*	*1970*	*1981*	*1986*
100 largest corporations	40.2	46.4	48.5	46.8	55.0
200 largest corporations	48.2	56.3	60.4	60.0	66.0

Source: Statistical Abstract of the United States

It hardly comes as a surprise that the main trend of the past 80 years has been the emergence of big business. More interesting is the question of whether big business is continuing to grow. This is a more difficult question to answer, for it depends on what we mean by "growth."

Certainly the place of the biggest companies within the world of corporations has been rising. Marx was indubitably right in predicting this trend. Indeed, as Table 3 shows, the top 100 companies in 1970 held approximately as large a share of total corporate wealth as the top 200 companies in 1948.

Merger Mania

Until recently, economists generally believed that the concentration movement had leveled off. Between 1960 and the early 1980s, the percentage of assets held by the top 100 corporations remained fairly steady, and the concentration of sales likewise showed no signs of significant change.

Beginning in the early 1980s, however, this condition of overall stability changed suddenly and dramatically. A new merger wave broke out—a wave of such immense proportions as to dwarf all earlier periods of corporate acquisition (see Figure 7). During the quiet years before this wave, the annual number of mergers in the ranks of the nation's larger corporations averaged less than 100, and the total amount of assets involved in all mergers amounted to something like $5 billion per year. Then merger mania began. In 1984, 2,999 "big" mergers took place, involving $124 billion in total assets. In 1985 and 1986 the numbers were *still* higher—about $180 billion in each year—and 1987, despite the market crash in October, saw mergers amounting to over $150 billion. By that year billion-dollar mergers—**mergers that were individually larger than the merger totals of the premerger decade**—**had become commonplace.** (See box for details.)

Behind the Merger Wave

What brought about this extraordinary and quite unforeseen merger frenzy? Two factors seem to underline the boom—one financial, the other legal. The financial impetus came originally from the combination of high interest rates and slow

FIGURE 7
Number of Mergers 1895–1987
The number of corporate mergers has risen to new heights in the 1980s.
Source: *Cited in Barrie A. Wigmore, "Speculation and the Crash of 1987, "presented to the American Economics Association, December 28, 1988. From Devra L. Golbe and Lawrence J. White, "Mergers and Acquisitions in the U.S. Economy: Aggregate and Historical Overview," in Alan J. Auerbach (ed.),* Mergers and Acquisitions, *a NBER Report, p. 37;* © *1988 by the University of Chicago Press.*

growth in the middle 1980s. Together these factors depressed profitability and the price of corporation shares to the point where the market value of the existing assets of many corporations (e.g., the oil reserves of the big oil companies) was far less than what it would cost to recreate those assets with new investments (oil exploration). This presented aggressive companies and shrewd financiers with the opportunity to acquire existing assets cheaply by buying out the corporations that owned them. Later in the decade, when the stock market began to boom again, a purely *speculative* motive made an appearance: Merger artists sought profits by bidding for companies that they could sell off later in the rising market. Even at the market's peak in 1987, it was still more profitable to buy existing assets on the stock market than to create assets with new investments.

The persistence of the merger mania may also be due to a changed attitude on the part of the federal government. Deregulation set the stage for a general competitive consolidation within the industries affected, such as trucking and airlines. And under President Reagan, the Justice Department effectively stopped enforcing the antitrust laws, thus removing an obstacle that had formerly dampened merger enthusiasm.

1988'S BILLION-DOLLAR DEALS

Announced Bids, Jan. 1 to Mar. 7

Buyer	Target	Price (Billions)
R. H. Macy	Federated Department Stores	$6.2
Eastman Kodak	Sterling Drug	5.1
Bat Industries	Farmers Group	4.3
Bernard F. Brennan	Montgomery Ward	3.8
Black & Decker	American Standard	2.3
Desert Partners	USG	1.9
Mesa	Homestake Mining	1.9
Pirelli	Firestone Tire & Rubber	1.9
Dun & Bradstreet	IMS International	1.8
Barris Industries	Media General	1.6
Beazer	Koppers	1.3
Kohlberg Kravis Roberts	Stop & Shop	1.2
American Brands	E–II Holdings	1.1
Forstmann Little	AFG Industries	1.1
New England Electric	Public Service of New Hampshire	1.0

Data: M&A Data Base, *Mergers Acquisitions Magazine; Business Week*

*Reprinted from March 21, 1988 issue of *Business Week* by special permission, copyright © 1988 by McGraw-Hill, Inc.

Hostile Mergers

The merger wave of the mid-1980s was often marked by "hostile" takeovers—purchases of one company by another, or by a financier, despite the objections of the first company's management. Hostile takeover bids succeed because existing shareholders find them profitable: The "raider" makes a buyout offer well above the current market price of the shares, and such lucrative prices cancel out whatever loyalty shareholders may feel toward existing management.

Where do the billions to take over a large company come from? Many hostile takeovers have been made possible because banks lent raiders very large amounts of money, often on frail security. After the takeover was consummated by buying out shareowners with the bank's money, the raider typically unloaded his debt on the company he had acquired, causing it to issue "junk bonds"—high-interest, ill-secured debt—whose proceeds were then used to reimburse the bank. Or the raider may have sold off the acquired company's assets to raise the cash to pay the bank that supplied the acquisition funds to begin with. Thus banks have provided the largest share of initial takeover financing.

Consequences of the Merger Wave

The effects of the merger wave cannot be described as clearly as its causes. It will be some time before we know to what degree the overall concentration of assets will be affected, or whether the domination of big companies in individual markets has changed. In the meanwhile the most important effect of the merger wave is likely to be on corporate profitability. Interest on the $173-odd billion of new debt that was issued in 1987 is an *expense* that must be met before profits can be realized. If this expense is not met—and in the case of junk bonds it may not be—any adverse turn of events, either in a single strategic company or in the overall economy, could possibly precipitate a panic comparable to those that shook the financial world in earlier periods of financial wheeling and dealing.

Is it possible that the merger wave may turn out to be a good thing, not a bad one? Its supporters claim that the effect will be the creation of larger, wealthier, and more efficient institutions, capable of better meeting massive competition from abroad. Its detractors worry about financial instability and about the wholesale elimination of jobs—including middle-management jobs—when companies merge. And in the background there is always the troublesome issue of the concentration of economic power. We are in the midst of a remarkable transformation of the corporate scene.

Explaining the Trend to Business Size

Can we explain the long-term trend toward the concentration of business assets, as we did the trend toward growth in GNP? By and large, economists would stress three main reasons for the appearance of giant enterprise.

1. ADVANCES IN TECHNOLOGY HAVE MADE POSSIBLE THE MASS PRODUCTION OF GOODS AND SERVICES AT FALLING COSTS. The rise of bigness in business, at least in the first instance, is very much a result of technology. Without the steam engine, the lathe, the railroad, it is unimaginable that big business would have emerged at all.

But technology went on to do more than make large-scale production possible. Typically it also brought an economic effect that we call **economies of scale.** That is, as production processes grew bigger, they also became more productively *efficient:* They came to yield more outputs in relation to the inputs of land, labor, and capital that they used.

THE RISE AND CRASH OF THE STOCK MARKET

The stock market is America's most closely watched, if not most reliable, index of economic performance. We watch the stock market not just from vicarious interest in other people's money, but also because it tells us (we think) about the prospects for a national economy that very much affect our own lives. A rising stock market reflects confidence: in future profits, investment, and growth. A falling market is depressing.

From the depths of recession in 1982, the stock market began one of its longest and most sustained recoveries in history: five full years of steady upward march. In 1987 the market soared to new highs, rising nearly 50 percent above its value on New Year's day, as measured by the Standard and Poor's index of 500 stocks.

Then, from October 13 through October 20, 1987, catastrophe struck. On October 19 alone the Dow Jones Industrial Index lost 508 points, or over 22 percent of its value. By whatever measure, all of the gains of a year were wiped out in a week. The total lost value of stocks in America's corporations was estimated at just over $1 *trillion* dollars.

What difference did it make? The answer, one year later, is: evidently not very much. Unlike the Great Crash of 1929, the Great(er) Crash of 1987 produced no recession, no panic, no wave of failures of brokerage firms and banks. In the words of President Reagan's Task Force on Market Mechanisms:

Two important points emerge from a comparison of the market decline of 1929 to that of 1987. First, structural change in the economy since the Depression—chiefly the changing composition of economic activity, the increasing roles of the government and the absence of chronic deflation—means that the economy now appears to be far more stable than it was in 1929. Second, the Great Depression appears to have been caused not by the stock market crash but by the interaction of a number of diverse circumstances (such as the declines in agriculture and housing) and misguided policies (such as the Smoot-Hawley Tariff, the tight monetary policy in late 1931 and the tax increase in the summer of 1932). Thus, as long as a similar set of circumstances and policy initiatives are avoided, a comparable economic contraction should remain only a remote possibility.

Economies of scale are perhaps most easily visualized in the vast increases over the past 30 years in the size of tanker ships that transport petroleum. Supertankers, now ranging in size up to over 220,000 tons, use no more crew (labor) than far smaller vessels. And because the volume of a container rises more rapidly than its surface area, the capital costs (the steel that goes into the ship) are also less per barrel of capacity. **Thus both capital and labor are reduced per unit of output as the size of tankers increases.**

Economies of scale exist in many other types of processes, such as mass assembly lines, where the economies in the use of labor time and in the specialization of capital goods are key factors. These economies provided a further powerful impetus to the growth of size. **The firm that pioneered in the introduction of mass-production technology often secured a competitive selling advantage because, having used fewer inputs per unit of output, it could offer its outputs at a lower price.**

2. CONCENTRATION IS ALSO A RESULT OF CORPORATE MERGERS. We have just looked into the merger wave of the 1980s. But ever since J. P. Morgan assembled U.S. Steel, mergers have been a major source of corporate growth. At the very end of the nineteenth century there was the first great merger wave, out of which came the first huge companies, including U.S. Steel. In 1890 most industries were competitive, without a single company dominating the field. By 1904 one or two giant firms, usually created by mergers, had arisen to control at least half the output in 78 different industries.

Again, between 1951 and 1960 one-fifth of the top 1,000 corporations disappeared—not because they failed, but mainly because they were bought up by other corporations. **In all, mergers account for about two-fifths of the increase in concentration between 1950 and 1970; internal growth accounts for the rest.**

3. DEPRESSIONS OR RECESSIONS PLUNGE MANY SMALLER FIRMS INTO BANK-RUPTCY AND MAKE IT POSSIBLE FOR LARGER, MORE FINANCIALLY SECURE FIRMS TO BUY THEM UP VERY CHEAPLY. Certainly the process of concentration is abetted by economic distress. When industries are threatened, the weak producers go under; the stronger ones emerge relatively stronger than before. Consider, for example, that three once-prominent American automobile producers succumbed to the mild recessions of the 1950s and 1960s, and to the pressure of foreign competition: Studebaker, Packard, and Kaiser Motors. More recently, American Motors was absorbed by Renault, and Chrysler only escaped demise by congressional bailout in 1979.

A New Trend Toward Smaller Industries?

Last, a possible countertrend. The long movement toward bigness may be peaking because of new technologies that favor smaller, more flexible firms. Perhaps symptomatically, while the large integrated steel firms have languished, "minimills" have been flourishing. Some economists have suggested that perhaps the day of the industrial Goliath is over, and that the Davids of the future will be firms capable of highly computerized "batch" operations instead of long mass-production runs. It will be a while before we know if this is the case, but the trend alerts us once again to the strategic role played by technology in establishing the basic structure of the economy. Moreover, it may be that today's emerging flexible-production companies will become the industrial giants of tomorrow!

HOW BIG IS BIG?

Just to get an idea of scale, the 36th largest industrial corporation in 1987 ranked by sales was Unisys. Its sales that year were $9.7 billion. It was not the 36th largest in terms of its assets, which were $9.9 billion. The 36th largest firm in assets was Rockwell International, with assets of $8.7 billion. Rockwell's sales of $12.1 billion ranked it 27th in terms of sales.

Thus it makes a difference whether we rank companies for size by sales or assets. At the very top of the heap, the top 9 firms in terms of sales are the top 9 in terms of assets. This coincidence weakens as we move down the list. Some examples: Chrysler was 10th in sales, 15th in assets; General Dynamics was 39th in sales, 68th in assets; North America Phillips was 86th in sales, 117th in assets; Conagra was 41st in sales, 150th in assets.

Which is more important, sales or assets? Sales measure the dominance of a company within its field; assets measure its overall financial strength. Actually, both sales and assets measure size, but what counts in the marketplace is profitability. Here the correct measure is the net rate of return—the rate of profit earned per dollar of capital. The average big business earns two to three times the return of the average small business, but really spectacular rates of return are usually found in smaller businesses on their way to stardom.

Last rule of thumb: To make it into the top 500 companies, your sales have to be about $460 million; your assets, $200 million.

Labor Unions

What about labor unions? Have they also shown trends comparable to the big corporation? Their history is parallel in many ways. Over the last 80 years, the percent of the labor force belonging to a union has increased from 3.2 to 18. Thus the twentieth century has seen the emergence of big labor alongside big business. Yet, as Table 4 shows, the peak came in the 1950s and the percent of unionized nonagricultural workers has actually declined since then.

TABLE 4
Labor Force in Unions
The importance of unions in the labor force has been falling, although unions remain powerful in key sectors.

	1940	*1950*	*1960*	*1970*	*1980*	*1986*
Percent unionized	27.2	31.9	31.4	27.3	22.0	18.0

Source: AFL-CIO *Directory of Labor Organizations.*

FROM PIN FACTORY TO ASSEMBLY LINE

We recall Adam Smith's pin factory. Here is a later version of that division of labor, in the early Ford assembly lines.

Just how were the main assembly lines and lines of component production and supply kept in harmony? For the chassis alone, from 1,000 to 4,000 pieces of each component had to be furnished each day at just the right point and right minute: a single failure, and the whole mechanism would come to a jarring standstill. . . . Superintendents had to know every hour just how many components were being produced and how many were in stock. Whenever danger of shortage appeared, the shortage chaser—a familiar figure in all automobile factories—flung himself into the breach. Counters and checkers reported to him. Verifying in person any ominous news, he mobilized the foreman concerned to repair deficiencies. Three times a day he made typed reports in manifold to the factory clearing-house, at the same time chalking on blackboards in the clearing-house office a statement of results in each factory-production department and each assembling department. *

Such systemizing in itself resulted in astonishing increases in productivity. With each operation analyzed and subdivided into its simplest components, with a steady stream of work passing before stationary men, with a relentless but manageable pace of work, the total time required to assemble a car dropped astonishingly. Within a single year the time required to assemble a motor fell from 600 minutes to 226 minutes; to build a chassis, from 12 hours and 28 minutes to 1 hour and 33 minutes. A stopwatch man was told to observe a 3-minute assembly in which men assembled rods and pistons, a simple operation. The job was divided into three jobs, and half the men turned out the same output as before.

As the example of the assembly line illustrates, the technology behind economies of scale often reduced the act of labor to robot-like movements. A brilliant account of this fragmentation of work will be found in Harry Braverman's *Labor and Monopoly Capital* (New York: Monthly Review Press, 1974).

*Allan Nevins, *Ford, the Times, the Man, the Company* (New York: Scribner's, 1954), pp. 1,507.

This does not mean, of course, that all unions today are diminishing. The last two decades have brought a boom in unions for white-collar workers, such as teachers and office workers; in unions for municipal employees, such as police, firefighters, and transit workers; in diversified union organization, such as the powerful Teamsters. The declines have come where industries are declining, as among railwaymen, clothing trades workers, and auto workers. Unions are certain to remain a major force in crucial areas of the economy.

THE TREND IN GOVERNMENT

We pass now to a consideration of the last great trend in the economy—the trend in government, whose end result has been the emergence of the modern public sector.

From Small to Large Government

First we must try to explain the rise of the government sector from its relative insignificance at the beginning of the century to the general magnitude and importance it enjoys today. What follows is an analysis of the historic trend that we believe most economic historians, conservative or liberal, would agree on.

1. THE GROWING SIZE OF BUSINESS PROVOKED A DEMAND FOR GOVERNMENT SUPERVISION. As business firms increased in size, private decisions became fraught with much larger social consequences. As business increased in size, the social impact of its activities steadily widened. Building or not building a plant came to spell prosperity or decline for a town, even for a state. Cutthroat competition could mean ruin for an industry on which whole regions depended. At the same time, as companies emerged with many thousands of employees and millions of dollars' worth of capital, fears grew about the possible misuse of power that so great a concentration of economic control seemed to imply. Thus one important reason for the long-term growth of government has been the public demand that it prevent or cope with problems that arose from the sheer increase in business size.

2. TECHNOLOGY BROUGHT A NEED FOR PUBLIC SUPERVISION. Much of the long-term growth of government stems from the impact of technology. Examples: As the automobile became commonplace, it created a need for traffic authorities to deal with it—some 10 percent of state and local government employment exists to deal with the automobile. The same effect followed the appearance of the airplane and the radio (how would access to ''channels'' be determined, what would stations be permitted to broadcast?). And of course in our own day we have seen the same effect from atomic energy, new drugs, space, and weaponry.

3. URBANIZATION INCREASED THE NEED FOR GOVERNMENT. City life has its appeals, but also its perils. People cannot live in crowded quarters without police, public health, and other facilities far more complex than those needed in a rural setting. Government has always been an urban phenomenon, and as every nation has urbanized, its reach of government has increased.

4. UNIFICATION OF THE ECONOMY GAVE RISE TO ADDITIONAL PROBLEMS.
Industrialization knits an economy together into a kind of vast, interlocked
machinery. An unindustrialized, localized economy is like a pile of sand: If you poke
a finger into one side of it, some businesses and individuals will be affected, but
those on the other side of the pile will remain undisturbed. The growing scale and
specialization of industrial operation turns the sandpile into a rigid structure. You
move one side of it, and the entire structure shakes. Problems can no longer be
localized. The difficulties of the economy grow in extent: There is a need for a
national, not a local, energy program, for national transportation, urban, and
educational programs. Government—largely federal government—is the principal means by which such problems have been handled.

5. ECONOMIC MALFUNCTION BROUGHT PUBLIC INTERVENTION. Seventy-five
years ago the prevailing attitude toward the economy was a kind of awed respect.
People felt that the economy was best left alone, that it was fruitless as well as
ill-advised to try to change its workings. That attitude changed with the Great
Depression. In the ensuing collapse the role of government greatly enlarged. The
trauma of the Depression and the determination that government had the
responsibility to prevent its recurrence were a watershed. Keynes's thinking played
a very important part in this transition.

**6. A NEW PHILOSOPHY OF "ENTITLEMENT" REPLACED THE OLDER ONE OF
"RUGGED INDIVIDUALISM."** Largely, but not wholly as a consequence of the
experience of the Depression, a profound change has been registered in public
attitudes toward the appropriate role of government. We no longer live in a society
in which old-age retirement, medical expenses, and income during periods of
unemployment are felt to be properly the sole responsibility of the individuals
concerned. For better or worse, these and similar responsibilities have been
gradually assumed by governments in all capitalist nations. Here lie crucial reasons
for the swelling volume of state, local, and federal production and purchase.

The Trend in Recent Years

What has happened to the trend toward big government in recent years? In most
people's minds, the trend of the past has continued or accelerated. The years since
1950 are popularly regarded as a time when the reach of government has vastly
increased.

Has it? In Figure 8(a) we trace the evolution of the public sector over the last 37
years. The first thing that strikes us is the tremendous increase in government
purchases. This surely seems evidence of an unprecedented growth of government
in modern times. But the upward-sweeping line is not corrected for inflation or real
growth. In Figure 8(b) we show the same dollar figures as a percentage of GNP. A
completely different picture now emerges. **As a share of the economy, there has
been no appreciable growth in government spending for goods and services
over the last 37 years.** The shift to "big government" came with the Depression
and World War II; since then government has grown along with, but not more
quickly than, the economy itself.

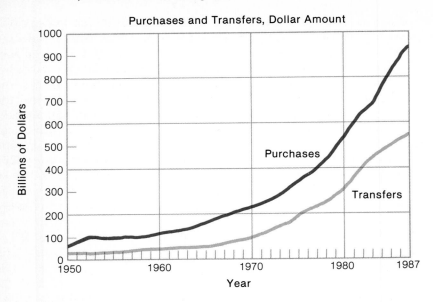

Purchases and Transfers, Dollar Amount

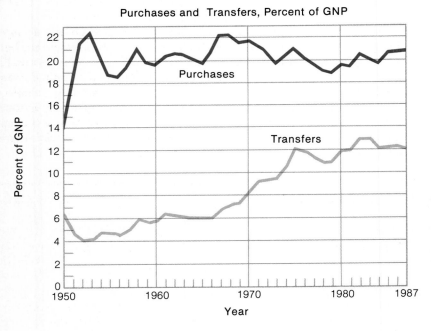

Purchases and Transfers, Percent of GNP

FIGURE 5.8
Government Buying or Spending Since 1950
Government trends are much more stable, as a percentage of GNP, than is apparent in the nominal data.
Source: *Economic Report of the President, 1988.*

The Trend in Transfers

The picture is somewhat different when we look at the growth of government transfers. Here we find a rise not only in the dollar totals but also in the size of transfers compared to GNP. In 1950 transfer payments of all kinds amounted to about 6.3 percent of GNP; in 1986 they had grown to about 12 percent of GNP.

But now we must distinguish between the growth of *programs* and the growth of *expenditures.* The number of welfare programs has not increased, particularly since the Reagan administration's effort to reduce the government's role to one of providing a relatively small "safety net." Expenditures have only grown because the costs of expanding a few large entitlement programs have far outweighed the savings from the abandonment of numerous smaller ones. Primary among these increases in expenditure have been the growth of social security payments, "indexed" to the cost of living, and the very rapid rise in Medicare costs. Together these two transfer programs have increased from $150 billion in 1980 to over $298 billion in 1988. An additional factor has been the mushrooming growth of interest payments on the national debt, up from $52 billion to $148 billion over the same eight years. This is a transfer from taxpayers to bondholders, who, as we have seen, come from the wealthiest stratum of our society.

Growth in Intervention?

Last comes a question that is not so readily answerable by graphs and figures. Has government intervention into the workings of the system followed the rising trend that marked the period from the late nineteenth century to the present?

That is a question we cannot answer because we have recently come through a history-making experiment. A great many regulatory efforts of the past have been undone—for example, the regulation of airline routes and trucking rates and the safety and environmental aspects of enterprise. In the 1980s the United States passed through a period of impatience with government intervention combined with a willingness to let the market mechanism itself serve as the great regulator of the system. It is too early to know how far this movement will go, or how permanent will be the changes it has already brought. This is an issue to which we will return.

LOOKING BACK

KEY CONCEPTS

This chapter has been concerned with the economy in movement—not in quick, month-to-month fluctuations of the kind that will concern us when we study macroeconomics, but in longer-run, year-to-year, or decade-to-decade changes. Here are the most important of them.

Real vs. nominal growth

More inputs and more productive inputs

1 There is a long-term growth pattern to GNP—a pattern that is much more striking in nominal GNP than in real GNP (that is, in figures uncorrected for inflation than in corrected figures), but remarkable even with all adjustments for rising prices. This growth can be attributed mainly to two factors: an increase in the quantity of inputs as our labor force and our stock of wealth have grown, and an increase in the quality and effectiveness of inputs as our productivity has increased. Here is Adam Smith's growth projection in reality.

Rise in incomes but little change in distribution

2 A second main trend is directly connected with the rise in output. It is the rise in dollar incomes for all levels of households—a rise that is, of course, much greater before we adjust for inflation than after. The distribution of income among classes has changed only very slowly, however. Poverty has been gradually eroded, but remains a stubborn problem, recently worsened.

Big-business share of assets has grown, but not its share of individual markets.

3 The share of total assets belonging to the biggest corporations showed a startling increase in the decades of the 1950s and 1960s. However, the increase in the share of sales in different markets going to the biggest firms has shown no significant change. Big firms get bigger by absorbing assets of companies in *different* branches of business, so that their degree of monopoly control within markets shows little change. The main sources of business growth have been technology (recall Chapter 2) and mergers.

A new merger wave in the 1980s may disrupt the corporate scene.

4 Starting in the mid-1980s, an unprecedented merger wave has brought enormous changes to the corporate world. The concentration of overall assets has certainly increased, but it is less certain that market concentrations have also increased. The merger wave has created a considerable threat of financial instability because mergers have often taken place through the issuance of ill-secured new bonds to finance company takeovers.

The reasons for a growing public sector are linked to the attributes of evolving capitalism.

5 The public sector has grown dramatically since the late nineteenth century. Here is a list of the most important causes:

☐ the growing size of business
☐ the disruptive effects of technology
☐ urbanization
☐ the unification of the economy
☐ a Keynesian remedy for economic malfunction
☐ a new philosophy of entitlement

For the last 37 years we have seen stability in the public sector, except for a few big entitlement programs.

6 There has been a striking stability in the trend of the public sector since 1950. The ratio of government spending to GNP has been virtually unchanged, although the dollar amounts are of course much larger. Transfer payments have risen as a fraction of GNP, but this is the result of indexing social security, the growth of Medicare, and higher interest payments on the national debt, not because of a growing number of transfer programs.

Can the trend be reversed?

7 We have recently seen an effort mounted by the Reagan administration to curtail further government growth and to cut back certain government programs. It is still too early to tell whether this effort will succeed, or be reversed under President Bush.

ECONOMIC VOCABULARY

Gross national product   74   Productivity   79
Real and nominal GNP   75   Economies of scale   89
Index numbers   77

QUESTIONS

1. Here are some raw data:

	GNP (Current $Billions)	Price Index (1982 = 100)	Population (Millions)
1970	$ 977	42.0	204
1980	2,633	85.7	227
1985	3,966	280	240
1987	4,486	117.5	—

What is real GNP per capita in 1980 and 1988 in 1982 dollars? In 1988 dollars? *Hint:* You will need a new price index with 1988 = 100.

2. If there were no change whatsoever in technology, do you think that a larger quantity of labor might result in GNP growing faster or slower than the sheer increase of man-hour input? *Hint:* Can people organize their activities better as their numbers change? Does this continue indefinitely?

3. Do you think it might be possible to construct a theory to explain why the pretax, pretransfer shares of income are so fixed? Could there be a kind of pecking order in society? Could different groups establish economic distances that satisfy them? Would they then strive only to retain, not to increase, those differences?

4. Can you imagine an invention that would result in rapid concentration in a very unconcentrated industry—say, the restaurant business? or the laundry business? Can you imagine an invention that could radically deconcentrate an industry? How might a watch-sized CB radio affect the telephone industry? What invention could do the same for Exxon? IBM?

CHAPTER 6

America in the World Economy

A LOOK AHEAD

With a rude shock, Americans have realized that our national economic health depends on events in the wider world. The United States is a trading nation. We have a need for foreign raw materials and a taste for foreign goods. We rely on foreign markets for the products of our agriculture, our aerospace, our capital equipment, and much else. We are affected by drought in the Soviet Union, by war in the Middle East, by depression in Latin America. It used to be said that when America sneezed, Europe caught pneumonia; now it is at least true that when the world economy catches cold, we sneeze.

This chapter is a first look at a problem that will concern us many times as we move through our studies. It focuses our attention on three main problems:

1 What is the position of the United States in the world economy today?
2 What has happened to our traditional competitive advantages?
3 What challenges lie ahead?

THE WORLD ECONOMY

Not many years ago, problems of international economics were largely relegated to the backs of textbooks, including this one, and it was understood that the busy instructor and the overworked student were both to be forgiven for letting them go by. There were two main reasons for this deliberate downplaying of the international side. The first was that America was still generally thought of as a **closed economy,** one that was able to get along quite well without worrying too much about the rest of the world. The second reason was that international economics introduced a new, seemingly unnecessary complication into the economic problem. It necessitated thinking about two kinds of money—ours and theirs.

For better or worse, the closed economy has become wide open. The rest of the world has moved from the backs of textbooks to the front pages of every newspaper. One does not have to be an economist to be aware of the "invasion" of foreign goods into American markets, an invasion that has not been forced on us, but that we have brought about freely by choosing to buy foreign cars, TV sets, shoes, and machine tools. All of us became aware of another aspect of America's international economic problems in August 1982, when Mexico nearly defaulted on its almost $100 billion debt to U.S. and foreign banks. We then realized for the first time the extent of our financial involvement with the rest of the world—we hold over $400 billion of loans, many of them very shaky. And in the years since, the debt problem of the developing countries has deepened and widened, and still seems far from a resolution.

So the era of the "closed" economy—it was never *really* closed—is over. Students and instructors, indeed all American citizens, must learn to think about a world where America's problems are tied into foreign problems, and where even the American dollar has to be understood as just one currency among many. That is what this chapter is about.

A SPECTRUM OF NATIONS

Let us begin by taking a look at the world economy as it might appear to an economist traveling at a planet-encompassing height. The first thing to be noted is that the United States is still the world's wealthiest economy. Our gross national product is about equal, each year, to that of *all* of Western Europe. We produce only a little more per capita than Japan, but more than twice as much overall, since Japan has only half of our population. We are twice as productive, both absolutely and on a per person basis, as our major strategic rival, the Soviet Union. We are 50 times more productive per worker than China, and 10 times more productive overall, since we have only one-fifth of its population. All in all, as Table 1 shows, we still possess the richest and most productive large industrial economy in the world.

TABLE 1
Population, GNP, and GNP Per Capita—Some Recent Figures.

Country	*Population 1987 (Millions)*	*GNP 1984 (Billions of $)*	*GNP per Capita (Actual $)*
Ethiopia	46.7	$ 4.7	$ 111
Bangladesh	107.1	12.6	128
Indonesia	180.3	82	484
Nicaragua	3.3	2.6	788
Mexico	81.8	139.4	1,795
Israel	4.2	21	5,070
USSR	284	1,998	7,035
Italy	57.3	360.7	6,330
Hungary	10.6	77.6	7,277
United Kingdom	56.8	466.4	8,270
Japan	122	1,249	10,237
W. Germany	60.9	674	11,020
Canada	25.8	329.4	13,100
U.S.	243.8	3,640	14,979
Switzerland	6.6	104.5	16,220

Source: *Statistical Abstract of the United States, 1988.*

Other Advanced Nations

Although we are the world's wealthiest nation, we are certainly not the world's only wealthy nation. Japan, for example, has made tremendous strides over the last 40 years. Its best manufacturing industries are second to none in efficiency. Its high rates of household saving and of investment are the envy of the world, and its economic growth rates have for decades averaged over twice our own. If Japan were not a crowded island chain with few natural resources, dependent on the Middle East and Indonesia for energy, on Australia and the Americas for food, and on the United States and Europe to provide markets for its manufacturing production, the Japanese would probably be richer than we are today.

Europe is not short of land or resources, but it has lacked the political and cultural unity that has so favored the development of Japan. Until the twentieth century, Europe was by far the most developed part of the world, dominant in world politics and in world trade. Nationalism, warfare, political upheaval, loss of colonial empires, economic depression, and an inability to integrate narrow national markets into a single economy brought a loss of Europe's competitive edge. But since World War II Europe has been overcoming these obstacles and building a stable, modern, integrated multinational economy. Today Europe is rich, peaceful, and self-sufficient, and looking ahead to full commercial integration in 1992. However, Europe also remains plagued by high unemployment, and worried about whether it can keep up with the Americans and the Japanese.

Among the advanced nations of the world, the Soviet Union is today perhaps the most interesting. Its history in this century up to the 1950s was remarkable—it went from peasant backwardness and war destruction to a capability in sophisticated space technology and impressive programs of social improvement. Then the first signs of a creeping disease became apparent, the disease of advanced bureaucratic arteriosclerosis. First the Russian economy lost momentum, then it stagnated, then it began to run in reverse. But the full story is not yet written. Under the leadership of Mikhail Gorbachev, the Soviet Union has entered the era of *perestroika*—restructuring. President Gorbachev has announced a radical program for dismantling the cumbersome structure of central planning and introducing many of the institutions of a freer—if not quite a free—market. Will these reforms work? Does perestroika mean the nose of the capitalist camel is under the communist tent? These are questions we will look into again in Chapter 38, but we raise them now as part of our first survey of the world economy.

The Third World

Beyond these giants there is the vast diversity of the Third World, where more than 3 billion of the world's people now live. The Third World encompasses every kind of economic experience, as well as every standard of living. Average living standards range from near-starvation (the per capita GNP of Ethiopia is $110 per year) to modest (Brazil, Chile, and Mexico have per capita incomes of $1,500 to $2,000 per year), but these averages are the result of lumping together the incomes of the affluent few and the indigent many. On this basis of averaging rich and poor, a few tiny principalities and sheikhdoms enjoy the highest living standards on the planet—the "average" per capita (not per household) income in the United Arab Emirates was $19,270.

Since 1970, Third World nations have demonstrated their importance in two ways. The first was their ability to extract an enormous flow of wealth from the West when the Organization of Petroleum Exporting Countries (OPEC) boosted oil prices from $2.59 to $11.59 per barrel in 1973 and again from $13.34 to $24.00 in 1979. The resulting transfer of wealth amounted to over $377 billion. It gave a tremendous boost to inflation in the West and produced some economic development in a few countries of the East and South. It also set into motion a spiral of lending, partly to help finance oil imports into countries like Brazil that had few domestic supplies, partly to finance industrialization in oil-exporting countries like Venezuela and Mexico. This lending spree ended in a vast overextension of credit that still hangs over the world. Perhaps most significant of all, OPEC made abundantly clear the vulnerability of all Western economies to any long-lasting interruption of oil supplies. Until the price of oil collapsed in 1986, the political geography of the planet was profoundly changed.

A second impact, less dramatic but no less significant, was the demonstration that the underdeveloped areas could combine low-wage labor with high technology to create export industries capable of challenging the Western economies. New techniques of transportation and communication made it possible to make circuit boards in Hong Kong, TV sets in Taiwan, automobiles in South Korea—achievements utterly impossible only a few years before. These countries soon became principal suppliers for their European and American markets. So far only a few of the underdeveloped countries have achieved this capability, but the more successful among them have become new and, to some, worrisome entrants to the advanced capitalist world.

FITTING INTO THE WORLD ECONOMY

How does the United States fit into this array of national economies? The United States has long been the largest trader in the world. In 1987 we imported $560.1 billion worth of goods, about as much as the entire gross domestic product of Great Britain! (We exported $425.8 billion, more than the whole GNP of Canada.) What's more, the American presence is felt in world trade even where the United States is not a direct party. The American dollar has been the unit of account for world trade since the end of World War II. Today it is estimated that up to a trillion dollars are held by foreigners who use them to finance world trade. Oil moving all over the world is priced in dollars, and the same is true of many other commodities traded on the international markets.

Nonetheless, until recently most Americans were not aware of the role the rest of the world played in their economic lives. That is because our participation in world trade and finance, vast though it was, was still small in comparison with the business we did internally, with ourselves.

Rising U.S. Involvement

But over the past 25 years that has changed. The change seems fairly modest when viewed against *total* GNP. In 1960 exports and imports amounted to only 5 percent of the total value of goods and services produced in the United States. By 1987, exports had risen to 11 percent of GNP and imports to 15 percent.

But look at manufacturing: Today one dollar of every five earned from the sale of U.S. manufactures comes from an export; one dollar of every two spent by Americans on manufactured products is spent on an import. These figures hit home harder when they are made more specific. One out of every three American-made jet planes, about one out of every two oil rigs, and approximately one of every three computers is destined for sales overseas. Taken together, exports are responsible for the jobs of 13 million Americans. At the same time, American consumers have acquired an enormous taste for imported manufactured goods, from automobiles to umbrellas, and American companies have come to rely more and more on raw materials, and intermediate goods such as steel, that are produced abroad. In 1960 foreign cars held only 4 percent of the U.S. market; in 1987 their share was 26 percent. In certain parts of the country, such as California, all the top-selling automobiles are imported. In steel, the share of imports in U.S. production has risen from 4.2 percent to 25 percent since 1960. Similar statistics could be cited for a host of other products—radios, televisions, bicycles and motorcycles, textiles, leather goods, and much more. We get a sense of this by looking at Figure 1.

The Trade Deficit

If our rising involvement in the world economy meant only a greater interweaving of American production and American consumption with world demand and

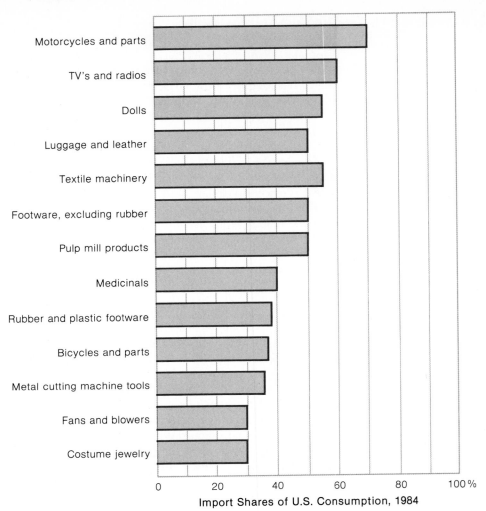

FIGURE 1
Americans Buy Many Foreign-Made Goods, as a recent survey shows.
Source: *Department of Commerce.*

world supply, we might still be able to put the international economy at the back of our textbooks. But something has happened in addition to a globalization of American economic activity. The globalization has taken place unevenly, with our imports rising much more rapidly than our exports.

We can see this in Table 2. Note that up to 1982 our exports were generally larger than our imports, so the *trade balance*—the net difference between what foreigners paid us for American goods and services and what we paid them for their goods and services—showed a sum in America's favor. In 1982, for example, the balance was $19 billion. If we think of the United States economy as a kind of national "firm" trading with (and competing against) other national "firms," that is

TABLE 2
U.S. Exports and Imports
Starting in 1983, there is a striking change in our balance of foreign trade.

| | Exports and Imports of Goods and Services | | |
Period	Exports	Imports	Net Exports
1974	146.2	132.8	13.4
1975	154.9	128.1	26.8
1976	170.9	157.1	13.8
1977	182.7	186.7	−4.0
1978	218.7	219.8	−1.1
1979	281.4	268.1	13.2
1980	338.8	314.8	23.9
1981	369.9	341.9	28.0
1982	348.4	329.4	19.0
1983	336.2	344.4	−8.3
1984	364.3	428.5	−64.2
1985	347.7	441.6	−94.0
1986	377.4	523.2	−145.8
1987	425.8	560.1	−134.3
1988	518.7	611.9	−93.2

Source: Economic Report of the President.

the net amount we earned that year. Now look at the years since then. Our purchases have far outrun our sales, so we have run up a very substantial deficit. In effect, we are no longer paying our way.

A Word about Trade Deficits

We now come to one of those complications that we used to skip: A nation is not a firm; and although individual businesses make or lose money in international trade, the nation runs no such profit and loss account. Instead, **a nation earns or loses claims against other countries from its exports and imports.** When we sell American goods abroad, we are paid in dollars by foreigners. Where do they get those dollars? Either from selling goods and services to us, or by borrowing from American lenders, such as investors who will buy their bonds or banks (probably American banks) who will extend them credit in dollars, or by spending any stores of previously earned dollars, called **reserves.**

If we buy more than we sell, we must also find the **foreign exchange**—the needed foreign currencies—to pay for what we have not earned. Where do we get that exchange? Exactly like foreigners, we have no choice but to spend any reserves we have accumulated or to borrow the money from banks who will lend us exchange or from investors who will buy our bonds.

What Table 2 shows is that in six years we have had to pay almost $550 billion more to foreigners than we have earned from them. This means that we have had to borrow that much from foreign banks and other lenders, mainly by selling them United States bonds. Even for a nation as large and wealthy as the United States, a debt of $550 billion to foreigners is beginning to be a serious problem, even though we have large investments abroad. If we go on piling up such debts, at some point our debt will seem so large that foreigners will no longer consider the United States a good risk. They will no longer be willing to buy our bonds or to extend credit for their currencies against IOUs in dollars.

A Trade Crunch

At that point America would have to bring its imports into line with its exports. America would have to "pay its way" because there would be no other source of foreign currencies with which to buy the foreign goods it wanted. We would then experience the same trade crunch that has been felt by countries such as Mexico or Brazil, whose economic plight has made them very poor credit risks.

Because Mexicans or Brazilians cannot borrow foreign currencies, they are forced to limit their imports to the amount that they can sell abroad—minus a very large fraction of those export earnings that must be paid to foreigners as interest on past debts. **The result is a severe fall in the standard of living.** The same result could be felt by this country if, let us say, our foreign debt was $2 trillion, and our ability to get foreign credits vanished. We would then have to bring our imports down to the value of our exports—minus the huge interest payments we would owe on our $2 trillion debt.

It is unlikely that the United States, with its vast strength, will ever experience a trade crunch like that of Mexico or Brazil. But it is not a scenario to be dismissed as "impossible," for that is the direction in which events are moving unless we bring order into our international economic relationships—an order that does not presently prevail.

Behind the Trade Deficit

How did the richest nation in the world become a debtor in the world economy? There is no simple answer, but we should become familiar with two main explanations.

1. THE DOLLAR WAS TOO HIGH. In the international economy currencies of different countries are constantly being exchanged for one another, and their prices often change dramatically. In the case of the United States, the rate of exchange of the dollar against other main currencies fell in the 1970s, and then moved sharply up after the turn of the decade. In 1980, for example, it cost $2.33 to purchase a British pound. In early 1985 the price of dollars had risen—and the price of pounds had correspondingly fallen—to the point where you could buy a pound for $1.24. Over the same five-year period the **exchange rate** for dollars against two other major European currencies had risen from 4.22 French francs to the dollar to over 10 francs, and from 1.82 German marks to 3.1 marks.

Why was the dollar so high? As with the prices of commodities, we explain movements of currencies in terms of supply and demand. A high price for dollars meant that foreigners were seeking to acquire dollars more than Americans were seeking to acquire other moneys. The main reason foreigners wanted dollars so strongly is that American interest rates became higher, and American inflation rates lower, than the corresponding rates in many European countries. Investors in those countries, or big international companies looking for a place to park their funds, bought dollars in order to purchase U.S. bonds or other investments. As this "portfolio" demand grew, the price of dollars rose.*

What is the effect of a high dollar? We will put ourselves first into the shoes of an American importer, then into those of an American exporter. Suppose we are a department store buyer shopping for sweaters in England. The English manufacturer doesn't quote us a price in dollars; he gives us a price in English pounds—don't forget that he probably sells the greater part of his sweaters to English stores, not American ones. Say that his price is £30. The high dollar becomes a wonderful break for our department store buyer. The higher the dollar goes, the fewer dollars she has to pay to acquire the pounds she needs. In 1980, for example, a £30 sweater would have cost $69.90. By early 1985, the same £30 sweater cost her only $37.20.

So high dollars mean cheap imports. Can you see that for the same reasons high dollars mean expensive exports? A French buyer of computers will be much less eager to pay $1,000 for an American computer when the dollar is high than when it is low, because it will cost him more francs to purchase that thousand dollars.

We have to leave a deeper examination of the exchange rate for Chapter 23. But we have seen one very important reason for the American trade deficit. A high dollar priced us out of a competitive position in exports and lured us into a vast import boom. Most experts believe that the dollar in 1985 was at least 30 percent over its normal relationship to other currencies.

From High Dollars to Low Dollars

Not surprisingly, the dollar began to fall in 1986. In fact, it did not merely fall—it plummeted, at least against the major currencies we use as benchmarks. In two years the price of a German mark rose from 46 cents to 56 cents; of 100 Japanese yen from 59 to 75 cents. As we write these words, the dollar has fallen so far that it is now American goods that are cheap in international trade and foreign goods that are expensive at home.

Then why hasn't the trade balance turned around? Why aren't American exports booming and U.S. imports from abroad shrinking? Part of the answer is that our exports *are* booming, but that our imports are *also* booming, mainly because foreign sellers have trimmed their profit margins to keep their foothold in the American market. Part of the answer is that important potential markets for U.S. goods, especially among the Third World countries, are stagnant because those nations remain trapped in their debt crisis and have no foreign exchange left to buy U.S. goods. Part of the answer may lie in a slow global shift in the location of production, away from former industrial centers to the burgeoning Pacific Rim and other newly industrializing areas.

---

*Later on we will find that American interest rates have been high because of American monetary and fiscal policy. That is a twist to the story which we must postpone for the moment.

TABLE 3
Manufacturing Productivity
The United States is no longer a world leader in productivity.

	Output per Hour (1983)	Rate of Growth (%) 1977–1982
United States	$18.21	0.6%
Germany	20.22	2.1
France	19.80	3.0
Italy	17.72	3.6
Japan	17.61	3.4
Canada	17.03	−0.3
U.K.	11.34	2.7

Source: Lester Thurow, *The Zero Sum Solution* (New York: Simon & Schuster, Inc., 1985), p. 49.

We will have to investigate these matters more carefully later in our book. Here it is enough to note that the falling dollar has not yet been enough to remedy our adverse trade flows, although sooner or later it is very likely to bring things into better balance.

2. PRODUCTIVITY GROWTH WAS TOO LOW. The high dollar is a big factor in the adverse American trade balance, but it is not the only reason for concern about America's position in the world economy. A second type of apprehension stresses real, not monetary, factors.

Behind the Productivity Lag

The data in Table 3 show that U.S. manufacturing productivity had already been bettered by Germany and France in 1983; it has probably further slipped since then. It has also probably been surpassed by a number of smaller European countries such as Sweden, the Netherlands, Switzerland, and Austria. Thus we are no longer the undisputed leader in productivity, at least not in the manufacturing sector. Even more disturbing are the data that show our rate of productivity growth to be slower than of most of our main competitors. We may recall from Chapter 5 how important growth rates are (look back for a moment to the box on page 00). U.S. figures during the five years shown in Table 3 reveal that we have been one of the worst performers in the advanced industrial world.

A country whose productivity is growing more slowly than that of its competitors will slowly find itself priced out of the market, exactly the same as a company whose efficiency is improving less rapidly than that of its competition. Although high exchange rates make our competitive position very difficult in the short run, low productivity growth makes it difficult in the long run.

Too Many Services?

What lies behind this laggard performance? Few important phenomena are less well understood. Some economists believe the reason lies in the failure of the American economy to save and invest as large a fraction of its GNP as its major competitor nations—Japan, for example, invests 28 percent of its GNP, Germany 20 percent —against our 19 percent.

This relatively low investment share in GNP reflects another big change in the U.S. economy—toward a lower share of manufacturing in total employment. We are shifting workers, in effect, from high-productivity-growth manufacturing jobs into lower-productivity-growth service jobs. In Chapter 4 we saw that three out of every four Americans today work in service occupations. These range from highly skilled occupations such as architect and engineer to low-skilled jobs in fast-food operations, but on the average, services produce less GNP per worker per year than either agriculture or manufacturing.

Hence the sheer movement into services pulls down our productivity average. This drift is visible in all advanced countries, but nowhere has it developed to the extent that it has in the United States—in France, Germany and Japan the service sector absorbs only 60 percent of the labor force. Moreover, the distribution of the labor force *within* the service sector is not helpful to the United States. Consider this comparison: For every 10,000 U.S. working people, there are 20 lawyers, 40 accountants, and 70 engineers. In Japan the numbers are 1 lawyer, 3 accountants, and 400 engineers.*

Other Explanations

Another explanation calls attention to our educational system. Much as with our relatively poor showing in capital formation, the United States compares badly with other advanced countries in its formation of human capital. In 19 international tests of educational achievement, Americans never scored at the top, and in 7 tests scored at the bottom.†

And there are still other explanations—adversarial rather than cooperative relations between American management and labor; the absence of a workable consensus on the role of government in the economy; inflexible management styles and failure to take full advantage of the flexible production techniques high technology makes possible; a decline of the old-fashioned work ethic; and more besides.

Moreover, unlike the problem of a high dollar, the productivity problem does not lend itself to a tidy solution. No matter what the root of the problem—capital formation, our occupational mix, our educational system, our labor-management structure—the cure involves our whole society, at every level and in every public and private dimension. **Some form of national policy will be needed to change the underlying configuration of American society in ways that encourage rather than discourage national productivity growth.**

*The New York Times, December 19, 1982, Sec. 12.
†Barbara Lerner, "American Education: How Are We Doing?" Public Interest, Fall 1982, p. 64.

A DEBTOR NATION?

In the summer of 1985 the Commerce Department announced that the United States had become a debtor nation for the first time since 1914. By a debtor nation, we mean that the value of U.S. assets held by foreigners—real plant and equipment, real estate, stocks and bonds, CDs, or just bank balances—exceeded the value of foreign assets of similar kinds held by Americans. Moreover, this net external debt was growing rapidly. By the end of 1985, it had already exceeded $100 billion, making us one of the world's largest net debtors. By the end of 1986, it was $400 billion. At the rate it was growing, our debt would reach $1 trillion by 1990. *The New York Times* called this "the most dramatic transformation in [the United States] financial position since world War I"; it may very well be the most dramatic turnabout in world financial history.*

The basic cause of the startling turnaround lies in our adverse balance of trade. As we know, the only way any nation can import more than it exports is to borrow the foreign exchange needed to pay for its import surplus. Our own borrowing took the form of selling many kinds of United States obligations to foreigners, from Treasury bonds to mutual funds or CDs. All these transactions made foreign currencies available to Americans because foreigners had to sell their own currencies in order to buy U.S. assets. The foreign funds they sold then became available through the banking system to U.S. importers.

Is the net U.S. debt a worrisome thing? There is no simple answer to this question. Insofar as our import surplus stimulates foreign production, our growing debt makes a sizable contribution to world economic growth, from which we benefit as well as others. In addition, the sale of Treasury bonds or bills and other

FINDING OUR PLACE

As we move through macro- and microeconomies and into international trade, we will have a chance to consider policies that may help us find a viable place in the world. In this introduction to the problem, let us end as we began, by trying to see the problem as a whole.

An Interdependent World

As we have seen, the importance of the rest of the world for the U.S. economy has risen sharply. Curiously, the importance of the U.S. economy *within* the rest of the world has not. In 1960 it was estimated that the United States accounted for 40 percent of all the production in the world. By 1984 this fraction had fallen to 24 securities to foreigners makes it possible for the United States to incur its own domestic debts, both private and public, without relying exclusively on its own savings. This eases the pressure on interest rates and helps growth at home.

The main danger is that the growth of foreign debt will eventually imperil America's international creditworthiness—its ability to borrow more foreign funds. That depends not so much on the size of our foreign borrowings as on the use to which we put them. In the nineteenth century we borrowed heavily from Europe to build a vast transcontinental railway system. But because foreign savings were put to such productive use, American international credit remained good despite the frequent bankruptcies of the railroads themselves. If our present and future international debt were put to equally productive use, the same optimistic forecast would seem appropriate today. Alas, that does not seem to be the case. Our foreign borrowings have not been earmarked for the creation of productive assets, public or private. Even though our borrowings have helped world economic recovery and have stimulated American growth, there is no reason for foreigners to feel that the value of their American assets is secure because those assets are "real wealth," like railways. The danger is that foreign lenders will appraise the soundness of their investments in the United States by the general condition of the American economy—*including its ability to make its exports pay for its imports.*

*As we will see when we look into multinational corporations (Chapter 30), the way we measure our international indebtedness is not altogether reliable. But there is no denying the trend.

percent. This is even more striking on an industrial basis. In 1960 U.S. steel companies produced 26 percent of the world's steel. In 1985 they produced only 11 percent. In 1960 we produced 52 percent of the world's automobiles; 25 years later, only 26 percent.

Up to now we have considered this global shift from America's point of view, where it appears as a formidable problem. But there is also the view of the rest of the world. From this perspective, the relative decline in U.S. importance appears as an opportunity, not a problem. It reflects the success of other nations—some left behind in the nineteenth century, some still in the ninth century—in finding a place in the world economy necessary for their own well-being. American policies in both Europe and the underdeveloped world have tried to stimulate growth. Thus America's relative decline in the world economy represents a political success, even though it presents an economic challenge.

We do not know at all what a truly integrated and well-functioning world economy would look like. Would it be knit together solely by market forces, or would there have to be a political framework of constraint over the whole? Would there be a single world monetary unit, or would each nation, as today, insist on its inviolable right to coin its own money? Would nations continue to define the boundaries of what we call "economies," or would there be such an intermingling of markets that national boundaries would have very little economic significance?

We cannot begin to answer these questions yet. Indeed, we hardly know whether they are the right questions to ask. But they give us some sense of the real significance of the relation between what we call the economy of the United States and the economy of the world.

LOOKING BACK

KEY CONCEPTS

The U.S. is no longer a closed economy.

1 The United States economy is still the richest and most productive economic entity in the world. But it is certainly not a "closed" economy. Both in trade and in finance, it is enmeshed in a world economy.

A spectrum of economies from rich to poor

2 The world economy is made up of a wide range of nations, from the Euro-Japanese group of "Western" economies through the underdeveloped, or Third World, countries where live most of the world's population. The Third World nations have made a significant impact through OPEC and as the location of new high-tech, low-wage industries.

Rising U.S. trade involvement

3 United States involvement in the world economy has been rising steadily in recent years, although, unhappily, imports have expanded much more rapidly than exports. More important is the very high ratio of manufacturing exports and imports: 20 percent of our manufactures are exported; 50 percent of domestic purchases of manufactured goods are imports.

The growing trade deficit

4 The United States has normally exported more goods and services than it has imported. During the last several years, however, it has incurred a very large and growing deficit in its balance of trade.

Deficits require using reserves or borrowing from abroad.

5 A deficit means that a nation has not earned enough from exports to pay for its imports. It must finance the deficit either by using its reserves of foreign exchange or by borrowing from abroad. If deficits become too large, a nation may no longer be able to borrow and will be forced to reduce its exports to the level of its imports—less any payments of interest on its debt abroad.

Our trade deficit began because of the high dollar, which cheapened imports into the United States and made U.S. goods expensive to foreigners.

6 Our trade deficit began because the dollar was too high. When the dollar is high, imports become cheap because we can buy many units of a foreign currency with each dollar; when the dollar falls, it takes more dollars to buy the same amount of foreign currency, and the price of imports goes up. By the same token, a high dollar makes our goods expensive for foreigners, while a lower dollar cheapens our goods in foreign money. The dollar was extremely high in the early 1980s, because of attractive U.S. interest rates.

Imports have remained high, despite the dollar's fall.	7 The cure for an adverse trade balance should be a fall in the exchange rate. But the American dollar dropped precipitously from 1985 to 1987 without remedying our situation. This is probably because of our stubborn propensity to import based on quality differentials and to the failure of world demand to magnify our export boom.
Lagging productivity has weakened the U.S. competitive position. National policy may be needed to correct lagging productivity.	8 A second general explanation for U.S. trade difficulties, especially in manufacturing, is lagging productivity. Numerous reasons have been offered for this lag, among them inadequate capital formation, a shift to low-productivity occupations in the service sector, and a comparatively poor education system. Policy changes affecting our whole society may be needed to bring about a shift in these (or other) causes of our low rate of productivity improvement.
A debtor nation	9 Largely because of our chronic trade deficit, the United States has suddenly become a net debtor to the world. If our trade deficit continues at the present level, we will owe the rest of the world huge amounts within a few years. International debts are not necessarily bad—indeed, they can be very useful when the borrowed money is put to productive use, as in the building of the railways in the nineteenth century. The worry about the present rise of international debt is that it has not been productively used, and that it might end in a panicky flight from the U.S. dollar.
An interdependent world is emerging	10 The United States economy no longer bulks so large in the world economy. This is due to the rise of Europe, Japan, and now some parts of the underdeveloped world to a position of greater well-being. This represents a political gain, even though it poses an economic challenge. What a fully interdependent world would look like we do not know.

ECONOMIC VOCABULARY

Closed economy   102
Reserves   107
Trade deficit   105

Foreign exchange   107
High and low dollar   108
Exchange rate   108

QUESTIONS

1. What do you think are the advantages of an open economy? The disadvantages?
2. Describe what is meant by a trade "deficit." What is a trade "surplus"? If one nation runs a deficit, must another run a surplus?

3. How does the United States manage to buy $130 billion more than it sells? Why cannot a country like Israel run up as large a deficit as the United States?

4. Suppose that it costs 50 francs to produce a bottle of French wine, and that the dollar buys 5 francs. What is the price of wine, ignoring transportation costs, to a New York retailer of wine? Now suppose that the dollar buys 10 francs instead of 5. Do we say that the dollar has gone up or down? Does a higher dollar make French goods cheaper or dearer? Will that increase imports or decrease them? Now put yourself in the shoes of a French importer of American wheat, which sells for $5 a bushel. Again forgetting transportation costs, what will the wheat sell for in Paris if 1 franc buys 20 cents? If 1 franc buys 5 cents? Can you see that a high dollar must mean a low franc? Are high dollars good for American grain exporters? Are high francs? Try to see international transactions as always involving two *differing* points of view.

5. Let us suppose you were convinced that the long-run cause of our trade deficit was a failure to build up our capital. What measures might help remedy this situation? Suppose you thought the trouble lay essentially in our education system. Now what would you recommend to make our performance as good as that of our main competitors?

6. Do you think economic relations tend to unite nations or divide them? Think about the effect on global living standards if there were no trade—and then think about the quarrels and wars that have been fought over economic spoils. Do you think it is possible that economic interrelations serves both to unite and to separate the world?

PART II

SOME BASIC ECONOMICS

CHAPTER 7

Economic Science

A LOOK AHEAD

Now that we have some background in the field, we are ready to take the next step toward becoming economists by learning something of the ways economists think. Here we are dealing with the abstract and analytic aspects of the field that we mentioned in Chapter 1.

Essentially this short chapter tells you that economic theory is about maximizing behavior that takes place against constraints. Acquisitiveness is a good first approximation of the meaning of "maximizing," and "constraints" implies limits, boundaries, or costs.

Economic reasoning consists of puzzling out what happens when rational acquisitors face constraints imposed by nature or society. Keep that in mind and the chapter will unfold step by step.

What is it that we are trying to understand as economists? Certainly it is not the economic attributes of *all* societies. Our first chapters focus on the United States, not merely because we are naturally interested in the economic aspects of our own country, but also because the United States is a kind of society that lends itself to economic analysis. Economic reasoning, we should note at the outset, applies most cogently to market societies, to capitalism.

However, economic reasoning will not try to come to grips with all of society. Our earlier survey paid little attention to vast areas of social life that we call sociological or political, still less to the religious or artistic. Economics mainly is concerned with the facts that bear on only one aspect of our social life: our efforts to produce and to distribute wealth. Boom and bust, inflation and depression, poverty and riches, growth or no growth—all can be described in terms of the production of wealth and its distribution.

MAXIMIZING VS. CONSTRAINTS

Our task, then, is to find some way of explaining production and distribution. Therefore economists observe the *human* universe, much as natural scientists observe the physical universe, in search of data and orderly relationships that may permit them to construct hypotheses.

What do economists see when they scrutinize the world of economic activity? Two attributes of a market society attract their attention:

1. Individuals in such a society display a particular behavior pattern when they participate in economic activities, as consumers or businesspeople. They behave in acquisitive, money-searching, "maximizing" ways.

2. A series of obstacles or constraints stands between the acquisitive drive of marketers and their realization of economic gain. Some are the constraints of nature; some are the obstacles of social institutions.

Thus an extraordinary conclusion begins to dawn. A great deal of the activity of a market society can be explained as the outcome of two interacting forces. One is the force of maximizing behavior—a force we have described in terms of the acquisitive behavior of men and women in a market society. The other is the constraining counterforce of nature or of social institutions—a series of obstacles that holds back or channels or directs the acquisitive drive. This suggests the daring scientific task that economics sets for itself. It is to explain the events of economic reality—even to predict some of the events of future economic reality—by *reasoning based on fundamental hypotheses about maximizing behavior and its constraints.*

HYPOTHESES ABOUT BEHAVIOR

Let us start with the economist's assumption about behavior. We can sum it up in a sentence: People are maximizers.

ACQUISITIVENESS

Remember that we are talking about the kind of behavior that we find in a market society. Perhaps in a different society of the future, another hypothesis about behavior would have to serve as our starting point. People might then be driven by the desire to better the condition of others rather than of themselves.

A story about heaven and hell is to the point. Hell has been described as a place where people sit at tables laden with sumptuous food, unable to eat because they have three-foot-long forks and spoons strapped to their hands. Heaven is described as the very same place. But in heaven, people feed one another.

Maximizing Utilities

What does that hypothesis mean? Essentially, it means that people in market societies seek to gain as much pleasurable wealth from their economic activity as they can. **We call this pleasurable wealth "utility." Thus we hypothesize that men and women are *utility maximizers*.**

Note that we define utility as *pleasurable* wealth. Economists do not argue that people try to accumulate the largest amount of wealth possible, regardless of its pleasures. We all know that after a certain point wealth-producing work brings fatigue, or even pain. Therefore we assume that as people work to maximize their wealth, they take into account the pains (or disutilities) of achieving it.

It is impossible to *prove* that people maximize in this fashion. But it seems plausible that most of us do seek wealth either as wage earners or as businesspeople and that we take account of the nuisances and difficulties of achieving it.

Satiable and Insatiable Wants

Economics not only assumes that men and women are maximizers, it also has a hypothesis about why they behave so acquisitively. **The hypothesis is that people's wants are insatiable; that human desires for utility can never be filled.**

Are our wants, in fact, insatiable? Does human nature keep us on a treadmill of striving that can never bring us to a point of contentment? As with maximizing, there is a prima facie plausibility about the assumption. For if we include leisure as well as goods among our aims, more time to enjoy ourselves as well as more income to be enjoyed, it seems true enough that something very much like insatiability afflicts most people. At least this appears true in societies that encourage striving for status and success and that set high value on consumption and recreation.

For example, surveys regularly show that men and women at all economic levels express a desire for more income (usually about 10 percent more than they actually have), and *this drive for more does not seem to diminish as we move up the economic scale.* If it did, we would be hard put to explain why people who are generally in the upper echelons of the distribution of wealth and income work just as hard as, sometimes even harder than, those on the lower rungs of the economic ladder.

There is, however, a very important qualification to the assumption that wants are insatiable for all wealth, including leisure. **The qualification is that economists assume human wants for *particular kinds* of wealth, including leisure, are indeed capable of being satisfied.** This idea of the satiability of *particular* wants will play a key role in our next chapter, when we see how we can derive the concept of demand and demand "curves" from our hypotheses concerning behavior.

Rationality

Equally important is an assumption about the way individuals think and act as they go about striving to fulfill their insatiable wants-in-general or their satiable wants-in-particular. **This assumption is that people are *rational* maximizers.** Economists mean by this that people in a market milieu stop to consider the various courses of action open to them and to calculate in some fashion the means that will best suit their maximizing aims. There may be two different ways of producing a good. As rational actors, people will choose the method that will yield them the good for the smallest effort or cost.

This concept of rational maximizing does not mean that human beings may not wish, on some occasions, to go to more trouble than necessary. After all, people could worship God in very simple buildings or out-of-doors, but they go to extraordinary lengths to erect magnificent churches and decorate them with sculpture and paintings. It is meaningless to apply the word *rational* to pursuits such as these, which may nevertheless have vast importance for society.

But when people are engaged in producing the goods and services of ordinary life, seeking to achieve the largest possible incomes or the most satisfaction-yielding patterns of consumption, the economist assumes that they *will* stop to think about the differing ways of attaining a given end and will then choose the one that is least costly. This is particularly true of businesspeople, whose activities are vital for a capitalist society.

The Economist's View of Humankind

Of course, economists do not believe that men and women, even in business life, are solely rational, acquisitive creatures. They are fully aware that people have many motivations: aesthetic, political, religious. If economists concentrate on the rational and acquisitive elements in people, it is because they believe these to be decisive for most economic behavior; that is, for the explanation of our ordinary productive and distributive activities.

Economic theory is therefore a study of the effects of one aspect of human behavior as it motivates people to undertake their worldly activities. Very often, as economists well know, other aspects will override or blunt the acquisitive, maximizing orientation. To the extent that this is so, economic theory loses its clarity or may even suggest outcomes different from those we find in fact. **But economists think that rational maximizing—the calculated pursuit of pleasurable wealth—is universal and strong enough to serve as a good working hypothesis on which to build their complicated theories.** To put it differently, economists do *not* think that political or religious or other such motives regularly overwhelm maximizing behavior. If that were so, economic theory would be of little avail.

Economists regard maximizing as a potentially useful mode of behavior. Of course they understand that there is a lot more to life than making as much money as possible. But economics allows us to see that maximizing can be a beneficial activity. Business schools exist, in part, to teach people to be better maximizers— that is, more efficient and productive.

HYPOTHESES ABOUT CONSTRAINTS

So far, we have traced the basic assumptions of economic reasoning about behavior. What about constraints? As we have seen, people do not maximize in a vacuum— or, to speak in more economic terms, in a world where all goods are available effortlessly in infinite amounts. Instead, people exert their maximizing efforts in a world where nature, technical limitations, and social institutions oppose those efforts. Goods and services are not free; they must be won by working with the elements of the physical world. Land, resources, and artifacts inherited from past generations are not boundlessly abundant. Laws and social organizations constantly impede our maximizing impulses.

Another way of putting it is that maximizing describes what we *want* to do, while constraints describe what we *cannot* do. Economics thus studies the problems, and sometimes the impossibility, of achieving what we want. That is why economics is often characterized as *maximizing subject to constraints*.

Constraints of Nature

Constraints are obviously very important. But we cannot sum them up as simply as the idea of maximizing.

Let us first think about two constraints on our maximizing desires that are imposed by nature. Later we will study these constraints in greater detail, but this is a good time to become generally familiar with them.

1. Diminishing Returns. Why can't you grow all the world's food in a flowerpot? Because there isn't room, obviously. But the economist sees something of considerable interest in this fact. It is that a *law of diminishing returns* describes what happens to output as you add more and more of one input—let us say seed—to a fixed amount of other inputs—in this case, the flowerpot.

Why is it, after all, that you can't produce ever-larger crops by adding more seed (or more labor or more fertilizer or more of any other single input) to a single field? The answer is that each seed needs to be complemented by a certain amount of soil, labor, and fertilizer; and that adding more and more seed brings you over that point of optimal combination. Thereafter, each additional unit of input yields less and less additional (or *marginal*) output (see Figure 1).

Once it is called to our attention, we find the workings of diminishing returns in many aspects of production. We cannot go on adding workers to a fixed number of machines without experiencing falling marginal (additional) output, once we pass the best mix of labor and machinery. On a larger scale, the Food and Agriculture Organization of the United Nations has noted that in the mid-1930s each additional ton of fertilizer improved output by 15 tons of grain. Forty years later, when annual inputs of fertilizer were far higher than before, each additional ton increased grain yields by only 5.8 tons. Diminishing returns was once more at work.

2. Increasing Cost. The second constraint is less familiar. It has to do with the fact that not all land or labor or resources are alike, so that **as we move from one kind of production to another, we are likely to find it more and more costly to produce each additional unit of the new output.** Costs are measured not in money, but in terms of alternative outputs forgone—what you have to give up in order to get an additional unit of the product whose output you are increasing.

Here a diagram can help us visualize the problem. In Figure 2 we see a community that can produce two kinds of output—milk and grain. If it puts all its labor and all its land into milk production, it can produce an amount of milk that we'll represent by the distance *OA* on the milk axis. If it puts all its land and labor into grain, it will produce *OB* of grain, as represented on that axis.

Now suppose that our community is producing nothing but milk and that it

FIGURE 1
Diminishing Returns
A production function shows the relationship between inputs and outputs. When diminishing returns prevail, each additional unit of input yields smaller and smaller additional units of output.

Units of Input

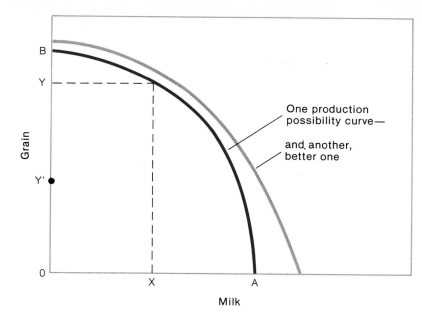

FIGURE 2
Increasing Cost

The curve AB is called a production possibility curve. It is an imaginary curve here, but it is meant to depict a real-life situation, in which we see how many tons of outputs, like milk or grain, a society could produce by using its resources in various combinations. The dotted line shows how better technology, for instance, could move such a curve out. What would an earthquake do to it? Draw in such a reduced production possibility curve. The curve bows because of the law of increasing cost—that is, because it becomes less and less efficient to move both labor and resources from one use to another. Compare how much grain we get (OY) as we cut milk production in half (moving from OA to OX), with how little we get (BY) as we move the remaining half (OX). Use a pencil to see if it works the other way around. Start from all grain (OB) and zero milk. First chart how much milk you get if you move the economy out of grain (from OB to OY'). Now eliminate all grain production. How much additional milk do you get?

decides to balance its output. It cuts milk production in half (to *OX*), moving land and labor into grain. We can see that it thereby gains *OY* amount of grain. Now notice what happens if the community moves the remaining half of its land and labor into grain. Output rises only a small amount, *YB*.

Why is the second half of the community investment in land and labor less productive than the first half? Because we have already plowed the best fields and availed ourselves of the most skilled farmers. The last bushels of grain are much harder to win than the first. And of course the same result would take place in reverse if we started from all grain, at *B*, and switched over into milk. **The constraint means that the more of any one product that we want, the more of some other product we have to give up to get it.**

How much of one thing do we have to surrender to get something else? That depends on a host of things—the resources available, the technology we can call on, the energy we can muster. The curve in Figure 2 shows us the grain-milk trade-off in our hypothetical community on some imaginary date, but a new invention, a change in climate, even a new economic system could change the efficiency with which we use our wealth. Thus the curve in Figure 2, which we call a **production possibility curve,** can move—loosening our constraints, as the dotted line shows, or possibly tightening them. We will come back to study this when we take up the subject of economic growth.

Opportunity Cost

Here is a good place to make a very important point about the constraint of cost:

The cost of the grain in Figure 2 is the milk we had to give up to get it, and the cost of the milk is the grain we had to forgo. That is why economists say "There is no such thing as a free lunch." Even if you did not pay money for it, someone had to produce that lunch, and the actual labor and materials that were used to make it can never be retrieved to make something else.

All costs, to economists, are opportunity costs. They are the utilities we must do without because we have chosen to devote our energies and wealth to creating other utilities. Later on, we will be talking about costs in dollars and cents, which is the way we usually think of cost. But when we say that something costs $10, what we really mean is that it costs us whatever utilities we might have enjoyed if we had spent the $10 on something else.

Have you ever hesitated over whether to buy this *or* that? Then you know what opportunity cost means.

Constraints and Costs

All these properties of nature set the stage for maximizing behavior. People seek wealth through the production and exchange of goods and services, but they do not maximize in a world where goods can be limitlessly and effortlessly obtained. Nature and our given technology offer us their services easily or reluctantly, depending on whether we are trying to maximize output by adding more and more of one kind of input (when we encounter diminishing returns), or whether we are trying to increase the output of one good or service at the expense of others (when the law of increasing cost comes into play).

Needless to say, different societies enjoy different settings in nature—rich or poor soils, cold or warm climates, easily available or scarce mineral deposits. These gifts of nature help establish the limits of productive activity.

Thus constraints will play a basic role in establishing costs or supplies. We return to these considerations in the next chapter, where we encounter a *supply curve,* the counterpart of the demand curve.

Constraints of Society

Perhaps we can already see the makings of a powerful analytic device in the interplay of maximizing drives and constraining influences. Before we move on, however, it is necessary to recognize that nature is not the only constraint on the maximizing force of behavior.

Society's constraints on our behavior are just as effective as nature's. The *law* is a major constraining factor on our acquisitive propensities. *Competition* also limits freedom of action, preventing us from charging as much as we would like for goods or services. The banking system, labor unions, the legal underpinnings of private property, are all *institutions* that operate like the constraints of nature in curbing the unhampered exercise of our maximizing impulse. So is the constraint of our available resources, our *budget*. Like technology, this is partly a constraint imposed by nature, partly one that is the consequence of man.

Not least, constraints affect us by our choice of the *social organization* of our productive efforts, as well as by their technical efficiency. The very same factory may have high or low output depending on whether employees' morale is good or bad.

BASIC HYPOTHESES

Let us briefly review the basic propositions in this first look into economic analysis. They can be summed up very simply.

Because economics generalizes about human behavior and the behavior of nature, it can theorize about, and to some extent predict, the operations of a market society. If we could not begin with the plausible hypothesis that people are rational maximizers and that nature (and social institutions) constrain their behavior in clearly defined ways, we could not hazard the simplest predictive statement about economic society. We could not explain why a store that wants to sell more goods marks its prices down rather than up or why copper costs will probably rise if we try to double copper production in a short period of time.

Economics as a Social Science

Perhaps these simple generalizations about behavior and nature do not seem to be an impressive foundation for a social science. Ask yourself, though, whether we can match these economic generalizations when we think in political or sociological terms. Are there political or social laws of behavior that we can count on with the same degree of certainty we find in laws of economics? Are there constraints of nature, comparable to the laws of production, discoverable in the political and social areas of life? There are not. That is why we are so much less able to predict political or sociological events than to predict economic events.

Although economic prediction has sharp limitations, its underlying structure of behavioral and natural laws gives it unique strength. We must now explore its capabilities. The place to begin must be obvious from our look into economic reality and our first acquaintance with supply and demand. It is the market mechanism.

LOOKING BACK

This chapter covers quite a few technical ideas, such as diminishing returns and increasing costs. Don't try to master them yet. Instead, be sure that you have the following simple conception of economic reasoning firmly in mind.

Economics is about production and distribution. It theorizes from two premises: utility maximizing and constraints.	1 Economic reasoning is mainly about production and distribution of wealth. It constructs hypotheses about this problem from two premises: (a) Men and women are maximizers of utility, and (b) they maximize in the face of well-defined obstacles or constraints.
Maximizing means an insatiable desire for utility in general, not for any one kind of utility.	2 Maximizing behavior means that individuals seek as much pleasurable wealth as possible. This pleasurable wealth is called *utility.* Economists believe that in a market society such as ours there is an insatiable desire for pleasurable wealth in general, although not for each particular kind of pleasurable wealth (after a certain point, more food makes us sick, more leisure is a bore).
Maximizing is guided by rational choice.	3 Economists also assume that individuals pursue their maximizing goals rationally—not in a haphazard, thoughtless way, but by making the best choices they can. Maximizing can therefore be socially useful.

Nature and technology impose two constraints:
• Diminishing returns
• Increasing costs
	4 Maximizing behavior has to contend with the obstacles set by nature and by society. Nature and technology together establish two important kinds of constraints:
	    The law of diminishing returns puts limits on the amount of output we can get from adding any one input—we can't grow all the world's food in a flowerpot.
	    The law of increasing costs limits our attempts to maximize because not all resources can be applied efficiently to any given purpose: We can't raise dairy cattle in Nevada. We can graph this in a production possibility curve.

Society applies institutional and social constraints.	5 Society imposes other constraints on maximizing—laws, institutional barriers, competition, and the like. Other important limits are imposed by budget considerations and morale.
Costs are missed opportunities.	6 Costs are basically missed opportunities. The term *opportunity cost* makes it clear that costs are not just sums of money, but possibilities for making wealth of various kinds that are forever lost because we have chosen to make wealth of one kind.
Maximizing subject to constraints is the analytic basis for much economics.	7 A powerful social science has emerged from the idea of interplay between maximizing and constraining forces. We shall see a demonstration of its power as we enter into a discussion of supply and demand in the next chapter.

ECONOMIC VOCABULARY

QUESTIONS

1. Do you feel like a maximizer? Are you content with your income? If you are not, do you expect that someday you will be satisfied?

2. Do you act rationally when you spend money? Do you consciously try to weigh the various advantages of buying this instead of that, and to spend your money for the item that will give you the greatest pleasure? Consciously or not, do you generally act as a rational maximizer?

3. How valid do you think the laws of economic behavior are? If they are *not* valid, why does economic society function and not collapse? If they *are* valid, why can't economists predict more accurately? (Chapter 9 has more about that!)

4. In what way is competition an institution? Are people naturally competitive? Would there be competition in a society that denied spatial or social mobility to labor, as feudalism did?

5. Can you think of any political activities or limits comparable to economic maximizing or constraints? Are there constraints of national size? Might it be possible to devise an economics of politics? For example, do you think politicians seek to maximize votes?

6. Suppose that you had a very large flowerpot and extraordinary chemicals and seeds. Could you conceivably grow all the world's food in it? Why would you still get diminishing returns?

7. What is the opportunity cost of undertaking a program such as space exploration? Of mounting a vast slum clearance program? Suppose the two cost the same amount of money? Does that mean the opportunity cost is the same?

Supply and Demand

A LOOK AHEAD

In this chapter you come to grips with the most important and powerful tool that economic reasoning gives us. The tool is an understanding of supply and demand and how they drive the market system.

It will help you to keep the following four steps in mind:

1 You will learn exactly what the word *demand* means, and what a "demand curve" represents.

2 You will learn the same thing about supply—what the word means and what a "supply curve" represents.

3 You will put the two together and see how demand and supply give rise to an *equilibrium* price.

4 You will begin to distinguish shifts of supply and demand curves from movements along those curves.

W hat impresses us first when we study the market as a solution to the economic problem? The striking fact is that the market uses only one means of persuasion to induce people to engage in production or to undertake the tasks of distribution. That means it is neither time-honored tradition nor the edict of any authority.

Prices and Behavior

Thus our first question: How is it that prices take the place of tradition or command, and become the guide to economic behavior?

The key lies in maximization. Through prices, acquisitive individuals learn what course of action will maximize their incomes or minimize their expenditures. This means that in the word *price* we include prices of labor and capital and resources which we call wages, profits, interest, and rent. Of course, within the category of prices we also include those ordinary prices that we pay for the goods and services we consume and the materials we purchase in order to build a home or to operate a store or factory. In each case, the only way that we can tell how to maximize our receipts and minimize our costs is by reading the signals of price that the market gives us.*

Therefore, if we are to understand how the market works as a mechanism—that is, how it acts as a guide to the solution of the economic problem—we must first understand how the market sets prices. For this, two distinct concepts are essential: *demand* and *supply*.

DEMAND

Taste and Income

When you enter the market for goods (almost every time you walk along a shopping street), two factors determine whether you will actually become a buyer and not just a window shopper. The first is your desire for the good. Economists call this "taste." It is your taste that determines whether a good offers you pleasure or utility, and if so, how much. The windows of shops are crammed with things you could afford to buy but which you simply do not wish to own. Perhaps if some of these were cheaper, you might wish to own them; other goods you would not want even if they were free. For such goods, for which your tastes are too weak to motivate you at the price at which they are offered, your demand is zero. The pleasure or utility they afford is not offset, for you, by what they cost. **Thus taste determines your willingness to buy.**

Yet taste is not the only component of demand. Shop windows are also full of

---

*In the real world reading prices can be very complicated, for it involves not only how much we know about the market, but also how much we *think* we know about it. Here we simplify matters and assume, to begin with, that we all have the knowledge that we need.

goods that you might very much like to own but cannot afford to buy. Thus your "effective demand" for Rolls-Royces is apt to be zero. The demand of the poor for food, shelter, clothing, and other necessities is small, even though their need and desire for such items may be very large. **In other words, demand also hinges on your ability to buy—on your possession of sufficient wealth or income as well as on your own taste.**

Diminishing Marginal Utility

Note that your demand for goods depends on your willingness and ability to buy goods or services *at their going price.* From this it follows that the amounts of goods you demand will change as their prices change, just as it also follows that the amounts you will demand change as your wealth or income changes. There is no difficulty understanding why changing prices should change our ability to buy: Our wealth simply stretches further or less far, our budget is less or more constrained by our income.

But why should our *willingness* to buy be related to price? The answer lies in the nature of utility. People are maximizing creatures, but they do not want ever more of the *same* commodity. On the contrary, as we saw, economists take as a plausible generalization that additional increments of the same good or service, within some stated period of time, will yield smaller and smaller increments of pleasure. **These increments of pleasure are called *marginal utility*, and the general tendency of marginal utility to diminish with rising consumption of any good is called the law of *diminishing marginal utility*.** Remember: Diminishing marginal utility refers strictly to behavior and not to nature. The units of goods we continue to buy are not smaller—it is the pleasure associated with each additional unit that is smaller.

Demand Curves*

In the bar chart on the left of Figure 1, we show the ever-smaller amounts of money we are willing to pay for additional units of some good or service, because each additional unit gives us less utility than its predecessor. In the graph on the right, we have drawn a *demand curve.* You will see that a demand curve generalizes this basic relationship between the quantity of a good we are interested in acquiring and the price we are willing to pay for it.

Figure 1 deserves a careful look. Note that each *additional* unit affords us less utility, so we are not willing to pay as much for the next unit as for the one we just bought. This does not mean that the *total utility* we derive from all 3 or 4 units is less than that we derived from the first. Far from it. It is the *addition* to our utility from the last unit that is much lower than the *addition* from the first or second.

---

*Anyone unfamiliar with graphs should turn right now to page 167 –168 and learn how to read them and use them. Look as well into the extra word on graphs on page 174–178.

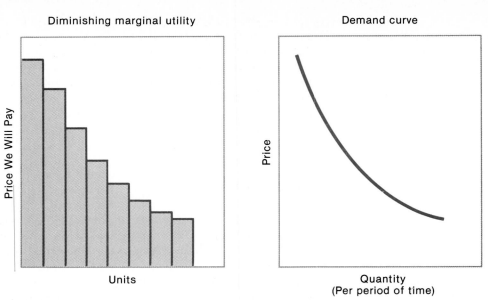

FIGURE 1
Diminishing Marginal Utility and a Demand Curve
Notice, on the left, how the marginal utility of each additional unit of a good diminishes as units are added to a purchase. The curve on the right simply generalizes the fact that each additional unit yields less pleasure than the one before it, and will therefore command a smaller price.

The Puzzle of Bread and Diamonds

The notion of diminishing marginal utility clears up an old puzzle of economic life: Why is it that we are willing to pay so little for bread, which is a necessity for life, and so much for diamonds, which are not? The answer is that we have so much bread that the *marginal* utility of any loaf we are thinking of buying is very little, whereas we have so few diamonds that each carat has a very high marginal utility. If we were locked inside Tiffany's over a long holiday, the prices we would pay for bread and diamonds, after a few days, would be very different from those we would have paid when we entered.

SUPPLY

What about the supply side? Here, too, willingness and ability enter into the seller's actions. As we would expect, they bring about reactions different from those in the case of demand.

At high prices, sellers are more *willing* to supply goods and services because they will take in more money. They will also be more easily *able* to offer more goods because higher prices will enable less efficient suppliers to enter the market, or will cover the higher costs of production that may result from increasing outputs.

Therefore we depict normal supply curves as rising. These rising curves present a contrast to the falling curves of demanders: Sellers respond eagerly to high prices; buyers respond negatively. Figure 2 shows such a typical supply curve. Note that a supply curve, like its demand counterpart, represents a functional relationship: how much we will offer at different prices. Time does not enter into this curve—the curve does not show changes that would require time-consuming activity, such as changing our scale of operation. For this reason it is called a *short-run* supply curve.

Supply and Demand

The idea that buyers welcome low prices and sellers welcome high prices is hardly apt to come as a surprise. What is surprising is that the meanings of the words *supply* and *demand* differ from the ones we ordinarily carry about in our heads. It is very important to understand that when we speak of demand as economists, we do not refer to a single purchase at a given price. **Demand in its proper economic sense refers to a** *schedule of quantities* **that we are willing and able to buy at different prices at a given time. That relationship is shown by our demand curve.**

The same relationship between price and quantity enters into the word *supply.* When we use the word *supply,* we do not mean the amount a seller puts on the market at a given price. We mean the *differing* amounts offered at *different* prices. Thus our supply curves, like our demand curves, portray the relationship between willingness and ability to enter into transactions at different prices.

Supply curve

Price

Quantity
(Per unit of time)

FIGURE 2
The Short-run Supply Curve
A typical supply curve slopes upward because each additional unit tends to be more difficult or expensive to make, at least in the short run.

Balancing Supply and Demand

We are now ready to see how the market mechanism works. Undoubtedly you have already grasped the crucial point on which the mechanism depends. **This is the opposing behavior that a change in prices brings about for buyers and sellers. Rising prices will be matched by an increase in the willingness and ability of sellers to offer goods, but by a decrease in the willingness and ability of buyers to take goods.**

It is through these opposing reactions that the market mechanism works. Let us examine the process in an imaginary market for shoes in a small city. In Table 1 we show the price-quantity relationships of buyers and sellers: how many thousand pairs will be offered for sale or sought for purchase at a range of prices from $50 to $5. We call such an array of price-quantity relationships a *schedule of supply and demand.*

As before, the schedules tell us that buyers and sellers react differently to prices. At high prices, buyers are either unwilling or unable to purchase more than small quantities of shoes, whereas sellers would be only too willing and able to flood the city with them. At very low prices, the quantity of shoes demanded would be very great, but few shoe manufacturers would be willing or able to gratify buyers.

If we now look at *both* schedules at *each* price level, we discover an interesting thing. **There is one price at which the quantity demanded is exactly the same as the quantity supplied.** This price is $25 in our example. At every other price, one quantity—that supplied or demanded—is larger, but at $25 the amounts in both columns are the same: 30,000 pairs of shoes. We call this balancing price the **equilibrium price.** We shall soon see that it is the price that emerges spontaneously in an actual market where supply and demand contend.

EQUILIBRIUM PRICE

How do we know that an equilibrium price will be brought about by the interaction of supply and demand? The process is one of the most important in all of economics, so we should understand it very clearly.

Interplay of Supply and Demand

Suppose in our example above that for some reason or other the shoe retailers put a price tag on their shoes not of $25 but of $45. What would happen? Our schedules show us that at this price shoe manufacturers will be pouring out shoes at a rate of 90,000 pairs a year. But customers would be buying them at the rate of only 5,000 pairs a year. Shortly, the shoe factories would be bulging with unsold merchandise. It is plain what the outcome of this situation must be. In order to unload their stocks, shoe manufacturers will begin to cut their prices. They will do so because this is their rational course—they can make a higher profit, or take a smaller loss, by selling more shoes, even though the price per shoe is lower.

TABLE 1
Demand and Supply Schedules for Shoes
Go down the price schedule and notice that quantities demanded do not equal quantities supplied—until you get to $25. Below $25 they are also unequal. $25 is the equilibrium price.

Price	Quantity Demanded (thousands)	Quantity Supplied (thousands)
$50	1	125
$45	5	90
$40	10	70
$35	20	50
$30	25	35
$25	30	30
$20	40	20
$15	50	10
$10	75	5
$ 5	100	0

As they reduce the price, their situation will begin to improve. At $40, demand picks up from 5,000 to 10,000, while at the same time the slightly lower price discourages some producers, so that output falls from 90,000 pairs to 70,000. Shoe manufacturers are still turning out more shoes than the market can absorb, but the difference between the quantities supplied and the quantities demanded is smaller than it was before.

Let us suppose that the competitive pressure continues to reduce prices so that shoes sell at $30. Now we have a much more satisfactory state of affairs. Producers will be turning out 35,000 pairs of shoes. Consumers will be buying them at a rate of 25,000 a year. Still there is an imbalance. Some shoes will still be piling up, unsold, at the factory or in stores. Prices will therefore continue to fall, eventually to $25. At this point, the quantity of shoes supplied by the manufacturers—30,000 pairs—is exactly that demanded by customers. There is no longer a surplus of unsold shoes hanging over the market and acting to press prices down.

The Market Clears

Now let us trace the interplay of supply and demand from the other direction. Suppose that prices were originally $5. Our schedules tell us that customers would be standing in line at the shoestores, but producers would be largely shut down, unwilling or unable to make shoes at such a price. Customers, many of whom would gladly pay more than $5, will let it be known that they would welcome a supply of shoes at $10 or even more. They too are trying to maximize—in this case, utilities rather than profits. If enough customers bid $10, a trickle of shoe output begins. Still, the quantity of shoes demanded at $10 far exceeds the available supply. Customers snap up the few pairs around and tell shoe stores they would gladly pay $20 a pair. Prices rise. Now we are getting closer to a balance of quantities offered and bid for. At $20 there will be a demand for 40,000 pairs of shoes, and output will have risen to 20,000 pairs. Still the pressure of unsatisfied demand raises prices further. Finally a price of $25 is tried. Now, once again, the quantities supplied and demanded are exactly in balance. There is no further pressure from unsatisfied customers to force the price up further, because at $25 no customer who can afford the going price will remain unsatisfied. We say that the market "clears."

Characteristics of Equilibrium Prices

Thus the interaction of supply and demand brings about a price at which both suppliers and demanders are willing and able to sell and buy the same quantity of goods. We can visualize the equilibrating process more easily if we now transfer our supply and demand schedules to graph paper. Figure 3 is the representation of the shoe market we have been dealing with.

The graph shows us at a glance the situation we have analyzed in detail. At the price of $25, the quantities demanded and supplied are equal: 30,000 pairs of shoes. The graph also shows more vividly than the schedules why this is an *equilibrium* price.

Suppose that the price were temporarily lifted above $25. If you will draw a horizontal pencil line from any point on the vertical axis above the $25 mark to represent this price, you will find that it intersects the demand curve before it reaches the supply curve. In other words, **the quantity demanded is less than the quantity supplied at any price above the equilibrium price, and the excess of the quantity supplied means that there will be a downward pressure on prices, back toward the equilibrium point.**

The situation is exactly reversed if prices should fall below the equilibrium point. Now the quantity demanded is greater than that supplied, and the pressure of buyers will push the price up to the equilibrium point.

Thus equilibrium prices have two important characteristics:

1. They are the prices that will spontaneously establish themselves through the free play of the forces of supply and demand.

FIGURE 3
Determination of an Equilibrium Price
Demand and supply curves only show what the schedule has already revealed: There is one price at which the two quantities are equal. This is the equilibrium price.

2. Once established, they will persist unless the forces of supply and demand themselves change.

Does "Demand" Equal "Supply"?

There is one last thing to be noted carefully about equilibrium prices. They are the prices that bring about an equality in the *quantities demanded* and the *quantities supplied*. They are not the prices that bring about an equality of "supply and demand."

Probably the most common beginning mistake in economics is to say that supply and demand are equal when prices are in equilibrium. If we remember that both supply and demand mean the *relationships* between quantities and prices, we can see that an equality of supply and demand would mean that the demand schedule and the supply schedule for a commodity were alike, so that the curves would lie one on top of the other. In turn, this would mean that at a price of $50, buyers of shoes would be willing and able to buy the same number of shoes that suppliers would be willing to offer at that price, and the same for buyers at $5. If such were the case, prices would be wholly indeterminate and could race high and low with no tension of opposing interests to bring them to a stable resting place.

Hence we must take care to use the words *supply* and *demand* to refer only to relationships or schedules. When we want to speak of the effect of a particular price on our willingness or ability either to buy or to sell, we use the longer phrase *quantity demanded* or *quantity supplied*.

The Role of Competition

We have seen how stable, lasting prices may emerge spontaneously from the flux of the marketplace, but we have passed over in silence a basic condition for the

SUPPLY AND DEMAND, AGAIN

Here is one of the oldest "puzzles" in economics. Suppose that the price of A.T.&T. stock rises. Because the price rises, the demand for the stock falls. Therefore the price of A.T.&T. must decline. It follows that the price of A.T.&T. should never vary or at least should quickly return to the starting point.

Tell that to your broker. Better, tell it to your instructor and show him—and yourself—with a graph of supply and demand, where the fallacy of this puzzle lies. If you have trouble, think again about the distinction between "demand" and "quantity demanded."

formation of these prices. This is the role played by *competition.*

Competition is often discussed as a somewhat unpleasant feature of economic life. Now, however, we can see that, although competition may well be unpleasant, it is indispensable—if we are to have socially acceptable outcomes for a market process.

Competition is the regulator that "supervises" the orderly working of the market. But economic competition (unlike the competition for prizes outside economic life) is not a single contest. It is a *continuing process.* It monitors a race that no one ever wins, a race where all must go on endlessly trying to stay in front, to avoid the economic penalties of falling behind.

Moreover, unlike the contests of ordinary life, economic competition involves not just a single struggle among rivals, but two struggles. One is between the two sides of the markets; the other is among the marketers on each side. **The competitive marketplace is not only where the clash of interest between buyer and seller is worked out by the opposition of supply and demand, but also where buyers contend against buyers and sellers against sellers.**

SHIFTS IN DEMAND AND SUPPLY

Prices, emerging from the unsupervised competition of buyers and sellers, are now a part of our understanding. These prices, once formed, silently and efficiently perform the necessary social task of allocating goods among buyers and sellers. Yet our analysis is still too static to resemble the actual play of the marketplace, for one of the attributes of an *equilibrium* price, we remember, is its lasting quality, its persistence. Things are different in the real world around us, where prices are often in movement. How can we introduce this element of change into our analysis of microeconomic relations?

The answer is that the word *equilibrium* does not imply changelessness. Equilibrium prices last only as long as the forces that produce them do not change. To put it differently, if we want to explain why any price changes, we must always look for changes in the forces of supply and demand that produced the price in the first place.

What makes supply and demand change? If we recall the definition of those words, we are asking: What might change our willingness or ability to buy or sell something at any given price? Having asked the question, it is not difficult to answer it. If our *incomes* rise or fall, that will clearly alter our *ability* to buy. A change in the *price* of *other* commodities will have a very similar effect: When food goes up, we go to the movies less often. Finally, a change in *tastes* will change our willingness to buy.

On the seller's side, things are a bit more complicated. If we are owners of the factors of production (labor, land, or capital), changes in incomes or tastes will also change our ability and willingness to offer these factors on the market. If we are making decisions for firms, changes in *cost* will be the main determinant.

Shifts in Curves vs. Movements along Curves

Thus changes in tastes or prices or in income or wealth will shift our whole demand schedule. The same changes, plus any change in costs, will shift our whole supply schedule.

Note that this is very different from a change in the quantity we buy or sell when *prices* change. **In the first case, as our willingness and ability to buy or sell is increased or diminished, the whole demand and supply schedule (or curve) shifts bodily. In the second place, when our basic willingness and ability is unchanged, but prices change, our schedule (or curve) is unchanged, but we move back or forth along it.**

Here are the two cases to be studied carefully in Figure 4. Note that when our demand schedule shifts, we buy a *different amount at the same price.* If our willingness and ability to buy are enhanced, we will buy a larger amount; if they are diminished, a smaller amount. Similarly, the quantity a seller will offer will vary as his willingness and ability are altered. Thus demand and supply curves can shift about, rightward and leftward, up and down, as the economic circumstances they represent change. In reality, these schedules are continuously in change, since tastes and incomes and attitudes and technical capabilities (which affect costs and therefore sellers' actions) are also continuously in flux.

Price Changes

How do changes in supply and demand affect prices? We have already seen the underlying process at work for shoes. Changes in supply and demand will alter the *quantities* that will be sought or offered on the market at a given price. An increase in demand, for instance, will raise the quantity sought. Since there are not enough goods offered to match this quantity, prices will be bid up by unsatisfied buyers to a new level. At that level, quantities offered and sought will again balance. Similarly, if supply shifts, there will be too much or too little put on the market in relation to the existing quantity of demand, and competition among sellers will push prices up or down to a new level at which quantities sought and offered again clear.

In Figure 5 we show what happens to the equilibrium price in two cases: first, when demand increases (perhaps owing to a sudden craze for the good in question); and second, when demand decreases (when the craze is over). Quite obviously, a rise in demand, other things being equal, will cause prices to rise; a fall will cause them to fall.

We can depict the same process from the supply side. In Figure 6 we show the impact on price of a sudden rise in supply and the impact of a fall. Again the diagram makes clear what is intuitively obvious: An increased supply (given an unchanging demand) leads to lower prices; a decreased supply to higher prices.

And if supply and demand *both* change? Then the result will be higher or lower prices, depending on the shapes and new positions of the two curves; that is, depending on the relative changes in the willingness and ability of both sides.

Figure 7 shows a few possibilities, where S and D are the original supply and demand curves, and S' and D' the new curves.

Changes in Quantities Demanded or Supplied vs . . . . Changes in Demand or Supply

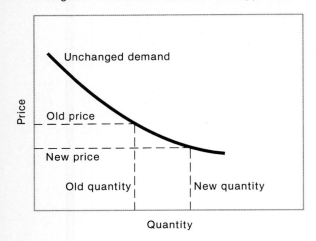

A change in price alone changes the *quantity* we demand.

A change in our willingness or ability to buy changes our whole *demand schedule*.

A change in price alone changes the *quantity* we supply.

A change in our willingness or ability to sell changes our whole *supply schedule*.

FIGURE 4

Here is where we can see the difference between a change in demand or supply, and a change in the quantity demanded or supplied. This is a graph that should be studied until you fully understand it.

FIGURE 5
Shifts in Demand
An increase or decrease in our demand schedule changes the equilibrium price, raising it in the first case, lowering it in the second.

FIGURE 6
Shifts in Supply
Shifts in supply also change equilibrium prices. Increased supplies lower them; decreased supplies raise them.

Long and Short Run

There is one point we should add to conclude our discussion of supply and demand. Students often wonder which "really" sets the price—supply or demand. Alfred Marshall, the great turn-of-the-century economist, gave the right answer: *Both do,* just as both blades of scissors do the cutting.

Yet, whereas prices are always determined by the intersection of supply and demand schedules, we can differentiate between the *short run,* when demand tends to be the more dynamic force, and the *long run,* when supply is the more important force. In Figure 8 we see (on the left) short-run fixed supply, as in the instance of

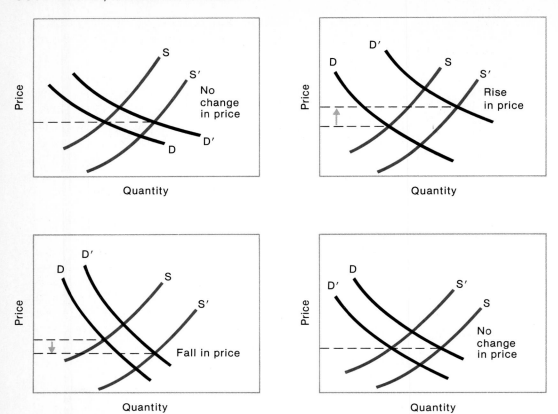

FIGURE 7
Shifts in Both Supply and Demand
When both supply and demand change, prices may rise, fall, or remain unchanged. The outcome is determined by the intersection of both *curves, so that we can never tell what will happen to price if we only know what has happened to one curve, but not to the other. It will help greatly if you try different combinations.*

fishermen bringing a catch to a dock. Since the size of the catch cannot be changed, the supply curve is fixed in place, and the demand curve is the only possible dynamic influence. Broken lines show that changes in demand alone will set the price.

Now let us shift to the long run and draw a supply curve representing the average cost of production of fish (and thus the supply price of fish) in the long run. We make, for the purpose of illustration, a crucial simplifying assumption: that in the long run the unit cost of catching fish does not increase as boats and nets and new fishermen are added to the fleet. Thus the long-run supply curve is horizontal. Fluctuations in demand now have no effect on price, whereas a change in fishing costs that would raise or lower the supply curve would immediately affect the price.

In all cases, do not forget, *both* demand and supply enter into the formation of price. In the short run, as a rule, changes in demand are more likely to

affect changes in prices. In the long run, changes in supply are apt to be the predominant cause of changes in price, as when technology lowers the cost of commercial fishing.

A Last Word on Maximizing

Does the market mechanism bear a relation to the general notion of maximizing? Indeed it does. Buyers and sellers both are *willing* to respond to price signals because they wish to maximize their utilities. But neither can maximize at will. Buyers are *constrained* by their budgets, and sellers are *constrained* by their costs. Thus the *ability* of buyers or sellers to respond to price signals is limited by obstacles of budgets or cost.

In addition, buyers and sellers are both constrained by the operation of the market. A seller might like to sell his goods above the market price, and a buyer might like to buy goods below the market price. But the presence of competitors means that a seller who quotes a price above the market will be unable to find a buyer, and a buyer who makes a bid below the market will be unable to find a seller.

Thus the market mechanism embodies what economists call "maximizing subject to constraints." We will learn more about this in Part Four. Already we can see that the very interaction of the maximizing drives and the constraining

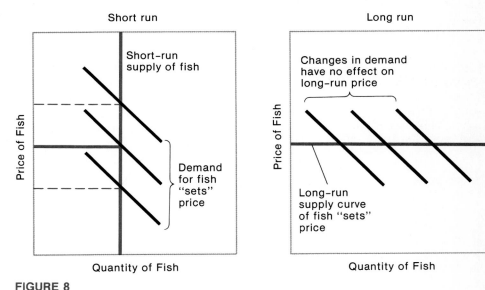

FIGURE 8
Short- and Long-run Supply Curves
Short-run supply is represented by a vertical curve since the same amount is offered no matter what the price. Here, demand "sets" the price, although without the supply curve there would be no price. In the long run, supply is horizontal, and demand has no effect on price. Yet without a demand curve there would be no sales of fish—and therefore no price at all! Both supply and demand are essential for all prices.

obstacles leads the market to establish equilibrium prices. We can also see that if we could know these maximizing forces and constraints beforehand, we would know the supply and demand curves of a market and could actually predict what its equilibrium price would be! In actual fact, our practical knowledge usually falls far short of such omniscience. But often we can use this principle for the next-best purpose, which is to predict the *change* in an existing equilibrium price that will result from particular changes in the forces of supply and demand. We will encounter this mode of analysis in the pages ahead.

LOOKING BACK

KEY CONCEPTS

You can now see that the purpose of this chapter is to show how maximizing subject to constraints works in terms of demand and supply. Here are the main points that you should carry away from what you have read:

Demand is the willingness and ability to buy at a given price.

1 Demand is a central idea of economics. It means the willingness and ability of any person or group of persons to buy a good or service at a particular price. Your demand schedule reflects your desire to maximize your utilities for that good, within the constraint of your budget.

Marginal utility typically falls.

2 Our willingness or ability to buy more of any kind of good reflects the marginal utility that another unit of that good will yield. The marginal utility means the additional utility—the pleasures of the *next* movie, the *next* pair of shoes, the *next* dollar of income—within a given period of time. A basic assumption of economic reasoning is that the marginal utility of any one thing diminishes: The second movie, pair of shoes, or dollar will not give as much pleasure as the first one.

Therefore typical demand curves fall.

3 This gives rise to normal, downward-sloping demand curves, showing that we are only willing to buy more units of the same goods at cheaper prices. These curves represent our schedules in simplified form.

Supply curves typically rise.

4 Supply curves typically rise because suppliers are not able (or willing) to offer more and more goods within a given period of time, except at higher prices.

Supply and demand vs. quantities supplied or demanded

5 Supply and demand refer to the range of goods or services that sellers or buyers will offer at differing prices. At any given price we should refer to the *quantity supplied* or the *quantity demanded*. When we say supply or demand, we mean the whole schedule or the curve that represents that schedule.

The idea of equilibrium where quantities offered are equal to quantities demanded

6 When we compare schedules, or plot two supply and demand curves, we can find out if there is an equilibrium price. This is a price where the quantities offered or supplied are equal to the quantities demanded. Economists are often careless and say that at an

How equilibrium prices emerge and persist	equilibrium price "supply equals demand," but students should watch their language! In an equilibrium price, the *quantities demanded* equal the *quantities supplied,* and the market clears.
	7 Equilibrium prices are spontaneously established through the interplay of supply and demand, and they will persist unless the willingness or abilities of buyers and sellers change.
There is a two-sided aspect of competition.	8 There is a double-edged aspect to competition. Competition not only means that buyers oppose sellers, each trying to get the better of the other, but also that buyers have to win out against other buyers and that sellers have to outdo—or do as well as—other sellers.
Changes in supply or demand mean shifts in the entire curves, not movements along them.	9 Changes in price occur when there are shifts in supply and demand—that is, when the quantities that people are willing and able to buy or sell change at a given price. These changes are characterized by shifts in the supply and demand curves rather than by movements along these curves. Thus an increase (decrease) in demand means that we buy more (less) *at the same price*.
The price system	10 Last, bear in mind that you are learning the remarkable way in which an economic mechanism coordinates the very different objectives and activities of buyers and sellers through only one means—the signal of price. Prices inform people how to maximize rationally, given their constraints. The Invisible Hand does the rest!

ECONOMIC VOCABULARY

QUESTIONS

1. Fill out the schedule below by supplying reasonable numbers to show the quantities demanded and supplied for T-shirts in a small town, at prices ranging from $1 to $10, over a period of, say, one year. (You might assume that there are about 10,000 potential buyers in your market.) Now graph the schedule in the graph space provided. Be sure to indicate the quantities on the horizontal axis.

2. Choose any arbitrary price above the equilibrium. How will maximizing behavior change this higher price back toward equilibrium? Does it require a contest among buyers? Sellers? Both? Either?

3. Now do the same thing with a price below the equilibrium.

SCHEDULE OF SUPPLY AND DEMAND FOR T-SHIRTS, PER YEAR

Price of T-Shirts	Quantity Demanded	Quantity Supplied
$10		
9		
8		
7		
6		
5		
4		
3		
2		
1		

Quantity
(Indicate numbers)

4. Subtract the quantities in your supply schedule from those in your demand schedule. There will be a plus or minus at all prices except one. Why is that? Does that help explain why an equilibrium price clears a market?

5. Whatever quantity is sold must be bought; whatever is bought must be sold. Then how can we say that only one price will clear the market? *Hint:* Look again at your answer to question 2.

6. What changes in your economic condition would increase your demand for clothes? Draw a diagram to illustrate such a change. Show on it whether you would buy more or less clothes at the prices you formerly paid. If you wanted to buy the same quantity as before, would you be willing and able to pay prices different from those you paid earlier?

7. Suppose that you are a seller of costume jewelry. What changes in your economic condition would decrease your supply curve? Suppose that costs dropped. If demand were unchanged, what would happen to the price in a competitive market?

8. Draw a diagram that shows what we mean by an increase in the quantity supplied; another diagram to show what is meant by an increase in supply. Now do the same for a decrease in quantity supplied and in supply. (*Warning:* It is very easy to get these wrong. Check yourself by seeing if the decreased supply curve shows the seller offering less goods at the same prices.) Now do the same exercise for demand.

CHAPTER 9

Why Economists Disagree

A LOOK AHEAD

We have just seen that economics has many science-like aspects. Yet we all know that no two economists ever seem to agree. Why is this the case? This chapter talks about the inherent difficulties of forecasting; about the reasons why predictions concerning human behavior can never have the same degree of accuracy as predictions about natural processes; and about the ways in which our values color our perceptions and lead us to different expectations concerning economic events.

This is certainly not a difficult chapter to read or understand. But it is exceedingly difficult to apply. Indeed, the whole secret of being a good economist lies in the lessons it tries to teach.

*E*conomists are notorious for disagreeing. No two forecasts for the economy are alike. Liberal and conservative economists often seem to be looking at two entirely separate worlds. Different economists will recommend different, and sometimes diametrically opposed, policies as fervidly on one side as on the other. If economics is as analytic a study as we have made it out to be, why don't economists agree more?

Of course there is a quick rejoinder. Doctors disagree. Lawyers disagree. Physicists disagree. Even mathematicians disagree. Evidently there is nothing in the nature of science, or argument, or even abstract logic that forces unanimity of thought on all its practitioners. So an easy response to the question of this chapter is simply that disagreement is a common attritbute of human discourse. If economists didn't disagree, they would be supermen—or fools.

But that is not a wholly satisfactory answer because it does not tell us anything about the *reasons* why economists (or doctors or lawyers or mathematicians) differ. The reasons are interesting because they make us think about the foundations of economics.

ECONOMICS AND FORECASTING

Perhaps the first place where we notice the differences among economic opinions is in the general field of forecasting. We are all familiar with the clash of forecasts put out by the economists of the administration (any administration) and of Congress, or the divergences of views of well-known private economists in bank or industry or foundations.

Why do forecasts vary so frequently and by so much? A good answer is that economists' forecasts differ for exactly the same kinds of reasons as meteorologists'. Meteorologists typically differ as to their predictions, and even the most reliable of them make terrible mistakes. Asking why meteorological forecasting is so often mistaken or at odds with itself deepens our understanding of why economic forecasting is also often wrong. Here are two reasons that apply in both cases: the problem of data and the problem of complexity.

1. THE PROBLEM OF DATA. The meteorologist is often wrong because he or she doesn't have enough data. Moreoever, no meteorologist can ever have enough data. That would require him or her to know everything about the weather at any moment—the temperatures at every point in the country, the direction and intensity of each and every wind current. Thus every meteorologist is forced to make forecasts on the basis of partial information, and that which has been left out may turn out to have been decisive. "Ah! If I'd only know about *that*," says the weather person when asked why his "sunny day tomorrow" turned out to be a downpour.

The same is true for the economist. No economic forecaster can know the complete state of the economy at any moment. *Indeed, no one knows it.* Of necessity this introduces an element of uncertainty into every forecast. Something is *always* left out. If it is important, the forecast will be wrong.

2. THE PROBLEM OF COMPLEXITY. The second problem is closely allied with the first. Even if the weather person knows each and every fact about today's meteorological conditions, there is no way to combine the data to yield tomorrow's weather with absolute certainty. This is because the "systems" that constitute weather are too complex to be reduced to exact models. For example, atmospheric turbulence cannot be described except in very general terms, whose form is described by the new science of *chaos theory*. Such systems are characterized by the fact that very small errors in data can lead to very large differences in predictions.

The same problem applies to economics. Even if some gigantic computer had stored within it every bit of data concerning individual incomes and tastes, and every last iota of technical information about production techniques, and all the other facts that impinge on economic activity, there would still be no way of putting these billions of items into a precise model of the actual economy. It is not surprising, then, that economists' forecasts differ, because different economists combine—and simplify—the data at hand in different ways.

BEYOND METEOROLOGY

These are obvious reasons why economic forecasting, like weather forecasting, cannot be an exact science. But there are other reasons why economists disagree—reasons that are not to be found in meteorology, or for that matter in any other natural science.

1. WILL AND INTENTION. One reason is that the elements of the social world differ from those of the natural world in a very important respect: They possess wills and intentions. When the astronomer predicts the eclipses of the moon, she does not have to worry about how the moon feels about going into eclipse. If she did, astronomy would be a much less reliable science. But wills and intentions are very much part of what economists must constantly worry about. An economist who predicts that prices or GNP will rise has to make assumptions about the behavior of human beings, not of inanimate objects. Because no one can ascertain how the members of a society think or feel at any moment, an economist is forced to assume that human beings will act in the way economic theory assumes to be their normal behavior—as rational, maximizing beings.

But suppose that they do not. Suppose that whims or fads, or patriotic or revolutionary sentiments, sweep the country. Then prices may not behave in textbook fashion because consumers rush for or shun the commodity in question for no "good" reason at all; or GNP may fall because workers go on strike—perhaps "against their best interests." Such kinds of behavior are not an ordinary part of social life—if they were, we would not be able to talk about rational, maximizing behavior as the norm. But as long as individuals have wills and purposes, unexpected behavior will occur. Of course, when it does, forecasts will go wrong.

2. EXPECTATIONS. But let us suppose that behavior *is* nomal. Can forecasts still go askew?

They can and will if the forecaster does not correctly assess the frame of mind of the economic agents with respect to the future. Forecasting depends critically on *correctly assessing the expectations* of the actors on the marketplace.

This is such an important aspect of economic prediction that we must take a moment to illustrate it. Let us look at the operation of a simple market when the price of a commodity rises (perhaps beause of a rise in the cost of producing it). In Figure 1 we see the result. Price moves from *OA* to *OB;* the quantity bought declines from *OX* to *OY;* and that is that. A new stable equilibrium has been reached.

But now let us introduce the matter of expectations. Suppose that consumers interpret the rise in the price of the commodity as indicating a futher rise to come. They think: "This is only the beginning. Prices will be soon be even higher." **Because of these changed expectations, a rational, maximizing pattern of behavior will lead to a different course of action.** Instead of buying less, consumers will buy more to stock up on the item before its price goes higher. In that case, the same increase in prices will lead to a shift in the demand curve, from *DD to D'D.* The quantity demanded will not fall, but will actually rise, as Figure 2 shows.

Hence a major element in all economic forecasting involves assumptions about the way actors in the market think about the future. Car manufacturers cut prices. Will that lead to a rise in sales? It will, if households expect that prices will rise again in the future, or will at least stay at their new levels. But if buyers read the cut in prices as a forerunner of future cuts, their national maximizing behavior will lead them to hold back and wait for bigger bargains to come. In that case, the price cut will result in a drop in auto sales, not an increase.

One last complication. Expectations not only play a critical role in determining how markets behave, but they are also beyond direct observation. There is no way of knowing what consumers think about the future because expectations are subject

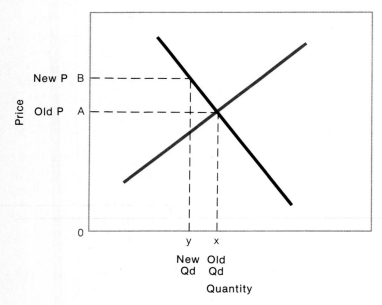

FIGURE 1
A Normal Price Response
A normal response to higher prices is a fall
in the quantity demanded (Q_d).

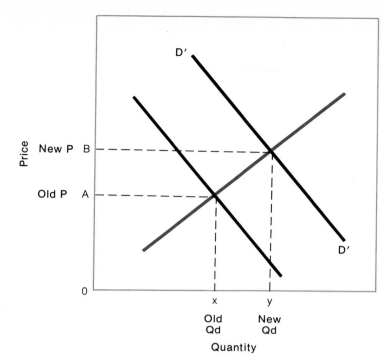

FIGURE 2
How Expectations Change
Market Behavior
If expectations move the demand curve out to D′D′, higher prices will result in an increase in Q_d.

to lightning changes. One of the biggest difficulties in political polling is that voters change their minds at the last minute—often right in the voting booth. The same problem complicates the "polling" of economic expectations—a complication magnified by the fact that we cast economic votes much more frequently than we do political ones.

3. THE SPEED OF ECONOMIC ADJUSTMENT. A third problem that plagues economic forecasting involves the speed at which economic changes take place. When scientists predict the outcome of natural processes, they often know very clearly how long it will take for the process under observation to reach its expected conclusion. We know how rapidly the earth spins, the speed at which light travels, and a number of other such constants that involve time. Even then, natural scientists cannot always predict how rapidly changes will occur—the rain predicted for today may arrive tomorrow.

Economists are in a much worse fix because they have no constants that involve time. There are no regularities in economic life by which we can set our clocks. We do not spend our incomes or respond to price changes or even work with clocklike regularity. As a result, economic processes can take place slowly or rapidly. Markets, disturbed by some outside shock like a bad harvest, may restore order in a matter of days or hours, or may fluctuate irregularly for weeks. Workers who have been thrown out of their jobs may rapidly find new work, or may suffer unemployment for long periods of time. Businesspeople may respond to optimistic news quickly or slowly.

The speed at which the economy adjusts to changes—including the very important changes of government policy—profoundly affects forecasting. How many times have we not heard an economist whose predictions have failed to come true say: "Wait!" The difficulty is, of course, that no one can say how long to wait. Yet we can see that the pace of economic adjustment is bound to affect the rightness or wrongness of our economic pronouncements.

FROM PREDICTION TO UNDERSTANDING

It is clear that economic prediction is inherently fraught with problems. No one can foresee with 20-20 vision tomorrow's price of apples or next week's Dow Jones average, or next month's GNP. Indeed, we can see that exact prediction is beyond the capabilities of the science.

Commonsense Prediction

Is all prediction therefore illegitimate for economists? That is certainly not our conclusion. **In a powerful sense, it is impossible not to predict.** When we declare ourselves in favor of, or opposed to, any form of policy—a tax increase or decrease, high tariffs or no tariffs—it is because we are predicting the effect of such a policy on our nation's fortunes. On a smaller scale, when we decide to buy more or less of an item when its price changes, it is because we are predicting that the given change will or will not be followed by further changes in the same direction.

But how can we predict when we have just declared that prediction is beyond the reach of economics? Part of the answer lies in the degree of precision we expect of prediction. Exact prediction is impossible, but not workable predictions on which we can rely with a fair degree of certainty. A good many economic processes display a kind of stability that makes it possible to forecast their course within boundaries that are fairly narrow; others have no such built-in stabilizing properties. No one has yet invented a system for predicting the stock market, which can—and sometimes does—show tremendous jumps or declines. On the other hand, the day-to-day course of GNP cannot fluctuate like the stock market as long as 100 million Americans get up in the morning and go to work (as economist Herbert Stein has put it).

Thus we can make much more reliable forecasts about the course of GNP than about that of the stock market. By the same token, however, our demands for accuracy rise, so that a forecast for GNP a year from now that is 10 percent off is deemed a failure, whereas such a forecast for the stock market would be a triumph.

Prediction vs. Expectations

A second approach to the problem draws a distinction between precise prediction and a general state of reasoned expectations. Even if we cannot predict the movements of the economy with a high degree of accuracy and a strictly fixed time schedule, **we can have informed anticipations of economic developments.** To the degree that we grasp the underlying forces and constraints of economic life, we can understand economic events as parts of a "system." The workings of the economy do not appear as inexplicable events but as happenings that reveal—however deep below the surface—the presence and influence of economic regularities.

Not predictions, but reasoned expectations based on understanding, are therefore the goal of economic science. These reasoned expectations can never attain the precision of an astronomer's calculations, so that two economists telling us what tomorrow's economic weather will be are as likely to disagree as to agree. Indeed, as long as observers differ in their assessments of such noneconomic factors as the nation's frame of mind, or its adaptability to change, or its stability of purpose and intention, they *must* come to different answers about the economic future.

Nevertheless, they will each try to reach reasoned conclusions about the shape of things to come, based on the application of economic laws (such as supply and demand or diminishing return) to the situation as they perceive it. They will talk about the future as emerging from a set of forces and constraints, not as mere chance.

FROM UNDERSTANDING TO ADVOCACY

A great deal of economic preditions is, in fact, economic advocacy. Or to put it the other way around, we often advocate economic policies, such as higher or lower taxes, because we predict that the effect of these changes will be favorable for the system. This introduces the question of values into the question of why economists disagree.

Values

Values are an inextricable part of all social thinking. We are "for" or "against" such things as economic equality among citizens or among nations in much the same way that we are for or against political equality. One can argue endlessly about such matters, but there is no final court of appeal. In the end, values remain—values. They are social arrangements that we prefer, sometimes mildly, sometimes passionately. They are not conclusions that are irrefutably thrust upon us by logic.

Value judgments permeate many of our economic determinations. They deeply affect the manner in which economists perceive the social world, and as a result they also affect the ways in which economists tell us that the economy will behave. Here are a few examples.

Producer vs. Consumer Well-Being

Many economic events affect us in two different ways—for instance, as producers and as consumers. When prices go up, they favor us if we are producers of that commodity, but not if we are consumers of it. When imports are taxed or otherwise restrained, we are grateful if we are workers in an industry whose existence is threatened by foreign competition, but resentful if we want to buy those goods as inexpensively as possible.

Which side of this clash of interests is entitled to preference—workers in American automobile plants or would-be buyers of Nissans and Hondas? As we will see when we study the specifics of microeconomics and again when we look into foreign trade, that is a very hard question to answer. To a large degree it depends on the assumptions we make about how quickly and easily our economy will adjust to imports. If we think the adjustment will be quick and relatively painless, we will favor the consumer side. If not, we are likely to be more sympathetic to the producer side. Since some economists feel one way and some the other, they will disagree as to the policy we ought to follow—and as to the consequences of doing one thing or another.

Concentrated Pains, Diffuse Benefits

Another common case in which economists differ involves situations in which a given policy, or course of economic events, inflicts considerable pain on a few individuals, but benefits the general public. An instance in point might be a reduction in welfare payments that hurts poor families but lightens general taxes, or the lifting of rent controls that penalizes occupants of those apartments but stimulates the construction of new dwellings.

Once again, values come to the forefront. There is no cut-and-dried way of comparing the cost to those individuals who are adversely affected by the events or policies in question with the benefits for those who will gain. As with the opposed interests of producers and consumers, different economists will judge the situation differently, in part depending on their values—their "affinity" for those on each side; in part on their appraisal of how quickly and easily individuals and firms will respond to one set of arrangements or the other. The result is that one economist will be all for reducing welfare payments and easing our tax burdens, while another will be against it; one economist will seek to protect rent control and another will urge getting rid of it.

Values and interests

Of course values enter here, too. There is no purely objective criterion that guides us when we decide whether the pains of unemployment or of relocation are justified by the gains to society. Our value judgments reign in these matters, although they may be buttressed by facts and figures. Yet, as we know from our own experience, there are often facts and figures on the other side too.

In this difficult question we can often rely on one guide. **Our values are frequently, although not always, affected by our interests.** We learn to look with skepticism on the "disinterested" opinion of someone who stands to gain from one side or another of a dispute. The same applies, of course, to economic disputes. It would be a true cynic who declared that our judgments always reflect our selfish interests, but it would be a fool who declared that there was no connection between them. The fact that values normally and naturally incline us to one side or the other of issues adds another degree of clarification to economic disagreements. Does the advocate of a policy stand to gain from its adoption? Do two economists in debate have affiliations with opposing economic groups? To the extent that that is the case, of course they will disagree. The only disreputable aspect of such a disagreement is to conceal one's interest or to pretend that it plays no role in one's judgment.

FROM VALUES TO CONCEPTIONS

Beneath values lies a still more deeply buried substratum on which differences are also based. There are fundamental perceptions about the nature of the economic system itself. We have already seen how differently capitalism looked to Adam Smith and Marx and Keynes. Those deeply divided perceptions continue to the present day, giving rise to many of the differences in economic pronouncements.

What are some of these ground-level disagreements? One of them is of special importance: the inherent stability or instability, self-correcting or self-destroying, property of capitalism.

Is Capitalism Inherently Workable?

Adam Smith certainly believed in the workability of the system. Its success derived, in his view, from the inherent tendency of a market society to grow because of the driving force of its thrust for accumulation, and to adapt to change because of the mobility of its market institutions. Marx believed it was not workable because the very process of expansion, in the absence of any plan, would lead to crises of one sort or another. Keynes thought that capitalism might be workable, provided that government intervened to prevent it from undergoing long-lasting unemployment.

Many economists today strongly believe that Smith was essentially right, and that capitalism will work—if it is left alone. Obviously such economists predict a different outcome for the system than those who believe, along with Keynes, that the economy tends to settle down into a condition of persisting unemployment unless the government steps in to remedy this state of affairs. And neither the Smith-nor the Keynes-oriented economist will expect or predict the same outcome as someone influenced by Marx.

Which view of capitalism is correct? Economists have debated these matters for a long time, and have not come to any agreement. **Moreover, as we see it, one can legitimately perceive the economy from each of these (and perhaps still other) perspectives. There are aspects of the system that are strongly self-stabilizing and corrective, other aspects that are powerfully self-destabilizing and destructive, and still others in which the workability of the system appears to depend on the policies we undertake.**

At any rate, that is the point of view that wil appear in this book, which adheres to no single school of thought. Recognizing the existence—and in our view, the validity—of multiple perspectives sheds still more light on the question of why economists disagree.

A Last Look at Disagreement

So it is clear that economists will continue to disagree. But it should also be clear that what they disagree about is not the nature of economic inquiry itself. Economists of all schools use the same basic tools of inquiry, talk about supply and demand and constraints of various kinds, rely on the idea of "maximizing" as the force that drives the system and of "rationality" as the mind set that guides its actors. **There is, in other words, a language of economics common to all economists—the language we have set out to learn in this introduction to the subject.**

To speak the same language, however, is not to say the same thing. Economists disagree about matters that are fundamentally political or social, matters that are fraught with value suppositions and deeply held views about the economic world that are neither provable nor disprovable. From this point of view, being a good economist requires more than merely speaking the language of economics well. One also has to have a keen sense of what the world is all about. That is a matter no introductory text can teach—nor any advanced one either.

LOOKING BACK

KEY CONCEPTS

Disagreement is commong among scientists.

Forecasters often rely on different facts.

Humans possess wills and intentions and form expectations concerning the future. That also often makes their behavior unpredictable.

Uneven speeds of adjustment also cloud economic predictions.

1 The fact that economics has science-like aspects does not exempt economists from disagreement. Scientists also disagree, as do philosophers and other scholars.

2 Economic forecasters often differ for exactly the same reasons as do meteorologists. The data of the economic universe are too numerous to be completely gathered, and too complex to be understandably ordered.

3 In addition, economists deal with human beings, whose actions are influenced by wills and intentions and by expectations concerning the future. Expectations can turn our actions around 180 degrees, because our rational maximizing impulse will cause us to hold back when prices fall and to rush in when prices rise—if we expect the fall or rise to worsen. If we expect the price change to be short-lived, our behavior will be just the opposite.

4 Further, accurate predictions are made more difficult because there are no constant speeds of behavioral adjustment in economic processes. Markets may move quickly or slowly—making predictions right or wrong, depending on the time frame of the predictor.

Workable predictions are made on the basis of inertia.	5 Nonetheless, we all ''predict'' economic outcomes, both in our daily lives and as practicing economists. Often we do so on the basis of the natural stability or inertia of social processes. The question then is how accurately we can speak of their future course.
Reasoned explanation is the economists' goal, not exact prediction.	6 Because exact predictions are impossible, the goal of economics might be better described as its ability to form reasoned explanations. These enable us to speak about the future as determined, however inexactly, by the kinds of regularities and processes we have previously looked into.
We often base advocacy on prediction. Values usually enter these decisions, as well as interests.	7 Economic advocacy often involves prediction—we favor certain policies because we expect certain consequences to follow from their adoption. Advocacy also involves value judgments—deep-seated preferences concerning the desirability of various economic (or social) outcomes. Very often these values are revealed in our preferences for one side or another when economic processes benefit some people but not all. In turn, our values are often determined by our interests.
Preconceptions about the workings of capitalism also affect our judgment.	8 As deep as our values are, our basic conceptions about the nature of the economic system itself, in particular about the inherent tendencies of a capitalist system. There is no general agreement among economists as to whether the system has stabilizing, destructive, or correctible aspects. Our own belief is that it contains all three, so that different conceptions are legitimate concerning different aspects of its workings. This, too, introduces a reason for disagreement among economists.
Despite these disagreements, economics provides a language of discourse.	9 Disagreements are therefore built into the nature of economic understanding. Nonetheless, economists have devised a language that enables them to speak in widely shared meanings about the properties of their subject. This language is economics.

ECONOMIC VOCABULARY

Chaos theory　153	Prediction　156
Expectations　153	Values　157

QUESTIONS

1. What is the difference between the ''behavior'' of an atomic particle and that of a buyer or seller?
2. Describe a scenario in which expectations make prices rise when we would normally expect them to fall. And vice versa.

3. What characteristics would we have to expect of stock traders to give us the grounds for a reliable prediction of stock prices?

4. Can you suggest some general attributes of our economic system that seem to have self-stabilizing tendencies? Self-destabilizing ones? How about sales of commodities like salt for one, and runs on banks for another?

5. Are you aware of your own value-laden preconceptions? For example, do you think that men and women are entitled to equal pay for equal work? That economic inequality is acceptable, but not political inequality?

CHAPTER 10

An Economist's Kit of Tools

A LOOK AHEAD

This is a chapter about concepts and techniques. It isn't about "economics," but about some ideas, simple statistical devices, and other tools with which every economist must be familiar. There is no single, large idea to keep in mind as you go through this chapter. We suspect that for most students it will be very easy; easy or hard, it has to be mastered. Keep a list of the six ideas as they come, and check them off against the review in "Looking Back" after you have finished.

*T*his chapter will give us a series of concepts and techniques that we will use in thinking clearly about economics. Some of them seem very simple but are more subtle than they appear at first. Others look demanding at first, even though they are actually very simple. There are six of these intellectual tools. Try to master them, for we will be using them continuously from now on.

CETERIS PARIBUS

The first concept is the need to eliminate outside influences that might invalidate our efforts to make scientific statements about economic behavior. If we were physicists trying to arrive at the formula for gravitation, for instance, we would have to make allowances for wind or air resistance in calculating the force that gravity really exerts. So in economics we have to eliminate disturbing influences from our observations. We do so by making the assumption that "other things" remain constant while we focus on the particular relationships we're interested in.

This assumption of holding "other things equal" is called by its Latin name, *ceteris paribus.* It is extremely easy to apply in theory and extremely difficult in practice. In our examination of the demand curve in Chapter 8, for example, we assumed that the *income* and *tastes* of the person (or of the collection of persons) were unchanged while we examined the influence of price on the quantities of shoes they were willing and able to buy. The reason is obvious. If we allowed their incomes or tastes to change, both their willingness *and* their ability would also have changed. If prices doubled but a fad for shoes developed, or if prices tripled but income quadrupled, we would not have found that demand decreased as prices rose.

Ceteris paribus is applied every time we speak of supply and demand, and on many other occasions as well. Since we know that in reality prices, tastes, incomes, population size, technology, moods, and many other elements of society are continually changing, we can see why this is a heroic assumption. It is one that is almost impossible to trace in actual life or to correct for fully by special statistical techniques.

Yet we can also see that unless we apply *ceteris paribus,* **at least in our minds, we cannot isolate the particular interactions and causal sequences that we want to investigate.** The economic world then becomes a vast Chinese puzzle. Every piece interlocks with every other, and no one can tell what the effect of any one thing is on any other. If economics is to be useful, it must be able to tell us something about the effect of changing *only* price or *only* income or *only* taste or any *one* of a number of other things. We can do so solely by assuming that other things are equal and by holding them unchanged in our minds while we perform a particular intellectual experiment.

FUNCTIONAL RELATIONSHIPS

Economics, it is already very clear, is about relationships—relationships of human beings to nature and relationships of individuals to one another. The laws of diminishing marginal utility or diminishing returns or supply and demand are all statements of those relationships, which we can use to explain or predict economic matters.

We call relationships that portray the effect of one thing on another *functional relationships.* Functional relationships may relate the effect of price on the quantities offered or bought, or the effect of successive inputs of the same factor on outputs of a given product, or the effect of population growth on economic growth, or whatever.

STATICS AND DYNAMICS: THE IMPORTANCE OF TIME

Of all the sources of difficulty that creep into economic analysis, none is more vexing than *time.* The reason is that time changes all manner of things and makes it virtually impossible to apply *ceteris paribus.* That is why, for example, we always mean "within a fixed period of time" when we speak of something like diminishing marginal utility. There is no reason for the marginal utility of a meal tomorrow to be less than one today, but good reason to think that this will be true of a second lunch today on top of the first.

So, too, supply and demand curves presumably describe conditions that prevail within a short period of time, ideally at one instant. The longer the time period covered, the less is *ceteris* apt to be *paribus.*

This poses many difficult problems for economic analysis because it means that we must use a "static" (or timeless) set of theoretical ideas to solve "dynamic" (or time-consuming) questions. The method we will use to cope with this problem is called *comparative statics.* We compare an economic situation at one period with an economic situation at a later period, without investigating in much detail the path we travel from the first situation to the second. To inquire into the path requires calculus and advanced economic analysis. We'll leave that for another course.

One important point: Functional relationships are not logical relationships of the kind we find in geometry or arithmetic, such as the square of the hypotenuse of a right triangle being equal to the sum of the squares of the other two sides, or the number 6 being the product of 2 times 3 or 3 times 2. Functional relationships cannot be discovered by deductive reasoning. They are descriptions of real events that we can discover only by empirical investigation. We then search for ways of expressing these relationships in graphs or mathematical terms. In economics, the technique used for discovering these relationships is called *econometrics*.

IDENTITIES

Before going on, we must clarify an important distinction between functional relationships and another kind of relationship called an *identity*. We need this distinction because both relationships use the word *equals*, although the word has different meanings in the two cases.

A few pages ahead we shall meet the expression

$$Q_d = f(P)$$

which we read "Quantity demanded (Q_d) *equals* or *is a function of* price (=$f(P)$)." This refers to the kind of relationship we have been talking about. We shall also find another kind of "equals," typified by the statement $P + S$ or purchases equals sales. $P + S$ is *not* a functional relationship, because purchases do not "depend" on sales. They are *the same thing* as sales, viewed from the vantage point of the buyer instead of the seller. P and S are identities: Q and P are not. The identity sign is $+$.

Identities are true by definition. They cannot be "proved" true or false, because there is nothing to be proved. On the other hand, when we say that the quantity purchased will depend on price, there is a great deal to be proved. Empirical investigation may disclose that the suggested relationship is not true. It may show that a relationship exists but that the nature of the relationship is not always the same. Identities are changeless as well as true. They are logical statements that require no investigations of human action. The signs $+$ and $=$ do not mean the same thing.

Sometimes identities and behavioral equations are written in the same manner with an equal sign ($=$). Technically, identities should be written with an identity sign ($+$). Unfortunately, the sign also reads "equals." Since it is important to know the difference between definitions, which do not need proof, and hypotheses, which *always* need demonstration or proof, we shall carefully differentiate between the equal sign ($=$) and the identity sign ($+$). **Whenever you see an equal sign, you will know that a behavioral relationship is being hypothesized. When you see the identity sign, you will know that a definition is being offered, not a statement about behavior.**

As definitions, identities deserve our attention because they are the way we establish a precise working language. Learning this language, with its special vocabulary, is essential to being able to speak economics accurately.

SCHEDULES

We are already familiar with the next item in our kit of intellectual tools. It is one of the techniques used to establish functional relationships: the technique of drawing up *schedules* or lists of the different values of elements.

We met such schedules in Chapter 8, in our lists of the quantities of shoes supplied or demanded at various prices. **Schedules are thus the empirical or hypothetical data whose functional interconnection we wish to investigate.** As working economists, we would experience many problems in drawing up such schedules in real life. We often use them, however, in economic analysis, as examples of typical economic behavior.

GRAPHS

The depiction of functional relationships through schedules is simple enough, but economists usually prefer to represent these relationships by graphs or equations. This is so because schedules show the relationship only between *specific* quantities and prices or specific data of any kind. **Graphs and equations show *generalized* relationships, relationships that cover all quantities and prices or all values of any two things we are interested in.**

The simplest and most intuitively obvious method of showing a functional relationship in its general form is through a graph. Everyone is familiar with graphs of one kind or another, but not all graphs show functional relationships. A graph of stock prices over time, as in Figure 1, shows us the level of prices in different periods. It does not show a behavioral connection between a date and a price. Such a graph merely describes and summarizes history. No one would maintain that such and such a date *caused* stock market prices to take such and such a level.

On the other hand, a graph that related the price of a stock and the quantities that we are willing and able to buy *at that price, ceteris paribus,* is indeed a graphic depiction of a functional relation. If you look at the hypothetical graph in Figure 2, you will note the dots that show the particular price-quantity relationships. Now we can tell the quantity that would be demanded at any price, simply by going up the price axis, over to the demand curve, and down to the quantity axis. In Figure 2, at a price of $50, the quantity demanded is 5,000 shares per day.*

---

*Technically, we would need a schedule of survey results showing the quantities demanded for every conceivable price in order to draw a graph. In fact, we obtain results for a variety of prices and assume that the relationship between the unmeasured points is like that of the measured points. The process of sketching in unmeasured points is called *interpolation.*

Amsterdam
From Jan. 1, 1982 to Nov. 12, 1987 (Weekly)

Australia
From Jan. 1, 1982 to Nov. 12, 1987 (Weekly)

Frankfurt
From Jan. 1, 1982 to Nov. 12, 1987 (Weekly)

Hong Kong
From Jan. 1, 1982 to Nov. 12, 1987 (Weekly)

London
From Jan. 1, 1982 to Nov. 12, 1987 (Weekly)

New York
From Jan. 1, 1982 to Nov. 12, 1987 (Weekly)

FIGURE 1
Stock Market Prices
Some graphs like these, show how a given variable behaves over time.
Source: *Report of Presidential Task Force on Market Mechanisms.*

UPWARD-SLOPING DEMAND CURVES

Although most demand curves slope downward, in two interesting cases they do not. The first concerns certain *luxury* goods in which the price itself becomes part of the "utility" of the good. The perfume Joy used to be extensively advertised as "the world's most expensive perfume." Do you think its sales would have increased if the price had been lowered and the advertisement changed to read "the world's second-most expensive perfume"?

The other case affects just the opposite kind of good: certain basic staples. Here the classic case is potatoes. In nineteenth-century Ireland potatoes formed the main diet for very poor farmers. As potato prices rose, Irish peasants were forced to cut back on their purchases of other foods to devote more of their incomes to buying this necessity of life. More potatoes were purchased, even though prices were rising, because potatoes were still the cheapest thing to eat.

Such goods have upward-sloping demand curves. The higher the price, the more you (are forced to) buy. Of course, when potatoes reach price levels that compete with, say, wheat, any further price rises will result in a fall in the quantity demanded, since buyers will shift to wheat.

**FIGURE 2
Price-Quantity
Relationship of a
Given Share**
Other graphs, like this one, depict relationships. There is more about this in the extra word following this chapter.

EQUATIONS

A third way of representing functional relationships is often used for its simplicity and brevity. **Equations are very convenient means of expressing functional relationships, since they allow us to consider the impact of more than one factor at a time.** A typical equation for demand might look like this:

$$Q_d = f(P)$$

Most of us are familiar with equations but may have forgotten their vocabulary. There are three terms in the equation above: Q_d, f, and P. Each has a name. We are interested in seeing how our quantity demanded (Q_d) is affected by changes in price (P). In other words, our "demand" is dependent on changes in price. Therefore the term Q_d is called the **dependent variable:** "variable" because it changes; "dependent" because it depends on changes in P. As we would imagine, the name for P is the **independent variable.**

Now for the term f. The definition of f is simply **function** or "function of," so that we read $Q_d = f(P)$ as "quantity demanded is a function of price." If we knew that the quantity demanded was a function of both price *and* income (Y), we would write $Q_d = f(P,Y)$. Such equations tell us what independent variables affect what dependent variables, but they do not tell us *how* Q_d changes with changes in P or Y.

The "how" depends on our actual analysis of actual market behavior. Let us take a very simple case for illustrative purposes. Suppose that a survey of consumer purchasing intentions tells us that consumers would take 100 units of a product if its price were zero—that is, if it were given away free—and that they would buy one-half unit less each time the price went up by \$1. The demand equation would then be:

$$Q_d = 100 - .5(P)$$

Thus, if price were \$10, buyers would take $100 - .5 \times 10$, or 95 units.*

We should stop to note one important property of ordinary price-quantity demand or supply functions. It is that they have opposite "signs." A normal demand function is negatively sloped, showing that quantities demanded *fall* as prices rise. A supply function is usually positively sloped, showing that quantities supplied *rise* as prices rise. A survey of producers might tell us that the quantity supplied would go up by 2 units for every \$1 increase in price, or

$$Q_s = 2(P)$$

Note that the sign of the coefficient 2 is positive, whereas the slope of the demand function was negative, $-.5$.

---

*Suppose we wanted an equation that would measure the effect on quantity demanded of both price and income (see box page 172). Such an equation might be:

$$Q_d = 100 - .5(P) + .1(Y) \text{ where } Y = \text{income}$$

In this equation the quantity demanded goes *up* by 100 units whenever incomes rise by \$1,000. As before, it goes *down* by ½ unit as prices rise by \$1. If incomes were \$2,000 and P were \$10, the quantity demanded would be $(100 - .5 \times 10 + .1 \times 2,000) = 295$ units.

ECONOMIC TECHNIQUES REVIEWED

The basic assumptions that economics makes regarding economic society can be summed up in two sets of general propositions or laws—laws about behavior and laws about production. What we have been learning in this chapter are the *techniques* of economic analysis—the ways in which economics uses its basic premises.

These techniques, as we have seen, revolve around the central idea of functional relationships. Because behavior or production is sufficiently regular, functions enable us to explain or predict economic activity. Their relationships are presented in the form of graphs or equations derived from the underlying schedules of data.

As we have seen, the ability to establish functional relationships depends critically on the *ceteris paribus* assumption. Unless we hold other things equal, either by econometric means or simply in our heads, we cannot isolate the effect of one variable on another.

ECONOMIC FALLACIES

No chapter on the mode of economic thought would be complete without reference to *economic fallacies*. **Actually, there is no special class of fallacies that is called *economic*. The mistakes we find in economic thought are only examples of a larger class of mistaken ways of thinking that we call fallacies.** But they are serious enough to justify a warning in general and some attention to one fallacy in particular.

The general warning can do no more than ask us to be on guard against the sloppy thinking that can make fools of us in any area. It is easy to fall into errors of false syllogisms,* of trying to prove an argument *post hoc, ergo propter hoc* ("after the fact, therefore because of the fact"). An example would be "proving" that government spending must be inflationary by pointing out that the government spent large sums during periods when inflation was present, ignoring other factors that may have been at work.

The gallery of such mistaken conclusions is all too large in all fields. One fallacy that has a special relevance to economics is called the **fallacy of composition.** Suppose we had an island community in which all farmers sold their produce to one another. Suppose further that one farmer was able to get rich by cheating: selling his produce at the same price as everyone else, but putting fewer vegetables into his bushel baskets. It must follow, then, that all farmers could get rich if all cheated.

We can see that there is a fallacy here. Where does it arise? In the first part of our example, when our cheating farmer got rich, we ignored a small side effect of his action. The side effect was that a loss in real income is inflicted on the other members of his community. To ignore that side effect was proper so long as our

---

*See the questions at the end of this chapter.

EQUILIBRIUM IN EQUATIONS

It is very easy to see the equilibrium point when we have a supply curve and a demand curve that cross. But since equations are only another way of representing the information that curves show, we must be able to demonstrate equilibrium in equations. Here is a simple example:

Suppose the demand function, as before, is:

$$Q_d = 100 - .5(P)$$

and that the supply function is:

$$Q_s = 2(P)$$

The question is, then, what value for P will make Q_d equal to Q_s? The answer follows:

$$\text{If } Q_d = Q_s, \text{ then } 100 - .5(P) = 2(P).$$

Putting all the P's on one side,

$$2(P) + .5(P) = 100, \text{ or } 2.5p = 100. \text{ Solving, } P = 40.$$

Substituting a price of 40 into the demand equation, we get a quantity of 80. In the supply equation we also get 80. Thus 40 must be the equilibrium price.

focus of attention was what happened to the one farmer. But when we broadened our inquiry to the entire community, as we had to in order to examine the effect of widespread or universal cheating, the loss of income should have become a consideration. Everyone loses as much by being shortchanged as he gains by shortchanging. The side effect has become a central effect. What was true for one turns out not to be true for all. Later on, in macroeconomics, we will find a very important example of exactly such a fallacy when we encounter what is called the Paradox of Thrift.

LOOKING BACK

KEY CONCEPTS   This is a chapter about the concepts and techniques of economic analysis, not about the basic assumptions underlying economic theory. We should become familiar with a few of these ideas, or tools.

Ceteris paribus	1 *Ceteris paribus* is the assumption that everything other than the two variables whose relationship is being investigated is kept equal. Without *ceteris paribus* we cannot discern functional relationships.
Functional relationships	2 Functional relationships showing that X depends on Y lie at the very center of economic analysis. They are not logical or deductive relationships but relationships that we discover by *empirical investigation*.
Identities	3 Identities are purely definitional, therefore not subject to proof or to empirical investigation. Such definitions can, however, be very important.
Schedules, graphs, and equations	4 The three techniques used to present functional relationships are: (a) schedules, or lists of data; (b) graphs, or visual representations; and (c) equations.
Independent and dependent variables functions	5 You should know the meaning of three equational terms: the *independent variable,* the causative element that interests us; the *dependent variable,* the element whose behavior is affected by the independent variable; and the *function,* a mathematical statement of the relation between the two. Read the sentence $x = f(y)$ as "x is a function of y." Here, x is the dependent variable; y is the independent variable.
Fallacy of composition	6 Finally, learn to be on guard against economic fallacies, especially against the fallacy of composition.

ECONOMIC VOCABULARY

QUESTIONS

1. Suppose you would acquire 52 books a year if books were free, but that your acquisitions would drop by 5 books for every $5 that you had to pay. Can you write a demand function for books?

2. Can you write a hypothetical function that might relate your demand for food and the price of food, assuming *ceteris paribus?*

3. "The quantity of food bought equals the quantity sold." Is this statement a functional relationship? If not, why not? Is it an identity?

4. Here is a schedule of supply and demand:

Price	Units Supplied	Units Demanded
$1	0	50
2	5	40
3	10	30
4	20	25
5	30	20
6	50	10

Does the schedule show an equilibrium price? Can you draw a graph and approximate the equilibrium price? What is it?

5. How do we read aloud the following? $C = f(Y)$ where C = consumption and Y = income. Which is the independent variable? The dependent?

6. Which of the following statements is a fallacy?
All X is Y
   Z is Y
Therefore Z is X
All X is Y
   Z is X
Therefore Z is Y
Try substituting classes of objects for the Xs and Y, and individual objects for the Zs. Example: All planets (Xs) are heavenly bodies (Y). The sun (Z) is a heavenly body (Y). Therefore the sun (Z) is a planet (X). Clearly, a false syllogism.
Other fallacies:
   If I can move to the head of the line, all individuals can move to the head of the line.
   If I can save more by spending less, all individuals should be able to save more by spending less. *Hint:* If all spend less, what will happen to our incomes?
   The fact that Lenin called inflation a major weapon that could destroy the bourgeoisie indicates that inflations are part of the communist strategy for the overthrow of capitalism.

AN EXTRA WORD ABOUT

Graphs and Economic Causation

Many students worry a great deal about drawing graphs and worry very little about what graphs show. They are wrong on both counts. The technique of graphing is essentially simple. What graphs show is not.

USES OF GRAPHS

Some graphs show the movement of a variable over time—for example, stock market prices. No one is perplexed by graphs of this kind. But other graphs show relationships. These are the graphs that worry students. Here are some hints to help you to draw these kinds of graphs.

1. Always begin by labeling the axes of a graph. Even the most common supply and demand type of graph should have one label identified as price (or *P*) and another as quantity (or *Q*). No mistake is as frequent as omitting *P*s and *Q*s or whatever identifying symbols are called for on a graph.

2. Each point on a graph represents two variables. Each point shows what value of *X* is related to a given value of *Y*—e.g., what quantity is offered (or bought) at a given price. Therefore every point must always be referred to *both* axes. In Figure 1, for example, point *H* shows 5 units of quantity offered at a price of 6 dollars. 5 units and 6 dollars are called the *coordinates* of point *H*.

3. Curves show how relationships vary. A given dot shows the relation of only one pair of coordinates, such as 5 units and 6 dollars. A curve shows the relationship of many pairs of coordinates for the function we are interested in. The upward curve *FGH* in Figure 1 shows how *P* and *Q* vary for sellers, for instance. Another curve, *ABC*,

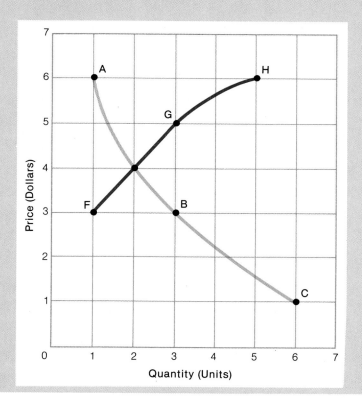

shows a relationship with a downward slope, perhaps for buyers. What are the actual values of *P* and *Q* at points *A, B,* and *C*? What, if any, coordinates are shared by both curves?

4. Graphs should be carefully drawn. Very often a graph represents an important idea visually. It may show that a pair of coordinates lies on *two* curves, as does the equilibrium point in the standard supply-demand graph. Or it may show that one curve touches another at just one point, which also means that the two curves have one pair of coordinates in common. When you draw a curve, you are *describing* a relationship: Be sure you describe it right. Figure 2 gives two freehand examples for you to study.

5. Professor Edwin Dolan writes in *Basic Economics,* "When you come to a chapter in this book that is full of graphs, how should you study it? The first and most important rule is *do not ever memorize graphs.*" Professor Dolan is so right! Graphs come last, to capsulize what you know. They never come first, to tell you what you *should* know. Graphs are a pictorial shorthand for ideas, usually ideas about functional relationships (curves) and their interconnections. Learn the economics and the graphs will follow. Learn the graphs—and you will know only geometry.

CORRELATION

That was the easy part of understanding graphs. Now for the hard part. Most students think that graphs "explain" things. They look at a graph of a demand curve and say "The lower price *causes* us to buy more." They look at a graph showing a nice regular pattern between variable *A* and variable *B,* and they assume that this pattern of "correlation" implies an explanation.

Here's an example. On the left side of Figure 3, we have plotted the shoe size and

Note that axes are labeled. This graph shows that there is one point (X), where there is a common pair of coordinates, M and N, for two functions or curves.

Note axes are not labeled. The graph shows that there is a no point where one pair of coordinates relates to both curves. Is that what you want to show?

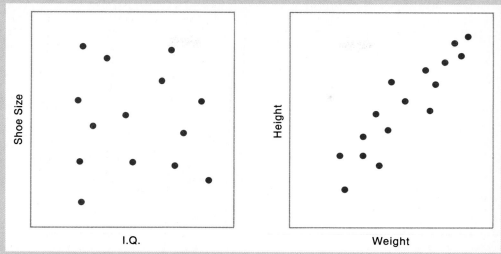

No pattern or correlation exists here.   *A clear pattern or correlation is visible.*

the IQs of a group of seniors. No pattern—no "correlation"—is visible.

Hence no one assumes that large shoe sizes cause high IQs. On the right side of Figure 3 we correlate a sample of the heights and the weights of a number of individuals. There is a clearly visible pattern or correlation.

Does this mean that height causes weight to increase? Yes and no. Height is associated with weight, but height *and* weight both depend, in part, on age. Our graph happens to cover a population that includes both infants and adults, and so of course there is a correlation, but it is not purely a causal one. Height is associated with weight partly through the mediating factor of maturity. Lesson: Be very, very careful of jumping to conclusions about causes just from the evidence of associations, or correlations.

Here are a few examples for you to think about.

1. Wrong-way causation.   It is a statistical fact that there is a positive correlation between the number of babies born in various cities of northwestern Europe and the number of storks' nests in those cities. Is this evidence that storks really do bring babies? The answer is that we are using a correlation to establish a causal connection the wrong way. The true line of causation lies in the opposite direction. Cities that have more children tend to have more houses, which offer storks more chimneys to build their nests in!

2. Spurious causation.   Suppose there was a positive correlation all during the 1970s between the cost of living in Paris and the numbers of Americans visiting there. Does that imply that American visitors were the cause of price increases in that city?

Here at least there is little danger of getting the causal links back to front. Few people would argue that more Americans visited Paris *because* its prices were going up. It would be equally difficult to argue that American tourists were the cause of rising Parisian prices, simply because the total amount of American spending was small in relation to the total amount of expenditure in Paris.

The answer, then, is that the correlation is spurious in terms of causality, although it is real in terms of sheer statistics. The true explanation for the correlation is that the rising numbers of American visitors and the rising costs of living in Paris were both aspects of a worldwide expansion in incomes and prices. Neither was the "cause" of the other. Both were the results of more fundamental, broader-ranging phenomena.

3. The problem of ceteris paribus. Finally, we must consider again the now familiar problem of "other things being equal." Suppose we correlate prices and sales in order to test the hypothesis that lower prices "cause" us to increase the quantities we buy. Now suppose that the correlation turns out to be very poor. Does that disprove the hypothesis? Not necessarily. First we have to find out what happened to income during this period. We also have to find out what, if anything, happened to our tastes. We might also have to consider changes in the prices of other, competitive goods.

As we know, this problem affects all scientific tests, not just those of economics. Scientists cannot test the law of gravitation unless "other things" are equal, such as an absence of air that would cause a feather to fall much more slowly than Galileo predicted. The trouble with the social sciences is that the "other things" are often more difficult to spot—or just to think of—than they are in the laboratory.

WHAT CAN CORRELATION TELL US?

These (and still other) pitfalls make economists extremely cautious about using correlations to "prove" causal hypotheses. *Even the closest correlation may not show in which direction the causal influences are working.*

So, too, the interconnectedness of the economic process often causes many series of data to move together. In inflationary periods, for example, most prices tend to rise, and in depression many indexes tend to fall, without establishing that any of these series was directly responsible for a movement in another particular series.

Finally, economists are constantly on the lookout for factors that have not been held constant during correlation, so that *ceteris paribus* conditions were not in fact maintained.

Is there an answer to such puzzling problems of correlation and causation? There is a partial answer. We cannot claim that a correlation is proof that a causal relationship exists. But every valid hypothesis—economic or other—*must* show a high and "significant" correlation coefficient between "cause" and "effect," provided that we are reasonably certain that our statistical test has rigorously excluded spurious correlations and unsuspected "other things."

This exclusion is often very difficult, sometimes impossible, to achieve with real data. A physicist can hold "other things equal" in his laboratory, but the world will not stand still just so an economist can test his theories. *The net result is that correlations are a more powerful device for disproving hypotheses than for proving them.* All we can say on the positive side is that a causal relationship is likely to exist (or at least has not been shown *not* to exist) when we can demonstrate a strong correlation backed by solid reasoning.

MICROECONOMICS

CHAPTER 11

Prices and Allocation

A LOOK AHEAD

With Chapter 11, we enter the world of microeconomics—or rather, we reenter it, because we already learned some basic microeconomics when we studied supply and demand in Chapters 7 and 8. In this three-part section, we extend that basic knowledge considerably. In Chapter 11 we investigate the market mechanism as a vast coordinating device, a rationing and allocating mechanism for society. In Chapter 12 we add the necessary concept of elasticity, which will enable us to speak of the market's functions with much greater precision. Chapter 13 will then turn the coin over and show us some of the inherent limitations of the market.

In our present chapter we learn simple but central things:

1 The market mechanism is a device for organizing the production and distribution activities of society. It does so through two vast networks: the factor market, in which businesses, households, and government agencies are brought together to produce and distribute wealth; and the goods market, in which products and services are allocated.

2 The market is a rationing device. This is one of the most important ideas in microeconomics. The price mechanism is a way of determining who will participate in economic activity as buyer or seller, and who will not.
Bear in mind as you read the chapter that all societies must find some means of solving this rationing, or allocation, problem. The things to look for here are the strong points and the weak points of *price* rationing.

THE WEB OF TRANSACTIONS

We began our study of economics by learning how the economy looked from a macro perspective. Now that we are about to start a study of microeconomics, there is no more effective way to illustrate the difference between the two approaches than to look over the economic panorama from our new vantage point.

Once again, our eye is caught by the enormous activity taking place in the offices, factories, and fields of the nation. But now our micro perspective brings a hitherto unnoticed aspect of the process to the fore. We are no longer much interested in the river of total output or its component parts. Instead, we direct our attention to the activity taking place in a thousand corners of the economy where individuals and firms are conducting their daily business. We look at the economic flow as a *vast web of transactions* into which virtually everyone enters as either a buyer or a seller.

Production

We are all familiar with this *market system* in which we participate as buyers of goods and services. We are not as used to thinking about it as a mechanism for organizing production. Yet that is actually one of the two vital services the market performs.

Figure 1 shows us how the market takes charge of production. Let us first look at the black arrows that go clockwise from households to business, and then from business to households. These arrows represent the movement of *actual services or products* from one place to another. Starting from households, these services consist of the skills and energies of labor (and the physical services of capital goods or land) that householders produce and make available to business. Thereafter, as the black arrows show, the products that business has made from these services of labor and resources move back to the households, where they will be consumed.

Thus we can see that the market mechanism organizes the indispensable economic activity of production as a great circular motion of economic activity. Labor, land, and capital—the factors of production—are combined into commodities that will return to the owners of these resources as goods and services needed for the renewal or growth of society.

Distribution

The other vital service the market performs is *allocation,* for the goods and services that have been produced must be shared in the community. This leads us to take notice of a second loop in Figure 1 which goes in the opposite direction from the production loop. This is the flow of money payments. With every individual market transaction, goods or services move in one direction and money moves in the other.

Our blue arrows show us this second circular flow of payments going in the opposite direction to the flow of real activity. With every household purchase of a business product, money moves from the hands of householders to the hands of business. And with every purchase of the services of the factors of production,

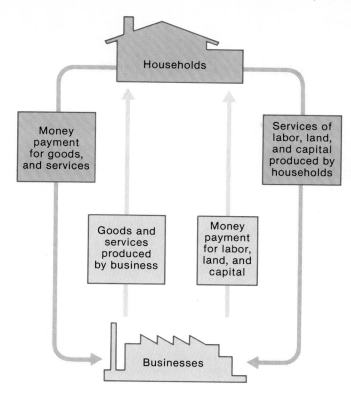

FIGURE 1
The Basic Market Mechanism
This diagram shows us two loops. The black loop represents production. Real labor and other services move from households to firms, and return as real goods and services. The blue loop represents distribution. Money payments leave businesses for households and return to firms as payments for business output.

money moves from business to the owners of these factors—wages and salaries going to labor, rent to landowners, profit or interest to owners of capital resources. **Thus we can see that in addition to organizing production, the market mechanism organizes the distribution or sharing of incomes.**

Of course, Figure 1 does not depict the entire market mechanism. It has omitted a vital flow of goods and services from one business to another, matched by a return flow of payments from business to business. No less vital, government has been left out, both as a buyer of goods and services and as a producer of outputs of its own, thereby linking it with households and business. Figure 2 shows these complicated interlocks.

Two Kinds of Markets

Another way of revealing how the market mechanism works is to divide its activities into two kinds of market: a factor market and a goods market, as in Figure 3.

The factor market is another name for the loop where production takes place. Here the services of labor, land, and capital are bought and sold, hired and fired, offered and withheld in a vast number of transactions whose outcome is the production of goods and services.

The market for goods and services is the loop where allocation is organ-

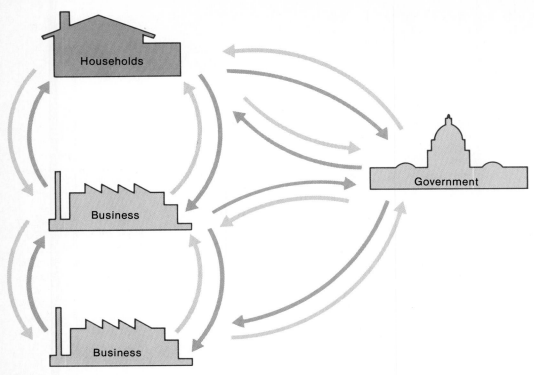

FIGURE 2
The Complete Business Mechanism
Here we begin to get some idea of how complex the flow of the market mechanism actually is.
But notice that the maroon and black flows are essentially the same as in Figure 1.

ized. Here shoes and ships and sealing wax are sold to, and thereby distributed among, the buyers of society.

Breaking the market system down into two kinds of markets further clarifies the working of the overall mechanism. For we can see that households and firms (including government units) both participate in each of the two basic markets, *but on different sides of each market.* In the market for goods, the household is a buyer. In the market for factors, the household is a seller as its members offer their services for hire. In the market for goods, the firm is a seller. In the market for factors, the firm buys. Thus we can redraw our model of the circular flow as in Figure 4, with supply and demand curves that show the twofold participation of each of the basic participants in the two markets.

Here we can see that the household is the source of the demand curve in the market for goods. We also see it is the source of the supply curve in the market for factors. On the other hand, the firm shapes the supply curve in the goods market, and the demand curve in the factor market.

Thus, far from being a chaos of buying and selling, the market system is a network of transactions with demand on one market reflected in supply in another, and supply in one market reflected in demand on another. This

circular flow—this link of demand and supply—will be one of the main keys to understanding how the economy works as a whole.

Looking at the System as a Whole

Now for a last important insight. The two markets—for factors and for goods—are also connected. This is because the household income that will be spent in the goods market is earned in the factor market. For businesses, the income that will be spent on hiring factors has to be earned in the goods market. **Production and distribution are therefore mutually dependent, not wholly independent,**

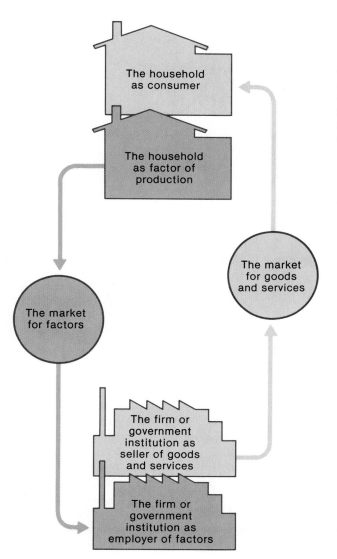

FIGURE 3
Circular Flow in Two Markets
Here we see how households, businesses, and government agencies participate in two markets, acting as buyer in one and as seller in the other.

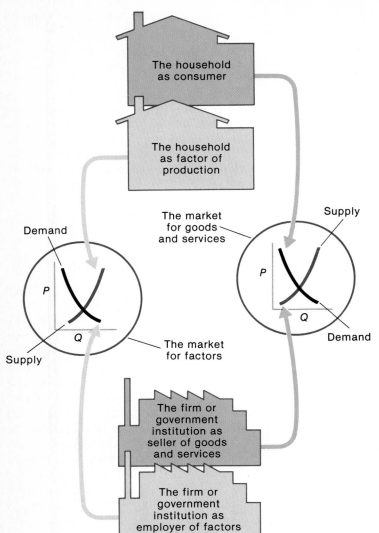

FIGURE 4
Demand and Supply Curve in the Circular Flow
Our final diagram shows how supply and demand curves represent the activities of the participants in the market mechanism. Notice especially that the household is the source of the demand curve in the goods market and of the supply curve in the factor market. What is the role of business?

activities. The outcome of the production circuit determines how the distribution circuit will operate; and the outcome of the distribution circuit determines the ability of business firms to enter the factor market.

Thus once again we see the market mechanism as a complex system, a network of actions that impose order and pattern on the economic life of society.

Like many models, ours operates at a very high level of abstraction. It lumps together the richest investor and the poorest laborer in the market for factors. It jumbles the sale of caviar and hospital care into one undifferentiated market for goods and services. Nevertheless, this abstract conception begins to untangle the flux of market activities in the world around us. It even clarifies our task in the chapters ahead. We must study the two different markets and the two different institutions, one at a time, to find out the actions and motivations characteristic of each. We begin in our next chapter by taking a searching look at households and their demand for goods and services.

THE ALLOCATION PROBLEM

From Chapter 8, "Supply and Demand," we know how prices are formed in the marketplace. We understand in general that prices for goods reflect the interplay of the demand schedules of consumers and the supply schedules of producers. In the next chapter we will see how changes in demand affect prices and how various characteristics of demand exert different influences on the price structure.

Individual and
Collective Supply and Demand

We must add one word before we investigate the market at work. Thus far, we have considered only the factors that make an *individual* more willing and able to buy or less willing and able to sell as prices fall. Generally, when we speak of supply and demand, we refer to markets composed of *many* suppliers and demanders. That gives us an additional reason for relating price and behavior. If we assume that most individuals have somewhat different willingnesses and abilities to buy, because their incomes and their tastes are different, or they have unequal willingnesses or abilities to sell, then we can see that a change in price will bring into the market new buyers or sellers: **As price falls, it will tempt or permit one person after another to buy, thereby adding to the quantity of the good that will be purchased at that price. Conversely, as prices rise, the number of sellers drawn into the market will increase, and the quantity of goods they offer will rise accordingly.**

We can see this graphically in Figure 5. Here we show three individuals' demand curve. At the going market price of $2, A is either not willing or not able to buy any of the commodity. B is both willing and able to buy 1 unit. C buys 3 units. If we add up their demands, we get a *collective or market demand curve.* At the indicated market price of $2, the quantity demanded is 4 units. What would it be (approximately) for each buyer, and for the group, at a price of $1?

The same, of course, applies to supply. In Figure 6 we show individual supply curves and a collective or market supply curve that is 7 units at $2 market supply. What would total supply be at a price of $1? What would seller A's supply be at $1?

Rationing

In one form or another, *rationing*—or the allocation of goods among claimants—is a disagreeable but inescapable task every economic system must carry out; for in all societies, the prevailing reality of life has been the inadequacy of output to fill the wants and needs of the people. In traditional economies rationing is performed by a general adherence to rigidly established rules. Whether by caste or class or family position, these rules determine the rights of various individuals to share in the economic product. In command societies the division of the social product is carried out in a more explicitly directed fashion, as the governing authorities determine the rights of various groups or persons to share in the fruits of society.

A market society, as we know, minimizes the heavy hand of tradition and the authoritative one of command. It cannot escape some system of rationing, though, to prevent what would otherwise be an impossibly destructive struggle among its citizens. This critical allocative task is also accomplished by the price mechanism. One of the prime functions of a market is to determine who shall be allowed to acquire goods and who shall not.

How the Market Rations

Imagine a market with 10 buyers, each willing and able to buy 1 unit of a commodity, but each having a different maximum price. Imagine 10 suppliers, each also willing and able to put 1 unit of supply on the market, again each at a different price. Such a market might look like Table 1.

Remember that the maximum prices may differ because different people have different desires for the commodity or because they have different incomes. Those willing to pay the highest prices may not desire the commodity the most. They may simply have the most income and be willing and able to pay more for everything.

As we can see, the equilibrium price will lie at $6, for at this price there will be 5 suppliers of 1 unit each and 5 purchasers of 1 unit each. Now let us make a graph

FIGURE 5
Individual and Market Demand Curves
The demand curve for a product on a market is the sum of the individual demand curves for it. Note that the addition is horizontal: We are adding quantities, not prices!

FIGURE 6
Individual and Market Supply Curves
Like market demand curves, market supply curves sum up the willingness and ability of individuals into a market total.

and let each bar stand for one person. The height of the bar tells us the maximum each person will be willing to pay for the unit of the commodity or the minimum he or she would sell it for. If we line up our marketers in order of their demand and supply capabilities, our market will look like Figure 7.

What we have drawn is in fact nothing but a standard supply and demand diagram. But look what it shows us. All the buyers who can afford and are willing to pay the equilibrium price (or more) will get the goods they want. All others will not. So, too, all the sellers who are willing and able to supply the commodity at its equilibrium price or less will be able to consummate sales. All those who cannot will not.

Thus the market, in establishing an equilibrium price, has in effect allocated goods among some buyers and withheld goods from others. It has permitted some sellers to do business and denied that privilege to others. Remember in our example in Chapter 8 that anyone who could pay $25 or more

TABLE 1

The table shows a lineup of buyers and sellers, each one with a different maximum or minimum price (also called a "reservation price"). Can you see why $6 is an equilibrium price?

Price	$11	$10	$9	$8	$7	$6	$5	$4	$3	$2	$1
Number willing and able, at above price, to:											
buy one unit	0	1	2	3	4	5	6	7	8	9	10
sell one unit	10	9	8	7	6	5	4	3	2	1	0

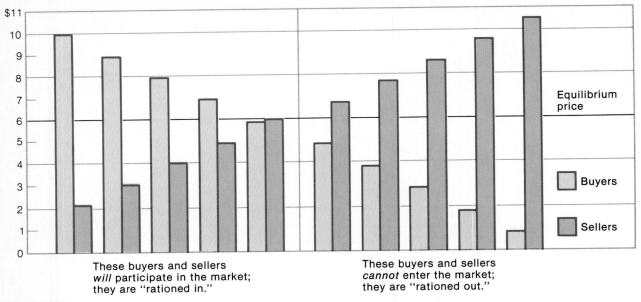

FIGURE 7
How the Market Rations

got a pair of shoes. Those who could not pay that much were unable to get shoes. All producers who could turn out shoes for $25 or less were able to do business, and those who could not meet that price were unable to make any sales at all.

Note that the market is in this way a means of *excluding* certain people from economic activity; namely, customers with too little money or with too weak desires and suppliers unwilling or unable to operate at a certain price.

Later we will see that the market mechanism allocates incomes in much the same way as it allocates goods. Those who successfully enter the market as factors of production get paid wages, rents, or interest. Those who do not, don't.

PRICE VS. NONPRICE RATIONING

The rationing system of the market is both its triumph and its trouble.

Let us look first at the triumphs. Nonmarket systems typically suffer from two difficulties. If they are run mainly by tradition, they tend to be inert, passive, changeless. It's very hard to get something done in a traditional economy if it has to be done in a new way.

A command system has a different inherent problem. It is good at getting things done, but it acquires its problem-solving capacity at a price. The price is the presence of political power in the economic mechanism, either as a large bureaucracy or as an authority capable of sticking its nose into daily life.

Against these two difficulties, the price system has two great advantages: (1)

It is highly dynamic and (2) it is self-enforcing. **That is, on the one hand, it provides an easy avenue for change to enter the system; on the other, it permits economic activity to take place without anyone overseeing the system.**

The second (self-enforcing) attribute of the market is especially useful with regard to the rationing function. In place of ration tickets with their almost inevitable black markets and cumbersome inspectorates and queues of customers trying to be first in line, the price system operates without any kind of visible administration apparatus or side effect. The energies that must go into planning and the frictions that come out of it are alike rendered unnecessary by the self-policing market mechanism.

Market Problems

Now for the troubles. The market system has the defects of its virtues. It is efficient and dynamic, but it is also devoid of values. It recognizes no valid claim to the goods and services of society except those of wealth and income. Those with income and wealth are entitled to the goods and services the economy produces; those without income and wealth receive nothing.

This blindness of the market to any claim on society's output except wealth or income creates very serious problems. It means that those who inherit large incomes are entitled to large shares of output, even though they may have produced nothing themselves. More important, it means that individuals who have no wealth and who cannot produce—perhaps because they are ill or simply because they cannot find work—have no way of gaining an income. To abide strictly by the market system of distribution we would have to be willing to tolerate individuals starving on the street.

Therefore every market society interferes to some extent with the outcome of the price rationing system. In times of emergency it issues special permits that take precedence over money and thereby prevent the richer members of society from buying up all the supplies of scarce and costly items. In depressed areas it may distribute basic food or clothing to those who have no money to buy them. And to a certain extent it uses taxes and transfer payments to redistribute the ration tickets of money in accordance with the prevailing sense of justice, or of overriding political pressures.

Shortages

Our view of the price system as a rationing mechanism helps to clarify the meaning of two words we often hear as a result of intervention into the rationing process: *shortage* and *surplus.*

What do we mean when we say there is a *shortage* of housing for low-income groups? The everyday meaning is that people with low incomes cannot find enough housing. Yet in every market there are always some buyers who are unsatisfied. We have previously noted, for instance, that in our shoe market, all buyers who could not or would not pay $25 had to go without shoes. Does this mean there was a shoe shortage?

FIGURE 8
The Shortage: Gas
Here is a graphic portrait of a shortage of a critical commodity such as gasoline. The supply of gas in the short run is fixed, as the vertical supply curve SS shows. That is, there is only so much gas on hand, no matter what the price. (We'll discuss such vertical curves in our next chapter.) The demand for gas (DD) indicates that quantity OS' is sought at the going price OA. There isn't that much gas. A shortage of SS' exists, creating lines of cars at the gas pumps. Suppose the government puts on a gas tax AA', raising gas prices from OA to OA'. At the new higher price the quantity demanded is OS, just equal to supply. There is no more shortage. But there are a lot of complaints about high prices!

Certainly no one uses that word to describe the outcome of a normal market, even though there are always buyers and sellers who are excluded because they cannot meet the going price. Then what does a "shortage" mean? **We can see now that shortage usually refers to a situation in which some nonmarket agency, such as the government, fixes the price below the equilibrium price.**

An Example in Gasoline. Figure 8 shows us such a situation in gasoline—for instance, after the OPEC shock of 1973. Note that the established price was *below* the price that would have cleared the market.* As a result, the quantity of gas demanded (*OS'*) was greater than the quantity supplied (*OS*). The result was that people waited in long lines at the pumps and that those who failed to get to the pumps on time had to do without gas.
How could the shortage have been "cured"? Perhaps by raising the price to an equilibrium level. At a price of, say, \$3 including taxes, the lines would probably have disappeared.

*Why did the companies not set the price at *OA'*? Simply because they feared the public outcry that would have accompanied this price. It would have been an economic equilibrium price, but not a political one.

Why did we not do that? Because the public would have objected violently to paying such high prices, and this was a *political* risk that neither the oil companies nor the government wanted to take. People preferred to wait in line and take their chance of going without gas to paying the amount needed to remove the shortage.

Price Controls

This bears directly on the problem of price controls. The problem with such controls is that they tend to fix prices below the level that would be established in a free market. As a result, some buyers who would ordinarily have been priced out of the market remain *in* the market, although there are not enough goods offered to satisfy their demands. The result tends to be queues in stores to buy things before they are gone, under-the-counter deals to get on a preferred list, or black or gray markets selling goods illegally at higher prices than are officially sanctioned. We show this in Figure 9.

Surpluses

The opposite takes place with a surplus. In this situation the quantity supplied is greater than that demanded (note we should *not* say that "supply is greater than demand"). In a free market the price would fall until the two quantities were equal. If the government continues to support the commodity, for example, wheat, then the quantity bought by bakeries will not be as large as the quantity offered by farmers. Unsold amounts will become a surplus bought up by the government.

Thus the words *shortage* and *surplus* mean situations in which there are

FIGURE 9
Shortages
The graph makes clear that a "shortage" means that prices are not able to rise to equilibrium levels, so that quantity demanded exceeds quantity supplied.

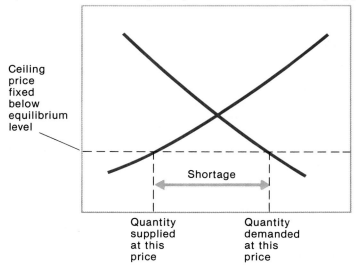

Ceiling price fixed below equilibrium level

Shortage

Quantity supplied at this price

Quantity demanded at this price

RATIONING BABIES

Because the market is such an efficient distributive mechanism, it has been proposed as a means to achieve zero population growth, assuming that this were the declared national policy. Since a sizable minority (probably about 15 percent) of all families voluntarily choose to have no children or only one, a country can achieve ZPG even if some families have more than two children. The question is how to decide which families should be allowed to have the extra children. Professor Kenneth Boulding has ventured an answer that leans heavily on the market mechanism. He proposes that each girl and boy at adolescence be given 110 green stamps, of which 100 are required if a woman is to have a legal child. (The penalty for having an illegal child would be very severe.) Unwanted or surplus stamps would then be sold in a market organized for that purpose. It can be seen that the total number of stamps would permit the population as a whole to have 2.2 children per family—the ZPG rate. The market would therefore serve to ration the extra stamps, making them available to those with higher incomes or a greater desire for children. "As an incidental benefit," writes Boulding, tongue in cheek, "the rich will have loads of children and become poor, and the poor have few children and become rich."*

When this scheme was first published, it provoked a storm of criticism. Commenting on its reception, Boulding observed: "This modest and humane proposal, so much more humane than that of Swift, who proposed that we eat the surplus babies, has been received with so many cries of anguish and horror that it illustrates the extraordinary difficulty of applying rational principles to processes involving human generation."

*Kenneth E. Boulding, *Economics as a Science* (New York: McGraw-Hill, 1970), p. 39.

sellers and buyers who are willing and able to enter the market at the going price but who remain active and unsatisfied because the price mechanism has not eliminated them. This is very different from a free market where there are unsatisfied buyers and sellers *who cannot meet the going price* and who are therefore not taken into account. Poor people, who have no demand for fresh caviar at $60 per pound, do not complain of a caviar shortage. If the price of fresh caviar were set by government decree at $1 a pound, there would soon be a colossal "shortage."

When Price Rationing Fails

What about the situation with low-cost housing? Essentially what we mean when we talk of a shortage of inexpensive housing is that we view the outcome of this particular market situation with noneconomic eyes and pronounce the result distasteful. By the standards of the market, the poor who cannot afford to buy housing are simply buyers at the extreme lower right end of the demand curve. Their elimination from the market for housing is only one more example of the rationing process that takes place in *every* market. **When we single out certain goods or services (such as dialysis or private nursing care) as being in "short supply," we imply that we do not approve of the price mechanism as the appropriate means of allocating scarce resources in these particular instances.** An economic problem becomes a social problem. This does not imply that the market is not as efficient a distributor as ever. What we do not like is the social outcome of the market rationing process. The underlying distribution (or maldistribution) of income clashes with other standards of the public interest that we value more highly than efficiency.

LOOKING BACK

KEY CONCEPTS

Market mechanism: two loops or circuits

The production loop: Business buys factor services and makes goods that are used by the factors.

The distribution loop: payments to factors who buy business's output

Two kinds of markets: factors and goods

Households enter the factor market as sellers; business as a buyer. In the goods market, households shape demand and business determines supply.

One central idea of this chapter has been to show that the vast array of buying and selling activity we call "the market" is actually a *system*—that is, a social institution that displays regular, orderly patterns of operation. We follow the operations of this mechanism by observing that it can contain two loops or circuits, one having to do with production, the other with distribution.

1 First, production. The market network is the means by which a market society organizes its factors of production so as to bring about production. This shows up as a flow of services (labor power or the services of capital or land) from households that own them to businesses that put them to productive use. The loop is completed when the goods that business produces return to the household to be consumed or put to further use.

2 The distribution loop is a circuit of money payments, not of real services or goods. It goes in the opposite direction to the production loop as businesses pay households for their services as factors of production, and as households pay businesses for the products they buy.

3 Another way of revealing the connectedness of the market mechanism is to divide the complex totality of market activity into two kinds of markets: the market for factors and the market for goods (and services). The factor market regulates production; the goods market organizes allocation.

4 In the factor market, households offer their services to business as labor or as owners of land and capital. Their activities therefore shape the supply curves in that market. It is just the reverse in the market for goods and services. Here it is business that shapes the supply curve because businesses are the sellers in this market, whereas demand is formed by the factors of production (behaving as households).

The market as rationing or allocation mechanism	**5** The second central idea of this chapter is one of the most important in this entire section. It is the idea of the market as a rationing system—a means of allocating output (or, as we will later see, income).—This is fundamental to understanding our form of economic society.
Price as rationer	**6** The rationing device used by the market is simplicity itself. Price determines who will and who will not enter the market, whether as buyer or seller. Those who cannot or do not wish to sell or buy at existing prices are rationed out of the marketplace.
Strengths of the market system: flexibility and self-governance	**7** The price system of allocation has two great advantages. It avoids the stodginess and unresponsiveness of tradition-bound systems, and it makes unnecessary the bureaucracy or political intervention of command-run systems. Markets govern themselves. Those who are rationed in and those who are rationed out usually—although not always—acquiesce in the market's determinations.
Weaknesses: no social conscience or political awareness	**8** Price rationing has one great disadvantage: It recognizes no claim on output except the ability to enter the market. Therefore it has no "heart," no political awareness. As a result, all market systems make allowances for those it considers are unfairly or unwisely kept out of the market.
Shortages: when prices are below equilibrium, $Q^d > Q^s$	**9** The function of price as an allocator throws light on shortages and surpluses. What we mean by a shortage is that price is held below an equilibrium or clearing level by government or other means. As a result, the quantity demanded is greater than that supplied. The result of this is queues or black markets or a scramble to get to the front of the line.
Surpluses are just the opposite: $Q^d < Q^s$	**10** A surplus comes about just the other way. When prices are held up above clearing levels by price supports or some other means, more is supplied to the market than is demanded. The supply for which there are no buyers at the support price is called a surplus.

ECONOMIC VOCABULARY

QUESTIONS

1. What is the difference between the market for goods and the market for factors? Can a household be a buyer in the market for factors? Suppose it hires a maid?

Are a maid's activities a factor of production or a kind of service? Can a household be a seller in the goods market? Suppose it sells homegrown vegetables? In that case, is it acting as a household or a firm?

2. Can you describe other ways in which the factor and the goods markets interact? Will a firm's behavior on the goods market (its supply curve) be affected by a household's behavior on the factor market (the household supply curve or the price that a household asks for its services)? How about a firm's behavior as a buyer of factors being determined by a household's behavior as a buyer of goods?

3. What is meant by describing the market as a "system"? What exactly do we mean by a system? Does it imply that there is something mechanical—machinelike—about the way a social organism works? Can you see that all these words—*system, mechanism,* even *works*—imply a regular, orderly, predictable process?

4. Why is rationing an inescapable problem in our kind of society? Is it inescapable even in traditional societies, like the Eskimo? How is it solved there?

5. Explain how the market rations automobiles. What other means of allocating cars could you imagine in a capitalist society? In a socialist one?

6. Under what circumstances is the market not regarded as a good rationer? Take a newly perfected vaccine as an example. Why would people object to selling it to the highest bidder? Why don't the same arguments apply to aspirin?

7. Is there a shortage of low-cost housing? High-cost housing? What do we mean by the term?

8. Would you be in favor of a gas tax that would remove any shortages or do you prefer rationing on a nonprice basis? Which basis strikes you as best?

9. Diagram a situation in which a government subsidy holds up farm prices and creates a surplus. (You might check your diagram with Figure 7 on page 190.)

AN EXTRA WORD ABOUT

Optimal Allocation and Marginal Utility

There is another way in which a market allows us to allocate income efficiently. Let us see how the market mechanism maximizes the total utilities of a person who shops in many markets for many goods.

An intuitive example may help us begin. Suppose you had to spend your weekly income each Monday, but you had to make up your shopping list, once and for all, before leaving your house. If you had enough price catalogs, that would not be impossible to do, although you might debate the merits of this item versus that one. *Suppose you had to make up the list without knowing what prices were!*

Two problems would present themselves. First, you would not know how many goods you could buy *in toto* because you would not know whether your income would suffice to buy a few goods or many. Second, you would have no way of ranking the priority of your purchases. Knowing the prices of bread and cake, you can decide how much you want to spend on each. Not knowing these prices, how could you make a rational decision whether to buy many units of bread and no cake, or 50-50 or some other combination?

You might think, perhaps, that a rational man would buy bread first, then cake. But suppose after he had made his irrevocable decision he found that bread was very expensive and cake very cheap. He might then regret having decided to buy so much bread and wish he had chosen cake instead.

This seemingly trivial example contains more than may at first meet the eye, for it shows us how the existence of prices enables us to behave as rational maximizers in disposing of our incomes. Therefore let us pursue this line of reasoning a little further.

In Figure 1 we show our reservation prices for three commodities. *Reservation price* is a term meaning the highest price that we are willing to offer as buyers or the lowest price we'd take as sellers. In each case, our reservation price for another unit of the same good diminishes because the good gives us less marginal utility. At the same time, as the diagram makes clear, the schedule of reservation prices is very different for each good. Good A is very important to us, so our initial reservation price is very high; good B less so; good C still less. (We have drawn our reservation prices in steplike fashion and overlaid a generalized schedule of reservation prices, which is, of course, our familiar demand curve.)*

MARGINS VS. TOTALS

The question we want to elucidate is this: *How much of each good will we buy to get the largest possible satisfaction from our income?*

Suppose we had an unlimited income. This is the same thing as supposing that the goods were free, that their prices were zero. How much of A, B, and C would we then acquire? An unlimited amount? Certainly not. As our diagram shows, we don't want unlimited quantities of A, B, and C. Beyond a certain point, their marginal utilities are negative. They are nuisances. We could even have negative reservation prices: We would pay someone to take the stuff away. Thus, with no budget constraint, we consume quantities OA + OB + OC.

Now notice something interesting about this unlimited consumption. The three demand curves reflect differing marginal utilities of the three goods. Looking at these curves, we see that the *total* utility we get from A will be greater than that we get from B or C, and that the *total* utility of B will be greater than that of C. Why, then, don't we take more of A and B, since their total utility is so large? The answer, also apparent from the graph, is that after we have acquired quantity OA of good A, *we don't get any further utility from it.* The same is true of B after we have OB of it, and of course of C, after OC.

This begins to clarify a very important point. To get the maximum amount of enjoyment from our income—even from an *unlimited* income—we need pay no attention to the total utilities we get from various commodities. Their marginal utilities are all we need to know. We will reach a maximum of satisfaction from our total expenditure when we get as much utility from the marginal unit of one good as from

---

*Remember that each of these schedules of reservation prices depends on our income as well as our tastes. With different incomes we might have a different set of desires for the three goods.

FIGURE 1
Allocating Income
The graph shows us different schedules of reservation prices (the most we would pay) for successive units of three commodities. At price OX we will just be tempted to buy an amount OQ_1 of good A, OQ_2 of good B, but none of good C. At zero price, how much do we want of each?

another. **Indeed, the rule for maximizing our total satisfaction is to acquire goods until their marginal utilities per dollar of expenditure are equal.**

THE EQUIMARGINAL RULE

This equimarginal rule has many applications in economics, for it has an astonishing property. It means that we don't have to stop to compare totals when we maximize values. *We need compare only margins.* Later we will see that this applies to entrepreneurs trying to maximize total revenues and to minimize total costs. They, too, will need to look at only marginal costs and incomes. For ourselves as consumers, it means that we do not have to try to compare whether we get more "total" satisfaction out of bread or out of cake. All we have to do is worry about whether we want one more loaf of bread or one more piece of cake. If we buy whichever we want more of at the moment, we will automatically be maximizing our total well-being. When we equally desire another unit of each, we have spent our income as efficiently as possible.

BUDGET CONSTRAINTS

So far, we have imagined that we had no budget constraint. Of course we do have such constraints. Our incomes are limited, and prices are not zero. Then how does the equi-marginal principle apply?

If you will turn back to Figure 10, you will see an X on the price axis of good A. We can imagine that this is the price of goods A, B, and C. We picture them having the same price: e.g., $5 for a basket of fruit (good A), a necktie (good B), a movie ticket (good C). (We could draw different prices for each good, but that would only complicate the diagram without changing the principle.)

Now how much of A, B, and C do we buy? You can see that we buy (approximately) OQ^1 of good A, and OQ^2 of good B. We buy none of good C. Why? Because the price is higher than our top reservation price. We don't want to go to the movies at $5, given our budget constraint.

Now look at goods A and B. You obviously have much more total utility from A than from B. Why, then, don't you buy more of A and less of B? The answer is that you are getting as much satisfaction *at the margin* for good A as for good B. If you bought another unit of good A and one less unit of good B, you would be giving up more utility than you would be getting. *Thus budget constraints limit the amount of goods we can buy, but we still maximize our well-being by seeking equal marginal utilities from those we buy.*

EQUALIZING MARGINAL UTILITIES

Now let us take one last step. We have just seen that we maximize our personal well-being by equalizing the marginal utilities of goods, not their total utilities. *We can then see that we will spend our income optimally when we get the same satisfaction from the last dollar spent on each good.* If the marginal utility of a dollar's worth of bread is equal to that of a dollar's worth of cake, we will then have achieved our aim.

When we speak of "a dollar's worth" of bread, we are speaking of its price. Therefore we can set up a formula that will describe the way we allocate our incomes to maximize our satisfactions.

$$\frac{\text{marginal utility of good A}}{\text{price of good A}} = \frac{\text{marginal utility of good B}}{\text{price of good B}}$$

or in more abstract terms:

$$\frac{MU_1}{P_1} = \frac{MU_2}{P_2} = \frac{MU_n}{P_n}$$

where *MU* stands for the marginal utilities of goods 1, 2 . . . *n,* and $P_1, P_2 . . . P_n$ stand for their respective prices.

Here is the equimarginal principle at work. We are maximizing our well-being by equating the *marginal* utilities of different goods in proportion to their prices, so that each dollar expenditure for each good gives us the same enjoyment. We may still get a much larger amount of enjoyment from one kind of good than from another, but we will only decrease our total welfare if we lose sight of the equimarginal principle.

CHAPTER 12

Market Dynamics

A LOOK AHEAD

We have already learned how the interaction of supply and demand schedules establishes price, and how movements in these schedules (and in the curves that represent them) help explain changes in price. Now we need to explore the concept of price formation a little more deeply.

In this short but important chapter we concentrate on two problems:

1 The idea of elasticity, one of the most useful notions in the economist's kit of tools. Elasticity will provide a much more complete understanding of how supply and demand work.

2 The idea of substitution. It has been said that substitution is one of the central organizing concepts of economics. We will use it here to shed light on the much misunderstood words *necessity* and *luxury*.

We have seen how shifts in demand or supply affect price, but *how much* do they affect price? Suppose, for example, that demand schedules have increased (shifted rightward) by 10 percent. How do we know how large an effect this change will have on price?

This question leads us to a deeper scrutiny of the nature of supply and demand by way of a new concept called elasticity, or more properly, **price elasticity.**

Elasticity and Slope

We already know that when we describe a supply or demand curve as "steep" or "flat," we are making a statement about its *slope*. And it is easy to see that the steeper one such curve, the less the effect of a given shift in the other will be on the quantity supplied or demanded.

Figure 1 illustrates the case with two supply curves. Our diagrams show two commodities selling at the same equilibrium prices and facing identical demand schedules. Note, however, that the two commodities have very different supply curves. In both cases, demand increases by the same amount. Notice how much greater is the price increase (and how much less the quantity increase) for the good with the steep supply curve.

Elasticity is simply a way of measuring this difference. It is the *proportional* change in quantity supplied, divided by the *proportional* change in price. Thus, if quantity supplied increased by 20 percent when the price offered increased by 5 percent, we would say that the price elasticity of supply equals 4—a very high figure for a

FIGURE 1
Slope of Supply Curves and Elasticity of Supply
Elasticity depends in part on the slope of supply or demand curves. These shapes, in turn, represent the sensitivity of buyers or sellers to price changes. On the left, we have a steep supply curve. The increase in demand from DD to D′D′ brings a big jump in prices. On the right, the same increase in demand coaxes forth a lot of additional supply. We say that the price elasticity of supply is greater for the second commodity.

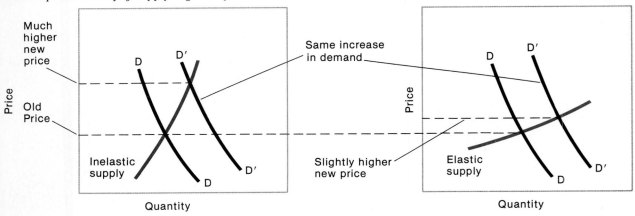

supply elasticity. If, on the other hand, it takes a 20 percent price increase to yield a 5 percent increase in supply, we say that the price elasticity is only 25 percent, or one-quarter, a low value.

Notice we do not say that a curve or line is elastic or inelastic. That is because price elasticity is generally not constant as you move along a line or curve. Indeed, elasticities for any *linear* demand curve will range from very large at low values of output and high prices (since even small absolute and proportionate declines in price yield large proportionate increases in demand) to very low at high values of output. This is true irrespective of the slope of the demand curve, which in the case of linear demand is everywhere the same.

Because elasticity measures sensitivity of response to price changes, it is a powerful factor in explaining price movements. An elastic demand (or supply) means that changes in price strongly affect buyers' or sellers' willingness or ability to buy or sell. Inelasticity means that the effect of price on quantity is small. When a change in price of X percent yields a change in quantity (demanded or supplied) of just X percent, we say that demand or supply is **unit-elastic** at that point.

The Elasticity Formula

It is helpful to have a precise idea of how we measure elasticity. The method is simple enough. **We measure the percentage change in the quantity demanded over the percentage change in price.** If the percentage change in quantity demanded is greater than that of price, our measure of elasticity will be greater than unity, and we have an elastic curve. If it is less than unity, we have an inelastic curve. If the two variables are equal, we have unit elasticity.

In algebra*

$$\frac{\Delta Q/Q}{\Delta P/P} = \text{measure of elasticity}$$

where

ΔQ is the *change* in quantity demanded

Q is the *original* quantity demanded

ΔP is the *change* in price

P is the original price

It helps if we see what elasticities of different kinds look like. Figure 3 is a family of supply and demand curves that illustrates the range of buying and selling responses associated with a change in prices.

---

*A footnote for the mathematically inclined student. You have probably noticed that the change in quantity is likely to be a positive number when the change in price is a negative number—we buy more when the price goes down. Therefore the measure of demand elasticity will also be a negative number. For convenience' sake, economists disregard this and speak as if the measure were positive. You should also note that there are a number of refinements in measuring elasticity that we do not go into here. The main one concerns the difference between measuring elasticity at a single point—point elasticity—and measuring it along a section of the curve—arc elasticity.

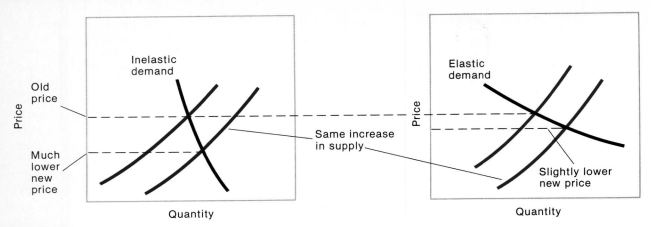

FIGURE 2
Slope of Demand Curves and Elasticity of Demand
Elasticity obviously applies to demand as well as to supply. Rule: The more elastic demand is, the less will a given
shift in supply curves affect prices.

Elasticities and Business Fortune

In Chapter 31 we will discover a very important effect of elasticities in determining
the incidence of taxation—that is, who pays a given tax. But while we are still
studying the marketplace, we should note that elasticities have a great effect on the
fortunes of buyers and sellers. It makes a big difference to a buyer whether the
supply curve of a desired commodity is elastic or not, for that will drastically affect
the amount the buyer will have to spend on that particular commodity if its price
changes. It makes an equal amount of difference to a seller whether the demand
curve for his output is elastic or not, for that will determine what happens to total
revenues as prices change.

Here is an instance in point. Table 1 shows three demand schedules: elastic
demand, demand, and unit elasticity. Let us see how these three differently
constituted schedules would affect the fortunes of a seller who had to cater to the
demand represented by each.

A very interesting result follows from these different schedules. The amounts
spent (price times quantity) are in Table 2. **The total amount spent for each
commodity (and thus the total amount received by a firm) will be very
different over the indicated range of prices.**

To a seller of goods it makes a lot of difference whether or not the demand he
faces is elastic. If demand is elastic and he cuts his price, he will take in more
revenue. If his demand is inelastic and he cuts his price, he will take in *less* revenue.

Conversely, a business that raises its price will be lucky if the demand for its
product is inelastic, for then receipts will actually increase. Compare the fortunes of
the two businesses depicted in Figure 4. Note that by blocking in the change in
price times the change in quantity, we can show the change in receipts. (Because we
have ignored changes in costs, we cannot show changes in profits.)

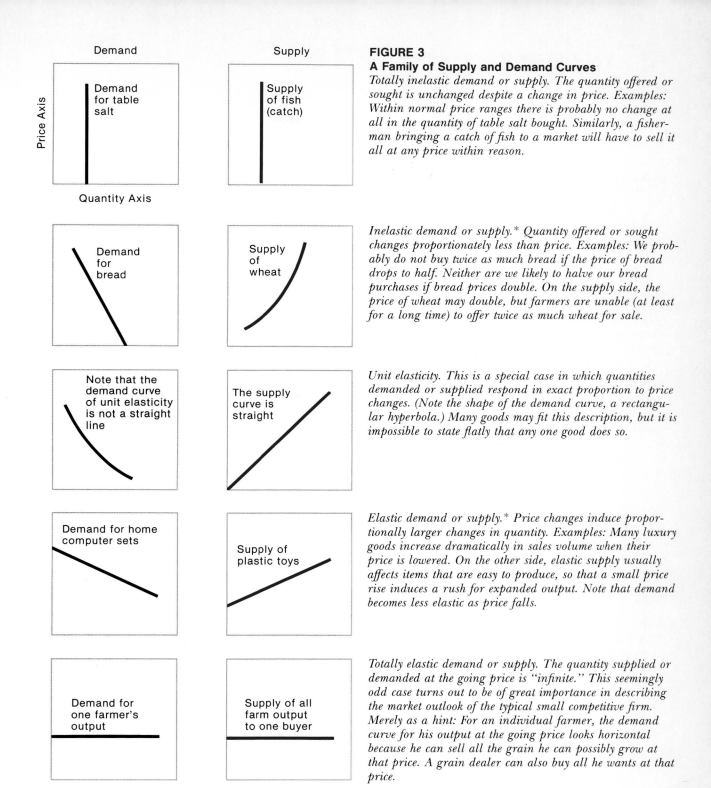

FIGURE 3
A Family of Supply and Demand Curves

Totally inelastic demand or supply. The quantity offered or sought is unchanged despite a change in price. Examples: Within normal price ranges there is probably no change at all in the quantity of table salt bought. Similarly, a fisherman bringing a catch of fish to a market will have to sell it all at any price within reason.

Inelastic demand or supply.* Quantity offered or sought changes proportionately less than price. Examples: We probably do not buy twice as much bread if the price of bread drops to half. Neither are we likely to halve our bread purchases if bread prices double. On the supply side, the price of wheat may double, but farmers are unable (at least for a long time) to offer twice as much wheat for sale.

Unit elasticity. This is a special case in which quantities demanded or supplied respond in exact proportion to price changes. (Note the shape of the demand curve, a rectangular hyperbola.) Many goods may fit this description, but it is impossible to state flatly that any one good does so.

Elastic demand or supply.* Price changes induce proportionally larger changes in quantity. Examples: Many luxury goods increase dramatically in sales volume when their price is lowered. On the other side, elastic supply usually affects items that are easy to produce, so that a small price rise induces a rush for expanded output. Note that demand becomes less elastic as price falls.

Totally elastic demand or supply. The quantity supplied or demanded at the going price is "infinite." This seemingly odd case turns out to be of great importance in describing the market outlook of the typical small competitive firm. Merely as a hint: For an individual farmer, the demand curve for his output at the going price looks horizontal because he can sell all the grain he can possibly grow at that price. A grain dealer can also buy all he wants at that price.

*As the text explains, these curves have different elasticities at different points. Our illustrations are only suggestive, not strictly accurate.

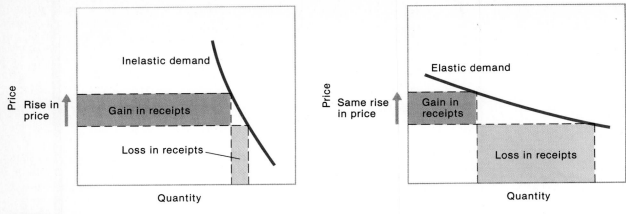

FIGURE 4
Elasticities and Receipts
Notice the striking difference in the receipts of two businesses facing demand of different elasticities if each firm raises price by the same amount.

TABLE 1
Demand Schedules for Three Goods
The three demand schedules are different in elasticity because each reveals a different ability or willingness to buy as prices change.

		Quantities Demanded	
Price	Inelastic Demand	Unit Elasticity	Elastic Demand
$10	100	100	100
9	101	111⅑	120
8	102	125	150
7	103	142⁴⁄₇	200
6	104	166⅔	300
5	105	200	450
4	106	250	650
3	107	333⅓	900
2	108	500	1,400
1	109	1,000	3,000

TABLE 2
Total Expenditures (or Receipts)
Compare what happens to receipts of the three goods when price drops from $10 to $9.

	Goods with Demand Schedules That Are		
Price	Inelastic	Unit-Elastic	Elastic
$10	$1,000	$1,000	$1,000
9	909	1,000	1,080
8	816	1,000	1,200
7	721	1,000	1,400
6	624	1,000	1,800
5	525	1,000	2,250
4	424	1,000	2,600
3	321	1,000	2,700
2	216	1,000	2,800
1	109	1,000	3,000

Our figure shows something else. If we reverse the direction of the price change, our businesses' fortunes suffer a sharp change. A demand curve that is elastic spells bad news for a business that seeks to raise prices, but the same demand curve brings good fortune to one that intends to cut prices. Just the opposite is true with an inelastic demand curve: Here the condition of demand is favorable for a price rise, since the seller will hold most customers even at the higher price; but it is bad for a price cut, since the seller will gain few additional customers (or the old ones will increase their purchases only slightly) when prices fall.

BEHIND ELASTICITIES OF DEMAND: SUBSTITUTION

Because elasticities are so important in accounting for the behavior of prices, we must press our investigation further. We will leave the supply side of elasticity to be studied when we look into the behavior of factors and firms. Here we will ask why demand curves are shaped the way they are. Why is our price (or income) sensitivity for some commodities so great and for others so slight?

If we think of a good service for which our demand might be very inelastic—say, eyeglasses (assuming we need them)—and compare it with another for which our demand is apt to be highly elastic—say, a trip to Europe—the difference is not difficult to grasp. One thing is a necessity; the other is a luxury. But what do we mean by *necessity* and *luxury?*

One attribute of a necessity is that it is not easily replaced by a substitute. If we need eyeglasses, we will spend a great deal of money, if we must, to acquire a pair. Hence such a necessity has a very inelastic demand curve.

Marginal Utility Again

Necessities are never absolute in the sense that nothing can be substituted for them. High enough prices will drive buyers to some substitute, however imperfect.* Just when will the buyer be driven to the "next best thing"? As we know, economists say that the decision will be made by a comparison of the marginal utility derived from a dollar's worth of the high-priced item with that derived from the lower-priced substitute. As the price of wine goes up and up, there comes a point at which we would rather spend our next dollar for a substantial amount of beer than a sip of wine.

---

*What *would* be the substitute for eyeglasses? For a very nearsighted person, the demand for one pair of glasses would be absolutely inelastic over a considerable price range. But when glasses got to be, say, $500 a pair, substitutes would begin to appear. At those prices, one could hire a helper to guide one around or to read aloud. Admittedly this is less satisfactory than having glasses; but if the choice is between spending a very large amount on glasses and on personal help, the latter might seem preferable. Of course, there are some goods without any substitutes—air, for example. Such goods are "free goods," because no one owns them. If a good such as air could be owned, it would have to be subject to stringent public control to prevent its owners from exacting a horrendous price for it. On that same basis, what is the rationale for allowing food to be privately owned in a starving country?

INCOME ELASTICITIES

We should notice that we can use another term—*income elasticity*—to describe how our willingness or ability to buy or sell responds to a change in *income*, rather than price. With many commodities, income elasticities of both demand and supply are more significant than price elasticities in actual economic life.

The idea of income elasticity is exactly the same as that of price elasticity. Sales of an income-elastic good or service rise proportionately *faster* than income. Sales of an income-inelastic commodity rise *less than proportionately* with income. These relationships are graphed in the accompanying figure.

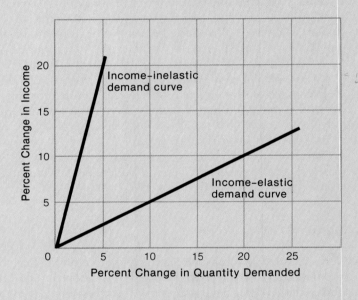

FIGURE 5
Income Elasticities

Do not be fooled into thinking that these are supply curves because they slope upward. "Income" demand curves show a functional relation different from that of "price" demand curves. In the curves shown, we assume that prices are unchanged, otherwise we would not have *ceteris paribus*.

Necessities and Elasticity

We have seen that necessities have inelastic demand curves, so that we stick to them as prices rise. What about when they fall? Won't we rush to buy more necessities, just because they *are* necessities? Won't that make their demand curves elastic?

Surprisingly, we do not rush to buy necessities when their prices fall. Why? The answer is that necessities are the things we buy *first,* **just because they are necessities.** Having bought what we needed before the fall in price, we are not tempted to buy much more, if any more, after the fall. Bread, as we commented in an earlier chapter, is a great deal more valuable for life than diamonds. But we ordinarily have enough bread, so the marginal utility of another loaf is no greater than that of an equivalent expenditure on any other good. Thus, as the price of bread drops, the quantity we seek expands only slightly. So too with eyeglasses.

Compare the case with a luxury, such as a trip to Europe. There are many substitutes for such a trip: trips out West, trips East, or some other kind of vacation. As a result, if the price of a European trip goes up, we are easily persuaded to switch to some alternative plan. Conversely, when the price of a European trip gets cheaper, we are quick to substitute *it* for other possible vacation alternatives, and our demand accordingly displays its elastic properties.

Do not make the mistake, however, of thinking that elasticity is purely a function of whether items are expensive or not. Studies have shown that the demand for subway transportation in New York City is price-elastic, which hardly means that riding in the subways is the prerogative of millionaires. The point, rather, is that the demand for subway rides is closely affected by the comparative prices of substitutes—bus fares and taxis. **Thus it is the ease or difficulty of substitution that always lies behind the various elasticities of demand schedules.**

The Importance of Substitutes

Time also plays an important role in shaping our demand curves. Suppose, for example, that the price of orange juice suddenly soared owing to a crop failure. Would the demand for orange juice be elastic or inelastic?

In the short run, it would generally be more inelastic than in the longer run. Lovers of orange juice would likely be willing to pay a higher price for their favorite juice because (they would believe) there was really no other juice quite as good. As weeks went by, they might be tempted to try other breakfast juices, and no doubt some of these experiments would take. Substitutes would be found after all.

The point is that it takes time and information for patterns of demand to change. Thus demand curves generally become more elastic as time goes on and the range of discovered substitutes becomes larger.

Because substitutes form a vast chain of alternatives for buyers, changes in the price of substitutes change the position of demand curves. Here is a new idea to be thought about carefully. Our existing demand curve for bread or diamonds has the shape (elasticity) it does because substitutes exist at various prices. When the prices of those substitutes *change,* the original commodity suddenly looks "cheaper" or "more expensive." If the price of a subway ride rises from $1.00 to $1.50 while the price of a taxi ride remains the same, we will be tempted to switch part of our transportation from subways to taxis. If subway rides went to $2.00, there would be a mass exodus to taxis.

Thus we should add changes in taste and in income when we consider the possible causes of a shift in demand. If the price of a substitute commodity rises, the demand for the original commodity will rise. As the price of the substitute falls, demand for the original commodity will fall. This may, of course, bring changes in the price of the original commodity.

Complements

In addition to substitution, there is another connection between commodities. This is the relationship of *complementarity*. **Complementarity means that some commodities are technically linked, so that you cannot very well use one without using the other, even though they are sold separately.** Automobiles and gasoline are examples of such complementary goods, as are cameras and film.

Here is another instance of change in the price of one good actually affecting the position of the demand curve for the other. If the price of film goes up, it becomes more expensive to operate cameras. Hence the demand for cameras is apt to drop. Note that the price of cameras has not changed in the first instance. Rather, when the price of the complementary good, the film, goes up, the whole demand curve for cameras shifts to the left. Thereafter the price of cameras is apt to fall too.

Behavior and Nature, Again

There is a last point we should make before we leave the subject of elasticity. We have seen that the substitutability of one product for another is the underlying

THE SEARCH FOR SUBSTITUTES

The search for substitutes is a complicated process that can lead to equally complicated supply and demand reactions. Just after a taxi strike in New York City, when fares went up 50 percent, people switched to substitutes (they rode buses and subways or walked) and the taxi business suffered severely. Then after the shock of the increase wore off, business revived. People got used to higher fares; that is, they discovered that the marginal utility of a high-priced taxi ride was still greater than the marginal utility of the money they saved by using other transportation, plus the marginal utility of the time they wasted or the business they lost because they weren't taking taxis. In other words, the substitutes weren't satisfactory. Gradually, people began taking more cab rides, and taxi receipts were higher than before the fare hike. The quantity of taxi service consumed was down somewhat, but not by as much as the original drop. In this case, demand proved to be more *inelastic* over time than it was in the very short run.

cause of elasticity. Indeed, more and more we are led to see products themselves as bundles of utilities surrounded by competing bundles that offer a whole range of alternatives for a buyer's satisfaction.

What is it that ultimately determines how close the substitutes come to the commodity in question? As with all questions in economics that are pursued to the end, the answer lies in two aspects of reality before which economic inquiry comes to a halt. One of these is human behavior, with its tastes, drives, and wants. One person's substitute will not be another's.

The other ultimate basing point is the technical and physical nature of the world that forces certain constraints upon us. Cotton may be a substitute for wool because they both have the properties of fibers, but diamonds are not a substitute for the same end use, because they lack the requisite physical properties. Diamonds, as adornment, may be a substitute for clothes made out of cotton; but until we learn how to spin diamonds, they will not be a substitute for the cloth itself.

LOOKING BACK

KEY CONCEPTS

Elasticity measures our quantity response to price changes:
$\Delta Q/Q$
$\Delta P/P$

1 The use of curves gives us a quick, graphic sense of the market at work. In particular, it highlights our responsiveness as buyers or sellers to changes in price (or income). We call this responsiveness the elasticity of supply or demand. You should learn the formula for this elasticity.

Elasticities affect receipts and expenditures.

2 Elasticities greatly affect the way markets work. One important effect is the relation between elasticities and business receipts. A firm facing an inelastic demand will be glad to raise prices, sad to lower them. Why? A buyer with an elastic demand for a commodity will be sad when prices go up, glad when they go down. Again why? (If you don't know, review pages 202–203.)

Substitution lies behind elasticity.

3 Finally, we go behind elasticity to find the all-important element of substitution. It is the ease of finding substitutes that shapes our behavior as buyers and sellers. If we can't find substitutes, we change our buying habits relatively little even if prices go up. This is another way of describing a necessity. If substitutes abound, even a small price rise will bring a larger reduction in the quantity we consume—we have given up a luxury.

Necessities and luxuries are created by ease of substitution.

It has been said that substitution is the law of economic life, the key to everything. Think about the kinds of substitutes we have for even the most necessary items. What are the substitutes for water? Bread? There are surprisingly many. Indeed, it is hard to find items, like eyeglasses, for which substitutes are very few.

4 *Last, be sure you do the questions to this chapter.* They will help you discover what you know—and don't yet know.

ECONOMIC VOCABULARY

QUESTIONS

1. Draw the following: a perfectly inelastic demand curve and a perfectly elastic supply curve; a demand curve of infinite elasticity and a totally inelastic supply curve. Now give examples of commodities each one of these curves might represent.

2. Show on a diagram why elasticity has so much effect in determining price changes. (Refer back to the diagrams on pages 000–000 to be sure that you are right.)

3. Draw a diagram that shows what we mean by an increase in the quantity supplied; another diagram to show what is meant by an increase in supply. Now do the same for a decrease in quantity supplied and in supply. (*Warning:* It is very easy to get these wrong. Check yourself by seeing if the decreased supply curve shows the seller offering less goods at the same prices.) Now do the same exercise for demand. Refer back to Chapter 8 if you have forgotten.

4. Show on a diagram (or with figures) why you would rather be the seller of a good for which demand was elastic if you were in a market with falling prices. Suppose prices were rising—would you still be glad about the elasticity of demand?

5. How does substitution affect elasticity? If there are many substitutes for a product, is demand for it elastic or inelastic? Why?

6. If you were a legislator choosing a product on which to levy an excise tax, would you choose a necessity or a luxury? Which would yield the larger revenue? Show how your answer hinges on the different elasticities of luxuries and necessities.

7. By and large, are luxuries apt to enjoy elastic or inelastic demands? Has this anything to do with their price? Can high-priced goods have inelastic demands?

8. Why is demand more apt to become elastic over time?

9. The price of pipe tobacco rises. What is apt to be the effect on the demand for pipes? On the demand for cigars?

CHAPTER 13

Where the Market Fails

A LOOK AHEAD

We have been learning about how the market works as an efficient allocator of goods. Now we must learn about how the market fails to work in certain instances. Two general categories of cases will interest us in this chapter:

1 The first has to do with situations in which the market operates badly or inefficiently.

2 The second concerns a class of transactions that entirely escape the market's organizing powers. In the second class we come across the very important problem of pollution, and we will consider ways of coping with it.

*U*p to this point we have been concerned with learning about the ways in which the market operates as a self-enforcing mechanism for allocating goods. We have noted that the results of its allocation may not necessarily please us because the market has a very mercenary attitude toward allocation, but we have made a point of stressing how efficiently and effectively it operates compared with other rationing systems.

In this chapter we must round out our understanding of the market by probing two areas of economic activity where the market works very inefficiently or not at all. One of these has to do with instances where marketers have no way of making intelligent decisions, and where therefore the results of the market will reflect ignorance, luck, or accident rather than informed maximizing behavior. The second case involves a large category of production that we call public goods— goods that escape the ministrations of the market entirely.

INFORMATION PROBLEMS

The whole market system is built on the assumption that individuals are **rational maximizers.** But buried in that assumption is the implicit expectation that marketers will have at least roughly accurate information about the market. A good example to the contrary is the situation faced by the tourist in a bazaar of a country where he or she doesn't know a word of the language. Such a buyer has no way of knowing what the price of an article "ought" to be. That's why tourists so often return triumphantly with their bazaar trophies—only to discover that they were for sale in their hotel at half the price.

The Prevalence of Ignorance

Without correct or adequate information, marketers obviously cannot make correct decisions. But often marketers do not have adequate information. Consumers guide themselves by hearsay, by casual information picked up by random sampling, or by their susceptibility to advertising. Who has time to investigate which brand of toothpaste is really best or even tastes best? Even professional buyers, such as industrial purchasing agents, cannot know every price of every product, including all substitutes.

The lack of information can be remedied, at least up to a point; but the remedy costs money or its equivalent—time. Few of us have the resources or patience to do a complete research job on every item we buy. Would it even be rational to do so? **Thus a certain amount of ignorance always remains in all markets, causing prices and quantities to differ from what they would be if we had complete information.** These differences can be very great, as anyone knows who has ever discovered, with sinking heart, that he or she paid "much too much" for a given article or sold it for "much too little."

MARKET INSTABILITY

One important class of market failure that stems from inadequate information is market instability. We have concentrated thus far on the tendency of markets to gravitate toward an equilibrium price. But markets may not equilibrate if the information marketers have is faulty; instead, they may gyrate or race back and forth, as the stock market does when investors are particularly "nervous" about the future.

Cobwebs

One interesting kind of market instability is called a *cobweb,* for reasons that become clear when we look at Figure 1. In this graph we show the supply and demand curves for some commodity that is produced a long time before it is sold, so that producers can't quickly change their outputs to correspond with the state of the market. They have to gear production to the demand they *expect* six months or even longer into the future. If these expectations are unfounded, trouble can ensue.

In Figure 1 we begin by supposing that Christmas tree growers initially put the quantity *OA* on the market. We can see that quantity *OA* will sell at price *OB*. Figuring that this will be *next year's* price, tree growers now plant the amount they are willing and able to offer at price *OB*—quantity *OC*. Alas, when the harvest comes, it is found that quantity *OC* will fetch only price *OD*. Now the process goes

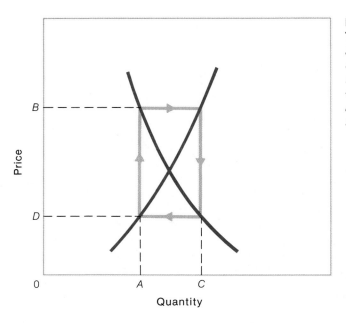

FIGURE 1
The Cobweb
See text for the explanation of this cobweb. If expectations and information remain unchanged, producers will go on chasing their tails forever.

into reverse. Growers will figure that next year's price will be *OD,* and they plant amount *OA,* since at price *OD* the quantity they wish to supply is no more than that. Thereupon, next harvest time the price goes back to *OB* and around we go. If the supply and demand schedules were differently sloped, we could have a cobweb that converged toward equilibrium, as we show on the left of Figure 2; or we could have one that "exploded," as we see in the diagram on the right.

EXPECTATIONS AND SPECULATION

Expectations are so important in making markets work smoothly that we must spend a little more time with them.

Let us quickly learn how expectations work. Suppose buyers of a commodity discover that its price is rising. If they expect that this rise in price will be short-lived or even if they think that the new higher price will persist for a fairly long time, they will behave the way textbooks say they should. In the face of higher prices, quantities demanded will decline, a new equilibrium price will be established, and that will be that. The market will have performed its task.

FIGURE 2
Stabilizing and Explosive Cobwebs
The cobweb on the left spirals into an equilibrium and the one on the right "explodes." The reason in both cases lies in the position and shape of the supply and demand curves. In other words, if supply and demand are favorable, a cobweb can lead to stability. If they are wrong, terrible instability can result.

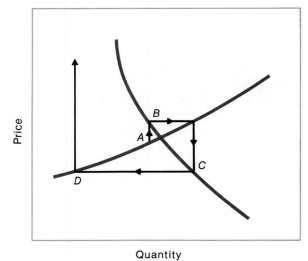

Perverse Reactions

Now suppose that the rise in prices sets off expectations that prices will rise still more. This is a common experience in inflationary times, when the mounting prices of goods leads us to believe that prices will be still higher tomorrow, not that they will be lower or remain at their new levels. **In this case of inflationary expectations, we do not behave as normal demanders. Instead of curtailing our willingness to buy, the rise in prices spurs it on. Better to buy more today than wait till tomorrow when prices will be higher still. Thus expectations can induce perverse reactions in the marketplace.** Of course, the same kinds of perverse reactions can affect the supply curves of sellers. Ordinarily, a rise in prices brings about an increase in the quantities offered. Not, however, if expectations point in the direction of still higher prices. Then sellers will hold back, causing the supply curve to shift leftward.

The result, as we can see in Figure 3, is that prices can move violently upward and that the movement of prices can continue to feed upon itself, because demand and supply curves (D^1, D^2, D^3 and S^1, S^2, S^3) are themselves being shifted by the very fact that prices have changed. In deflationary times, the same process can work in reverse.

Such perverse price movements can lead to very dangerous consequences. They play a major role in the cumulative, unstable processes of speculation or collapse. They can cause commodity prices to shoot to dizzying heights or plummet to the depths. At its worst, perverse behavior threatens to make an entire economy go out of control, as in the case of hyperinflations or panics. At best, it

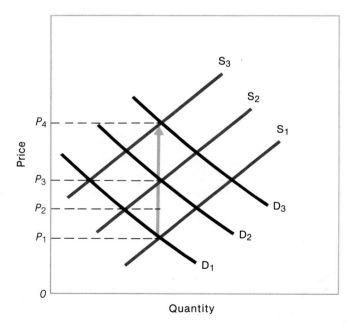

FIGURE 3
A Self-Feeding Price Rise
Suppose we have a market in which D_1 is the demand curve and S_1 the supply curve, with price at P_1. Now suppose that supply shifts to S_2, as when the OPEC countries in 1973 raised their prices. If D_1 did not change, we would simply have a new stable market with price at P_2. But if the change in supply serves as a trigger to move demand upward to D_2, price will rise to P_3. And if OPEC sellers, seeing that the market is buoyant, contract offerings further—the S_3 supply curve—prices will continue to go up if demand also shifts to D_3. This kind of market instability, based on expectations, can also work in reverse. Can you see its relevance to a "collapse" in stock prices?

disrupts smooth, orderly markets and brings shocks and dislocations to the economy.

Remedying Information Lacks

Can these market failures be remedied? Some can; some cannot. Ignorance can certainly be reduced by better economic reporting or by truth-in-advertising laws. Cobwebs can be mitigated by accurate economic forecasting or just by learning from experience. Perverse behavior can be lessened—perhaps—by persuasive pronouncements from important public figures.

But we must recognize that there is a residue of arbitrariness even in the best-intentioned remedies. Take the matter of consumer information. We "inform" the consumer, through labels on cigarette packages, that smoking is dangerous; but we do not prohibit the advertising of cigarettes. We spread "market information" by having the incomprehensible contents of medications printed on their containers, but we allow the consumer to be misinformed through advertising that claims superiority of one kind of aspirin over another.

Why? There is no clear rationale in these cases. Essentially we are trying to repair omissions in the market system—injecting information so that consumers can make better choices—without becoming paternalistic. Maybe we think it is better to allow the consumer to make some mistakes than to allow the government to make them for him.

That is perhaps as it should be. But the consequence is that the market will continue to produce less than wholly satisfactory or efficient results because a residue of ignorance or misinformation is allowed to remain—or remains despite our best efforts.

PUBLIC GOODS

Now we must turn to the range of problems that derive from the fact that certain kinds of output in our system do not have the characteristics of ordinary goods or services because they are not sold. That is, they never enter the market system in the first place, so it is not surprising that the market cannot allocate them. We call such outputs *public goods*. Since public goods are not easy to define, let us start by illustrating the properties of goods such as defense, the national weather service, and lighthouses. Such goods have these peculiar characteristics:

1. **The consumption of a public good by one individual does not interfere with its consumption by another.** A lighthouse is as effective for ten boats as for one. A weather service is as useful for 100 million TV viewers as for 100. By way of contrast, private goods cannot be consumed in the same way. Food, clothing, or doctors' services that I use cannot also be consumed by you.

2. **Private individuals have no control over the use of a public good.** I can deny you the use of my car. There is no way of denying you the use of "my" national defense system or of "my" road system.

3. **Most important of all, public goods can be provided only by collective decisions.** My private consumption depends on my individual decision to spend or not spend my income. But there is no way that I can, by myself, buy defense, weather services, or a lighthouse service.* We must not only agree to buy the public good or services, but agree *how much* to buy!

Not all public goods are entirely "pure." Highways, education, the law courts, and sanitation services are not so universally available as lighthouses or defense. The amount of education, road space, court time, or garbage service that I consume does affect the amount left over for you. It is possible to exclude some citizens from schools or roads. But even these less perfect examples share in the third basic attribute of public goods: They must all be produced by collective decisions, usually by the voting system of the community; the market, left to itself will not provide them. We see why in the new section.

Free Riding

Because of their characteristics, all public goods share a common difficulty. *Their provision cannot be entrusted to the decision-making mechanism of the market.*

In the use of ordinary goods, each person can consume only as much as that person buys. Here the market works very well. The marginal utility of the goods the individual consumes determines how much he or she will spend. By way of contrast, in the use of public goods, the utility calculus doesn't work. Each person will not buy an amount that he or she really wants, because each can enjoy the goods *someone else* buys. Do not forget that there is no way of excluding others from the use of a pure public good (or from most not-so-pure ones). Therefore each of us would try to get a free ride if we attempted to use the market to determine the level of output.

An example may help. Lighthouse service is a pure public good. Why couldn't we make it a private good? The answer is that no boat owner would be willing to pay what the lighthouse is actually worth to him. Why should he? So long as someone else builds a lighthouse, the boat owner can enjoy its services free!

Voting Instead of Buying

How do we then determine the level of provision of such goods? By eschewing the useless market mechanism and availing ourselves of another means of decision-making: voting. **We vote for the amount of public goods we want; and because**

---

*Not even if I were immensely rich or an absolute monarch? In that case, we would not have a market system, but a command economy catering to one person. Then indeed there would be no distinction between public and private goods.

voting is a curious mechanism, sometimes we oversupply ourselves with these goods and sometimes we undersupply ourselves. We feast on defense and starve on prison reform because defense has "friends in Congress" and prisons do not.

Is there a remedy for the problem? Some economists have suggested that we try to bring as many public goods as possible into the market system by getting rid of their "public" characteristics. We could charge admission to the city's parks, and then produce only as much park service as people were willing to buy. We could charge tolls on all roads, even streets, and limit the building or repair of highways to the amount of private demand for road services. We might limit the use of law courts to those who would hire the judge and jury, or ask the police to interfere on behalf of only those citizens who wore a badge attesting to their contribution to the police fund.

Privatizing Public Goods

Such a **privatization** of public goods might indeed bring the level of their production up, or down, to the amount that we would consume if they were strictly private goods, like cars or movie tickets. The problems are twofold. First, there are innumerable technical difficulties in making many public goods into private ones. Imagine the problems in charging a toll for each city street!

Second, and more arresting, the idea offends our sense of justice. Suppose we could convert defense into a private good. The defense system would then defend only those who bought its services. Presumably the more you bought, the better you would be defended. Few believers in democracy would like to see our national defense converted into a bastion for the rich. Nor would we remove from public use the law courts, the schools, the police, and so on. Unlike private goods, which we have the *privilege* of buying from our incomes, public goods are thought of as our *rights*.

There are valid arguments and clever techniques for returning *some* public goods into the market's fold. **The main point to keep in mind is that it is impossible to make all goods private; and for the ones that should remain public, the market cannot be used to establish a desirable level of output. Here the market mechanism must give way to a political method of making economic decisions.**

EXTERNALITIES

Our next instance of market failure is closely connected with the attributes of public goods. It is the problem of allowing for the "externalities" of production; that is, for the effects of the output of private goods and services on persons other than those who are directly buying or selling or using the goods in question.

Pollution

Externalities bring us to one of the most vexing and sometimes dangerous problems in our economic system—controlling pollution.

What is pollution, from an economic point of view? It is the production of wastes, dirt, noise, congestion, and other things that we do not want. Although we don't think of smoke, smog, traffic din, and traffic jams as part of society's "production," these facts of economic life are certainly the consequence of producing things we do want. Smoke is part of the output process that also gives us steel or cement. Smog arises from the production of industrial energy and heat, among other things. Traffic is a by-product of transportation. In current jargon, economists call these unwanted by-products "bads" to stress their relation to things we call "goods."

"Bads" Escape the Market

Why do externalities exist? The basic answer is technological: We do not know how to produce goods "cleanly"; i.e., without wastes and by-products such as smoke—at least within acceptable cost limitations. But the economic answer calls our attention to another aspect of the problem. **Externalities refer to the fact that the output of bads does not pass through the market system.** A factory may produce smoke, etc., without having to pay anyone for producing these harmful goods. Certain inputs used by firms—air, water, even space in an aesthetic rather than an economic sense—are available without charge, so that there is no constraint to urge a firm to use air or water sparingly or to build a handsome rather than an ugly factory or building.

In other words, pollution exists because it is the cheapest way to do many things, some having to do with producing goods, some with consuming them. It is cheaper to litter than to buy waste cans (and less trouble, too); cheaper to pour wastes into a river than to clean them up. That is, it is cheaper for the individual or the firm. But it may not be cheaper for the community. A ship may dump its wastes "for free" into the ocean, but people on the beach will suffer the costs of having to cope with debris that washes ashore.

Marginal Private and Social Costs

The point is so fundamental it is worth elaborating. In back of the conception of the marketplace as an *efficient* allocator of goods and incomes is a silent assumption. It is that all the inputs going into the process are owned by some individual and that all the outputs are bought by some person or firm or agency. Presumably, then, the price at which commodities are offered will include all the costs that are incurred in the process. Presumably also, the price that will be offered will reflect all the prospective benefits accruing to the buyer. **In other words, prices established in the marketplace are supposed to take into account *all* the disutilities involved in the process of production, such as fatigue or unpleasantness of work, and *all* the utilities ultimately gained by the final consumer of those goods.**

What the problem of pollution has brought home is that the market is not a means for effectively registering a great many of these costs and benefits. The examples of the damage wrought by smoke that is not charged against the factory or of a neighborhood nuisance such as a loud bar or a hideous advertising sign are instances of economic activities in which *private costs are less than social costs.* These social costs are, of course, private costs incurred by other people. Contrariwise, when a person spends money to educate himself, he benefits not only himself but also the community, because he becomes a more productive citizen and presumably a more responsible one. Thus the *social benefits* of some expenditures may be greater than their *private benefits.*

Some externalities are not "bads," but "goods." A refurbished apartment building may increase the property value of a neighborhood. Here is a positive externality. The benefit gained by others results from the reconstruction but is not paid to the owners of that building. Such externalities give some private goods the partial attributes of public goods.

CONTROLLING EXTERNALITIES

How can we bring the process of pollution under social control? Basically, we can attack the problem in three ways. We can

1. regulate the activity that creates it;
2. tax the activity that creates it; or
3. subsidize the polluter to stop (or lessen) the activity.

1. Regulation

Faced with the ugly view of smoke belching from a factory chimney, sludge pouring from a mill into a lake, automobiles choking a city, or people being injured by contaminants, most ecologically concerned persons cry for regulation: "Pass a law to forbid smoky chimneys or sulfurous coal. Pass a law to make mills dispose of their wastes elsewhere or purify them. Pass a law against automobiles in the central city."

What are the economic effects of regulation? **Essentially the idea behind passing laws is to internalize a previous externality. That is, a regulation seeks to impose a cost on an activity that was previously free for the individual or firm, although not free, as we have seen, for society.** This means that individuals or firms must either stop the polluting activity entirely, bear the cost of whatever penalty is imposed by law for pollution, or find ways of carrying out their activities without giving rise to pollution.

Costs of Regulation. Let us take the case of a firm that pollutes the environment as a joint product of producing goods or services. Suppose a regulation is passed enjoining that firm to install antipollution devices—smoke scrubbers or waste treatment facilities. Who bears this cost?

The answer seems obvious at first look: The firm must bear it. But if the firm passes its higher costs along in higher selling prices, we arrive at a different answer. Examine Figure 4. Our firm's original marginal cost (or supply) curve is S^1. The need to install new antipollution equipment raises it by an amount *ac* to S^2. Now a little economic analysis will show us that the cost is in fact borne by three groups. First, the firm will bear some of the cost because at the higher price, it will sell less output, *OY* instead of *OX*. How much less depends on the elasticity of demand for its product. But unless demand is totally inelastic (a vertical line), its sales and income must contract.

Two other groups also bear part of the cost. One group is the factors of production. Fewer factors will be employed because output has fallen. Their loss of income is therefore also a part of the economic cost of antipollution regulation. Last, of course, is the consumer. Prices will rise from P^1 to P^2. Note that consumers lose satisfaction in two ways: They must pay a higher price, *bc,* for the units that they do buy, and some of them will be discouraged by the higher price from buying as much of the good as before or from buying at all. (The satisfaction they lose is measured by the area under the demand curve, *abc.*)

Gains from Regulations. Offsetting all these costs is the fact that each of these three groups, above with the general public, now has a better environment. There is no reason, however, why any of these groups, should think that *its* benefit outweighs *its* costs. Most of the benefit is likely to go to the general public, rather than to the individuals actually involved in the production or consumption of the polluting good or service.

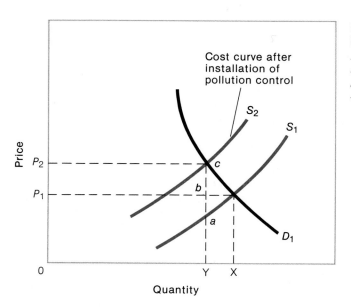

FIGURE 4
Effects of Regulation
Regulation imposes costs on buyers, sellers, and employees. See text if you don't understand why.

Thus a regulation forcing car manufacturers to make cleaner engines will cost the manufacturers some lost sales, will cost consumers added expense for a car, and will cost lost income for whatever land, labor, and capital are no longer employed at higher production costs. As part of the public, all three groups will benefit from cleaner air, but each is likely to feel its specific loss more keenly than its general gain.

Is Regulation Useful? Regulations are good or bad, partly depending on their ease of enforcement. Compare the effectiveness of speed limits, which attempt to lessen the externality of accidents, and of regulations against littering. It is difficult enough to enforce speed laws, but it is almost impossible to enforce antilittering laws.

Ease of enforcement is largely a matter of cost. If we were prepared to have police posted on every mile of highway or every city block, regulation could be fully effective for speed violations or for littering. Obviously the cost would be horrendous, and so would people's reaction to being overpoliced.

2. Taxation

A second way to cope with pollution is to tax it. When a government decides to tax pollution (often called *effluent charges*), it is essentially creating a price system for disposal processes. If an individual company found that it could clean up its own pollutants more cheaply than paying the tax, it would do so. If the company could not clean up its own pollutants more cheaply than the tax cost (which is often the case because of economies of scale in pollution control), it would pay the necessary tax and look to the state to clean up the environment.

The effluent charge looks like, but is not, a license to pollute. It is a license that allows you to give some of your pollutants to the state *for a price.*

As a result of effluent charges, an activity that was formerly costless is no longer so. Thus, in terms of their economic impacts, these charges are just like government regulations. In fact, they are a type of government regulation. They raise the supply curve for the good in question, with all the corresponding ramifications. The difference is that each producer can choose to install clean-up equipment and not pay the tax or to pollute and pay whatever tax costs are imposed.

Antipollution Taxes vs. Regulations. Which is better, regulation or taxation? As we have seen, regulation affects all polluters alike, and this is both its strength and its weakness. Taxation enables each polluter to determine what course of action is best. Some polluters will achieve low-pollution targets more cheaply by installing antipollution equipment, thereby avoiding taxes on their effluents, while other polluters will find it more profitable to pay the tax.

Here practical considerations are likely to be decisive. For example, taxation on effluents discharged into sewers is likely to be more practical than taxation on smoke coming from chimneys. The state can install a sewage treatment plant, but it cannot clean up air that is contaminated by producers who find it cheaper to pay a pollution tax than to install smoke-suppressing equipment. Moreover, to be effective, a pollution tax should vary with the amount of pollution—a paper mill or a utility plant paying more taxes if it increases its output of waste or smoke. One of the problems with taxation is installing monitoring equipment. It is difficult to make accurate measurements of pollution or to allow for differences in environmental harm caused by the same amount of smoke coming from two factories located in different areas.

3. Subsidies

The third way of dealing with pollution is to subsidize polluters to stop polluting. **In this case, the government actually pays the offending parties to clean up the damage they have caused or to stop causing it.** For example, a township might lower the taxes on a firm that agreed to install filters on its stacks. This is, of course, paying the firm to stop polluting.

Economists typically object to subsidies because they camouflage the true economic costs of producing goods and services cleanly. When regulations or taxes increase the price of paper or steel, the individual or firm becomes aware that the environment is not free and that there may be heavy costs in producing goods in a way that will not damage the environment. The increased price will lead them to demand less of these goods. But when they get clean environment through the allocation of a portion of taxes, there is no price signal to show them the cost of pollution associated with particular commodities.

Nevertheless, there are cases when subsidies may be the easiest way to avoid pollution. For example, it might be more effective to pay homeowners to turn in old cans and bottles than to try to regulate their garbage disposal habits or to tax them for each bottle or can thrown away. Therefore subsidies are sometimes expedient means of achieving a desired end, even if they are not the most desirable means from other points of view.

Externalities in Review

In one way, the problem of externalities differs markedly from the problem of public goods. The difference is that it is sometimes possible to allow the market system itself to handle the otherwise hidden costs of pollution by using the various techniques we have examined.

Therefore, in offsetting externalities in the production of private goods, we avoid some of the arbitrariness that troubles us in the provision of public goods. We can internalize the costs of pollution in a way that we cannot privatize the costs or benefits of pure public goods.

Nonetheless, we must remember that a market system has weak spots or ineffective areas peculiar to its institutional nature. **Its inability to put a price on external effects or to give a producer the rewards of producing external benefits means that the system, left to itself, may work poorly or even dangerously. The remedy requires political intervention of one kind or another—regulation, taxation, or subsidy. As we have seen, practical considerations determine which method is likely to be the best.**

Market Strengths and Weaknesses

This conclusion should not be interpreted as a kind of general plea for more government. Many economists who severely criticize the market want less government—certainly less bureaucratic, nonparticipatory, nondemocratic government. The point, however, is to recognize that the existence and causes of market malfunction make some government intervention inescapable. We can then seek to use government power to repair individual market failures in order to strengthen the operation of the system as a whole.

After so much criticism of the market system, perhaps we should conclude by recalling its two basic strengths. **First, the market encourages individuals to exert energies, skills, ambition, and risk-taking in the economic pursuits of life. This gives to market systems a high degree of flexibility, vitality, inventiveness, and change.** For all their failures, market economies have displayed astonishing growth, and the source of that growth lies ultimately in the activities of their marketers.

Second, the system minimizes the need for government supervision, although for reasons we now understand, it cannot dispense with it. It would be a mistake to suppose that every instance of government intervention is an abridgment of freedom or that every area of market activity is an exemplar of liberty. The truth is that government and market are equally capable of promoting liberty or giving rise to oppression. Nonetheless, in a world in which the concentration of government power has been one of the greatest scourges of humankind, there is clearly something to be said for a mechanism capable of handling the basic economic tasks of society without exaggerated dependence on political authority.

LOOKING BACK

KEY CONCEPTS

This chapter is a very important complement to our previous chapters. There we stressed the advantages of the market as a rationing device. Here we point out its shortcomings or inadequacies.

Inadequate information yields poor market results.

1 The first class of serious market failure arises from inadequate or erroneous information. Without correct information, marketers cannot make correct decisions and market results may be seriously deficient.

Cobwebs result from erroneous expectations.

2 One consequence of inadequate information is a tendency to generate instability under certain conditions. One of the most interesting of these is the cobweb, where prices may rise and fall and may never zero in on equilibrium.

Expectations can also lead to inflationary markets.

3 Cobwebs, in turn, reveal the importance of expectations in making markets work smoothly. When expectations are inflationary, we get perverse behavior, so that rising prices make the entire demand curve shift outward. This can be an important element in perpetuating inflation.

Public goods escape the market and cause free riding. Privatization is sometimes possible but may offend our sense of justice.

4 A second large category of market failure arises when the market cannot allocate at all because outputs have no price. One of these cases concerns public goods—goods collectively bought. Public goods result in free riding. In some cases, this can be corrected by privatizing public outputs. Often, however, we do not wish to sell public goods because they are deemed to be a citizen's right, and therefore felt to be properly available without specific charge.

Externalities are "bads" that exist because there is no charge based on polluting behavior.

5 Externalities have certain of the attributes of public goods. The production of "bads" is a kind of free ride for polluters. Pollution arises because there is no way of charging for the "bads" that production or consumption create—the litter a consumer throws on the road, the smoke a factory generates, the congestion to which each automobile adds.

Regulation, taxation, and subsidy are three ways of coping with externalities.

6 There are three basic ways of coping with externalities. The first is to regulate; the second is to tax; the third is to subsidize. No one of these is always superior to the others, but each has its strengths and weaknesses. Each situation must be judged separately to discover which method is most likely to be effective.

ECONOMIC VOCABULARY

Rational maximizing 214
Cobwebs 215
Perverse reactions 217
Public goods 218
Free riding 219
Privatization 220

Externalities 220
Bads 221
Regulation 222
Taxation 224
Subsidies 225

QUESTIONS

1. As a seller who seeks to maximize, would you increase or decrease your offerings if prices rose and you expected them to rise further? Suppose you expected them to fall—then what is your rational maximizing response?

2. Can you imagine an industrial process that might result in a cobweb? How about a process in which you had to make heavy commitments in plant and equipment long before production actually took place? Suppose hydroponic farming takes over, so that agriculture becomes more industrialized and less dependent on seasons. Would you expect the cobweb type of reaction to become less common? Why?

3. Explain the mechanism of a free ride. Are there free rides in private goods? How about window displays? Skywriting? Network TV?

4. Explain carefully why the market system will not work in supplying the appropriate level of goods that have "public" characteristics.

5. What kinds of public goods do you think should be made private? The national parks? Public schools? Public beaches? Public hospitals? (By "private," we mean charging a user fee sufficient to cover costs.) Explain your preference in each case.

6. Can you think of an externality imposed by a producer on a consumer? (That's easy.) One imposed by one producer on another? One consumer on another?

7. What do you think would be the best way to handle the following externalities: (a) a smoky factory, (b) roadside littering, (c) overfishing a pond, (d) noise from an airport, (e) radiation hazards in a hospital, (f) billboards, (g) pornography, (h) overcutting forests, (i) noise from motorcycles, (j) disruption to traffic caused by parades. In each case, discuss the relative advantages of regulation, taxation, and subsidy.

Operating a Competitive Firm: I

A LOOK AHEAD

With Chapter 14 we begin a new section in our microeconomic studies. We leave behind the market mechanism as a whole (though we return to it in the Challenge section ahead) to consider an area of microeconomics heretofore unexamined. This is the manner in which the basic unit of production, the competitive business firm, is run. In this and the next chapter we take a look at this kind of firm and go over its operation at two levels. Then in Chapter 16 we move to a tour of big business, and of smaller but less than perfectly competitive firms. And last, in Chapter 17, we apply our microeconomic scrutiny to taxing and government spending. There we shall find that the vocabulary and techniques we have mastered will apply to the public as well as the private sector.

In this chapter we meet for the first time a decisive economic personage. This is the entrepreneur, the person who makes the decisions that affect the business enterprise. Our task in this chapter is to analyze the three main tasks the entrepreneur must carry out:

1 Deciding on the scale of operations.
2 Combining the factors of production as profitably as possible.
3 Determining the volume of output.

In this visit we do no more than familiarize ourselves with the entrepreneur's task in general terms. In Chapter 15 we return, pad and pencil in hand, to calculate the firm's course.

*M*ost of us have firsthand knowledge of the household, whose role is crucial in determining the demand for goods. We know a lot less about the firm, whose function is to supply us with goods. In this chapter we enter the gates of a competitive firm for a quick look around. We will come back in our next chapter to study the operation in greater detail.

ECONOMICS OF THE FIRM

The first person we encounter inside the factory gates is an economic personage we have not previously studied. It is the boss of the works, the organizer of the firm, the *entrepreneur.*

Entrepreneurship

An entrepreneur is not necessarily a capitalist; that is, the person who has supplied capital to the business. The entrepreneur *may* act as the risker of capital, but so may a bank. The capitalist may be a group of people who have lent money to the business but never visited the premises. **An entrepreneur provides a service that is essentially different from that of putting up capital. His or her contribution is** *organizational.* Indeed, some economists have suggested that it is proper to think of four factors of production: labor, land, capital, and entrepreneurship, instead of the first three alone.

Economic Profit

As a fourth factor of production, the entrepreneur is paid a wage, *the wage of management.* It can, of course, be very high, since entrepreneurship is a valuable skill, the skill of maximizing a firm's *economic profit.*

This is not the profit of everyday usage. In ordinary usage we call "profit" any sum left over after a firm has paid its wages and salaries, rents, cost of materials, taxes, etc. Included in that ordinary profit is an amount an economist excludes from the definition of a true economic profit. This is the interest owed to the capitalist for the use of his or her capital. In other words, if a firm has a plant and equipment worth $1 million and makes a profit of $50,000, an economist, before declaring the $50,000 to be a true economic profit, would first ask whether the firm had taken into account the interest owing to it on this capital. If interest rates were 5 percent, and no such allowance had been made (and it usually is not the ordinary accounting practice to do so when the firm owns its own capital), an economist would say that no economic profits were earned. **Economic profit is what is left after paying all explicit costs and after allowing for implicit interest. It is the final residual.**

Our analysis shows us how an entrepreneur tries to create economic profits after appropriately remunerating all the factors, including capitalists, and how the operation of the market constantly tends to make this economic profit disappear, despite the best entrepreneurial efforts. (That will become clear in our next chapter rather than in this one.)

One last point. Who gets the residual? It goes to the owner of the business, who is legally entitled to any profits it enjoys. That owner, as we have said, may or may not be the entrepreneur. In a cooperatively owned factory it might be the workers. Usually it is a proprietor, a group of partners, or shareholders, including, of course, the management, to the extent that it owns shares. In all cases this residual economic profit is over and above any recompense for the services these factors supply, including the service of making capital available.

THE TASKS OF THE ENTREPRENEUR

What does our entrepreneur do for his wages of management? In actual practice, he will do many things: bargaining with labor unions, establishing credit lines with a bank, arranging complex real estate deals, hiring production and design experts, gauging "what the market will bear" when it comes to pricing and selling output. Some of these tasks we shall investigate in Chapter 16, when we look into the operation of firms that are not perfectly competitive.

But we must begin with a simpler model. We are going to start by analyzing the basic tasks of an entrepreneur in an environment of *pure competition*. As we shall see later, this is more the exception than the rule. Nevertheless, studying the operation of a firm in pure competition reveals more clearly than any other model the essential tasks of entrepreneurship.

Pure Competition

Exactly what do we mean by pure competition? In general, economists mean three things:

1. LARGE NUMBERS OF SELLERS OR FIRMS. A *monopoly*, as we shall see in Chapter 16, means there is only one firm in an industry. An *oligopoly* means there are a few firms. **But a competitive market means that there are many firms. By "many" we mean enough so that no single firm by itself can affect the prices it pays for the factors of production or the prices it receives for its output, regardless of how much or how little it produces.**

Are there such markets? Of course. Farms operate in a market situation very close to that of pure competition. So do many small businesses, where the field is so numerous each entrepreneur knows that he or she has no power to influence the market for the firm's outputs.

2. EASY ENTRY AND EXIT. A competitive industry is not only characterized by large numbers of firms. **It is also an industry into which new firms can move with ease and out of which unsuccessful firms can easily exit.**

This has very important consequences for the conduct of business. We can readily see why. In a competitive industry, if profits are high, there will soon be an invasion of entrepreneurs from other fields seeking to reap some of that profit. If business is bad, there will be a general exodus toward greener pastures.

3. The Outputs of Competitive Firms Are Undifferentiated. A differentiated output.is one that is recognizable as belonging to its producer. A cereal with a brand name, an automobile with a distinctive look, and fashion garments with their labels are all differentiated goods. The ability of a producer to differentiate his output gives him the ability to gain a loyal clientele and to charge prices that may differ from those of competitors.

No such advantage of differentiation exists in a market characterized by pure competition. One output is exactly like another. Thus wheat is wheat and bears no identification of the farm it comes from; paper clips are paper clips (although they may have differentiated boxes); coal is coal; one taxi ride is like another.

The absence of product differentiation carries a consequence of great importance. It means that competition among firms must be carried out entirely by trying to beat the prices offered by rivals. There is no way of attracting buyers to a particular output except by price.

Pure Competition and the Entrepreneur

As we can see, the conditions for pure competition are stringent indeed. In effect, they rob the entrepreneur, as the chief executive of the business, of much of the power he would like to have (and that he *does* have in industries that are not so competitive, as we shall see). In fact, in a market of pure competition—farming, much wholesale trading, and small retail business, for example—the operating powers of an entrepreneur are reduced to three:

1. **The entrepreneur can decide on the scale of the enterprise.**
2. **He can determine how best to combine the factors of production.**
3. **He can choose the level of output that will maximize profits.**

And that is all he can do! There is no chance of striking a special arrangement with the factors of production, such as signing a sweetheart contract with a labor union. There is no point in hiring a design expert or an advertising firm because it is impossible to differentiate his firm's corn, paper notebooks, or wire coat hangers from his competitors'. There is no strategy in pricing because if he is as much as a penny over his competitors, he will not sell any of his production.

HOW AN ENTREPRENEUR OPERATES

What does an entrepreneur actually do under such demanding conditions?

Task No. 1: The Decision on Scale

The first task lies in the determination of the scale of output—how big the firm is to be. In each industry a certain minimum size, mainly dictated by technology, is needed to operate in the existing market. Suppose we were considering opening a bookstore. A bookstore may be very small, but it must occupy *some* space. It must stock a reasonable number of books and someone must sell them. If we were in agriculture, we would need a farm of at least a certain area, depending on the crop, and a basic amount of capital in the form of buildings, equipment, fertilizer, seed. If we were in manufacturing, there would be a minimum size of plant or machinery essential for our operation. If we were in a mass-production business, such as steel, the smallest efficient plant might run into an investment of millions of dollars and a work force of thousands; but that would take us well out of the world of atomistic competition to which we are still devoting our attention.

In other words, the first decision of an entrepreneur involves the physical (or engineering) fact that there is a certain amount of each factor that must be hired for technical reasons. This is what we mean by minimum scale. If problems of scale did not exist, we could produce television sets as efficiently in a garage as in a vast plant or raise cattle as cheaply in our backyard as on a range.

Economies of Scale. The choice of a scale of operation has important consequences for the costs the entrepreneur's firm will incur. Every plant has a cost curve that describes how much it costs to produce one unit of output at various levels of production. In Figure 1 we see such a curve. Notice that when we are producing only small quantities (such as *OX*), the cost for each unit of output is high (*OY*); and that costs per unit typically fall as production increases, after which they eventually rise again. This produces a dish-shaped curve.

We will learn a lot more about curves as we move along. **Here we should note that a cost curve applies to a given scale of output. A bigger plant may well**

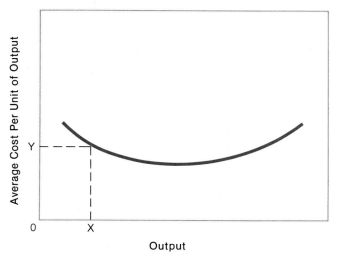

FIGURE 1
Typical Average Cost Curve
A curve of average costs usually falls at first and then rises. We call such curves "dish-shaped" or "U-shaped." Remember that they show how average costs change as we vary output. Total cost is shown by multiplying average cost by the number of units produced. At output OX, total cost is OY × OX.

lower unit costs because it can utilize technologies in large-scale production that are unavailable to small producers. If a small firm is successful, it may be able to gain these *economies* of scale by building a larger plant. In Figure 2 we show how successively bigger plants can reduce costs, at least up to the point where the limits of efficiency are reached and mounting costs per unit of output are encountered, creating *diseconomies of scale*.

The actual choice of an appropriate scale of plant is more important for big, oligopolistic firms than for small, competitive ones. But even in atomistic competition there are decisions to be made with regard to scale. A farmer has to decide whether to build another barn. A stationery store owner has to decide whether to buy additional space. The decision on scale, with its economies and diseconomies, is a very important first task of entrepreneurship.

Task No. 2: Combining the Factors

Having chosen the appropriate scale, our entrepreneur now has to make two decisions on how to combine labor, land, and capital; or in more ordinary business language, how much to pay in wages, rent, and interest.

The Profitability Rule: MR > MC. The first decision is whether it is profitable to hire a given factor, say an additional salesperson or an additional amount of inventory. This decision is very simple to make. Our entrepreneur merely compares two figures: (1) the cost of adding the additional factor and (2) the income he expects to gain from the additional factor. In economic language, he compares

FIGURE 2
Long-Run Cost Curve or Envelope Curve
Cost curves change as the scale of output changes. This long-run cost curve, or "envelope" curve, shows how a larger scale first lowers unit costs, then increases them. These curves refer to individual plants, not to firms, which may have many plants.

the *marginal cost* of a factor with the *marginal revenue* he expects from the factor.

By "marginal" we mean the additional cost or the additional revenue in question. If the entrepreneur is thinking of taking on a salesperson and the wage for salesclerks is $10,000, then the marginal cost of such a unit of labor is $10,000. Obviously the person will not be hired unless the entrepreneur expects that the clerk will bring into the firm at least $10,000 of marginal revenue—that is, of additional income.

Hence the cardinal rule for hiring is: Compare marginal cost and marginal revenue. If marginal revenue is greater than marginal cost, hire the factor. If not, get rid of the factor because it is costing more than its keep.

Comparing Factor Returns. And now for the second decision. Assuming that marginal revenue is greater than marginal cost for all factors, the entrepreneur has to decide whether to spend the firm's money on one factor or another. Suppose an additional salesperson costs $10,000 and is expected to bring in $12,000 of additional income; 100 square feet of space would cost $1,000 and would yield $1,300 of new income; and a new piece of equipment would cost $10,000 but would increase revenues by $15,000.

Here all the factors are profitable buys. But which is the *most* profitable? The answer is not difficult. Our entrepreneur simply compares the return per dollar for each factor or the percentage return on each factor. A dollar of additional labor cost brings in $1.20 ($12,000 of revenue divided by $10,000 of cost); a dollar of space brings in $1.30 ($1,300 divided by $1,000); and a dollar of capital expense yields $1.50. Clearly the most profitable use of the firm's money will be to put it all into equipment, as long as the ratios of marginal cost and marginal revenue stay the same.

Maximizing Profits. Will they stay the same? For reasons we will investigate more closely in the next chapter, they will not. As the entrepreneur hires more and more equipment (or more and more of any one factor), its marginal revenue will eventually decline because it will be used beyond the point of greatest efficiency. Our entrepreneur will then switch to some other factor that has become more profitable at the margin. In the end he will maximize his profits by mixing factors so that their marginal returns are all equal, with no special advantage accruing to any one.

Here is a rule to remember. The entrepreneur maximizes profits first by seeking equal marginal revenues.* If returns at the margin are not equal, there must exist opportunities for greater profit by adding more of the factor whose marginal return is highest. This is true whether the entrepreneur is running a competitive business or a monopoly. It is how the entrepreneur ensures that the firm will be as efficient as possible, getting as much return as possible from every dollar it spends.

---

*This is just like a consumer seeking to maximize total utilities by equating the marginal enjoyments of different goods. See the Extra Word section after Chapter 25.

Task No. 3: Determining the Level of Output

Now we come to the last and most complicated part of the entrepreneur's task. We have seen how he determines the initial scale of the enterprise, and decides whether to hire factors, and if so, which factors to hire. Now we must see how the entrepreneur determines how much output to produce.

The basic rule for determining output is very simple, and resembles the basic rule for hiring factors. An entrepreneur is constantly comparing marginal costs and marginal revenues for his output, just as he is comparing them for the factors he hires. The price at which he sells his last unit of output is his marginal revenue. The amount it costs him to produce that last unit of output is his marginal cost.

It's not difficult to see that he will decide on his volume of production by comparing the two. **If marginal revenue (*MR*) is greater than marginal cost (*MC*), he will be making money on that unit of output and will want to increase his production to make more money. If *MR* is less than *MC*, he will be losing money on his marginal output and will want to contract production.**

The Marginal Revenue Curve. It is possible to describe this task of the entrepreneur in a very revealing and helpful graph. Let us start by showing what marginal revenue looks like to a farmer, a small businessman, or another competitive entrepreneur.

Remember, the conditions of pure competition rule out any possibility that the small firm, by itself, could affect the level of prices. The prices of wheat or corn, paper clips or coal, are just *there,* and the entrepreneur has no choice but to take them as the market offers them. Therefore the demand curve for his product looks to him like Figure 3. It is a horizontal line, showing that the market will absorb all the corn or paper clips he can produce at a given price. The price may not be a profitable one, but that is another matter we will look into in the next chapter.

The point is that the competitive firm's selling price does not change, whatever its levels of output. Each unit therefore brings in exactly as much revenue as the one before or after. That is why the firm's marginal revenue curve is a horizontal line.

**FIGURE 3
Demand Curve for a Competitive Firm**
Because a competitive firm by definition cannot affect the market whether it sells all or nothing at all, each unit of item will fetch the same price. Therefore the marginal revenue of each unit will be the same. This means that the demand curve and the marginal revenue curve are one and the same—perfectly elastic, horizontal lines.

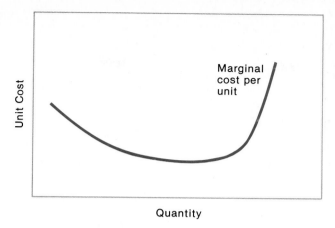

FIGURE 4
A Typical Marginal Cost Curve

A marginal cost curve shows the additional costs of each unit as we increase output. Usually the marginal cost of the first units is high; then it falls; and finally rises, often sharply. Our next chapter will analyze this curve more carefully.

When we study monopolies and oligopolies we will see that this is not the case for them.

The Marginal Cost Curve. Perhaps we can anticipate what comes next. We are going to discover what the marginal cost curve looks like, and by putting that curve against the marginal revenue curve, we will find out how the entrepreneur solves his third task, determining the level of output.

We already know that *average* costs of output give us a dish- or U-shaped curve (refer back to Figure 1 if you've forgotten). Not until the next chapter will we analyze the reasons for the similar shape of the marginal cost curve. But in this first look around a competitive plant, it will suffice if we intuitively understand that it's likely to cost an entrepreneur a lot to start up production, so that marginal costs per unit—the cost of each additional unit—are apt to start out high. We can further see that it is plausible for marginal costs to fall as output gets up to the levels for which the scale of the plant is designed, and that marginal costs are likely to rise beyond that point. Thus we get the idea that a marginal cost curve will look like Figure 4.

Marginal Revenue and Marginal Cost. Finally we have all the information we need to understand how an entrepreneur performs the last of this three basic tasks. We have a marginal cost profile that tells us what happens to unit costs as we hire or fire factors. We have a marginal revenue profile that tells us what happens to the firm's income as we do the same. It remains only to put the two together to discover just how much output a firm should make to maximize its profits.

We can do this very simply by superimposing the revenue diagram on the cost diagram. **The point where marginal revenue and marginal cost meet indicates exactly where the most profitable volume of output lies.** If our entrepreneur were producing to the left of this point, he would be missing the chance to make more money by expanding output. We can see that this is the case because up to point *OX* in Figure 5 each additional (marginal) unit of production will bring in more than it costs. If production goes beyond *OX*, on the other hand, the entrepreneur will have miscalculated, because each unit of output beyond *OX* will cost more than it yields.

FIGURE 5
Point of Optimum Output
Marginal cost and marginal revenue provide the guide to the level of output where profit is maximized. Think about costs and revenues for units marked X′ and X″. Can you see why X′ makes money and X″ does not? What should the entrepreneur do in each case?

End of the Tour

There is a great deal that remains to be explained. Is our firm making money? Why do the curves have the shapes they do? Is there an equilibrium level of operation for the firm?

These questions will necessitate a second trip with pad and pencil in hand, ready to do some calculations. Our first visit has prepared the way by showing us in bold terms what the entrepreneur has to do. Now we should be ready to put ourselves more directly into his or her shoes.

LOOKING BACK

KEY CONCEPTS

The entrepreneur seeks an economic profit.

1 The key person within the firm is the entrepreneur, the organizer of production. The entrepreneur (who may or may not be a capitalist) seeks to make an economic profit. An economic profit is a residual—what is left after paying all costs, including the implicit costs of interest on the firm's capital.

Three conditions of pure competition: large num-

2 We first study the entrepreneur's task under pure competition. Pure competition refers to a market in which three conditions prevail: a large

bers, easy entry and exit; no product differentiation

Competition by price alone

Three entrepreneurial tasks: Choosing the right scale

Hiring factors if their MR > MC. The factor whose profitability is highest is always hired.

Expanding output until MC = MR

number of firms, easy entry or exit of firms, and no differentiated products. The only competitive weapon available to the firm, therefore, is price.

3 The entrepreneur in such a competitive milieu has only three variables under his command. The first is scale. A plant must be the right size to enter the market in the first place.

4 Second, the entrepreneur must combine factors as profitably as possible to get costs as low as possible. He does so by applying two simple rules: (a) He hires a factor only if its marginal revenue is greater than its marginal cost (if *MR > MC*). (b) He always hires the factor whose profitability is greatest, giving the largest return per dollar of cost.

5 Third, the entrepreneur determines the level of output. He does this by comparing the marginal cost of each unit of additional output with the marginal revenue obtained from that unit. The marginal cost of most firms has a dish or U shape. We shall investigate the reasons for this more carefully in the next chapter. By expanding output until marginal revenue equals marginal cost, the entrepreneur maximizes the firm's profit.

ECONOMIC VOCABULARY

Entrepreneur   230
Economic profit   230
Pure competition   231
Entry and exit   231
Undifferentiated output   232
Scale   233

Economies of scale   233
Profitability rule: *MR > MC*   234
Marginal cost   235
Marginal revenue   235
MR curve   236
MC curve   237

QUESTIONS

1. Suppose you were about to open a small business—say, a drugstore. What do you think would be the factors critical in determining the scale of your operation? Suppose it were a farm? A factory?

2. Why does pure competition require a large number of sellers? Does this mean that a drugstore is not competitive if it is the only such store in town? What does this suggest about the difficulties of defining a market?

3. Which of the three conditions for pure competition do you think is missing from

the following industries: (a) aircraft construction; (b) fashion design; (c) gold mining?

4. Suppose a manufacturer had the following alternatives. It would be possible to (a) spend $1,000 on a machine that would add 115 units to sales (each unit selling at $10); (b) spend $5,000 to hire a new worker who would increase output by 510 units; (c) rent new space for $10,000 that would make possible an increase in output of 1,100 units. How would one know which was the best factor to hire? Show that the manufacturer would begin by asking what the dollar return would be per dollar of cost for each factor. What is this in the case of the machine? The new worker? The land?

5. Why is the demand curve the same as the marginal revenue curve for a manufacturer of wire coat hangers? Draw the demand curve for such a firm. Draw a separate diagram for its marginal revenue curve. Are they exactly the same? (They should be.)

6. Superimpose a firm's MR curve on its MC curve and explain carefully why the point of highest profit is where the curves intersect.

AN EXTRA WORD ABOUT

Helping the Farmer

The farmer is the very prototype of the entrepreneur of a competitive firm. But farming is an industry with very special problems. Traditionally, it has been a trouble-ridden occupation. All through the 1920s, the farmer was the "sick man" of the American economy. Each year saw more farmers going into tenantry, until by 1929 four out of ten farmers in the nation were no longer independent operators. Each year the farmer seemed to fall further behind the city dweller in terms of relative well-being. In 1910 the income per worker on the farm had been not quite 40 percent of the nonfarm worker. By 1930 it was just under 30 percent.

Part of this trouble on the farm, without question, stemmed from a difficult heritage. Beset now by drought, now by the exploitation of powerful railroad and storage combines, now by his own penchant for land speculation, the farmer was proverbially an ailing member of the economy. In addition, American farmers had traditionally been careless of the earth, indifferent to the technology of agriculture. They were not model entrepreneurs. Between 1910 and 1920, for instance, while nonfarm output per worker rose by nearly 20 percent, output per farm worker actually fell. Between 1920 and 1930, farm productivity improved somewhat, but not nearly so fast as productivity off the farm. For the great majority of the nation's agricultural producers, the trouble appeared to be that they could not grow or raise enough to make a decent living.

INELASTIC DEMAND

If we had looked at farming as a whole, however, a very different answer would have suggested itself. Suppose farm productivity *had* kept pace with that of the nation. Would farm income as a whole have risen? The answer is disconcerting. The *demand* for farm products was quite unlike that for manufactured products generally. In the manufacturing sector, when productivity rose and costs accordingly fell, the cheaper prices of manufactured goods attracted vast new markets, as with the Ford car. Not so with farm products, however. When food prices fell, people did not tend to increase their actual consumption very greatly. Increases in overall farm output resulted in much lower prices but not in larger cash receipts for the farmer. Sellers faced with an *inelastic demand* find that a flood of output only leaves them *worse* off than before.

That is very much what happened during the 1920s. From 1915 to 1920 the farmer prospered because World War I greatly increased the demand for his product. Prices for farm output rose, and his cash receipts rose as well; in fact, they more than doubled. After the war, when European farms resumed production, American farm crops simply glutted the market. Although prices fell precipitously (40 percent in the single year 1920–1921), the purchases of farm products did not respond in anything like equal measure. As a result, the cash receipts of the farmer toppled almost as fast as prices. In turn, an ailing farm sector contributed to a general economic weakness that would culminate in the Great Depression.

THE NEW DEAL

At its core, the trouble with the farm sector was that the market mechanism did not yield a satisfactory result for farmers. Two causes were evident. One was the inelastic demand for food. The second was the inability of a vast, highly competitive industry like agriculture to limit its own output so that it would not constantly "break the market" every time a bumper crop was harvested.

This chronic ailing condition of agriculture was one of the first problems attended to by Franklin Roosevelt's New Deal administration. The New Deal could not alter the first cause, the inelasticity of demand, for that arose from the nature of the consumer's desire for food. However, it could change the condition of supply, which hurled itself, self-destructively, against an unyielding demand. One of the earliest pieces of New Deal legislation—the Agricultural Adjustment Act—sought to establish machinery to be used by farmers, as a group, to accomplish what they could not do as competitive individuals: curtail output.

The curtailment was sought by offering payments to farmers who agreed to cut back their acreage or in other ways hold down their output. In the first year of the act there was no time to cut back acreage, so that every fourth row of growing cotton had to be plowed under and 6 million pigs had to be slaughtered. In a nation hungry and ill-clad, such a spectacle of waste aroused sardonic and bitter comment. Yet if the program reflected a society's appalling inability to handle its distribution problem, its the attack on overproduction was not without results. In both 1934 and 1935 more than 30 million acres were taken out of production in return for government payments of $1.1 billion. Farm prices rose as a result. Wheat, having slumped to 38 cents a bushel in 1932, rose to $1.02 in 1936. Cotton doubled in price, hog prices tripled, and the net income of the American farmer climbed from the fearful low of $2.5 billion in 1932 to $5 billion in 1936.

SUPPORT PRICES

Later the New Deal sought to raise farm incomes by establishing *support prices* at which the government would, if necessary, buy farm output. Because the New Deal aimed to raise incomes, not to stabilize production, these prices were set at a level *higher* than equilibrium market prices. Given these support prices, farmers could confidently plan their future production, since they knew their output would be bought. But because prices were above equilibrium levels, they chose to grow more than the consumer was willing to consume at the support price. In other words, surpluses emerged, as in Figure 1.

To avoid these surpluses, the government limited the acreage that farmers could plant if they wanted to qualify for support payments, as Figure 2 shows. The strategy might have worked were it not for the extraordinary increase in agricultural productivity resulting from new technologies. Between 1940 and the late 1960s, harvested acreage declined by 15 percent, but the yield per acre increased by over *70 percent*. The result was a flood of output. Huge quantities had to be purchased and stored by the government. Only the massive distribution of these supplies to the underdeveloped lands during the early 1960s prevented the surplus problem from becoming a permanent national embarrassment. Even so, the problem of surpluses, and huge agricultural subsidy payments, re-emerged in the 1980s.

THE FARM PICTURE IN PERSPECTIVE

As any agricultural economist can tell you, the farmer leads anything but a serene life. He must make difficult guesses about the course of prices years into the future. Prices take large swings, seldom settle into stable patterns, and may not be a very good guide to the future.

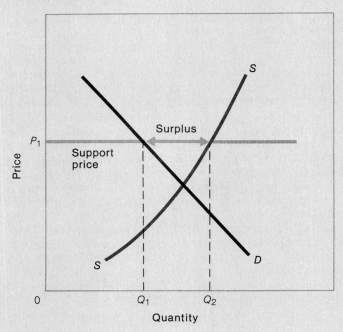

FIGURE 1
Price Support Surplus
At support price P_1 consumers want to buy quantity Q_1. Farmers, however, produce quantity QQ_2. The difference, Q_1Q_2, has to be bought and stored by the government. In 1960, government warehouses bulged with unsold crops worth \$6 billion.

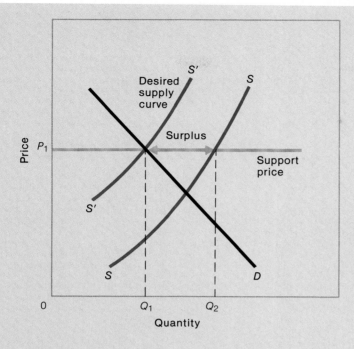

FIGURE 2
The Effort to Limit Supply
The government tried to eliminate the surplus by restricting acreage. It sought to move SS to S'S' to bring about equilibrium output OQ_1.

Yet, in all this it is important to gain a sense of long-term perspective. We have seen that the farmer, unable to control economic swings, has traditionally been their victim. What we have tried to do in the last four decades is to intervene in the market process to make it yield results more in accord with our conceptions of social justice. Despite all the difficulties we have discussed, the results are substantial. In 1940 only a third of all farm families had electricity and only a quarter had telephones. Today these are virtually ubiquitous. The present standard of living of the independent farm operator is close to that of urban middle-class families.

The important lesson is that it is possible to intervene in the market process to bring about desired social ends, although, as our discussion should have made clear, the process of intervention is far from simple and full of unexpected pitfalls.

It would be misleading, however, to leave this brief discussion of farming with the impression that all is now well. Small-scale farming (say, under 200 acres), once the mainstay of the American economy, is in a precarious state, and the majority of the million-odd small farmers now depend as much or more on income from nonfarm jobs—perhaps tending a gas pump—as they do on selling their small crops. Middle-scale farming (200 to 500 acres) is sorely pressed by rising costs and heavy debts. Meanwhile the importance of food exports has increased as a portion of total American foreign sales. The farm sector has been severely hurt in recent years by a high dollar, which cost the United States much of its traditional agricultural export market. How much of this will return with the dollar's decline, we do not know. The average American farmer has by no means achieved a degree of financial security commensurate with the contribution he makes to the national economy; and he will not achieve this security until the United States has again established a competitive place in the world economy.

CHAPTER 15

Operating a Competitive Firm: II

A LOOK AHEAD

In this chapter we will go over some material we have already covered, but much more carefully. There are a lot of numbers and a lot of graphs, but you should already be generally familiar with the situation that they analyze.

Three big questions tie the chapter together:

1 Why do unit costs rise after their initial fall? This will bring us the very important role of the law of diminishing returns.

2 What are the conditions for equilibrium of the competitive firm? This will again bring home the need to equate *MC* and *MR* and will introduce a new criterion for equilibrium in the industry: Average cost must equal average revenue (or price).

3 How can profit be earned by a firm in a competitive setting? Here we will learn about intramarginal earnings, or quasi rents.

Keeping these three main ideas in mind will help you move steadily through the analysis.

THE COST PROBLEM

*O*nce again, let us become imaginary entrepreneurs. Since we are familiar with the firm's calculations about buying factor services, let us extend our knowledge to a full appreciation of what the cost problem looks like.

Fixed and Variable Costs

We know that a firm's *total* costs must rise as it hires additional factors. Yet as businesspeople, we can see that our total costs will not rise proportionally as fast as our additional factor costs because some costs of production will not be affected by an increase in factor input. Real estate taxes, for example, will remain unchanged if we hire one person or 100—so long as we do not acquire additional land. We can assume that the depreciation cost of machinery will not be affected by additions to land or labor. Rent will be unchanged unless the premises are expanded. The cost of electric light will not vary appreciably despite additions to labor or machinery. Neither will the salary of the president. **Thus some costs, determined by legal contract or by usage or by the unchanging use of one factor, do not vary with output. We call these fixed costs.**

In sharp contrast with fixed costs is another kind of cost that does vary directly with output. Here are many factor costs, for generally we vary inputs of labor and capital (and sometimes land) every time we seek a new level of production. To increase output almost always requires the payment of more wages and the employment of more capital (if only in the form of inventories or goods in process) and sometimes the rental of more space. **All costs that vary with output are called variable costs.**

Average Costs

Now we must move from considering *total* costs—fixed or variable—to considering costs *per unit* of output. These are called *average costs*. Instead of thinking about the costs of bringing in a crop or producing a batch of output, we fasten on the costs per bushel or per item of manufacture. Both variable and fixed costs can be translated from their total amounts to their average basis by dividing the total by the number of bushels or items the firm makes. We shift from total to average costs because they allow us to focus on, and to compare, *marginal* revenues and expenses in a way that total costs do not.

There is certainly no difficulty in picturing what happens to *fixed costs* per unit of output as output rises. By definition, they must fall. Suppose a manufacturer has fixed costs (rent, certain indirect taxes, depreciation, and overhead) of $10,000 a year. If 5,000 units of the product are produced per year, each unit will have to bear $2 of fixed cost as its share. If output rises to 10,000 units, the unit share of fixed costs will shrink to $1. At 100,000 units it would be a dime. Thus a curve of average fixed costs would look like Figure 1.

We notice that the curve of fixed costs per unit falls steadily. This stands to reason because the costs *are* fixed and they are spread over an ever-larger output. But this does not explain why the cost curve eventually turns up—why it has a dish or U shape. That question brings us to the question of variable costs.

Variable Costs and Diminishing Returns

Variable costs must be the reason that cost curves per unit eventually turn up. This means that variable costs per unit—wages, for example—must rise after a time. Why should that be the case?

The answer takes us away from the firm, for a moment, to think again about a constraint of nature we encountered in Chapter 7—the law of diminishing returns.

Let us begin with a case that is very simple to imagine. Suppose we have a farmer who has a farm of 100 acres, a certain amount of equipment, and no labor at all. Now let us observe what happens as he hires one man, then a second man of the same abilities, then a third, and so on. Obviously, the output of the farm will grow. What we want to find out, however, is whether it will grow in some clearly defined pattern that we can attribute to the changing amount of the factor that is being added.

What would such a curve of productivity look like? Assume that one man, working the 100 acres alone as best he can, produces 1,000 bushels of grain. A second man, helping the first, should be enormously valuable, because the two men can begin to specialize and divide the work, each doing the jobs he is better at and saving the time formerly wasted by moving from one job to the next. As a consequence of this division of labor, output may jump to 3,000 bushels.*

Marginal Productivity

Since the *difference* in output is 2,000 bushels, we speak of the *marginal productivity of labor* when two people are working as 2,000 bushels. Note that we should not (although in carelessness we sometimes do) speak of the marginal productivity of the *second* person. Alone, his efforts are not more productive than those of the first person; if we fired the first worker, worker number 2 would produce only 1,000 bushels. What makes the difference is the jump in the combined productivity of the *two* men, once specialization can be introduced. Hence we should speak of the changing marginal productivity of *labor,* not of the individual.

It is not difficult to imagine an increasing specialization taking place with the third, fourth, and fifth worker, so that the addition of another unit of labor input in each case brings about an output larger than was realized by the average of all the previous workers. Remember that this does not mean the successive factor units themselves are more productive. **It means that as we add units of one factor, the**

*With each additional worker, the proportions of land, labor, and capital are altered, so that the change in the level of output should rightfully be ascribed to new levels of efficiency resulting from the interaction of *all three factors.* But since labor is the factor whose input we are varying, it has become customary to call the change in output the result of a change in "labor productivity." If we were altering land or capital alone, we would call the change the result of changes in their productivities, even though, as with labor, the real cause is the changing efficiency of *all* factors in different mixes.

FIGURE 1
Profile of Fixed Costs per Unit
As output increases, fixed costs are spread over a larger number of units, and therefore fixed costs per unit steadily decline.

total mix of these units plus the fixed amounts of other factors forms an increasingly efficient technical combination. Remember Adam Smith's pin factory!

We call the range of factor inputs over which average productivity rises a range of *increasing average returns.* It is, of course, a stage of production that is highly favorable for the producer. Every time he adds a factor, efficiency rises. (As a result, as we shall shortly see, costs per unit of output fall.) The rate of increase will not be the same, for the initial large marginal leaps in productivity will give way to smaller ones. But the overall trend of productivity, whether we measure it by looking at *total* output or at *average* output per person, will still be up. All this keeps on happening, of course, because the factor we are adding has not yet reached its point of maximum technical efficiency with the given amount of other factors.

Diminishing Returns

At a certain point the farmer notices a disconcerting phenomenon. Marginal output no longer rises when he adds another worker. Total output will still be rising, but a quick calculation reveals that the last person on the team has added less to output than his predecessor.

What has happened is that we have overshot the point of maximum technical efficiency for the factor we are adding. Labor is now beginning to crowd land or equipment. Opportunities for further specialization have diminished. **We call this condition of falling marginal performance a condition of decreasing or diminishing returns.** As the words suggest, we are getting back less and less as we add the critical factor—not only from the "marginal" worker, but also from the combined labor of all workers.

If we now go on adding labor, we will soon reach a point at which the contribution of the marginal worker will be so small that average output per man will also fall. Now, of course, costs will be rising per unit. If we went on foolishly adding more and more workers, eventually the addition of another worker would add nothing to total output. In fact, the next worker might so disrupt the factor mix that *total* output would actually fall, and we would be in a condition of negative returns.

Total, Average, and Marginal Product

This changing profile of physical productivity is one of the most important generalizations economics makes about the real world. It will help us to think it through if we now study the relationships of marginal and average productivity and of total output in Table 1. All three columns are integrally related, and it is important to understand the exact nature of those relationships.

1. **The column for total output is related to the column for marginal productivity, because the rise in total output results from the successive marginal increments. For instance, the reason total output goes from 7,800 bushels with 4 workers to 9,800 with 5 workers is that the marginal output associated with the fifth worker is 2,000 bushels. Thus, if we know the schedule of total outputs, we can always figure the schedule of marginal productivity simply by observing how much total output rises with each additional unit of factor input.**

2. **It stands to reason, therefore, that if we know the schedule of marginal productivity, it is simple to figure total output: We just add up the marginal increments.**

3. **Finally, the meaning of average productivity is also apparent. It is simply total output divided by the number of workers (or of any factor unit in which we are interested).**

. One thing must be carefully studied in this example. Note that marginal productivity begins to diminish with the fourth worker, who adds only 2,300

TABLE 1

It is important to understand the relation among the three columns. If you knew only the successive totals, how would you calculate the marginal products? If you knew the marginal column, how do you figure the total? From there, how do you get the average?

Number of Workers	Total Output	Marginal Productivity (Change in Output	Average Productivity (Total Output ÷ No. of Workers)
1	1,000	1,000 Increasing	1,000
2	3,000	2,000 marginal	1,500 Increasing
3	5,500	2,500 productivity	1,833 average
4	7,800	2,300	1,950 productivity
5	9,800	2,000 Decreasing	1,960
6	11,600	1,800 marginal	1,930 Decreasing
7	13,100	1,500 productivity	1,871 average
8	14,300	1,200	1,790 productivity

bushels to output, and not 2,500, as did his predecessor. Average productivity, however, rises until we hire the sixth worker, because the fifth worker, although producing less than the fourth, is still more productive than the average output of all four previously hired workers. Thus marginal productivity can be falling while average productivity is still rising. That is a sentence worth reading twice—or even three times—until it sinks in.

The three curves in Figure 2 all show the same phenomenon, only in a graphic way. The top curve shows us that as we add workers to our farm, output at first rises very rapidly, then slowly, then actually declines. The marginal productivity curve shows us *why* this is happening to total output. As we add people, the contribution they can make to output changes markedly. At first each worker adds so much that average output grows rapidly. Thereafter marginal output falls, although average output still rises. Finally, each worker adds so little that he actually pulls down the average obtained before his hiring. The average curve, as we have just indicated, merely sums up the overall output in an arithmetical way by showing us what the average person contributes to it.

The Law of Variable Proportions

To sum up: If we add successive units of one factor to fixed amounts of others, marginal productivity will at first increase and then decrease. We call this the

FIGURE 2
The Law of Variable Proportions
The graph simply enables us to visualize the relationships of Tabel 1. Note that marginal productivity falls before average productivity.

TABLE 2

Can you see the law of diminishing returns at work in these figures?

Number of Workers	Total Output (Units)	Marginal Product
0	0	
1	5,000	5,000
2	13,000	8,000
3	23,000	10,000
4	32,000	9,000
5	39,000	7,000
6	44,000	5,000
7	47,000	3,000
8	49,000	2,000

law of diminishing returns, or the law of variable proportions (both terms are used).

Bear in mind two things about the law. (1) It applies to all factors, land and capital as well as labor; and (2) we can't speak of the law in operation if we don't hold all factors fixed except one. Otherwise, we do not know the cause of any change in output.

Average Variable Costs

Now we return to our firm. Perhaps we can already anticipate that the law of variable proportions will explain why average costs turn up despite falling average fixed costs. Let us work our way through the actual figures.

We will begin by setting up an imaginary but plausible schedule of output for our manufacturer in Table 2. Once again, we see the law of variable proportions at work. The total number of units produced will rise at first rapidly, then more slowly, with the addition of labor input to the plant.

TABLE 3

Total variable costs rise steadily at $5,000 per worker. Average costs first fall, then rise. Why? Because changing marginal productivity first makes output rise rapidly, then more slowly. Therefore the $5,000 increments of variable cost at first get spread more thinly, lowering cost per unit from $1 to $.63. Then (starting with the fifth worker, the share of variable costs begins to rise, from $.63 to over $.80.

Number of Workers	Total Variable Cost @ $5,000 per Worker	Total Output (Units)	Average Variable Cost (Cost ÷ Output)
1	$5,000	5,000	$1.00
2	10,000	13,000	.77
3	15,000	23,000	.65
4	20,000	32,000	.63
5	25,000	39,000	.64
6	30,000	44,000	.68
7	35,000	47,000	.74
8	40,000	49,000	.82

To convert this schedule of physical productivity into a curve of average costs, we must do two things:

1. Calculate the total cost for the variable factors used for each level of output. This is total variable cost.

2. Then divide the total variable cost by the number of units, to get average variable cost.

Let us assume that the going wage is $5,000. Table 3 then shows the total, marginal, and average costs for different levels of output. Notice that average variable costs decline at first and thereafter rise. The reason is by now clear enough. Variable cost increases by a set amount: $5,000 per worker, as factors are added. Output, however, obeys the law of variable proportions, increasing rapidly at first and then displaying diminishing returns. **It stands to reason, then, that the variable cost *per unit* of output will be falling as long as output is growing faster than costs, and that it will begin to rise as soon as additions to output start to get smaller.**

If we graph the typical variable cost curve per unit of output (or average variable cost), it will be the familiar dish-shaped or U-shaped profile Figure 3 shows.

Total Cost per Unit

We can now set up a complete cost schedule for our enterprise by combining fixed and variable costs, as in Table 4. Notice how marginal costs begin to turn up *before* average costs.

If we graph the last two columns of figures—average and marginal cost per unit—we get the very important diagram in Figure 4.

TABLE 4
Here we show total cost—fixed plus variable—and total output. It's simple thereafter to figure average and marginal costs. Technical note: *Ideally, we should like to show how marginal cost changes with each additional unit of output. Here our data show the change in costs associated with considerable jumps in output as we add each worker. Hence we estimate the marginal cost by taking the change in total costs and dividing this by the change in total output. The result is really an "average" marginal cost, since each individual item costs actually a tiny fraction less, or more, than its predecessor. We have shown the data this way since it is much closer to the way businesspeople figure.*

Number of Workers	Total Cost ($10,000 Fixed Cost + $5,000 per Worker)	Output (Units)	Average (Total Cost ÷ Output)		Marginal (Change in Total Cost ÷ Change in Output)	
1	$15,000	5,000	$3.00		$	Falling
2	20,000	13,000	1.54	Falling	.63	marginal
3	25,000	23,000	1.09	av.	.50	cost
4	30,000	32,000	.94	cost	.55	
5	35,000	39,000	.90		.71	Rising
6	40,000	44,000	.91	Rising	1.00	marginal
7	45,000	47,000	.96	av.	1.67	cost
8	50,000	49,000	1.02	cost	2.50	

FIGURE 3
Profile of Changing Variable Costs per Unit (Average Variable Cost)
This is simply a graph of the last column in Table 3. We now see that the upward slope of the dish-shaped curve is the result of the law of diminishing returns.

The Cost Profile

We have reached the end of our cost calculations, and it will help to take stock of what we have done. Actually, despite all the figures and diagrams, the procedure has been quite simple.

1. We began by seeing what would happen to our *fixed costs* per unit as we

FIGURE 4
Average and Marginal Cost
When we graph average and marginal costs, we really see what a difference the phenomenon of diminishing returns makes.

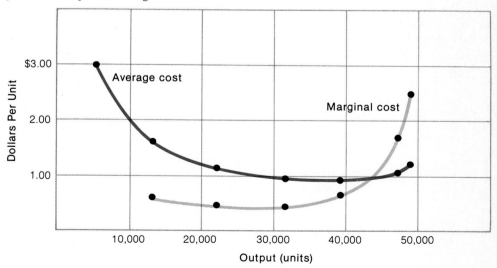

expanded output. Since fixed costs, by their nature, do not increase as production increases, the amount of fixed cost that had to be charged to each unit of output fell as output rose.

2. Next we calculated the *variable costs* that would have to be borne by each unit as output increased. Here the critical process at work was the law of variable proportions. As the marginal productivity of factors increased, variable cost per unit fell. When the inevitable stage of diminishing returns set in, variable costs per unit had to rise.

3. Adding together average fixed and variable costs, we obtained the average *total cost* of output. Like the variable cost curve, average total costs are dish-shaped, reflecting the changing marginal productivity of factors as output grows.

4. Finally, we showed the changing *marginal cost*—the increase in total costs divided by the increase in output. As before, it is the changing marginal costs that the entrepreneur actually experiences in altering output. It is the increase at the margin that alters total cost and therefore determines average cost.

The Common Sense of Changing Average Cost

Actually, the cost profile we have worked out would be known by any businessperson, even one who had never studied microeconomics. Whenever a firm starts producing, its cost per unit of output is very high. A General Motors plant turning out only a few hundred cars a year would have astronomical costs per automobile.

As output increases, unit costs come down steadily, partly because overhead (fixed cost) is now spread over more units, partly because the factors are used at much greater efficiency. Finally, after some point of maximum factor efficiency, average costs begin to mount. Even though overhead continues to decline, it is now so small a fraction of cost per unit that its further decline does not count for much, while the rising inefficiency of factors steadily pushes up variable cost per unit. If General Motors tries to jam through more cars than a plant is designed to produce, the cost per auto will again begin to soar.

So much for the *average* cost. By directing our attention to the changes that occur in total cost and total output every time we alter the number of factors we engage, the *marginal* cost curve simply tells us why all this is happening. In other words, as our plant first moves into high gear, the cars we add to the line (the marginal output) will cost considerably less than the average of all cars processed previously. Later, when diminishing returns begin to work against us, we would expect the added (marginal) cars to be high-cost cars, higher in cost than the average of all cars built so far.

Average and Marginal Costs

Since the cost of marginal output always "leads" the cost of average output in this way, we can understand an important relationship that all marginal and average

FIGURE 5
Relation of Marginal and Average Cost
The marginal cost curve cuts the average cost curve at its lowest point. For reasons, read the information on the graph.

cost curves bear to each other. **The marginal cost curve always cuts the average cost curve at the lowest point of average cost.**

Why? Because as long as the additional cars are cheaper than the average of all cars, their production must be *reducing* average cost; that is, as long as the marginal cost curve is lower than the average cost curve, the average cost curve must be falling. Conversely, as soon as additional output is more expensive than the average for all previous output, that additional production must *raise* average costs. Again (look at Figure 4), as soon as marginal cost is above average cost, average cost must begin to rise. Hence it follows that the *MC* (marginal cost) curve must cross the AC (average cost) curve at the minimum point of average cost. This relationship has nothing to do with economics as such, but with simple logic, as Figure 5 may elucidate.*

FROM COST TO REVENUE

The cost profile gives us a clear picture of what happens to unit costs as our firm hires additional factors. But that is only half the information we need to understand how a firm operates with one foot in the factor market and the other in the market for goods. Now we need a comparable profile of what happens to revenues as the firm sells the output its factors have made for it.

---

*It follows that the marginal productivity curve always crosses the average productivity curve at its peak. Look at Figure 2. As long as marginal productivity is *higher* than average productivity, the average curve must be *rising*. As soon as additional (marginal) output is *less than* the preceding average output, the lower marginal output must *diminish* the average. The relation is exactly that of Figure 5, only upside down.

Average and Marginal Revenue

We already know what the demand curve looks like for a competitive firm. It is a horizontal line, reflecting the fact that the firm's output is too small to affect the market price of the good. Let's now assume that our firm makes such a competitive product—say, a metal stamping whose price is $1.50.

The entrepreneur can easily calculate his revenue curves, knowing there is a limitless demand for his product.* Each unit will sell at the same price as the one before or the one after. The revenue brought in by each unit—the marginal revenue—will therefore be unchanged. So will the average revenue, which is the same thing as the selling price. As the schedule of Table 5 and the graph of Figure 6 show, marginal and average revenues are the same. (They won't be when we get to less-than-competitive markets in the next chapter.)

Marginal Cost and Supply

Now we have all the information we want. We have a cost profile that tells us what happens to unit costs as we hire or fire factors. We have a revenue profile that tells us what happens to unit revenues as we do the same. It remains only to put the two together to discover just how much output the firm should make to maximize its profits. As we can see in Figure 7, it is just about at 45,000 units.

We already know why this is the most profitable level of output. But we can now see a new meaning for the marginal cost curve. **The rising portion of the marginal cost curve is the firm's supply curve.**

Suppose price rises from P_1 to P_2 in Figure 8. As far as the firm is concerned, it does not matter where its average cost is. What counts is whether additional production will be profitable. Further, it will be profitable only if the marginal cost of that additional production does not exceed marginal revenue. Therefore, when price rises, the firm's output increases from Q_1 to Q_2, a point determined by the intersection of the MC curve and the new price.

The point we must bear in mind is more than just a geometrical demonstration. **It is that marginal costs, not average costs, determine most production decisions.** When prices rise or fall, the change in quantity will reflect the ease or difficulty of adding to or diminishing production, as that ease or difficulty is reflected in the shape of its MC schedule.

TABLE 5

Output (Units)	Price	Marginal Revenue	Total Revenue	Average Revenue
5,000	$1.50	$1.50	$ 7,500	$1.50
10,000	1.50	1.50	15,000	1.50
20,000	1.50	1.50	30,000	1.50
40,000	1.50	1.50	60,000	1.50

*So why doesn't an ambitious firm produce a limitless amount and become limitlessly rich? Because rising unit costs will soon bring it limitless losses.

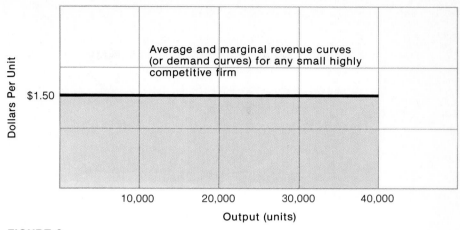

FIGURE 6
Average and Marginal Revenues Under Competition
This is the same flat curve we saw in the previous chapter. We reproduce it here because its flatness holds the key to analyzing the competitive firm's situation. (Can you anticipate why the marginal and average revenue curves will not be flat, and will not be the same, when we get to monopolistic markets?)

Profits

Now let us return to the firm producing the quantity of stampings that just equates marginal cost and marginal revenue. What is the total amount of economic profit at the firm's best level of output? This is very difficult to tell from diagrams that show only marginal costs and marginal revenues. As we have just seen, these curves tell us

FIGURE 7
The Point of Optimum Output
Here is the same MC = MR diagram we used in the previous chapter, this time calibrated to show the actual number of units at optimal output.

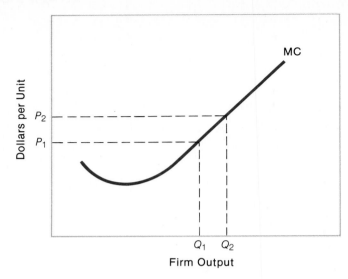

FIGURE 8
The Firm's Supply Curve
We have often talked about a firm's supply curve. Now we can see that the rising portion is its marginal cost curve.

how large *output* will be. But we must add another curve to enable us quickly to see what the *profit* will be at each level of output.

This is our familiar average cost curve. Average costs, we know, are nothing but total costs reduced to a per unit basis. Average revenues are also a per unit basis. **Hence, if we compare the average revenue and cost curves at any point, they will tell us at a glance what total revenues and costs look like at that point.**

Figure 9 reveals what our situation is at the point of optimum output. (This time we generalize the diagram rather than putting it into the specific terms of our illustrative firm.) The diagram shows several things. First, as before, it indicates our most profitable output as the amount *OA*—the output indicated by point *X*, where the marginal revenue and marginal cost curves meet. Remember: We use marginal costs and marginal revenues to determine the point of optimum output. Second, it shows us that at output *OA,* our *average cost* is *OC* (=AB) and our *average revenue* is *OD* (=AX), the same as our marginal revenue, since the demand curve for the firm is horizontal. Our profit on the *average* unit of output must therefore be *CD* (=BX), the difference between average costs and average revenues at this point. The *total* profit is therefore the rectangle *CDXB,* which is the average profit per unit (*CD*) times the number of units. Remember again: We use average costs and average revenues to calculate profits.

Working Out an Example

We can translate this in terms of our firm. At the point where *MC = MR,* it is making about 45,000 stampings, as Figure 7 shows. Table 4 does not show us the exact cost at 45,000 units, but we will assume it is 1 cent more than the 91-cent cost of making 44,000 units. We will therefore estimate average cost for 45,000 stampings to be 92 cents per unit. Since the selling price is $1.50, we are now taking in a total of $1.50 × 45,000 units, or $67,500, while our total cost is 92 cents ×

45,000 units or $41,400. Our profit is the difference between total revenues and total costs, or $26,100.

Entry and Exit

However satisfactory from the point of view of the firm, this is not yet a satisfactory stopping point from the point of view of the system as a whole. If our firm is typical of the metal stamping industry, small firms throughout this line of business are making profits comparable to ours. In other lines of endeavor, though, numerous businesses do not make $26,100 in economic profit. Hence entrepreneurs in these lines will now begin to move into our profitable industry.

Perhaps we can anticipate what will happen now. **As other firms move into our line of business, output will increase. The supply curve of the industry will move to the right. The price of our product will therefore fall, as Figure 10 shows.**

How long will this influx of firms continue? Suppose it continues until price falls *below* the average cost curve of our representative firm. Now its position looks like Figure 11. Output will still be set where *MC = MR* (it always is), but now the average cost curve is above the average revenue curve at this point. The unavoidable result is a loss for the firm, as the diagram shows.

What will happen? Clearly, we need a reverse adjustment process—an exodus of firms into greener pastures, so that the supply curve for our industry can move to the left, bringing higher prices for all producers. This may not be a rapid process, but eventually the withdrawal of producers should bring about the necessary adjustment shown in Figure 12.

FIGURE 9
The Firm in Equilibrium with Profits
How well is our firm doing? Total costs = OABC: output times average costs. Total revenues = OAXD: output times average revenue. Profits equal the difference, or CBXD—a profit of BX per unit times the number of units.

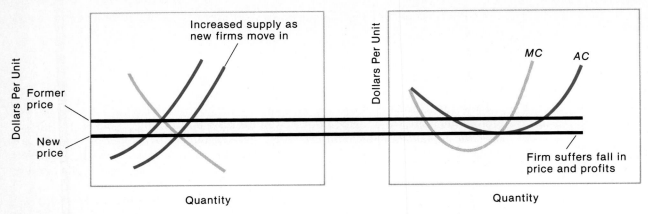

FIGURE 10
Industry in Adjustment to Profits
On the left we see that supply and demand lower the price as new firms move in. On the right we see how this affects each individual firm.

Minimizing Losses

The process of minimizing losses (which is as close as an unfortunate entrepreneur can get to maximizing profits) is worth a careful look. Figure 13 shows two curves: *AC* is our familiar curve of average costs. *AVC* is the curve of average variable costs (Figure 3). It is not *total* cost because it does not include the items like rent that go into fixed cost.

Suppose that price falls to P_1. Should the firm quit? No, because it covers its out-of-pocket expenses (*AVC*) and even makes a little over to cover some, although

FIGURE 11
The Firm Suffering a Loss
If price sinks too low, the firm will seek optimum output (MR = MC), but its price will fail to cover average costs. It will make a loss.

FIGURE 12
Industry Adjustment to Losses
As firms gradually leave an industry, the supply curve moves to the left, prices rise, and firms' losses are reduced.

not all, fixed cost. **As long as price is high enough to cover variable costs, a firm will continue to produce. Only when price fails to cover out-of-pocket AVC costs will it be rational to shut down.**

How long can a firm go on incurring losses? The answer depends on how rapidly it can terminate its fixed costs, such as getting rid of its buildings, machinery, etc., or how long it can incur losses without going bankrupt. The firm may limp along for an extended period, continuing to add production to the market and thereby delaying the leftward shift of the industry's supply curve.

Long-Run Equilibrium

Sooner or later, whether through the entry of new firms or the gradual withdrawal or disappearance of old ones, we reach a point of equilibrium for both the firm and the industry. It looks like Figure 14. Note that this position of equilibrium has two characteristics for the firm:

1. **Marginal cost equals marginal revenue, so there is no incentive for the individual entrepreneur to alter output.**
2. **Average cost equals average revenue (or price), so there is no incentive for firms to enter or leave the industry.**

Thus we can state the condition for the equilibrium resting point of our firm and industry as being a four-way equality:

$$MC \quad = \quad MR \quad = \quad AC \quad = \quad P$$

$$\frac{\text{marginal}}{\text{cost}} = \frac{\text{marginal}}{\text{revenue}} = \frac{\text{average}}{\text{cost}} = \frac{\text{price}}{\text{(average revenue)}}$$

We have reached an equilibrium for the firm and for the industry. It is certainly

FIGURE 13
Adjusting to Losses
If price is at P₁, the firm is covering variable costs, although not total costs. Perhaps it makes enough to cover its wages and some of its rent. It stays in business despite its economic loss. At price P₂ it can't even cover out-of-pocket costs. It has to shut down.

an uncomfortable one for us as typical manufacturers, for at the final resting point of the firm, it is clear that *profits have been totally eliminated.* We are driven to the conclusion that in a "perfect" competitive market, the forces of competition would indeed press toward zero the returns of the *marginal* firms in all industries, so that the cost and revenue profile of the last firms able to remain alive in each industry would look like our diagram.

Quasi Rents

Note, however, that these are marginal firms. Here is a clue to how profits can exist even in a highly competitive situation. In Figure 15 we show the supply curve of an industry broken into the individual supply curves of its constituent firms. Some of these firms, for reasons we will discuss below, will be lower-cost producers than others. When the industry equilibrium price is finally established, they will be the beneficiaries of the difference between the going price, which reduces the profits of the *marginal* firm to zero, and the lower unit costs attributable to their superior efficiency. Industry equilibrium leaves them in the enviable position of the firm shown in Figure 9.

These intramarginal profits are called quasi rents. * **They are the only true economic profits we find in competitive industries.**

Sources of Quasi Rents

Whence do these quasi rents arise? From several sources. One source may be personnel. Workers hired at the same wage are not always equally productive. A superior manager will recruit or organize a superior work force and gain rents as a result. Another source can be location. A retail store may enjoy a movement of population into its area. The value of its location increases, but its actual rental

---

*Sometimes they are called "economic rents" or even plain "rents."

FIGURE 14
Marginal Firm in Equilibrium with No Profits
Here is a diagram to be fully grasped. It shows the conditions for equilibrium of the competitive firm: (1) no incentive to change output (MR = MC); (2) no incentive for entry or exit (AC = P).

payments may not rise until a new lease is signed. Third, just plain luck or the uncertainties of the business world constantly create positive or negative quasi rents. Not all prices adjust quickly to changed conditions. An entrepreneur goes into a business having calculated costs and revenues, then finds that costs have fallen or revenues risen for reasons that could not be anticipated. Positive or negative quasi rents—profits or losses—will ensue. Uncertainty is, in fact as well as in proverb, fundamental to life and a major source of the good or bad fortune that

FIGURE 15
Quasi or Economic Rents
Even though the marginal firm makes no profit, intramarginal firms may realize quasi rents. Entry into the industry will tend to eliminate them.

besets the best-laid plans of entrepreneurs.

Thus economic profits enter the competitive world from changes in the economic setting, from random runs of good and bad luck, from unequal distributions of talent or resources. As a general rule, these sources of quasi rent are ephemeral, and the normal, profit-seeking movement of the industry will erode and eventually erase them. Badly run firms will go out of business or hire a better manager. Badly located firms will pick up and move. Contracts will come to an end and be renegotiated to remove quasi rents. Movements of the marketplace that create positive rents one year will create negative ones the next. Luck evens out. **Thus in the long run we can expect a tendency in a competitive market to eliminate existing quasi rents, although new ones may be created as conditions change.**

And how about inventions? In the real world, firms spend a great deal of money on research and development, seeking to gain an edge, usually based on some technological advantage. Are such profits also quasi rents? Yes and no. If the advantage is an invention or a technological advance protected by a patent, it creates a *monopoly,* and that takes us into the terrain covered in our next chapter. But if the technological advantage is based on a new technique or innovative production or on general organizational superiority, it is likely to have a much shorter life. In any competitive industry some firms will always be more imaginative, inventive, innovative than others, yet competition has a way of eroding such quasi rents with great rapidity. Thus a transient cost advantage, or advantages in product design, earn profits that can best be described as quasi rents.*

*We'll come back to quasi rents in pages 596–598.

LOOKING BACK

| KEY CONCEPTS | There are a great many graphs and tables in this chapter, but they all dovetail into an overall concept. The concept is the idea of the competitive firm seeking to maximize its profit. Keeping that in mind will help organize your understanding. |

Fixed and variable cost

1 All firms have two kinds of costs, fixed and variable. Fixed costs, which do not vary with output, decline when figured on a per unit basis as output grows. Variable costs display the familiar U shape.

The law of diminishing returns gives first increasing, then diminishing returns.

2 Variable costs rise because of the law of diminishing returns—also called the law of variable proportions. This law tells us that as we add more and more of any one factor to a fixed amount of other factors, output will first rise—increasing returns—and then fall—diminishing returns.

This gives falling, then rising average variable costs.

3 This change in productivity means that costs per unit—average costs—first fall, then rise, as we add variable costs (usually labor) to a fixed amount of plant and equipment.

Eventually average and marginal cost both rise. MC curve always cuts AC curve at lowest point.
AR and MR curves are identical.

4 If we add variable to fixed costs, we get the familiar dish-shaped curve. As output increases, eventually both average and marginal cost will rise, marginal cost more sharply. The marginal cost curve always cuts the average cost curve at its lowest point.

5 Average and marginal revenues for a competitive firm are identical and horizontal. This is because the firm's output is too small to affect price, whether it expands or contracts output.

$MC = MR$ is always optimal output.

6 The firm maximizes its own profit by setting output where $MC = MR$. The marginal cost curve always determines the point of optimal output. It is the firm's supply curve.

Entry and exit will change the supply curve for the industry. A firm will produce as long as $AR > AVC$.

7 $MC = MR$ is the "solution" for the firm, but it may not be the equilibrium for the industry. If the firm is making profits, there will be entry from other firms. Supply will increase. Price will drop. Profits will tend to disappear. If there are losses, some firms will leave the industry. Supply will diminish, prices will rise, losses will be cut. A firm will continue to produce as long as price (average revenue) is greater than average variable cost (out-of-pocket expenses).

Long-run equilibrium: $MC = MR = AC = P$

8 Long-run equilibrium requires that the firm be at the $MC = MR$ point and that it also have $AC = AR$ (or price). The firm must have no incentive to change output, and there must be no incentive to enter or leave the industry.

Quasi rents are profits based on transient advantages.

9 Profits at the margin thus tend toward zero. But intramarginal profits, or profits based on transient advantages, will continue to appear. These profits are called quasi rents.

ECONOMIC VOCABULARY

Fixed costs   246
Variable costs   246
Unit costs   246
Diminishing returns   247
Marginal productivity   247
Marginal product   249

Law of variable proportions   250
Average and marginal costs   254
Average and marginal revenue   256
Entry and exit   259
Quasi rents   262

QUESTIONS

1. If you were a retail grocer, what kind of costs would be fixed for you? If you were a manufacturer who owned a large computer, would its maintenance be a fixed cost? If you *rented* the computer, would maintenance be a fixed cost?
2. Assume your fixed costs are $500 a week and your output can vary from 100 to

1,000 units, given the scale of your enterprise. Graph what happens to fixed costs per unit. Is this diminishing returns?

3. Assume your plant hires 6 workers successively and that output changes as follows:

Number of workers	1	2	3	4	5	6
Total units of output per week	100	300	550	700	750	800

What is the marginal product of each worker? The average product? If each worker costs $100 per week, what is the variable cost per unit as you add personnel? Explain the relation between the shape of the curve and the law of variable proportions.

4. If you add fixed costs of $500 per week to the variable cost you have just ascertained, what is the average cost? What is the marginal cost? (Remember, this is figured by dividing the *change in total cost by the change in total output.*)

5. Graph the curve of average total costs and marginal costs. Why does the marginal cost curve cross the average cost curve at its lowest point?

6. What does average revenue mean, and what is its relation to price? What is meant by marginal revenue? Why is marginal revenue the same as average revenue for a competitive firm?

7. Suppose (in the example above) you sell the output of your firm at $1.35 per unit. Draw in such a marginal revenue curve. Now very carefully indicate where the MR and MC curves meet. Show on the diagram the output corresponding to this point. What is the approximate average cost at this output? Is there a profit here? Indicate by letters the rectangle that shows the profit per unit of output and the number of units. Is it a quasi rent?

8. What will be the result, in a competitive industry, of such a profit? Draw a diagram showing how an influx of firms can change the ruling market price. Will it be higher or lower?

9. Draw a diagram showing how price could drop below the lowest point on the average total cost curve and indicate the loss the firm would suffer. Explain, by means of a diagram, why a manufacturer may remain in business even though the firm cannot sell its output for the full cost of producing it. What will determine whether or not it is worth the firm's while to quit entirely?

10. Carefully draw a diagram showing the equilibrium position for the firm. Explain how MR and MC are all the firm is concerned with. How do AR and AC enter the picture? Why do MR and MC, by themselves, fail to give an equilibrium price in a competitive industry?

11. Suppose you are a druggist and you know that the least efficient druggist in town makes virtually no profit at all. Assuming that you both sell in the same market at the same prices, and that you hire factors at the same prices, what could bring a profit to your enterprise? What would you expect to be the trend of these profits?

16

Operating a Big Business

A LOOK AHEAD

In this chapter we move from the world of perfect competition to that of imperfect competition—monopolies, oligopolies, and monopolistically competitive business. We will study the operation of these business firms and compare it with the operation of the perfectly competitive firm we have already studied.

The crucial difference, as we will soon see, is that firms operating in conditions of imperfect competition have falling marginal revenue curves rather than horizontal ones. This means that at optimum output, where $MR = MC$, average cost will not equal average revenue or price. The main objective of this chapter is to see what difference this makes.

In Chapter 18 we make a social assessment of big business and consider various ways to deal with the problems it presents.

MOTIVES AND MARKETS

*M*onopoly and oligopoly are bad words to most people, just as competition is a good word, although not everyone can specify exactly what is good or bad about them. Often we get the impression that the aims of the monopolist are evil and grasping, while those of the competitor are wholesome and admirable. In the popular imagination the essential difference between a world of pure competition and one of very impure competition seems to hinge on motives and drives: well-meaning competitors vs. ill-intentioned monopolists.

The truth is that exactly the same motives drive the monopoly and the competitive firm. Both seek to maximize profits. Indeed, the competitive firm, faced with the necessity of watching costs and revenues in order to survive, is apt to be, if anything, more pennypinching and more intensely profit-oriented than the monopolist, who (as we shall see) can afford to take a less hungry attitude toward profits. The lesson to be learned—and to remember—is that motives have nothing to do with the problem of less-than-pure competition. **The difference between a monopoly, an oligopoly, and a situation of pure competition is entirely one of market structure; that is, of the number of firms, ease of entry or exit, and the degree of differentiation among their goods.**

Price Takers vs. Price Makers

We have noted a very precise distinction between the competitive situation (numerous firms, undifferentiated goods) and markets with few sellers or highly differentiated goods. In the competitive case, as we have seen, each firm caters to so small a section of the market that the demand curve for its product is, for all intents and purposes, horizontal. By way of contrast, in a monopolistic or oligopolistic market structure there are so few firms that each one faces a downward-sloping demand curve. Each monopoly firm, in fact, faces the demand curve of its own *industry*. That means each firm, by varying its output, can affect the price of its product.

Another way of describing this difference is to call purely competitive firms, who have no control over price, *price takers* and to label monopolies or oligopolies or any firm that can affect the price of its product *price makers*.

"Pure Monopolies"

Before examining the economic problems of a "pure" monopoly, let us see how such a price maker operates. Why do we place the word "pure" in quotes? Because monopoly is not as easy to define as one might think. Essentially, the word means that there is only *one* seller of a particular good or service. The trouble comes in defining the "particular" good or service. In a sense, any seller of a differentiated good is a monopolist, for no one else dispenses *quite* the same utilities. Each shoeshine boy has his "own" customers, some of whom would probably continue to patronize his stand even if he charged slightly more than the competition.

Thus, at one end of the difficulty is the fact that there is an element of monopoly in many seemingly competitive goods, a complication we come back to later. At the other end of the problem there are so-called natural monopolies, where economies of scale lead to one seller supplying the whole market, such as a local utility company. Yet even here there are substitutes. If power rates become exorbitant, we *could* switch from electric light to candlelight. Hence, before we can draw conclusions from the mere fact that a company provides the "only" service of its kind, we need to know how easy or difficult it would be to find substitutes, however imperfect, for its output.

Limits of Monopoly

Evidently the problem of defining a "pure" monopoly is not easily resolved. Let us, however, agree to call the local power company a monopoly, because no one else sells gas and electricity to the community. In Figure 1 we show what the demand curve of such a monopoly looks like.

One point is immediately clear. **The monopolistic *firm* faces the same kind of demand curve the competitive *industry* faces.** That is so because both cater to *all* the demand for that particular product. A corollary follows. The demand curve itself imposes a fundamental limitation of the monopolist's power to control the market. Suppose a monopoly is selling quantity *OX* at price *OA*. The firm would prefer to sell quantity *OY* at price *OA,* but there is no way of forcing the market to take a larger quantity of its product—unless it lowers the price to *OB.*

The situation is very similar (on the seller's side) to a *union.* A union can raise the price of labor since it controls the supply of labor, but it cannot force employers to hire more labor than they want. Hence the question "Can unions raise wages?" must be answered "yes" as far as those who continue to be hired are concerned. But until we know the elasticity of the demand for labor, we cannot say if unions can raise the total amount of labor's revenues.

FIGURE 1
Demand Curve for a Monopoly
A monopolist's demand curve is never horizontal. It slopes like the demand curve of a competitive industry. A demand curve constrains the monopolistic firm as decisively as it constrains the competitive industry.

FIGURE 2
Advertising and Demand
*Any firm that advertises tries to
to do two things: (1) move DD to
the right, and (2) make D'D'
more inelastic than DD was.*

Advertising

There is one thing a monopoly can do, however, that neither a union nor a purely competitive firm can do. **A monopoly can advertise and thereby seek to move the demand curve for its product to the right, or to change its slope.** Advertising does not "pay" for a purely competitive firm selling undifferentiated goods because such a firm has no way of being sure that *its* goods—and not a competitor's—will benefit. But advertising *can* be profitable for a monopoly that will get all the demand it can conjure up. We can think of advertising as an attempt to sell larger quantities of a good or service without reducing prices, by shifting the demand curve itself. Figure 2 shows us this important effect, and we will talk about it further in a moment.

Cost Curves for the Monopolist

We have seen in what way the shapes of the demand curves faced by monopolists differ from those faced by competitive firms. Are cost curves similarly different?

In general, they are not. We can take the cost profile of a monopoly as being essentially like that of a competitive firm.* The monopoly, like the competitive firm, buys factors and exerts no control over their prices. The local utility does not affect the level of wages or the price of land or capital by its decision to expand or not to expand production. The monopolist, like the competitive entrepreneur, experiences the effects of changing productivity as he hires additional factors and, again like the competitive firm, shops for the best buys in the factor markets. Thus

---

*One difference is that monopolies (and oligopolies, to be discussed next) have *selling costs.* Some of their costs are variable, like advertising; others are fixed, such as long-term merchandising contracts.

HOW MONOPOLISTIC IS A MONOPOLY?

How do we recognize a monopoly? Because of the problem of substitutes, there is no very clear sign, except in a few cases such as the "natural" monopolies. Usually when we speak of monopolies we mean (a) very large businesses with (b) much higher than competitive profits and (c) relatively little direct product competition. Not many firms satisfy all three conditions. Exxon is a monopoly by criteria a and b, but not by c; Polaroid (until recently) by b but not a, and perhaps not by c (Kodak is its direct product competitor). Note, furthermore, that even small businesses can be monopolies, like "the only gambling house in town" famed in all westerns.

the same U-shaped average cost curve and the same more steeply sloped marginal cost curve will describe the cost changes experienced by a monopolist quite as well as those of a competitive firm.

FROM COST TO REVENUE

Monopoly Revenues

It is when we come to the revenue side of the picture that we meet the critical distinction of monopoly. **Unlike a competitive firm, a monopoly has a marginal revenue curve that is different from its average revenue curve.** The difference arises because each time a monopoly sells more output, it must reduce the price not just on the last unit sold, but on *all* units, whereas a competitive firm sells its larger output at an unchanged price. Therefore, as the monopoly's sales increase, its *marginal* revenues will fall.

A table may make this clear. Suppose we have a monopoly that is faced with an average revenue or price schedule as in Table 1. The graph of such a marginal revenue curve looks like Figure 3. Note that at an output of 6 units, AR (price) = $15; MR = $10.

What determines the shape of the marginal revenue curve? Obviously, the change in quantity demanded that will be brought about by a drop in price. In turn, this reflects—as we remember from our discussion in Chapter 15—the elasticity of demand which, in turn, hinges on our tastes and the availability of substitutes. The more inelastic the demand, the faster the marginal revenue curve will fall. Note

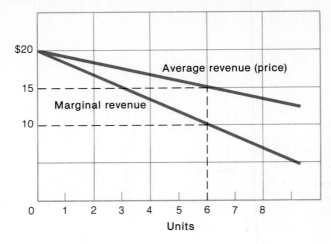

FIGURE 3
Average and Marginal Revenue for a Monopolist
When we graph the monopolist's situation we can see how a sloping demand curve creates an MR curve different from the AR curve.

especially that the *MR* curve lies below the *AR* curve because the monopolist must lower prices on *all* units sold, not just on the marginal unit. Thus each additional item drags down the revenue of all output.

Equilibrium for the Monopoly

The next step is obvious. We must superimpose the cost on the revenue profile to determine the equilibrium position for the monopolist. We can see this in Figure 4.

What will be the equilibrium position? **The monopoly seeking to maximize profit is guided by exactly the same rule as the competitive firm: It adds factors as long as the marginal revenue they bring in is greater than their marginal cost.**

Hence we look for the intersection of the *MC* and *MR* curves on Figure 4 to discover its optimum output.

We can see that optimum output is *OQ*. What about price? To discover this, we go up from the intersection of *MC* and *MR* to the *AR* (price) curve, and then over to the price axis. Optimum price obtainable for output *OQ* is *OA*.

As always, profit reflects the spread between average cost and average revenue. As we can see, this spread is *AZ*, the difference between average cost at output *OQ* and average revenue at that output. Total profit is therefore *AZ* times *OQ*, the rectangle we have shaded in.

TABLE 1
As price, AR, *falls,* MR *falls even more rapidly*

Quantity Sold	Price	Total Revenue	Marginal Revenue
1	$20	$20	$20
2	19	38	18
3	18	54	16
4	17	68	14
5	16	80	12
6	15	90	10

Monopoly vs. Competitive Prices

What is the difference between this price and that of a purely competitive market? We remember the formula for the equilibrium price of such a market: $MC = MR = AC$ = price. In the monopoly situation, MC still equals MR (this is always the profit-maximizing guide), but price certainly does not equal AC. Whereas the competitive firm is forced to price its goods at the lowest point on its cost curve, the monopolist will sell at a price above cost. If this were the case in a competitive market, we know what the remedy would be. An influx of firms would move the supply curve to the right and as a result, prices would fall until excess profits had been wiped out. **But in a monopoly situation, by the very definition of monopoly, there is no entry into the market. Hence the monopoly is able to restrict its output to the amount that will bring in the high profit it enjoys.**

OLIGOPOLY

Monopoly in its pure form is a rarity. Most big corporations operate in a market structure of oligopoly rather than monopoly. **In an oligopolistic market situation a few sellers divide the bulk of the market.** Sometimes there is a long tail of smaller competitors who share the leftovers.

The aircraft industry is a typical oligopoly. In 1982 there were 166 manufacturers of planes or airframes in the United States, but the top 5 accounted for two-thirds of all sales. There were over 723 makers of soaps and detergents, but the top 4 accounted for over half of the market. In tires and tubes, 164 companies made up the industry, but the top 4 had cornered two-thirds of all sales. In automobiles, the top four manufacturers out of 284 had 71 percent of the market.

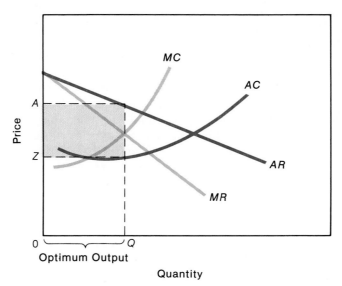

FIGURE 4
Monopoly Equilibrium
The intersection of MR and MC here tells us three things: (1) best output, OQ; (2) price at OQ = OA; and (3) average cost at OQ = OZ. Profit is the spread between price and cost (AZ) times the number of units sold (OQ).

Oligopoly Cost and Demand

What does a typical oligopoly look like under the lens of price theory? On the cost side, it is much the same as a monopoly, with a dish-shaped cost curve that includes selling expense. There is, however, an essential difference between the demand curve of a monopolist and that of an oligopolist. The demand curve for a monopolist, since it comprises the entire demand for the commodity, has the familiar downward-sloping shape. The demand curve for the oligopolist, although also downward-sloping, does not have the clear-cut position of the monopolist's curve.

On the contrary, the essence of the oligopoly's demand curve is that it is uncertain; and moreover, that its position depends on what the oligopoly and its competitors do. Like the monopoly, the oligopoly is free to raise or lower its price. Unlike the monopoly, the oligopoly does not do so against a fixed demand curve. If one firm raises its price, competitors may meet the competition by raising theirs. Or they may keep their prices unchanged. Or an oligopoly may ignore price raises or cuts and lure business away by altering the product or simply by changing its image in advertising. Each of these responses will have a different impact on the demand curves of all its competitors.

The Fight for Market Shares

This extreme indeterminacy brings its effects to bear on the character of oligopolistic competition. It makes price competition the least favored rather than the standard mode of competition. Instead of price wars, a fight for shares of the market becomes the normal mode of competition. This is, of course, totally unlike the other market structures we have examined. **No competitive firm fights for a share of the market, because its output is insignificant. A monopoly does not worry about its share, because it has the whole market for itself. But a fight for shares is the very heart of the oligopolistic struggle.** Figure 5 shows how intense this struggle has been in the automobile industry.

Moreover, because each producer tries to be better than its main competitors in one way or another, the fight usually takes the form of winning customers to a carefully *differentiated* product. A Ford is made to be distinguishable from a Chevy; a Chevy from a Chrysler.

In the fight for market shares, price cutting becomes a much feared means of competing resorted to only when the going gets very tough. Each oligopolist thinks he is better than the competition at designing or advertising or at serving customers. No one thinks he is better at price cutting. Moreover, each oligopolist fears that a price cut will be met by retaliatory price cuts, leaving market shares more or less unchanged and everyone worse off.

The Kinked Demand Curve

Thus we can see that it is not possible to arrive at neat models of oligopolistic behavior that predict how big companies will respond. But one among many

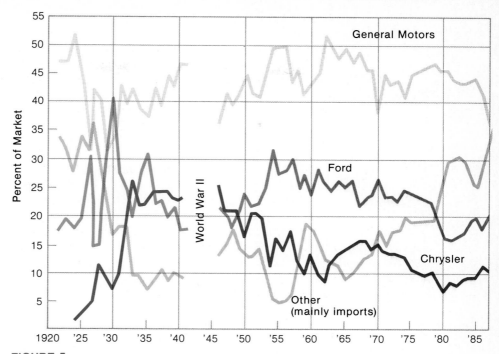

FIGURE 5

Fortune *magazine writes: "During the last half century, the auto industry has reached a few crucial turning points that affected the fortunes of competitors for many years. In the 1920s, Alfred Sloan of General Motors wrestled the lead from Henry Ford. Then, when car production resumed after World War II, Henry Ford II restored his company to a strong No. 2 position. The 'other category' now consists mainly of imports. The chart is based on R. L. Polk & Company's compilation of new-car registration figures."*

models of behavior has been worked out and is worth familiarizing ourselves with because it allows us to show graphically why oligopolists do not like to resort to price competition.

Suppose you were the president of a large company that, along with three other very similar companies, sold roughly 80 percent of a certain commodity. Suppose also that a price had been established for your commodity. It yielded you and your competitors a reasonable profit, but you and your fellow officers were trying to increase that profit.

One possibility that would certainly be discussed would be to raise the price of your product and hope your customers would continue to be loyal to you. Your company economists, however, might point out that their analyses showed a very elastic demand for your product *if you raised your price, but your competitors did not.* That is, at the higher price, many of your "loyal" customers would switch to a competitive brand, so your revenues would fall sharply and your profits decline.

Suppose, then, you took the other tack and gambled on that very elasticity of demand by cutting your prices. Would not other firms' customers switch to you and thereby raise your revenues and profits? This time your advisers might point out

CONCENTRATION RATIOS: WHAT IS AN INDUSTRY?

Economists generally measure the degree of concentration by comparing the ratio of total sales or assets of the top four or the top eight companies to the total sales or assets of their industry. But immediately we encounter the difficult problem of defining *industry*. Here are the figures in 1982, the last industry survey year. The top four companies made 81 percent of a commodity for which there is really no adequate substitute: salt. Yet if we put salt into an industrial classification called "chemical preparations not elsewhere specified," the share of the top four companies falls to a paltry 23 percent of the output of that larger group of products.

Take another example. A housewife shopping for salad dressing is a consumer in an "industry" in which the top four producers sell 57 percent of the product. If she thinks of herself as a consumer browsing in an industry called "pickles and sauces," the top four salad dressing makers' share of output is only 29 percent. A farmer looking for a tractor is buying in a "market" in which the top four companies make 72 percent of the total output: but if we think of a tractor as belonging to a larger industry called "farm machinery and equipment," the share of the top four is only 44 percent.

How *should* we draw lines around industries or products? One way is by measuring how much sales of product A increase if the price of product B rises. Here is the idea of substitution applied to an important problem of economic policy. We call the measure of interproduct influence the *cross-elasticity of substitution*. If a rise in the price of A leads *many* customers to switch to B, there is at least a prima facie case for drawing the line of the industry to include both. Of course, the argument then arises as to how many consumers it takes to make "many" of them.

that if you cut your price, your competitors would almost certainly do the same, to *prevent* you from taking a portion of their market. As a result, with prices cut all around, you would probably find your market share unchanged, and your demand curve inelastic.

As Figure 6 shows, you are facing a "kinked" demand curve. In this situation you might be tempted to sit tight and do nothing, for a very interesting thing happens to the marginal revenue curve that is derived from a kinked demand curve.

In Figure 7 we now get two marginal revenue curves: one applicable to the upper, elastic section of the demand curve; the other applicable to the lower, inelastic section. At the point of the kink, the marginal revenue curve is discontinuous, dropping vertically from the end of one slope to the beginning of

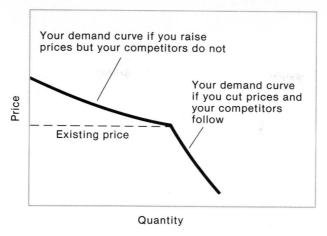

FIGURE 6
Kinked Demand Curve
The kinked demand curve is a graphic way of showing why oligopolies tend to shy away from price cutting. Their demand curve is elastic going up, inelastic going down—exactly the opposite of what they would like it to be.

the next. **As a result, there is no single point of intersection of the marginal revenue and marginal cost curves.** This means that an oligopoly's costs can change considerably before it is forced to alter its optimum volume of output or selling price.

The kinked demand curve helps explain why oligopoly prices are often so unvarying even without collusion among firms. It does not really explain how the existing price is arrived at; for once cost or demand conditions have changed enough to overcome oligopolistic inertia, a new kink will again appear around the changed price. The kinked curve thus shows what forces affect *changes* in the oligopolistic situation rather than how supply and demand originally determine the going price.

FIGURE 7
Discontinuous *MR* Curve
The kinked AR curve gives rise to a strangely shaped MR curve with a vertical discontinuity. Hence costs can change considerably (from MC_1 to MC_2) without altering optimum output, OQ.

Collusion and Price Leadership

Another way of avoiding price competition has probably already occurred to you. It is for the dominant firms to agree not to undersell one another.

Such agreements have existed, undoubtedly do exist, and certainly minimize price cutting. They are, however, illegal under the antitrust laws. When unearthed, they lead to prosecution, fines, and even jail sentences. Therefore outright collusion is probably used as a last resort. Moreover, outright collusion is often not necessary because a kind of tacit collusion called *price leadership* can do just as well.

Price leadership exists when one company sets prices for the entire industry. For years, CPC International set the price of corn starch. From time to time, when the market situation seemed to warrant it, CPC would announce a change in price. Immediately thereafter its two or three big competitors and its host of small fry competition would change their prices.

Did CPC confer with its major competitors over lunch before changing its price? Probably not. Its competitors were glad to follow the leader, because all recognized that this was the best way to maximize profits for the industry as a whole.*

Excess Capacity and Price Wars

Price leadership may lead to comfortable price relations within an industry, and it is a very common mode of pricing in oligopolistic markets. From time to time, however, the system breaks down. As long as business is good, firms gladly abide by a live and let live philosophy that permits competition to focus on the relatively safe means of product differentiation.

When business is poor, price leadership is not always accepted. This difference is generated by the fact that prices above the equilibrium for a competitive market lead to a condition known as *excess capacity*. Each seller within the industry is tempted to enlarge his production capacity to the size that the "administered" price indicates. The result, as Figure 8 shows, is excess capacity; that is, the ability to supply more output (Q_1) than the market will take at that price (Q_2). In desperation, the rivals turn to price cutting, and price wars are apt to break out until stability is once more achieved.

The Drive for Growth

We have concentrated on the tactics of competition among oligopolies, but we must not leave this form of industrial market structure without paying heed to a central aspect of oligopolistic life. This aspect is the drive for growth that characterizes virtually all oligopolistic firms.

To be sure, all firms in a market system seek to grow. But small competitive firms

---

*How are price leaders chosen? The situation varies from one industry to another. Sometimes it is the biggest firm, sometimes the most aggressive. Sometimes leadership shifts around. There is no fixed pattern.

GAME THEORY

A competitive firm has no strategy because it has no options. It is forced to maximize its short-run profits, or it will soon be forced out of business. But the introduction of market imperfections opens the way for numerous strategies.

The problems of strategy have led to the development of game theory, a new approach to economic analysis. Suppose we have two arch-rival firms who dominate an industry. The board of directors of firm A meets one day to decide on price policy. The president opens with, "Trustworthy sources I am unable to reveal inform me that if we raise our prices, firm B, our main competitor, will raise its prices. I calculate that firm B and ourselves will each boost profits by $10 million as a consequence. Therefore I recommend that we raise prices immediately."

At this point the president is interrupted by the company treasurer, who is a graduate of the Harvard Business School. "I must recommend against this proposal on two counts. First, firm B may well be baiting a trap for us. If we raise our prices, they will *not* raise theirs. We will thereupon lose a vast amount of business to B. I estimate that this will cause us a loss of $10 million, and that firm B will make a profit of $20 million.

"Second, suppose firm B *does* raise prices. Then, as profit-maximizing directors, we should certainly not raise ours; for in that case, by keeping our prices low, we will steal away a great deal of business from B, and we will make a profit of $20 million, while they lose $10 million."

"Well reasoned," says the chairman of the board. "It is not only clear that we should not raise prices, but I suggest that we inform company B—discreetly, of course—that we *will* raise prices, as they suggest, in order to tempt them to do so. That will make our strategy foolproof."

In due course, this information is transmitted to firm B, where a similar discussion takes place. Firm B resolves to "accept" firm A's offer, but in fact not to raise prices at all. Result: Neither firm raises prices because neither trusts the other. Instead of each gaining $10 million, which would have been the result of a price rise by both firms, the two firms stand pat and accept the much smaller profits that accrue from *minimizing risk.*

are hampered in their efforts because their rising marginal cost curves do not permit a single plant or business to expand very far. Monopolies, as we have seen, are few; and their growth, by definition, is limited to expansion of their industries. The growth situation is very different for an oligopoly. **To begin with, because an oligopoly is a large firm, it normally has many plants and therefore tends to enjoy economies of scale or long-run unit cost curves that are horizontal**

FIGURE 8
Excess Capacity
The ability of oligopolies to establish prices above equilibrium or clearing prices results in excess capacity. This is just like the "surplus" in earlier diagrams.

rather than upward-climbing. Thus there is no cost impediment to growth, at least not for a long time.

Second, the typical oligopolist is not as highly concentrated as the auto or tire manufacturers. The share of the industry served by the top four companies is frequently less than 50 percent, and the biggest single company often serves only about a quarter or less of the business. **Thus the field for expansion is very great, and the drive to widen one's share correspondingly powerful.** Growth may be the dream of the small business in a competitive industry, but it is the stuff of daily life for the oligopolist.

Finally, once again, technology may change the rules of the game. The increasing use of computers to supervise the flow of production opens the possibility that the most competitive firms in the future will not be those that have the lowest costs on long runs of standardized products, but those that can quickly change the specifications of "custom-made" shorter runs of output, designed to fit the particular needs of important customers. If indeed "batch" production becomes increasingly important, smaller firms may enjoy advantages of managerial flexibility that give them an edge over larger, more bureaucratic firms.*

---

*We recall from page 000 that long-run cost curves turned up at high levels of output. This is because they referred to economies and eventually diseconomies of scale for a *given plant.* It is indeed likely that unit costs increase in a given plant, because eventually it becomes so large that it is no longer convenient to administer. An oligopoly or a monopoly may, however, decide to build a new plant rather than to push an existing one beyond its economical size. Do big oligopolistic firms that spread production among several plants also experience rising unit costs? We really do not know. It may be that the new technology of information retrieval has so increased the efficiency of management that multiplant firms *never* experience rising unit costs. For all practical purposes, their long-run cost curves are horizontal or perhaps even falling.

*See Charles Sabel and Michael Piore, *The Second Industrial Divide,* (New York, Basic Books, 1984).

Growth within Markets

How is growth achieved? Usually by plowing back profits into more capital equipment or by buying up the ready-made plant and equipment of smaller companies in the field. It is virtually impossible to expand sales without an increase in capital assets, and therefore we find all successful oligopolies steadily building up the value of their capital.

For a considerable period a successful oligopoly can increase its share of the market in this way. But at a certain point, further growth within the market becomes difficult. The cost of gaining additional business rises, as indifferent customers are wooed and other customers remain loyal to competitive brands. Or the specter of an antitrust suit may loom because a company threatens, by virtue of its growth, to monopolize a market.

MNCs and Conglomerates

Two responses are open to the successful oligopoly. **First, it may transfer its fight for market shares from a national to an international basis.** The big corporation today considers the world to be its potential market—not merely a market to which it may ship its home-produced goods, but a market within which it may actually manufacture its product. We shall be investigating this extremely important aspect of modern competition in the extra word about multinational corporations following this chapter.

Or the oligopolist may decide to become a conglomerate; that is, to acquire capital in other industries. By diversifying its sales, it not only escapes the eye of the Justice Department's antitrust lawyers, but also avoids putting all its eggs in one basket.

The rise of the conglomerate helps explain a curious and seemingly contradictory state of affairs that we noticed in Chapter 5. There we saw that the share of total assets coming under the control of giant companies—virtually all of them oligopolists—had risen dramatically, so that the top 100 industrial companies in 1970 owned about 50 percent of all the assets of all manufacturing companies, about the same share as the top 200 companies had owned in 1948. We also noted that the concentration of sales did not parallel that of assets. Actually, a study of the nation's markets shows no overall drift toward a more highly concentrated pattern *within* markets.

Now we can understand the dynamics of this phenomenon. The concentration of assets is explained partly by the continued growth of some companies within their industries, and partly by the very rapid rise of conglomerates, often through mergers. From 1974 to 1984, there were some 23,000 mergers and acquisitions, and 82 of the largest 500 corporations disappeared. In 1985–1987, 21 of the Fortune 500 lost their corporate independence in the merger game.

Merger Mania Again

We took a look at the merger question in Chapter 5 (pages 86–87). The subject of power turns our attention there once again. Congress is now considering changes in the various laws affecting corporate mergers—changes designed to discourage takeovers whose effects are to yield large profits for the financial entrepreneurs who have arranged the takeover, but disappointing results—if any at all—for the combined corporations. One suggested way of coping with this problem is to legislate that a significant fraction of the directors of large corporations be nominated directly by *nonmanagement* owners. Since roughly half of most large corporations' shares are held by financial intermediaries such as pension funds, this means that substantial nominating power would be placed in the hands of managers of these funds. Such directors would likely have a considerable interest in preventing "their" corporations from being placed "in play," and might be expected to exercise their share of voting power to assure the best long-run strategy, rather than the tactic aimed at making the largest immediate gain.*

MONOPOLISTIC COMPETITION

We will return to the world of oligopolies, but first we must continue our survey of competition in the real world. For oligopoly, although perhaps the most significant departure from the ideal of pure competition, is not the most common. Once we pass from the manufacturing to the retail or service sectors where competition is still intense and characterized by numerous small units, we encounter a new kind of market situation, equally strange to the pages of a text on pure competition. **This is a situation in which there are many firms, with relatively easy entrance and exit, but where each firm sells a product slightly differentiated from that of every other.** Here is the world of the average store or the small competitive manufacturer of a brand-name product—indeed, of all sellers who can identify their products for the public and who must face the competition of many other makers of similar but not identical products.

Economists call this market situation tinged by monopoly *imperfect competition* or *monopolistic competition.* How does it differ from pure competition? Once again, there is no difference on the cost side. That is the same for both a perfectly competitive and an imperfectly competitive firm, except for the presence of selling costs in imperfect competition. The difference, again, comes in the nature of the demand curve.

We recall that the special attribute of the demand curve facing a firm in a purely competitive situation is its horizontal character. By way of contrast, **in a market of imperfect competition, the demand curve facing each seller slopes gently downward** because each seller's good or service is not exactly like that of competitors, and because each seller therefore has some ability to raise price without losing all his business.

---

*This suggestion, together with a sober estimate of the disappointing results of mergers to date, will be found in F. M. Scherer, "Corporate Takeovers: The Efficiency Argument," *Journal of Economic Perspectives,* Winter 1988, pp. 81 and *passim.*

Equilibrium in Monopolistic Competition

What is the equilibrium position of such an imperfectly competitive firm—say a dress manufacturer? In Figure 9 on the left, an imperfect competitor is obviously making substantial profits. Note that the firm's best position where $MR = MC$ is *exactly* like that of any firm, monopolies included. But our firm is not a monopolist and its profits are therefore not immune to erasure by entry into its field. In Figure 9 we show the same firm after *other entrepreneurs have moved into the industry* (with additional similar, although not identical, products) and taken away some of our firm's market and *moved its demand curve to the left.*

Note that our final position for the marginal dress firm has no more profit than that of a purely competitive seller because $AC = AR$. On the other hand, because its demand curve slopes, the equilibrium point cannot be at the lowest point on the average cost curve, nor will output have reached optimum size.

This outcome clearly dissipates economic well-being. The fact that firms are forced to operate to the left of the optimums on their cost curves means that they have not been able to combine factors to yield their greatest efficiency. This failure penalizes factors, once when they are paid too little because their potential marginal productivity has not been reached, and again when, as consumers, they are forced to pay too much for products that have not been produced at lowest possible cost. In addition, waste is incurred because the attempt to differentiate

FIGURE 9
Monopolistic Competition
Here we can see that initial equilibrium for a small dress manufacturer looks exactly the same as equilibrium for a monopoly. In both cases, MC and MR determine output. But unlike the case for monopolies, the dress manufacturer experiences the competition of entry. His demand curve AR_1 moves to the left to AR_2. Again, he seeks $MC = MR$, but now there is no spread between AC and AR. He has no profit and no advantage from his monopolistic MR curve.

Before other firms enter

After other firms enter

THE WORLD OF REAL COMPETITION IN COMPUTERS

Once we leave the world of homogenous products such as wheat, the problems of pricing and product design become much more complicated than any economics text can indicate. Let us take the case of the personal computer industry. At the moment there are over two hundred firms making computers. They range in price from a few hundred to several thousand dollars, and offer a wide range of options, "compatibilities," gadgets, service facilities, and the like.

Ten years from now, if past experience is a reliable guide, only a few dozen or so firms will have survived. What will determine which of the 200 firms will be among the survivors? Will it be price alone? That is very unlikely. Design alone? Equally unlikely. The winners will be those companies that have found a niche for themselves, where a combination of price and product design suits the needs of enough consumers to allow production to be carried on profitably.

What will that combination be? The managers of the present-day two hundred companies do not know—if they did, they would all be producing the "correct" product instead of searching to discover what the correct product will be. In the end we will probably have a spectrum of computers, just as we have a spectrum of cars or appliances or TV sets. The process of actual competition is one of "sorting out" and structuring the market itself, as well as finally locating oneself in it.

products leads in many instances to too many small units; for example, four gas stations at one intersection.

Inefficient though it may be, monopolistic competition yields no profit for the marginal firm in an industry. The entrepreneur therefore feels fully as hard-pressed as would the producer of an undifferentiated commodity. The difference is that a monopolistic competitive businessperson has the possibility of *further differentiating* a product in the hope of tilting the demand curve to a more inelastic position, thereby gaining a slight price rise to squeeze out a tiny "pure monopoly" profit. The result is that monopolistic competition fosters a tremendous variety of goods—the ladies' garment industry being a prime example.

Social Consequences

Are monopolies as evil as their reputations? Are oligopolies a bad thing? Are monopolistically competitive industries simply wasteful?

These are questions of major importance, but they take us outside the firm to a public point of view. We take up these issues shortly.

LOOKING BACK

KEY CONCEPTS

Markets vs. motivation
Price makers vs. price
takers

1 Imperfect competition—monopoly, oligopoly, and monopolistic competition—refers to different kinds of market structure than pure competition; it does *not* refer to different motivations. Competitive firms have no option but to take existing prices. Firms in imperfect competition can make prices—although not entirely as they would like.

Monopoly demand
curves are like those of
a competitive industry.

2 Monopolies are firms that cater to all the demand of a given market. They face the same demand curve as a competitive industry. By advertising, a monopolist hopes to move his demand curve out and to make it more inelastic.

$MR < AR$ for a
monopolist

3 Because a monopoly faces a sloping demand curve, its marginal revenue curve is not horizontal, but falling. This is because it must cut price to increase sales. For a competitive firm, $MR = AR$; for a monopoly, $MR < AR$.

Monopoly equilibrium:
$MR = MC$, $AR > AC =$
profit

4 Monopoly equilibrium is determined by the intersection of MR and MC. This gives optimum output. Optimum output indicates selling price. Profit is determined by the spread between selling price and average cost at the point of optimum output. This profit is not subject to erosion by entry because by definition our firm is the only one—a monopoly.

An oligopoly may have a
kinked demand curve
reflecting competitors'
reactions.

5 Oligopoly is much more common than monopoly. It is a market structure in which a few firms dominate the market. An oligopolist's demand curve is likely to be kinked. The kink simply tells us that each firm's price policy invites a response, so that if it raises prices, competitors won't, whereas if it cuts them, they will.

The fight for market
shares, diversification,
and multinationals

6 Oligopolies often use price leadership to avoid price competition. The fight for market shares is the most conspicuous feature of their strategies. To avoid undue concentration, oligopolies may diversify or go multinational.

Monopolistic
competition: entry
removes monopoly
profits

7 Monopolistic competition refers to market situations in which each firm has a monopoly (a sloping demand curve), but where entry is easy. The result is that demand is pushed to the left and equilibrium is reached without any monopoly profit.

ECONOMIC VOCABULARY

QUESTIONS

1. How would you define a monopoly? Are monopolies necessarily large? What constraints does a demand curve put on the behavior of a monopoly?

2. Suppose that you were the only seller of a certain kind of machinery in the nation. Suppose further that you discovered your demand curve looked like this:

   Price $100 $90 $80 $70
   Quantity of machines sold   1   2   3   4

   What is the average revenue at each price? What is the marginal revenue at each price? Draw a diagram showing the marginal and average revenues.

3. Now superimpose on this diagram a hypothetical cost profile for your business. Where is the point of equilibrium for the monopolist? Is this the same, in terms of *MC* and *MR,* as the point for the competitive firm? Now show the equilibrium output and price.

4. Does the equilibrium output of the monopolist yield a profit? What are the relevant costs for figuring profit, average cost per unit, or marginal cost? Show on your diagram the difference between average cost and selling price.

5. Why will a monopolist's selling price not be pushed to the lowest point on the cost curve?

6. What is the difference between monopoly and oligopoly? Between oligopoly and pure competition? Between pure competition and monopolistic (or imperfect) competition? Between the latter and oligopoly? Can these differences be expressed in demand curves?

7. What is a differentiated commodity? Give examples. Draw the demand curve for a farmer selling wheat and that for a toy manufacturer selling a special kind of doll. What will happen if the doll manufacturer makes a large profit? What will the doll maker's final point of equilibrium look like if there are many competitors?

8. Is excess capacity possible in a truly competitive industry? A monopoly? Why in an oligopoly?

AN EXTRA WORD ABOUT

The Multinational Corporation

The problem of big business is one of old standing, dating back to the period just after the Civil War. But recently that problem has been given a new twist by the appearance of enormous corporations whose business empires literally straddle the globe—the multinational corporations. Take PepsiCo, for example. PepsiCo does not ship its famous product around the world from bottling plants in the United States. It *produces* Pepsi Cola in more than 600 plants in 148 countries. When you buy a Pepsi in Mexico or the Philippines, Israel or Denmark, you are buying an American product that was manufactured in that country.

PepsiCo is a far-flung, but not a particularly large, multinational corporation: In 1987 it was the 150th largest company. More impressive by far is the Ford Motor Company, a multinational that consists of a network of 26 major subsidiary corporations, 19 of them foreign-based. Of the corporation's total assets of $45 billion, nearly one-half is invested in 19 foreign nations; and of its 350,000 employees (as of 1987), more than 210,000 were employed outside the United States. And if we studied the corporate structures of GM or IBM or the great oil companies, we would find that they, too, are multinational corporations with substantial portions of their total wealth invested in productive facilities outside the United States.

If we broaden our view to include the top 100 American firms, we find that two-thirds have such production facilities in at least six nations. Moreover, the value of output that is produced overseas by the largest corporations by far exceeds the value of the goods they still export from the United States. In 1986, assets of foreign affiliates of U.S. multinational firms (which means their wholly or partially owned overseas branches) came to over $260 billion.

INTERNATIONAL DIRECT INVESTMENT

Another way of establishing the spectacular rise of international production is to trace the increase in the value of U.S. foreign direct investment; that is, the value of foreign-located, U.S.-owned plant and equipment (not U.S.-owned foreign bonds and stocks). In 1950 the value of U.S. foreign direct investment was $11 billion. In 1986 it was over $260 billion. Moreover, this figure needs two upward adjustments.

The value of foreign direct investment is calculated by adding up the actual money spent each year in acquiring assets. But no adjustment is made for increases in the current value of those assets because of inflation. That is, the replacement value of American foreign assets would be much higher than its "book" value if assets were revalued according to current prices. Depreciation of the dollar, like foreign inflation, has raised the market value in dollars of U.S. overseas assets. Indeed, when domestic and foreign assets are measured at market prices, it is possible that dollar depreciations through the end of 1988 *entirely eliminated* the net debtor position of the United States.

A second correction to the value of foreign investment arises because the stated value of overseas assets includes only the dollars actually invested, not the value of the total enterprise the investment may control. It is frequently the case that a direct investment will control a larger amount of capital than the investment itself—it only takes 51 percent of the voting stock to wield decision-making power in a corporation, and frequently control is gained with a much smaller holding than that.

The actual value of American foreign direct investment (or its counterpart, European or Japanese foreign investment) is therefore difficult or impossible to calculate with exactitude. In all likelihood something between a quarter and a half of the real assets of our biggest corporations are located abroad, and probably the same ratio applies to other advanced capitalist economies.

THE INTERNATIONAL CHALLENGE

The movement toward the internationalization of production is not a strictly American phenomenon. If the American multinationals are today the most imposing (of the world's biggest 50 corporations, over 23 are American), they are closely challenged by non-American multinationals (see Table 1). Philips Lamp Works is a Dutch multinational company with operations in 68 countries. Of its 343,000 employees, 260,000 work in nations other than the Netherlands. Royal Dutch/Shell is another vast multinational, whose home is somewhere between the Netherlands and the United Kingdom (it is jointly owned by nationals of both countries): Shell *in the United States* ranks among "our" top 15 biggest companies. Another multinational is Nestlé Chocolate, a Swiss firm, 97 percent of whose $2 billion revenues originate outside Switzerland; and many multinationals are today Japanese.

MOTIVES FOR OVERSEAS PRODUCTION

What drives a firm to produce overseas rather than just sell overseas? One possible answer is straightforward. A firm is successful at home. Its technology and organizational skills give it an edge on foreign competition. It begins to export its product. The foreign market grows. At some point the firm begins to calculate whether it would be more profitable to organize an overseas production operation. By doing so, it would save transportation costs. It may be able to evade a tariff by producing goods behind a tariff wall. It may be able to take advantage of lower wage rates. Finally, it ceases shipping goods abroad and instead exports capital, technology, and management—and becomes a multinational.*

Calculations may be more complex. A successful company may change its point of view by degrees. First it thinks of itself as a domestic company, perhaps with a small export market. Then it builds up its exports and thinks of itself as an international company with a substantial interest in exports. Finally, its perspective changes to that of a multinational, considering the world (or substantial portions of it) to be its market. In that case, it may locate plants in other countries *before* the market is fully developed, in order to be firmly established abroad ahead of its competition.*

*This sequence, first described by Harvard's Raymond Vernon, is known as *product-cycle theory.*

*The internal dynamics that send some firms overseas, but not others, are by no means wholly understood. The internationalization of *production* is much more widely spread in some industries, such as glass, than in others, such as steel. Drugs are widely produced on an international basis; machine tools are not.

TABLE 1
THE TOP 15 MULTINATIONALS, 1984

Company	*Total Sales ($ Billions)*
1. Exxon Corporation	95.6
2. Shell/Royal Dutch Petroleum	94.3
3. General Motors	83.7
4. Mitsui	64.7
5. Mitsubishi Corporation	63.2
6. British Petroleum	57.2
7. Mobil	55.9
8. Ford	52.2
9. C. Itoh & Co.	51.9
10. Marubeni	48.1
11. Texaco	47.1
12. Sumitomo Corporation	47.1
13. IBM	45.8
14. Sears Roebuck	38.7
15. E. I. DuPont de Nemours	35.8

Source: The Times 1000, 1985–86, annual report.

ECONOMICS OF MULTINATIONAL PRODUCTION

Whether or not the multinational boom continues at its past rate, the startling rise of multinationals has already changed the face of international economic relationships. **One major effect has been a dramatic shift in the *geographic location* and the *technological* character of international economic activity.**

The shift away from exports to international production has introduced two changes into the international economic scene. One change is a movement of foreign investment away from its original concentration in the underdeveloped areas of the world toward the richer markets of the developed areas. Fifty years ago, in the era of high imperialism, most of the capital leaving one country for another flowed from rich to poor lands. Thus foreign investment in the late nineteenth and early twentieth centuries was largely associated with the creation of vast plantations, the building of railways through jungles, and the development of mineral resources.

But the growth of the multinational enterprise has coincided with a decisive shift away from investment in the underdeveloped world to investment in the industrial world. In 1897, 59 percent of American foreign direct investment was in agriculture, mining, or railways, mainly in the underdeveloped world. By the end of the 1970s, our investment in agriculture, mining, and railways, as a proportion of our total overseas assets, had fallen to about 20 percent; and its geographical location in the Third World came to only 36 percent of all our overseas direct investments. More striking, almost three-quarters of our huge rise in direct investment during the decades of the 1960s and 1970s was in the developed world; and the vast bulk of it was in manufacturing (and oil) rather than in plantations, railroads, or ores. **Thus the multinational companies have been investing in each others' territories rather than invading the territories of the underdeveloped world.** This is not to say that they do not wield great power in the less developed regions, as we shall see, but that their thrust of expansion has been in other industrial lands.

The second economic change is really implicit in the first. **It is a shift away from heavy- to high-technology industries—away from enterprises in which vast sums of capital were associated with large, unskilled labor forces, as in the building of railways or plantations, toward industries in which capital is perhaps less strategic than research and development, skilled technical manpower, and sophisticated management techniques typical of the computer, petrochemical, and other new industries.** Table 2 sums up the overall shift.

Note the dramatic shift away from Latin America and away from transport, mining, and agriculture into Europe and manufacturing, a shift that would be even more accentuated if we were not still dependent on oil as a major source of the world's energy. If nuclear power or the fuel cell displace oil within the next two decades, we can expect a still more rapid decline in investment in the less developed areas (especially in the Middle East), and a proportionately still larger concentration of foreign direct investment in manufacturing.

In recent years a still more dramatic trend has come to the fore. This is the capacity of big companies to combine high technology and low-wage labor by setting up modern production facilities in such areas as Mexico, Brazil, South Korea, and Singapore. This is by no means a movement confined to the multinationals. High-tech, low-wage operations have often been organized by companies of relatively small size. But the new capability of combining the two has often aided the big MNCs in consolidating their global positions.

Last, but certainly not least, is the increasing interlinking and interlocking of multinationals through joint ventures. Just as an instance, General Motors has a joint production venture in California with Toyota, and also owns a 34 percent interest in the Japanese firm Isuzu, a large supplier of auto parts. GM also has substantial interests in

TABLE 2
American Foreign Direct Investment

Total (Millions)	1929 $7,528	1950 $11,788	1987 $308,793
		Distribution by market (%)	
Canada	27	30%	18%
Europe	18	14	48
Latin America	47	41	14
Asia, Africa, other	8	15	20
		Distribution by industrial sector (%)	
Manufacturing	24	31%	19%
Petroleum	15	29	21
Transport and utilities	21	12	6*
Mining	15	9	2
Trade	5	7	10
Agriculture	12	5	4
Other**	8	6	38

*Transport only.
**Daily banking and finance.
Source: *Survey of Current Business,* June 1985, p. 30.

the firm of Suzuki and in Daewoo (an important Korean automaker), and has similar ownership interests in British and (reportedly) Italian companies.

This pattern of buying into the competition is by no means limited to General Motors. Walter Adams and James Brock cite this portion of a report of the International Trade Commission from 1980, before the joint venture movement attained its present importance:

> *In Australia . . . Renault assembles Ford vehicles and GM and Toyota produce engines for each other. While Renault supplies cabs for Ford H series trucks and Peugeot supplies diesel engines for Ford's European Granada, Ford has developed industrial diesels with Fiat. Volkswagen provides Chrysler with 4-cylinder engines, and Chrysler assembles Volkswagen products in Australia. . . .**

This interlinking of production makes it very hard to know what is "theirs" and what is "ours," or to separate a *company's* accounts from a *country's.* Even worse, it makes it difficult to tally up the national accounts in a meaningful way. What we count as an "import" may in fact be produced in whole or in part by the foreign branch of an American multinational. Thus part of the payments made abroad come back to American pockets—at least the pockets of the corporations. Similarly, our "exports" may contain a large amount of imported raw materials or parts. A portion of our export earnings will therefore go abroad rather than remaining at home. A new level of international economic activity has thus come into existence, arching over individual national economies—sometimes in concert with them and sometimes in opposition. Making sense of this new level of economic life is an important issue for economists, because until we have made sense of it, we cannot deal with it intelligently.

PROBLEMS FOR POLICYMAKERS

Multinationals have not only changed the face of international economic activity, they have also added considerably to the problem of controlling domestic economies. Assume that a country wants to slow down its economy through monetary policies designed to reduce plant and equipment spending. A restrictive monetary policy at home may be vitiated by the ability of a multinational to borrow *abroad* in order to finance investment at home. Conversely, a monetary policy designed to stimulate the home economy may end up in loans that increase production in someone else's economy. Thus the effectiveness of national economic policymaking is weakened. Moreover, it is not easy to suggest that monetary policies should be coordinated among countries, since the economic needs of different countries may not be the same: What is right for one country at a given time may be wrong for another.

HOST AND HOSTAGE

The jealous claims of nation-states who seek to retain national control over productive activity within their own borders and the powerful thrust of pan-national corporations for new markets in foreign territories introduces profound tensions into the political economics of multinational production. **On the one hand, the multinational is in a position to win hard bargains from the host country into which it seeks to**

---

*Walter Adams and James W. Brock, "The 'New Learning' and the Euthanasia of Anti Trust," *California Law Review,* October 1986, p. 1536, n. 100.

enter because the corporation is the main bearer of new technologies and management techniques that every nation seeks. Therefore, if one country—say France—refuses to give a would-be entrant the right to come in (and possibly to cause financial losses to its established firms), the multinational may well place its plants, with their precious economic cargo of productivity, in another country, leaving the recalcitrant nation the loser in the race for international growth.

On the other hand, the power is by no means entirely one-sided; for once a multinational *has* entered a foreign nation, it becomes a *hostage* of the host country. It is now bound by the laws of that country and may find itself forced to undertake activities that are "foreign." In Japan, for example, it is an unwritten law that workers engaged by giant corporations are *never* fired, but become permanent employees. Japan has been extremely reluctant to allow foreign capital to establish manufacturing operations on Japanese soil, to the great annoyance of foreign companies. But if, as now seems likely, Japan is opened to American and European capital, we can be sure that American or European corporations will be expected to behave in the Japanese way toward their employees. This will not be an easy course to follow, since these corporations are not likely to receive the special support the Japanese government gives to its own big firms.

Or take the problem of a multinational that is forced by a fall in demand to cut back the volume of its output. A decision made along strictly economic lines would lead it to close its least profitable plant. But this may bring very serious economic repercussions in the particular nation in which that plant is located—so serious that the government will threaten to take action if the plant is closed. What dictates shall the multinational then follow: those of standard business accounting or those of political accounting?

Or consider the multinational seeking to expand or to alter its operations in an underdeveloped country. This, too, may lead to friction, for as former Under Secretary of State George Ball has candidly asked, "How can a national government make an economic plan with any confidence if a board of directors meeting 5,000 miles away can, by altering its pattern of purchasing and production, affect in a major way the country's economic life?"

AN UNWRITTEN ENDING

There are as yet no answers to these questions. In all likelihood the tension between economic and political life will go unsatisfactorily resolved for a long time. The big corporations are certain to continue their multinational thrust. As global producers, they will be the main international carriers of efficiency and development, especially in the high-technology areas for which they seem to be the most effective form of organization. But if the power of the nation-state will be challenged by these international production units, it is not likely to be humbled by them. There are many things a nation can do that a corporation cannot, including, above all, creating the spirit of sacrifice necessary both for good purposes such as development and for evil ones such as war.

Perhaps all we can say at this stage of human development is that both nation-states and huge corporations are necessary, in that they seem to be the only ways in which we can organize ourselves to perform the arduous and sustained labor without which humanity would rapidly perish. Perhaps after the long age of capital accumulation has finally come to an end and sufficient capital is available to all peoples, we may be able to think seriously about dismantling the giant enterprise *and* the nation-state, both of which overpower the individual with their massive organized strength. However desirable that ultimate goal may be, in our time both state and corporation promise to be with us, and the tension between them will be part of the evolutionary drama of our period of history.

CHAPTER 17

Taxing
and Spending

A LOOK AHEAD

Taxing and government spending are usually thought to be macroeconomic problems—and of course they are when we consider the levels of taxing and spending in relation to the flows of gross national product. But there are also important microeconomic aspects to both of the great fiscal functions of government. Specifically in this chapter we look into:

1 The basic structure of the U.S. tax system.
2 The complicated question of tax incidence—who pays taxes.
3 The criteria for rational government expenditure.

All this should pave the way for some hard questions in the coming chapters.

THE STRUCTURE OF TAXATION

*T*axation in the United States is complex. It occurs on three basic levels of government—federal, state, and local—and through a myriad of entities and forms. There is a total of some 38,000 units of government in our country with taxing power. They tax sales, property, and income. There is no rhyme or reason to this system: It is simply the way our country grew up, and the way it is. That is partly why our system of taxation is so hard to justify or even to understand.

All in all, in 1987 federal, state, and local governments raised $1.46 trillion in taxes, or 32.2 percent of our gross national product. How does this figure compare with other industrial nations? Table 1 provides the answer: It is relatively low. Japan, with its heavier reliance on private pensions, manages to tax a smaller share of total income. Major European countries and Canada, with nationalized health care, take on a higher tax share than we do. For smaller, wealthy, social democratic states like Norway and Sweden, the tax share is highest of all.

One big difference, though, is the federal character of our tax system. Only 62 percent of all taxes raised in the United States in 1987 ($916 billion) went to the federal government. The remainder, $652 billion, was raised by states and localities. No other major industrial country has this degree of federalism and such diversity in tax raising.

Sources of Revenue

Moreover, the sources of taxation are diverse. The principal tax source of the federal government is the *personal income tax,* in existence since 1913. The personal income tax contributed $404 billion to the federal coffers in 1987, or nearly half of the total. Personal taxes (including personal property taxes) also contributed about one-quarter of their tax revenues to state and local governments in 1985.

The second largest source of tax revenue for the federal government—and the most rapidly growing in recent years—is *contributions for social insurance,* primarily social security, unemployment insurance, and Medicare. Social security is levied on payrolls—half on the employer, half on the employee; Unemployment insurance is levied on employers, and Medicare on individuals over age 65. Revenues go only toward the payment of retirement, health care, and unemployment insurance benefits. These sources contributed $348 billion to federal revenues in 1987, over a third of the total. State and local governments, in contrast, got only about one-fifteenth of their taxes from this source.

So far, we have accounted for over four-fifths of federal government revenues, but only for a third of state and local tax income. Where does the rest come from? We know the answer: from taxes on corporate income and on business sales, officially designated as *corporate profits taxes* and *indirect business taxes.*

Corporate profits taxes have been declining in relative importance in recent years. In 1960, for example, they contributed nearly a quarter of all federal revenues; by 1987, they were down to approximately a tenth. Corporate profits

TABLE 1
Taxes as Percent of GDP
Note that the United States ranks low in comparative terms. (Also note that GDP—gross domestic product—yields a smaller ratio than GNP. The rank order is the same.)

Country	Current Receipts
Japan	30.4%
United States	32.2
Canada	39.0
United Kingdom	42.5
Germany	45.2
Italy	45.3
Austria	46.6
France	47.0
Norway	52.6
Denmark	53.1
Sweden (1982)	59.3

Source: OECD Historical Statistics, p. 64. Data are for 1983 except where noted.

taxes are also a minor component—less than 4 percent—of state and local tax revenue. Figure 1 shows these trends.

That leaves "indirect business taxes"—primarily the city and state sales taxes that you pay on virtually everything you buy, unless you happen to live in one of the very few states that has managed to avoid adopting a sales tax. Federal excise taxes, such as the telephone tax, and taxes on cigarettes and alcohol account for the remaining tenth of federal revenues. But this source is vastly more important to the state and local sector, accounting for $313 billion in revenue in 1987, or approximately half of the grand total.

TAX INCIDENCE

Regressive, Progressive, and Proportional

What is a fair tax? As with so many questions that affect policy, there is no economic criterion for fair or unfair. But there are some objective measures that enable us to talk about the question more intelligently.

We start by recognizing that all taxes can be classified into three different kinds by their incidence—that is, by analyzing who pays them. Regressive taxes bear more heavily, in percentage terms, on low incomes than high ones: A highway toll, for example, is regressive because 50 cents is a bigger part of a poor driver's income than of a rich driver's. Proportional taxes bear equally on all income groups. Any tax that takes a fixed percent of all incomes—say 25 percent—would be a proportional tax. And a progressive tax is a tax that takes a larger bite—a larger percentage as well as a larger amount—as income rises.

There are no economic or even moral rules that enable us to say that one category of taxes is more fair than another. Yet there is no doubt that most economists, politicians, and members of the public do not openly admire regressive

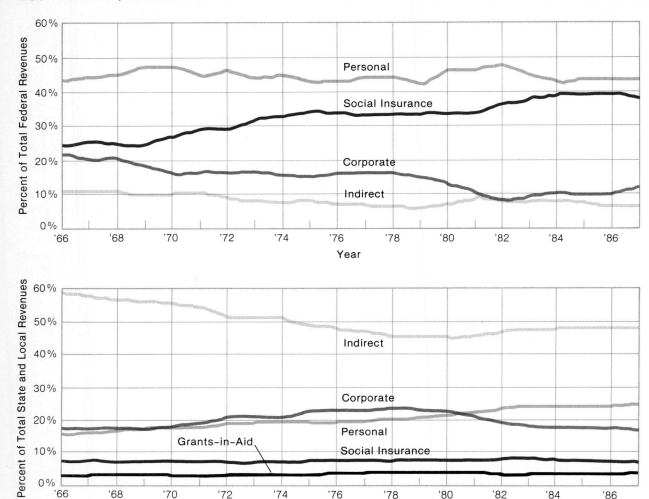

FIGURE 1
Tax Trends
This figure provides the basic data on federal and state and local tax trends over the past
twenty-five years. Note the rise in social insurance and the fall in corporate income taxes at
the federal level.

taxes. Sometimes we favor regressive revenue measures, such as lotteries, which tend to bear more heavily on the poor than the rich, but then we find ways of rationalizing our decision, such as the popularity of such measures or their convenience. On the whole, everyone favors proportional taxes or mildly progressive ones. But when progressivity goes "too far"—when very successful entrepreneurs are penalized by taxes that virtually wipe out all their incomes—we tend to call that unfair.

By these criteria, are our taxes fair or unfair? The answer depends, of course, on their incidence; and as we shall see, it is surprisingly difficult to determine what that incidence is. To take the most simple-looking case, suppose that the state levies a 5 percent sales tax on all commodities sold at retail. Who pays such a tax? The question seems nonsensical. Doesn't the consumer pay the tax? Not all of it. When the state levies a sales tax, the cost of commodities rises. This is the same thing as an upward shift to the supply curve, as we see in Figure 2. As a result, price rises from P_1 to P_2.

Now, who has paid the tax? The consumer has paid some, but not all. He pays the rise in price $P_2 - P_1$, and he also loses the utilities of the goods he can no longer buy, $Q_1 - Q_2$. But the producer has also paid some of the tax—the amount $P_1 - P_3$, and he has also suffered a loss in revenues because his sales have dropped.

And even this is not an end to the matter. Because the producer's income has fallen, his demand for factors has dropped from D_1 to D_2 (see Figure 3). Hence the prices of the factors and the quantities employed will fall. So *factors, too, bear part of the tax.* In Figure 3 factors of production suffer a cutback in price from L to M and a reduction in quantities employed from X to Y. Hence their incomes will fall from $OL \times OX$ to $OM \times OY$.

So the sales tax is actually shared by consumers, producers, and factors of production. The retail storekeeper, who actually makes out the check to the government, and the consumer, who pays his pennies of sales tax, are very likely not the sole bearers of the tax.

Product Market

FIGURE 2
Incidence of Sales Taxes
Sales tax per unit is $P_2 - P_3$. The consumer pays part, $P_2 - P_1$, and the producer part, $P_1 - P_3$. The consumer also suffers a fall in consumption from Q_1 to Q_2, and the producer a fall in sales of like amount. Both consumer and producer bear some of the tax.

Effects of Elasticity

How much of the tax will the consumer bear? That depends on the elasticity of demand for the product. If demand is very inelastic, the storekeeper will mark up items by the amount of the sales tax and will sell as many items as before. In that case, the consumer will pay it all, and the retailer or seller will simply act as the collection agency for the government, as Figure 4 shows.

More likely, when a sales tax is imposed, sellers will shave profit margins to avoid a serious loss of volume. They will mark up price by less than the tax and make up the difference out of profits. Sellers and consumers both will then bear the tax.

Complexity of Incidence

Are sales taxes fair or unfair? Perhaps we can now see how difficult it is to answer the question. Even in what seems to be a clear case we have to know two things:

1. **How much of the tax is shifted "forward" to the consumer, how much is absorbed by the seller or producer, and how much is shifted backward to the factors of production? That requires a knowledge of elasticities of demand and supply we often do not possess.**

2. **To determine how much of a sales tax is paid by any one person, we also have to know the extent to which that individual is a consumer, a producer, or a factor. Think about the impact of a 5-cent tax per pack of**

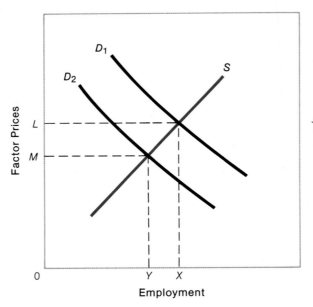

FIGURE 3
Impact of Sales Tax on Factors
Factors also bear some of the tax because a fall in the producer's revenues shifts his demand curve leftward. Factor income falls from OX times OL to OY times OM.

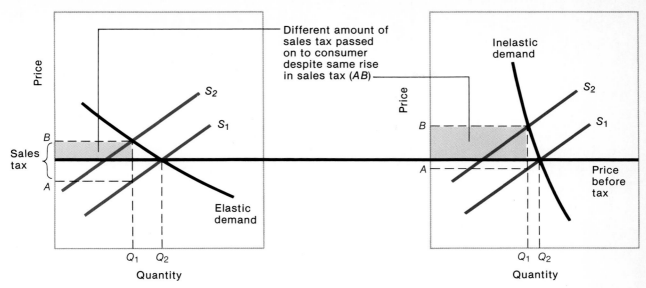

FIGURE 4
Effect of Elasticity on Tax Incidence for Consumers
Elasticity again makes all the difference. Compare the amount of tax that can be passed along to the consumer in the two cases above. Both goods bear the same sales tax. In the case on the left, demand is elastic, and therefore consumers find substitutes. Quantity sold falls markedly, and the actual rise in price—the amount of the sales tax passed on to the consumer—is only about half the sales tax. Observe how the inelastic demand curve on the right allows a much larger proportion of the tax to be shifted forward.

cigarettes on a tobacconist who does not smoke but who owns 10 shares of American Tobacco. Such are the difficulties of coming to clear-cut pronouncements about tax incidence.

Regressivity of Sales Taxes

Nonetheless, we can venture one generalization. **A sales tax on necessities is sure to be passed on to the consumer to a much greater extent than one on luxuries.** This is because the demand curve for necessities is, by definition, less elastic than the demand curve for luxuries. Most necessities, such as food, bulk larger in the budgets of low-income families than in those of high-income families. For example, food costs may absorb about 30 percent of a $12,000 family budget, in contrast with about 20 percent of a $25,000 budget. Therefore sales taxes on necessities are regressive.

Does this mean that a sales tax on luxuries is progressive? Not necessarily. Because the demand for luxuries is likely to be elastic, the sales tax on luxuries may not be shifted forward, but will fall instead on the yacht builder, the furrier, the Cadillac maker, and their employees—who may not be wealthy at all!

PERSONAL INCOME TAXES

Progressivity of Income Taxes

The income taxes levied by federal, state, or local (usually municipal) authorities are generally progressive in their structure. That is, the rate of taxes rises as income rises. The federal income tax, as we write these words, begins at 15 percent and increases to 33 percent at a taxable income of $43,151 for a single taxpayer. It then falls again, to 28 percent, on incomes over $89,560—a quirk in the tax structure that is definitely *not* progressive! Table 2 shows the tax rates for married and single taxpayers in various brackets.

There is, however, a great deal of difference between rates on paper and actual income taxes paid by families. This is because we do not pay taxes on our total or gross income, but on our taxable incomes. Taxable incomes are our gross incomes less various exemptions and deductions permitted by law. For example, we are allowed to deduct $1,950 for each dependent (including ourselves) in figuring our income tax. We deduct interest that we pay on our home mortgages. We can deduct all state and local taxes from our federal income tax. We can take off charitable contributions, legitimate business expenses, and a long list of other items.*

Effect of Deductions

Deductions affect the incidence of the income tax structure in two ways. In the first place, they often create "horizontal" inequities. Two families or individuals with identical incomes may pay very different taxes because one can use a deduction and another cannot. For years, owners of oil properties enjoyed a deduction known as a depletion allowance. It enabled them to reduce their taxable income from oil by as much as a third below the actual oil income. Owners of state and local bonds have for years enjoyed the privilege of not paying any federal tax on the interest from these bonds.

Thus two households, side by side in identical houses, enjoying identical incomes, may pay hugely different taxes. Because of deduction loopholes, a few—actually a very few—wealthy people escape taxation entirely.

In the second place, deductions greatly lessen the progressivity of taxes. Deductions have this antiprogressive effect because a deduction is worth much more to a high-income family than to a low-income one. Example: charitable donations. A rich family, whose marginal tax bracket is 28 percent, gives away $100. As a result, its pretax income is reduced by $100, but its tax is reduced by

---

*And what is a legitimate business expense? The cost of commuting to work? No. The money you lay out for lunch? No. The bill you pay for your client's lunch *plus* your own lunch? Yes—at least, 80 percent of it. The rules and regulations for determining what is and what is not "deductible" fill literally thousands of pages. They constitute a basis for the very comfortable living made by tax accountants and tax lawyers—professionals who owe their incomes largely to the interpretation of, and legal steermanship through, the Byzantine tax code of the United States.

$28. The net cost of the $100 gift is therefore $72 in reduced after-tax spendable income. A poorer family, whose marginal tax bracket is 15 percent, also gives away $100. It thereby saves a tax of $15. Its spendable, after-tax income is reduced by $85. Not only is this loss of spendable income larger in *absolute* terms than for the richer family, but it is certainly larger as a percentage of the poor family's total income.

Do Taxes Impinge on Effort?

Personal income taxes—particularly the high marginal rates on high incomes that prevailed until the mid-1980s—have come under intense attack in recent years. Does this reflect good economics? We look into the details of this attack again in Chapter 20; here we simply set down the outlines of the critics' case.

The essence of the argument has been that high tax rates on *income* are the equivalent of high tax rates on *effort*. Progressive income taxes, it is claimed, lessen the marginal utility of additional work because they take away an increasing proportion of the after-tax income that can be derived from it. Therefore they move those subject to high taxes up the classical supply curve of labor, encouraging the wealthy, in effect, to spend their time by the pool and on the golf course rather than in productive effort.

Studies—both before and after the tax reductions of 1981—have failed to support this "supply-side" case. Neither hours worked nor intensity of effort seems to respond to changes in marginal tax rates. And the reasons are easy to understand.

First, a change in taxes affects more than the relative value of labor as against leisure: It also affects *income*. After a tax cut, a wealthy person has more after-tax income than before, and this increase in wealth may induce him or her to work less, even though the after-tax return *from working* has risen.

Second, for many of the truly wealthy, there never was a strong connection between hours worked and income. Top-bracket income comes more from

TABLE 2
Tax Rates
The Tax Reform Act of 1986 produced the simplified structure of marginal rates shown here. Notice that the rate structure is not uniformly progressive: families in the highest-income categories pay a lower rate on their last dollar earned than do moderate-upper-income earners.

Adjusted Income (Married Taxpayers)	Marginal Federal Income Tax Rates
0–$29,750	15%
$29,751–71,900	28%
$71,901–149,250	33%
above 149,250	28%

(Single Taxpayers)	
0–$17,850	15%
$17,851–43,150	28%
$43,151–89,560	33%
Above $89,560	28%

nonwork—capital gains, interest and dividends, and other property income—than from active economic effort. Property income is not at all affected by the number of hours put in at the office, so lowering taxes on *income* (not just on salaries) offers no spur to work.

Turning the coin over, we find that lowering marginal tax rates also has little effect on factory or service workers generally because they do not control the number of hours they work. Work schedules are largely set by managers, not by the work force. In addition, whatever incentive might result from higher take-home pay owing to an income tax reduction is offset, under the 1981 tax changes, by increases in social security taxes on payrolls.

Income taxes may, however, change income tax payment habits. Unlike most other forms of taxation, the income tax demands a huge degree of voluntary taxpayer cooperation. High tax rates, accompanied by widespread distrust of the uses to which tax revenue is put, may foster tax evasion or lead taxpayers to resort to methods of exchange that evade the tax collector's notice. A lawyer will offer free advice to a carpenter in exchange for a weekend's work on the lawyer's garage. A housepainter will submit two estimates: a high one if the transaction is to be reported, a low one if it is to be under-the-table. At the top of the income ladder, a commodity speculator will work overtime on such devices as butterfly straddles to show paper losses each year and avoid the capital gains tax. At the bottom end, a housekeeper will take the weekly payment in cash, and not insist that the employer make the mandatory contribution to the social security system.

SOCIAL SECURITY TAXES

Social security taxes pose another problem. There is no question who pays them. They reduce the income of the wage earner and the employer, who may or may not be able to pass forward his share of the tax. The more interesting question is whether this tax is regressive.

At first glance there is no doubt in the matter. Social security taxes today take 15.02 percent of all wages, half paid by a reduction in the salary check, the other half by the employer. This percentage is the same on all taxed wages, so that the tax seems quite proportional. But there is no tax levied above an established level ($43,800 in 1987), so that high wage earners pay smaller proportions of their earnings. In addition, although social security taxes are taken from even the lowest earned income, property income of any kind—interest, rent, dividends, or royalties—is exempt from social security. Thus, measured against total income, the social security levy is regressive.

Yet in the end, matters are not quite that simple. The payout formula for social security is set to give low-income earners more dollars of benefit per dollar paid in than high earners. **Therefore, if we offset the regressive tax with the progressive payment schedule, the net impact of social security becomes progressive.**

The difficulty is that social security taxes are paid at one stage in an individual's life cycle and the benefits are received at another, later stage. It is not easy to compare the costs and benefits of such *intertemporal transfers* when they are separated by long periods of time. This problem is worsened because the ratio between the number of persons working (and paying tax) and those not working (and receiving benefits) is changing in favor of the retired population. An ever-larger proportion of our population is living on social security, at much higher benefit levels than formerly; and this trend will certainly continue.

CORPORATE INCOME TAXES

Let us next take a look at the corporate income tax, no longer a prime source of funds for the federal government.

Who pays a corporation's income tax? Few questions are more uncertain. Some economists think the corporate income tax is essentially a sales tax, borne partly by consumers, partly by the business (in the form of reduced income), partly by the factors of production who suffer a loss in earnings. Others think it is a tax on capital, serving to reduce the flow of capital into the corporate sector. Still others believe that its impact cannot be clearly observed because most corporate income taxes are paid by big oligopolistic companies, who may use tax increases as an excuse to raise prices in their industry, laying the blame for this on "the government." Some economists even go so far as to say that one of the virtues of the corporate tax is that since no one can state with certainty who pays it, it serves as an excellent way for the government to raise money without clearly imposing a tax on anyone!

Double Taxation

Many critics claim that corporate taxes are unfair because they tax the owners of corporations twice on the income their companies have earned. They are taxed once when the corporation pays income taxes to the government—money that would otherwise belong to the shareowner. And they are taxed again when personal income taxes are collected on the dividends received by shareholders.

Many who favor progressive taxes would protest the abolition of the corporate income tax would aid the rich. Actually, if corporate income taxes were abolished and all corporate earnings were distributed to shareowners, the bite on wealthy stockholders might well be greater, not smaller, than today!

PROPERTY TAXES

Property taxes are very important sources of revenue for states and localities—and hot political items since Proposition 13 put a ceiling on them in California in 1976, and Massachusetts followed suit with Proposition 2½ in 1980. One difficulty with property taxes is that inflation can raise the assessed value of real estate much more

MAKING MONEY OUT OF TAXES

Whether or not corporation income taxes are a useful means of raising revenues, they are certainly an effective way of *making* money for those corporations able to take advantage of the provisions of the tax code that allow for various kinds of write-offs, shelters, and other perfectly legal avenues of tax avoidance.

In 1984, for example, the 275 biggest corporate money-makers paid about 15 percent of their net income to the federal government—not the 46 percent that the tax code presumably levied. Of these companies, 129 paid no taxes or received tax rebates, although their profits amounted to $66.5 billion. Of this group, 9 companies paid no taxes at all for the years 1981–84. For example, the Boeing Corporation received rebates during this period of $285 million, although its reported income came to over $2 billion. General Electric received tax rebates of $98 million over the period, although its income came to $9,577 million. In all, the 9 companies with the biggest rebates earned $25.1 billion *before* federal income tax—and an additional $1.4 billion *after* taxes!

Donald Regan, at that time Secretary of the Treasury, reports that he persuaded President Reagan to support his tax reform proposals by explaining that the White House secretaries paid more income taxes than a long list of top corporations *combined*. Since tax reform, corporate income tax collections have risen substantially—up by 30 percent in 1987 over 1986 alone. But they remain less than 10 percent of federal receipts, compared with nearly 16 percent in 1960.

Source: Data from *Corporate Taxpayers and Corporate Freeloaders* (Washington, DC: Citizens for Tax Justice, August 1985).

rapidly than it increases the income of homeowners. What happened in California was that owners found themselves unable to meet taxes that were mounting steadily higher. To be sure, homeowners could sell their houses at a profit. But to buy a new house cost just as much, and did not get around the problem of rising real estate taxes.

Are property taxes always paid by homeowners? Not when they are levied on an owner who rents his property. Then the taxes are usually passed along as higher rents. Because rent payments are a more important budget item for low-income families than for high-income families, these tax-induced rent raises are regressive in their impact. For slumdwellers who cannot afford to move, they may be terribly high.

In the case of a landlord, property taxes are sometimes progressive, not regressive. Suppose property taxes are $250,000 per year on a building whose rentals yield $1 million a year. Net earnings are therefore $750,000. Like any capital asset, the building is worth a capital sum that will yield $750,000 at the going rate of return for similar properties. At 10 percent, it will be worth $7,500,000. If property taxes are now raised and cannot be passed along, the capitalized value of the building will fall. Even though the taxes may be passed forward to renters, the heaviest cost will fall on the owner of the building whose capital has been diminished.

So it is not altogether clear that property taxes are as regressive as they are thought to be. They are regressive only if we estimate their incidence on incomes. If we include their impact on wealth, they can be a very progressive form of taxation!

TOTAL INCIDENCE

Can we sum up total tax incidence in our tax system? It must be clear that it is difficult to do so for two reasons. First, the horizontal variances are so great that average figures are often very little guide to reality. Second, incidence depends on elasticities of supply and demand that are often unknown to us.

The actual incidence of taxation therefore remains a matter for conjecture. We should note, however, that the uncertainties relate to the very lowest and highest incomes. Generally, state and local taxes are regressive, and federal taxes are progressive—the two balancing each other out to produce an overall system that is roughly proportional.

Is this overall system fair? If by fairness we mean that our tax incidence should be mildly progressive, the answer is mixed. Some elements of the system, such as social security payroll taxation, are not fair in this sense. Other elements, such as the federal income tax, are fairer. Still others, such as the property tax, are sometimes fair and sometimes not.

To make things even more complicated, we must remember that the taxes people pay depend very much on where they live. There are, as we mentioned at the beginning of this chapter, some 38,000 taxing authorities in the United States. States, municipalities, water districts, school districts, transportation authorities, and a host of other agencies can impose public charges, fees, and taxes. The structure (and fairness) of one's tax situation is very much determined by accidents of geography.

Tax Reform

The tax system of the United States has been changing rapidly since the Reagan administration took power in 1981. At that time, the highest marginal rate on the personal income tax was 70 percent! President Reagan was determined to bring those marginal rates down, partly because he was persuaded by the "supply-side" arguments we reviewed briefly on page 303.

The Economic Recovery Tax Act of 1981 began the process, reducing the top income tax rate to 50 percent and phasing in three years of reductions in the effective tax burdens faced by most taxpayers, weighted to favor particularly those with high incomes. In addition, ERTA made sharp cuts in corporate income taxation, which fell from 9.9 to 6.3 percent of federal tax receipts from 1980 to 1982.

But ERTA created a big problem: federal budget deficits that ballooned up to $200 billion and were in danger of spinning out of control. As a result, the agenda in Congress changed, and in 1982 and 1984 major new laws increasing taxes were enacted.

The big challenge came in 1986. All of the relatively easy repairs to the federal revenue structure had by that time been made, such as elimination of a costly program to make additions to personal savings exempt from income taxation. Tax reformers and revenue raisers then faced the hard political economy of our tax system, which lay in the existence of hundreds of well-defended exemptions, deductions, and loopholes. The problem was this: Each special provision was comparatively small, so that to close it would mean a saving of only a few dollars for most taxpayers. Therefore most taxpayers could work up little enthusiasm for specific loophole-closing reforms. On the other hand, each beneficiary of loopholes gained enormously by them, and these people were therefore prepared to mount all-out campaigns in their defense. That is why lobbying for individual tax breaks is always intense, while lobbying against them is weak.

Nevertheless the tax reformers won. They did so by mobilizing their efforts against *all* of the loopholes in the tax structure at the same time. That way, the political sacrifice would be equally shared, and no one politician could be blamed for failing to defend any one particular special interest. This tactic, an ingenious application of game theory to congressional politics, proved successful. With comprehensive reform, the reformers were able to offer a further reduction in top marginal tax rates—to 33 percent, as we have seen—and that persuaded President Reagan to lend his authority to the campaign. Tax reform became law in 1986, greatly reducing the special provisions of the personal income tax and increasing the effective bite of corporate income taxes.

We have seen that tax reform further reduced marginal income tax rates. Did it also make the income tax less progressive than it had been before? The answer, surprisingly, is that it did not. *Effective* tax burdens were probably more progressively distributed after tax reform than before, despite the lower marginal rates. A first reason for this is that loophole closing reclaimed more upper-income revenue for the government than rate reductions lost. A second reason is that the new tax structure incorporated a more generous personal exemption. Thus 6 million people whose total incomes place them below the poverty line were taken off the income tax rolls altogether, and the effective income tax rates on the working poor fell.

PUBLIC SPENDING

Taxing is, of course, only half the government's activity. The other half is spending. Is government spending wasteful? Many people think so. But how can we answer such a question analytically? One way is to reflect on how we would decide if *private* expenditure were wasteful. But notice: **We do not judge whether a firm's output is wasteful!** If there is a demand for the product, that is presumed to be sufficient justification for its existence. Outputs may be illegal if they are forbidden by government, but economists do not speak of "wasteful" outputs as long as there is a market for them.

The public sector is intrinsically different from the private sector. With minor exceptions it does not sell its output and therefore cannot justify it by pointing to market demand. Moreover, as we have seen, much public output consists of public goods, such as defense, from which no individual can be excluded, even if he or she did not contribute to their cost. For such goods, there is no conceivable market test to determine whether the "right" level of output has been attained. In the absence of such a test, we tend to call "wasteful" all government spending we do not approve of.

Voting vs. Spending— The Public Choice Perspective

How do we determine, in the absence of a market, whether a program should be undertaken in the first place? The answer, as we know, is through the representative political process, through voting. We vote for or against the general economic programs of candidates or parties. Within Congress or the state legislatures, our representatives vote again. The voting process is the subject of intense efforts to influence its outcome: leadership (or lack of it) provided by the President and his administration, lobbying, pressure from constituents, log-rolling deals of many sorts. From this pulling and hauling emerges the national economic budget with its appropriations for different public purposes, a process duplicated at state and local levels.

Some economists argue that this process leads to an inherent bias in favor of increasing expenditures. The reason is that each proposed expenditure is touted in terms of the specific benefits it will create. This rallies a group of intense supporters. Since the increased expenditure means only a small average increase in taxes, it will not result in an equally vociferous lobby of opponents. The presence of staunch supporters and the absence of strong objectors for specific expenditures thus tips the scales in favor of raising, not lowering, total expenditures, according to the argument of the "public choice" school.

But if this were so, why wouldn't total expenditures rise without limit? Why have federal purchases in relation to GNP remained so stable over the years? The answer is that there are *many competing interests, each seeking a larger share of federal spending at any given time.* In a political process, albeit with much fuss and rhetoric, these interests strive for and eventually reach a workable bargain with each other over the relative shares each will receive. While such an implicit bargain lasts, no single interest can achieve a disproportionate increase in spending for its pet purpose without exciting the intense opposition of all the others. Only something like a war, or a major reform movement, is likely to disrupt this bargain. Thus total spending tends to rise, but at a fairly slow rate, restrained by the competition of many different interests for what all perceive to be a limited total spending pie.

Is Spending "Rational"?

There is nothing inherently "rational" about the public allocation of resources so achieved. But it is not "irrational" either. Perhaps the most that can be said is that our public expenditure decision-making process is legitimated by the support most of us give to our political system. We recognize that without some orderly, open mechanism—however imperfect—to settle the many nonmarket resource-allocation decisions and conflicts that we face, we would be much worse off—less democratic and less free—than we are. **Economic analysis alone can give us no ultimately correct division between public and private expenditure.**

COST-BENEFIT ANALYSIS

Still, at the level of the individual public project, we are not helpless. We do have certain analytical tools at our disposal. The most important of these is known as **cost-benefit analysis.**

Calculating Costs and Benefits

Because a public expenditure is rarely planned to make money, a legislator must try to estimate the public benefits that will flow from the expenditure as an offset against its cost. These benefits may be fairly easy to calculate, as when a government agency plans to build a hospital and estimates what a comparable private hospital might earn. Even if the public hospital provides its services free, these services are presumably worth approximately that much to the public, since it has been relieved of expenditures it would otherwise have made at a private facility.

But often the benefits of a project are exceedingly difficult to calculate. How can we estimate the benefits of a new road? By the tolls that might be collected? What about the indirect benefits gained by townspeople who are now served more rapidly and efficiently? What about improvements in the landscape if billboards are banned?

There is no perfectly objective way of adding up all the benefits of a public project. We can make more or less sophisticated guesses and estimates, but these estimates always contain a large element of uncertainty. We can easily overestimate—or underestimate—the benefit of a project.

Cost Effectiveness

Once a project is decided on—a road, a school, a training program—considerations of cost effectiveness are exactly the same as they are in a factory, a private house, or any other private venture.

The principle is the use of the most economical combination of inputs to achieve a given output. Here "wastefulness" has the same definition it has in the private sector. It is certainly not easy to translate principles of efficiency, as an economist describes them, into the complex specifications of a construction job. But the aim is in no way different between the public and private sectors.

Sunk Costs

Many public projects are large, uncertain, one-of-a-kind ventures whose costs and benefits cannot be accurately forecasted. Often, as work goes forward, new difficulties and new costs come to light. The concept of benefit-cost analysis often has to be applied at several stages in such a public project. This raises the question of how one should treat sunk costs—expenditures that have been made in the past and that cannot be undone.

Here, too, there is a parallel between public and private efficiencies. Suppose that you have a dam or a factory half built. A decision must be made whether to continue with the project or abandon it. At this point neither the public legislator nor the private entrepreneur should go back and review whether the project should have been started in the first place. The money that has been spent on it is irretrievably lost, both to the public and to the private enterprise. The only relevant question is whether the *remaining cost* will be justified by the benefits or revenues that are expected ultimately to accrue.

Although a private firm may regret having decided to start up a new branch, an intelligent decision on going through with the project will measure only the remaining costs against the expected revenues. A legislator may rue having voted for a public project, but he will intelligently vote to complete it if the remaining costs will be justified by the total ensuing benefits.

"Throwing Good Money after Bad"

In other words, **all sunk costs are irrelevant in making decisions about future actions.** Rather, they *should be* irrelevant. In fact, it is very difficult for decision makers, public or private, to understand that costs incurred in the past are now beyond recall and can be recouped, in part if not in full, only by continuing with a project even though the total undertaking is now deemed to be a losing proposition. The impulse is to stop a project once it has been decided that the initial decision was in error. The common phrases "don't throw good money after bad" and "cut your losses" are heard, even though, *at the margin,* the investment would be highly profitable (relative to the investment as a whole).

It only makes sense to cancel a project if the *remaining* costs are greater than the *total* benefits. Of course, such a situation will arise only when the original cost-benefit analysis was badly in error, or if circumstances have changed dramatically since the project was begun. In real life, where specialists often dispute each other's estimates of costs and valuation of benefits, such cancellation decisions are often highly controversial.

THE MARKET IN A FINAL RETROSPECT

This seems a good place to make a final assessment of the wastefulness with which resources are allocated through votes and through spending. Many people look askance at how the public sector allocates its resources. No one needs to be reminded of innumerable scandals having to do with influence peddling or abuse of the public trust by members of federal or state legislatures.

What we should remember, however, is that the voting process is a substitute rationing mechanism. Where one-dollar-one-vote does not work, or is deemed an improper rationing mechanism, a democratic society must choose one-person-one-vote.

The abuses of the voting mechanism may be many, and its problems are assuredly difficult. Nonetheless, voting is the way a democracy rations its public output, just as spending is the way a market system rations its private output. Before we wax too indignant about the shortcomings of the political process, pointing to the waste that accompanies government programs, etc., etc., we should remind ourselves of the inequities that accompany private rationing decisions.

The market mechanism has enormous strengths, but it is certainly not perfect. In fact, we know that it must be imperfect. There are problems the market cannot cope with at all. Moreover, those it does handle reveal the pervasive bias of a voting system in which individuals are measured by their incomes, not by any other gauge of their human value.

Thus all market systems must have public counterparts and complements. It is impossible to have an economic system in which government would play no role whatsoever. The exercise of the political will that is so much (and so properly) distrusted is also essential for social survival. In this struggle between the authority of politics and that of the market lies a central issue, not merely of microeconomics, but also of modern economic society itself.

LOOKING BACK

KEY CONCEPTS

The U.S. tax system is complex.

1 The United States has a diverse federalized tax structure. Personal income taxes and payroll taxes for social insurance are the most important federal tax sources. Sales taxes are the most important state and local tax sources, with personal taxes on incomes and property a distant second. Corporate profits taxes contribute a declining share of federal revenue.

Incidence of taxation is important for equity. Incidence depends heavily on elasticity, but is hard to determine.

2 The key question, from the point of view of fairness or equity, concerns the incidence of taxation—who actually pays a given tax. Most Americans favor proportional or mildly progressive taxes. But most taxes are shifted forward or backward—to the consumer or to the factors of production. The amount of shifting depends very

considerably on the elasticity of the demand curve or supply curves in the product or factor markets. Actual incidence is often very difficult to determine.

Regressive taxes hit low incomes hardest. Sales taxes are such a tax. Graduated income taxes are progressive, hitting upper-income groups proportionately harder than lower, but loopholes greatly lessen this effect.

3 Sales taxes tend to be regressive—to bear more heavily on lower incomes than higher ones. Individual income taxes tend to be progressive, although deductions and loopholes greatly lower the actual (as opposed to the scheduled) degree of progressivity. Corporate income taxes are so complex in their incidence that we do not know whether they are passed forward or backward, or are progressive or regressive. Social security taxes are very regressive, because they reach a ceiling on high incomes, but the payout formula makes up for this regressivity. Property taxes can be regressive when they are passed along as higher rentals, but they can also be progressive when they result in lower capitalized values.

The total tax system has large horizontal inequities.

4 The overall incidence of the total tax system is unclear. This is especially true because there is such a multiplicity of tax systems in the United States. There is no doubt that substantial horizontal inequities exist and that it is very hard to get rid of them.

Waste as an economic concept involves efficiency, not the justification of output.

5 Waste is an important economic idea. In microeconomics it describes the criteria for efficiency, but it does not refer to the justification for output. In the public sphere it often describes our judgment about the worthwhileness of public efforts, as well as their efficiency.

Allocation problems of voting: asymmetry of spending and taxing.

6 We allocate public funds among various purposes by voting, not by market decisions. Voting has many problems as an allocation mechanism. One is that we tend to vote for programs that increase our incomes, but not for programs that increase others' incomes. This leads to an asymmetry between spending and taxing. It is easier to raise budgets by stressing particular advantages, which rallies strong supporters, than to cut them, which spreads benefits diffusely and wins no strong support.

Cost-benefit considerations should ignore sunk costs.

7 Expenditures should be justified by weighing benefits against costs. This is often difficult to do, because sunk costs, although irrelevant to a rational decision, are hard to ignore.

Public and private sectors are both necessary.

8 It is impossible to have an economy without a public sector—that is, without taxation and government expenditure. The public sector has many problems—but it must not be forgotten that the private sector also has its allocational difficulties. This is an inescapable problem of modern society.

ECONOMIC VOCABULARY

QUESTIONS

1. Can you think of arguments that would incline you in favor of a regressive tax system? How about encouraging the rate of saving? Or the idea that those who are richer deserve to be given preference because they have made a larger contribution to society?

2. Assume a payroll tax is levied in all firms. Using supply and demand curves, show who might bear such a tax if the demand for factors was very price-elastic.

3. Suppose family A has $1 million in stocks and bonds and an income of $35,000. Family B has no property but an earned income of the same amount. How would you decide which tax system would yield horizontal equity for the two families? For example, would corporate income taxes affect each alike? Straight income taxes? Capital gains taxes? Is horizontal equity possible when the source of income differs, even though the amount is the same?

4. Suppose there were a flat tax of 20 percent on all corporate income. How would you go about determining whether a business's expenses were a legitimate deduction from its gross income? Assume that no entertainment expenses were allowed for any business. Would this result in horizontal inequities in different businesses? Would this be sufficient argument not to press for this tax change?

5. A congressional committee is considering the construction of a moving sidewalk in Washington, D.C. It is estimated to cost $1 billion, and will give benefits of an estimated $1.5 billion. After six months of work, $1 billion has been spent and the remaining costs are estimated to be $600 million. Should you throw "good money after bad" or discontinue the project? What are the project's opportunity costs and sunk costs?

AN EXTRA WORD ABOUT

Fair Taxation

Two thousand years ago, in Book One of *The Republic,* Plato wrote, "When there is an income tax, the just man will pay more and the unjust less on the same amount of income." Americans today widely agree with Plato's maxim. The income tax, that annual headache, has lost much of its moral authority, and despite the real successes of tax reform in 1986, that authority has not been regained.

What would constitute a good system of taxation? Are there broad principles around which reasonable people can agree? In a study for the Joint Economic Committee, economist William Buechner set forth seven such criteria, with which we are broadly sympathetic.*

1. Revenues.   First, and perhaps foremost, a tax system should have the potential to raise revenue adequate to cover most of the expenditures of government in normal times. Since 1981, our tax system has failed to meet this objective by a wide margin; hence a good tax law must include measures that increase revenue, or at least make it politically easier to raise revenues after the reforms are in place.

2. Stabilization.   A good tax system should help to stabilize demand in the economy, allowing tax burdens to fall sharply in recessions but causing them to rise sharply when inflation is the threat. Progressivity improves the stabilizing properties of the tax system; as the income tax has become less progressive in recent years, it has also become less stabilizing. Indexation of tax rates to inflation, enacted in 1981, also has destabilizing effects since it reduces tax rates by increasing amounts as inflation rises—putting fuel rather than water on the inflationary fires.

3. Fairness.   There are two basic criteria of fairness or equity in taxation: *horizontal equity,* meaning that those with nearly equal incomes pay a nearly equal tax; and *vertical equity,* or progressivity, meaning that those with higher incomes pay a higher proportionate tax.

Despite its many faults, the income tax that we have been paying during the last decade has been a broadly progressive tax, as we may recall from Table 2 in the chapter. It is when we come to the problem of horizontal equity that problems emerge. Buechner writes:

> *The main source of tax inequity is the long list of preferences that are not available to all taxpayers on even terms. The Joint Committee on Taxation lists 108 deductions, credits, exemptions, and other preferences in the tax code, including those affecting corporations, that can be used to shelter income from taxes. This is*

*Tax Reform, A Staff Study Prepared for the Use of the Subcommittee on Economic Goals and Intergovernmental Policy of the Joint Economic Committee, Congress of the United States (Washington, DC: GPO, November 29, 1984).

double the number listed in 1970. Many tax preferences, particularly those which reduce the rate of tax on capital income, primarily benefit those at the top of the income scale. In addition, according to the Joint Committee on Taxation, the benefits of even the most widely used itemized deductions are concentrated among those earning $30,000 or more.

Buechner was describing here the system that provoked, and was replaced by, the tax law enacted in 1986. That law eliminated dozens of major special interest provisions in the tax code, and so made a larger share of the incomes of the well-to-do subject to the income tax, while reducing their incentives to change their economic behavior in order to avoid tax. The new tax system is fairer, but there is still more that could be accomplished.

4. Efficiency.   Any tax system will influence economic activity and the allocation of resources. Still, our present tax system clearly attempts far too much in this area, spreading too many incentives too thinly over too vast a ground. It drains the government of needed resources, providing help only wastefully and inefficiently to activities ranging from business capital investment through solar energy development to charitable contributions. A good tax reform would strip away inefficient or wasteful incentives, replacing them where necessary with direct subsidies, and otherwise returning the functions they serve to the discretion of the free market.

5. Simplicity and 6. Compliance.   Elimination of many special preferences would also serve the basic goal of making the tax system comprehensible to the individual taxpayer. This would help reduce the nearly 2 billion hours spent each year on tax preparation in the United States, and the $3 billion spent on professional assistance. More important, it would help restore voluntary compliance with the code, since taxpayers would have less reason to feel that they were falling behind in a rat race to save every possible tax dollar. As Table 1 shows, compliance—voluntary reporting of taxable income—has been declining in recent years, with the worst offenders being taxpayers with income from personal services (informal supplies income) and capital gains.

7. Federalism.   Unlike most other countries, the United States raises more tax revenue at the level of state and local government than at the federal level. Our system of federalism must therefore also be considered in a discussion of tax reform.

The autonomy of our state and local governments is an established—though by no means unlimited—national principle. We foster it through the tax system in two ways: (1) by reserving to the state and locality certain types of taxation, such as property taxation; and (2) by permitting taxpayers to deduct taxes paid to other levels of government from their income for federal tax purposes. To change the federal tax system in either respect could have serious repercussions on the ability of states and localities to raise their own needed revenues.

What now? After tax reform, criteria 3 through 6 are better met than they were before. But there is still in our judgment a need for new tax revenues: The tax reform bill did little or nothing to close the deficits in the federal budget.

What new taxes would we favor? We explored the macroeconomic aspects of this question in the extra word after Chapter 17. Applying Buechner's criteria, we would oppose regressive taxes on oil and gasoline (unless the revenues were rebated to

TABLE 1
Voluntary Reporting Percentages for Individual Filers and Nonfilers, by Source of Income, 1973 and 1981

Category	Percent of Income Reported	
	1973	*1981*
Wages and salaries	95.4%	93.9%
Dividends	90.7	83.7
Interest	87.6	86.3
Capital gains	75.7	59.4
Nonfarm proprietor income and partnership and small-business corporation income	84.0	78.7
Farm proprietor income	88.6	88.3
Informal supplier income	20.7	20.7
Pensions and annuities	81.5	85.2
Rents	94.7	95.6
Royalties	74.3	61.2
Estate and trust income	82.0	76.2
State income tax refunds, alimony, and other income	66.0	62.0
Total income	91.2	89.3

Source: Internal Revenue Service, *Income Tax Compliance Research: Estimates for 1973–1981* (Washington, DC: Internal Revenue Service, July 1983), p. 10. Later data are not available.

offset the effect on poor people) or a regressive value-added tax (VAT). We would favor the simple, technically easy step of raising marginal tax rates, since an increase of just two or three points (to a top marginal rate of 35 percent) would raise $70 billion or more per year, which we believe would solve the deficit crisis. How unfortunate, in our view, is the bad repute from which the income tax still suffers!

CHAPTER 18

The Control of Market Power

A LOOK AHEAD

We end our study of microeconomics with a section of four chapters devoted to the central unsolved issues of the market mechanism. One of these, discussed in this chapter, concerns the control of market power—the perennial issue of ''big business.'' The next two chapters focus on the patterns of income that the market distributes in fact, compared with those that would be distributed if the criterion of marginal productivity were the sole determining factor. Finally, in Chapter 21 we look at our unemployment and poverty, in many ways the most important measures of the success or failure of any market system.

No single analytical problem comes to the fore in the present chapter. Instead, the central theme is power—economic power in the marketplace. As we shall see, the problem of power is not so easy to define, or to offset, as we sometimes tend to believe. The purpose of the chapter is to make you aware of the complexity of a public policy issue of great importance.

*C*hapter 16 was devoted to the problem of market power from the firm's point of view: How should a monopoly price its products to maximize profits? What is an oligopolist's best strategy? What can a monopolistically competitive firm do to hang on to its minuscule market advantage? Now we address ourselves to the issue of market power from the public's point of view. And here the place to begin is with a simple question: Why oppose monopoly or any other form of market imperfection? What difference does it make?

IS THE CONSUMER KING?

In theory, the answer is clear: The consumer is king. Each individual comes to the marketplace fully equipped with definite views, or *preferences,* about the goods and services she would like to consume and the range of prices she is willing to pay. *Consumer sovereignty* is the term we use to assert that the consumer's given preferences are the ultimate source and determinant of market behavior.

Consumer Sovereignty

Under pure competition, the business of competition consists of efforts to satisfy those preferences. The consumer enjoys goods that are sold as cheaply and produced as abundantly as possible. Each firm produces the goods consumers want, in the largest quantity at the lowest possible cost—given the levels of wages and materials costs and the limits of technology. As we have seen, in a purely competitive market there exist no profits (except transitory rents). Business, in short, has no economic power in this world.

In an imperfectly competitive market, the situation changes. Firms have leverage over total supply. Hence they develop *strategies,* including the strategy of restricting output and raising prices. Profits are not competed away to the benefit of consumers. **Output is reduced, prices rise above the competitive level, and some consumer satisfaction is transferred to producers.** Business power enters the scene, countering the power of the consumer. In this situation, it is important to realize that the consumer is still "sovereign," as we have defined the term. Preferences are not as well satisfied as they would be under pure competition, but they have not actually been *altered* by the absence of it. The consumer has become, as it were, a constitutional monarch. The control of business power in this situation is, then, straightforward in principle, if difficult to achieve in practice. It consists of finding ways to make monopolies and oligopolies behave "as if" they were competitive firms—through regulation, the pressure of public opinion, antitrust action, or other means.

For the most part in this chapter, we will stick with the concept of the sovereign consumer, and explore the responses that are available when this sovereignty comes under challenge because business wields market power. But first we need to explore a serious dissent from the entire conceptual framework. This dissent holds that the power of modern corporations goes well beyond the ability merely to *obstruct* consumer preferences. Rather, their power reaches the point of helping to determine how preferences are formed.

Producer Sovereignty: A Dissenting View

John Kenneth Galbraith, in a famous argument,* asserts that it is quite wrong to take preferences as "given" by forces outside the economic system. He argues that consumer preferences are determined, at least in part, *within* the economic system—by product design and differentiation, and by the advertising strategies of large corporations. Insofar as business *creates* the tastes of the public, we have *producer sovereignty* instead of consumer sovereignty. Not only must consumers pay the higher-than-competitive prices and accept the particular kinds of product design that business offers on the market, but they are also actually conditioned through advertising and social pressures to like the world that corporations have created. If widely accepted, Galbraith's view would overturn much of traditional economic analysis. Let us look into it more carefully by examining two means by which producer sovereignty may be exercised: advertising and product differentiation.

Advertising as Information

Galbraith's dissent can be seen in part as an argument over the social role of advertising. In 1867 we spent an estimated $50 million to persuade consumers to buy products. In 1900 advertising expenditures were $500 million. In 1986 they were $102 *billion,* roughly one-third as much as we spend on primary and secondary education. Advertising is not omnipotent—highly advertised products from the Ford Edsel to the IBM PCjr have been known to fail. But even if we are not slaves of advertising, few would deny that advertising is a powerful and pervasive force in our economic lives.

The question is: To what effect? Does advertising infringe on consumer sovereignty? The issue is perplexing. If one regards the consumer as coming to the marketplace in search of specific goods to satisfy already well-formed needs and values, then one can think of advertising as merely providing *information* to that consumer. For example, I may know I need furniture for my house. I may even know that I prefer traditional natural woods over modern stainless-steel-and-glass designs, without knowing *exactly* what model or which manufacturer is producing what I want. Advertising then tells me where to find what I want, at the best price. This kind of advertising does not change tastes; it merely informs them.

Advertising as Manipulation

Yet it is obvious that all advertising is not merely informational and that consumers' tastes can be shaped by appeals to their instincts, their insecurities—or to their

*John Kenneth Galbraith, *The Affluent Society* (Boston: Houghton Mifflin, first published 1957).

children: Is a four-year-old screaming for Cap'n Crunch cereal at the Safeway expressing a "natural" preference for this item?

Adults, too, can be manipulated. We are mainly creatures of brand preference, not because we have sampled all the choices and made up our minds, but as a result of advertising exposure. It is difficult to contemplate the bottles of aspirin, toothpaste, soup, soap (up to 10 percent of the price of soap is selling expense), cars, cigarettes, and whisky without recognizing that there is an element of what might fairly be termed consumer exploitation. Brand-name aspirin, for example, sells for as much as three times the price of nonbrand versions of the identical product.

Product Differentiation

Product differentiation is another such case. Corporations proliferate models and styles prodigiously, whether we are talking about cars or stereos or furniture or clothing. Are they doing so strictly to meet a comparable diversity of tastes? Or do they find that product differentiation, combined with advertising, *creates* a diversification of tastes, along with a little range of monopoly power—enabling companies to raise prices and make a little more profit on each item?

As with advertising, the question is where to draw the line. Should an affluent society aim to produce the largest possible quantity of a standardized product at the least possible cost, or to offer an array of differing products that please our palates, admittedly at somewhat higher prices? Most of us would say that American consumers do not want to dress in some kind of "uniform," however inexpensive, or to drive a standardized cheap car. Yet sometimes a company succeeds just because it does produce a commodity that is cheap and standardized—the Volkswagen Beetle and Levi Strauss jeans are cases in point.

Thus product differentiation, like advertising, poses a conundrum for theory. Do we take the diversity of consumer preferences as given, or as created? Sociologists and anthropologists tend to see tastes as formed by the cultural influences that surround us—including advertising and product differentiation. Economists tend to regard advertising as primarily informational, and product differentiation as a response to a preexisting diversity of tastes. Economists, however, do recognize the force of Galbraith's dissent, which is that the whole *theoretical* structure of consumer sovereignty depends on the assumption that consumer preferences are *given,* not made.

BUSINESS AND POWER

For the moment let us go along with the profession and accept consumer sovereignty as a point of departure. What happens when the monopolistic corporation comes into conflict with this "sovereign" consumer? To what extent does monopoly or oligopoly introduce inefficiency or restrictions on output, preventing consumers from buying goods as cheaply as possible in the quantity they desire? What, in other words, are the consequences of business power?

Do Profits Bring Progress?

Once again, the evidence is murky. For one thing, we tend to leap to the conclusion that the competitive firm, which has managed to combine its factors of production as profitably as possible, has also reached the frontiers of technological efficiency. Is this really so? Suppose the frontiers of technology are themselves variable—capable of being advanced by determined efforts in research, development, and product design? Will a small competitive firm, on the margin of existence with low, competitive profits, ever actually advance the state of technological knowledge? Or do such efforts require a cushion, resources to spare, a "monopoly" profit?

These are not idle questions. There is ample evidence that the diffusion of new technologies often—but not always—occurs in large corporations, capable of employing battalions of scientists and engineers. Thus the transistor came from Bell Labs and the research on the semiconductor occurred at IBM. The economist Joseph A. Schumpeter thought that this process of big-business advance represented the core mechanism of capitalist development—the "gales of creative destruction" in which today's monopoly profits are the price we pay for tomorrow's technological advance.

Coping with Power

This brings us again to the question of power—the ability to impose one's will on others. Power has long been an issue of central concern for political scientists and philosophers. It has not been so much an object of examination for economists because, as we have seen, they picture the world as tending to a competitive situation in which power disappears.

But obviously power in the marketplace is not going to disappear—neither the power to influence tastes and wants identified by Galbraith nor power as less than perfect competition in the conventional economic view. The question is what to do about it.

A CONSERVATIVE VIEW

The first suggestion is most prominently associated with the name of Milton Friedman. Professor Friedman is a philosophic conservative whose response to the question of how a corporation should discharge its social responsibility is very simple: Make money.

The function of a business organization in society, argues Friedman, is to serve as an efficient agent of production, not as a locus of social improvement. It serves that productive function best by striving after profit—conforming, while doing so, to the basic rules and legal norms of society. It is not up to business to "do good"; and it is up to government to prevent it from doing bad.

Moreover, says Friedman, as soon as a businessman tries to apply any rules other than money-making, he takes into his own hands powers that rightfully belong to others, such as political authorities. Friedman would even forbid corporations to give money to charities or universities. Their business, their responsibility to society, he insists, is *production*. Let the dividend receivers give away the money the corporations pay them, but do not let corporations become the active social welfare agencies of society.

The Corporation as Social Arbiter

It is interesting to note that few corporate heads espouse Friedman's position. They take the view that the corporation, by virtue of its immense size and strength, has power thrust upon it, whether it wishes it or not. The solution to this problem, as executives see it, is for corporations to act "responsibly" in using their power, doing their best to judge fairly among the claims of the many groups to whom they are responsible: labor, stockholders, customers, government, and the public at large.

Thus many top corporate executives think of themselves as referees among contending groups, and no doubt many of them use caution and forethought in exercising the power of decision. But the weaknesses of this argument are also not difficult to see. There are no recognized criteria for qualifying as a "responsible" corporate executive.* Nor is there any clear guideline, even for the most scrupulous executive, for defining the correct manner in which to exercise responsibility. Should an executive's concern for the prevention of pollution take precedence over a good year-end profit statement? Over labor's request for wage increases? Over reducing the price of the product? Is the company's contribution to charity supposed to represent the executives' preferences, or those of the owners or consumers or workers? On what grounds should a company decide whether to do business in South Africa? Has Mobil a right to help the cause of public broadcasting? The makers of firearms to support the National Rifle Association?

The questions begin to indicate the complexity of the issue of social responsibility and the problems implicit in allowing important *social* decisions to be made by private individuals who are not publicly accountable for their actions.

Antitrust

Only a few decades ago, there was virtually unanimous agreement among economists that a strict application of antitrust laws was one of the most effective remedies for the problems of oligopoly. Today this zeal is on the wane, although, as

---

*The plea of professionalism is further placed in doubt by considerable evidence of white-collar crime in high corporate places. In 1985 a rash of scandals, including a plan by E. F. Hutton to defraud banks in which it placed its deposits, led to an unprecedented admission of guilt by the company, accompanied by a heavy fine. Half the bank failures in the nation, according to the FDIC, arose at least in part from criminal conduct. A former cabinet official and board chairman of a major steel company was sent to jail for passing inside information. Quipped *Time* magazine: "The ways things are going, *Fortune* may soon have to publish a 500 Most Wanted list" (June 10, 1985). 1987 was another bumper year for white-collar crimes, as Wall Street trader Ivan Boesky and a host of smaller fry were found guilty of using inside information, a felony. Boesky paid a fine of $50 million and went to jail; the small fry paid smaller amounts and generally were sentenced to longer terms.

we shall see, it is probably too early to write *finis* to antitrust prosecutions designed to break big companies into little ones.

Why has the zeal for antitrust declined? There are a number of reasons. One is that economists have come to recognize that an industry with one or two giant firms and a tail of small firms does not operate very differently—if at all—from an industry with five or six leading members. Whether concentration ratios give the top four firms 30 percent or 60 percent of an industry does not seem to affect their oligopolistic decision making. Product differentiation continues. The struggle for market shares goes on. Price leadership persists. Even the breakup of the aluminum industry from a near-monopoly under the domination of Alcoa to an industry in which four firms have big shares of the market does not appear to have changed aluminum prices or aluminum pricing policies.

A second major factor in reconsidering antitrust is the pressure of international competition, mainly from very large, often state-backed, foreign firms. It is difficult for U.S. corporations without very large resources to seize, or hold, a place in the world market; and large corporations are, by definition, the ones to whom antitrust concerns apply. Antitrust advocates warn that big multinationals, with their global interlocks (see page 290), can serve to block competition as well as to make it—a warning that must be heeded. But the driving force of the fight for market shares seems greater than the defensive tactics of preserving one's own turf. **At any rate, many economists today view large corporate size as a necessary condition for effective participation in the world's economy.**

A third consideration is the tremendous time lag and cost involved in major antitrust cases. A big antitrust case may go on for 20 or 30 years before it is resolved. One may ask whether the eventual savings are worth the huge legal costs. Moreover, many antitrust actions seem to make little economic sense. For example, antitrust laws prohibit the merger of two firms whose combined assets would be less than those of the industry leader, but the courts do nothing to break up the leader itself. This situation exists because antitrust is against "combination" on principle, but not against bigness as such. Yet the price policies of one big business often restrain trade as much as if two former competitors were combined.

The Ghost of Senator Sherman

Defenders of antitrust legislation do not question these views. It is not really imaginable that General Motors, for example, will ever be broken into a thousand firms each with a capitalization of $50 million, even though GM is big enough to yield that many pieces. In all likelihood, trustbusting GM would result in the formation of three or four giant firms, each worth $20 billion or so and each still possessing enormous market power.

But the defenders of antitrust do not want to give up the implicit threat that antitrust prosecution carries. The ghost of Senator Sherman, the sponsor of the original antitrust legislation, sits on the board of directors of all large firms, according to George Stigler, an eminent economist. There the ghost exercises a cautionary influence against actions that might be taken if there were no threat of antitrust action. The ghost serves to prevent the rise of supergiant firms whose political and social power might be considered inimical to our democracy, if not injurious to our economy.

THE BREAKUP OF MA BELL

In 1984 history's biggest antitrust case came to an end with the breakup of the American Telephone and Telegraph Corporation. AT&T was a classic monopoly, dominating telephone service in the nation. But, interestingly, the antitrust case did not allege that AT&T had used its monopoly power to exploit the consumer. To the contrary: Before the breakup, nearly every U.S. household had relatively cheap, efficient access to the phone network. AT&T was, moreover, the world's top-quality telephone system, providing phones that never broke, and clear and instantaneous connections across the country and, via satellites, around the world.

AT&T had been accused instead of abusing its *technological* stranglehold on the U.S. telephone system. It had used its control of local telephone service in order to prevent the establishment of alternative long distance services, and to prevent alternative manufacturers of telephone equipment from attaching their products to AT&T lines. Thus households could not take full advantage of new microwave transmission technologies, nor of the full range of telephone equipment manufacturers were capable of providing. With its monopoly profits from equipment and long distance services, AT&T kept local telephone rates low and engaged in funding a wide range of research activities through Bell Labs.

The court decree split AT&T away from its equipment manufacturer (Western Electric) and split off seven companies to provide local service in different parts of the country. The results? MCI, Sprint, and Allnet soon began an aggressive campaign to expand their share of the long distance market. As a result, long distance costs fell. At the same time, telephone equipment costs also fell, though often so did the quality of the equipment. But local telephone rates rose, since local companies no longer had AT&T's deep pockets behind them. Phone bills suddenly got more complex, as did the business of getting phone equipment repaired. Perhaps the biggest loser was the AT&T research effort, which was cut back sharply in the new competitive environment.

Six years after the breakup a Brookings Institution study reported that some long distance rates are still being kept artificially high, despite the new competition. The reason: continuing political pressure, exercised through state-by-state rate regulation, to maintain low-cost local service. Thus while divestiture has occurred, deregulation has not.

Regulation

Regulation has been a traditional American response to the problem of business power. Regulation has sought to influence or prohibit business actions in many fields: pricing, advertising, product design, dealing with unions and minority groups, pollution, workplace and product safety, and still other areas. Given the variety of ways in which corporations are regulated, it is hardly surprising that the effectiveness of the regulatory process is very uneven.

It is useful to distinguish *economic regulation,* which is concerned with pricing and market access, from *social regulation,* which is concerned with a host of other issues, such as pollution and safety and civil rights. (Of course, the distinction is somewhat artificial, since social regulation may have strong economic effects.)

Economic Regulation

Historically, the United States government has been most concerned with economic regulation of industries providing transportation and communications services, and with "natural monopolies"—utilities such as electric power companies—that have declining cost curves through their whole range of output.

The first great regulatory agency was the Interstate Commerce Commission, established in 1887 to regulate the railroads, which were at that time a natural monopoly in much of the country. The ICC's role was dual: to prevent abuses of market power by the railroads, and also to ensure that the country was adequately served by rail transportation. Later, buses and trucks and pipelines came under ICC jurisdiction, but the dual function remained: The ICC both restricted and protected these transportation sectors.

The Civil Aviation Board (CAB) was designed in the same mold to promote the airline industry and also to protect it from "cutthroat competition"; still later, the Federal Communications Commission (FCC) came to play a similar role for television, as did the original Atomic Energy Commission for nuclear power. As time went by, many observers came to feel that the regulators were not doing both sides of their job. Having lived with their industries, the regulating agencies had come to adopt the industry viewpoint, protecting the industry against competition more than protecting the broader interests of the public.

Social Regulation

In contrast to economic regulation, social regulation is not industry-specific. Rather, it represents the efforts of government to lay down guidelines for conduct for whole classes of industries to promote one or another social purpose. The first social regulations were laid down in 1906 during the Progressive era with the establishment of the federal Food and Drug Administration (FDA). Today the list includes the Federal Trade Commission (FTC), concerned with advertising, truth-in-lending and other trade practices; the Securities and Exchange Commission (SEC); the National Labor Relations Board (NLRB); the Equal Employment Opportunity Commission (EEOC) and Office of Federal Contract Compliance (OFCC), concerned with civil rights; the Occupational Safety and Health Administration (OSHA); the Environmental Protection Agency (EPA); and the Consumer Product Safety Commission (CPSC). Quite a list!

Social regulations have often proved effective—as when FDA testing prevented the sedative thalidomide from being released on the U.S. market when it was found that its use by pregnant women resulted in badly deformed babies. Sometimes they have not been effective, as in the case of the FTC's campaigns against TV advertising aimed at children in the late 1970s, or the failure of the EPA under the Reagan administration to do something about the problem of toxic waste dumps. Sometimes a regulatory failure occurs because the regulation itself was ill-conceived; at other times, for lack of money necessary for effective enforcement.

Right or wrong, social regulation is usually controversial. It imposes an economic burden on business, and what is sometimes worse, it steps on businessmen's toes, offending their sense of independence. Often social regulations lead to court fights, as over affirmative action rulings, or to battles in Congress, as over proposed FTC rules governing used car dealers and funeral parlors. In many cases, an uneasy stalemate comes to exist, in which the regulatory agency remains in existence, but without the funding it would require to pursue its legal mandates to the full extent stipulated in the law.

Deregulation

Recently there have been great strides to curtail economic regulation, started in the late 1970s and continued under the Reagan administration. The Atomic Energy Commission was broken up and its safety functions delegated to the Nuclear Regulatory Commission (NRC), which is not intended to promote nuclear power. The CAB has been abolished, together with federal control over airline routes and fares. The ICC has relinquished much of its power over the trucking industry, and some of its power over railroads. The breakup of AT&T diminished regulation of telecommunications. With the rise of cable TV, the FCC has been granting much more leeway than heretofore to commercial television stations on their programming decisions. Banking services have become progressively deregulated and competitive.

To date, the best-documented example of economic deregulation has been in the airlines. Its immediate and dramatic effect was a sharp fall in airline prices on those routes where the demand for service was high, permitting the use of the largest and most efficient aircraft at the lowest per passenger costs. As a result, coast-to-coast travelers found themselves able to fly for bargain rates, especially during off-hours. Another result was the dramatic reorganization of route structures, as big airlines moved to systems of "hubs"—American Airlines at Dallas, United at Chicago, TWA at St. Louis, Delta at Atlanta—that maximized within-airline transfers and permitted the most efficient use of equipment. Finally, many new airlines sprang up, servicing smaller airports with a wide range of smaller equipment and competing on major commuter and shuttle routes with the established giants. Some survived; some did not.

This is not to say that everyone has come out ahead. One large company, Braniff, went out of business; others have hovered on the bankruptcy edge. Yet others—Continental and United—have used a bankruptcy proceeding or a strike to force pilots and other staff to take major pay cuts. Union membership in the industry has declined. And everyone has heard the complaints about how much more expensive it is to fly (on a per mile basis) between lightly traveled destinations (say, New York to Nashville or Richmond, or Indianapolis to St. Paul or Sioux City) than on the great routes.

Such complaints, and allegations that small-city travelers "subsidize" the intercontinental routes, overlook the economies inherent in high load factors, big aircraft, and efficient airports on those routes, and the fact that airport overheads —maintenance, baggage crews, catering and ticket services—do not depend on the distance you fly. On the whole, it seems that airline deregulation has reinvigorated the industry, providing better, cheaper, and more efficient service at a price that more closely reflects airline costs than before—pretty much what a competitive model would predict.

Other Possibilities

Thus the problem of social responsibility will not be easy to resolve, no matter what steps we choose. **It is part of the problem of social responsibility that no purely** *economic* **criteria can fully appraise the question.** Let us therefore look at a few other suggestions for dealing with the problem that have been put forward in the recent past and that may well come forward again in the future.

Nationalization of large industries is not a characteristically American response to this issue, but effective nationalization sometimes occurs. To all intents and purposes, the Reagan administration took over the Continental Illinois Bank when the bank came near folding in 1983. A massive wave of scandals has plagued the defense industries, from reports that the government was charged with country club fees to allegations of procurement fraud in submarine contracts totaling, in just two cases, over a billion and a half dollars. As a result, the Pentagon forced the resignation of the chairman of the board of the General Dynamics Corporation, the nation's largest military contractor. Even more decisive action in the future— nationalization *de facto* if not *de jure*—cannot be ruled out.

Expanded access to the courts for aggrieved citizens is another option. It was a private civil suit under the antitrust laws that brought about the dissolution of AT&T. And corporate liability to lawsuits is by no means limited to antitrust. The Ford Motor Company was tried for murder (though acquitted) in a case stemming from the vulnerability of its Pinto model to rear-end collisions. Another murder case was brought in Chicago against a photochemical firm, one of whose workers had died of cyanide gas poisoning. That case resulted in a conviction. Less spectacular but still effective has been a rash of liability suits in product safety cases, tending to establish that a manufacturer remains responsible for its products long after they leave its factory or warehouse.

Economic democracy is another course of action that has its advocates, who urge the appointment of public members to boards of directors of large companies. These public members would be charged with protecting consumer interests and with reporting behavior contrary to the public interest. A variant is to put union representatives on the board. For instance, UAW President Douglas Fraser joined the Chrysler board a decade ago. And in the past few years some corporations have actually been bought out, in whole or part, by their workers. Worker buyouts have often brought a surge of productivity, but this has not usually been enough to reverse an unfavorable market position.

Power: The Unresolved Problem

It would be a mistake to conclude this recital with the implication that corporate (or union or government) power can be easily brought under control through a few legal remedies or by the power of public opinion—although certainly many abuses can be curbed, and much better levels of social performance achieved.

Yet mass organizations seem to be an inescapable concomitant of our age of high technology and increasing social interdependence. Here we should note that, depending on our interests, we stress different aspects of this universal phenomenon. **To some, who fear the continued growth of very large scale business, the most significant aspect is that we have not managed to control business power. To others, concerned over the emergence of large labor unions, it is labor power that most dangerously eludes effective control. And to still others, who are most worried by big government, it is the growth of public power that is the main problem.**

Thus the question of economic power remains, at best, only partially resolved. As A. A. Berle has written: "Some of these corporations can be thought of only in somewhat the same way we have heretofore thought of nations." Unlike nations, however, their power has not been rationalized in law, fully tested in practice, or well defined in philosophy. Unquestionably, the political and social influence and the economic power of the great centers of production pose problems with which capitalism—indeed, all industrialized societies—will have to contend for many years to come.

LOOKING BACK

KEY CONCEPTS
In theory, the consumer is king.

1 Consumer sovereignty is the ultimate rationale for the market system. With perfect competition, consumer sovereignty implies that (a) the consumer, not the producer, determines the allocation of resources; and (b) the consumer is offered goods produced as cheaply and as abundantly as resources and technology permit.

Market imperfections reduce consumer sovereignty.

2 If monopoly or oligopoly are present, the consumer becomes a qualified sovereign. His or her preferences may be the same as before, but the market may not cater to these preferences at the lowest price.

Do advertising and product differentiation disprove consumer sovereignty?

3 Advertising is generally thought by economists to provide information consumers need, while product differentiation is generally held to reflect the diversity of preferences. John Kenneth Galbraith's dissenting view holds that advertising and product differentiation actually mold and create preferences. If so, consumer sovereignty would give way to producer sovereignty, and the whole basis of economic theory would have to change.

Business power has met many suggestions:

4 There are many views as to how business power should be dealt with. The view of conservatives who follow Milton Friedman is that big

Friedman suggests that profit-seeking is the only legitimate social function of business, but many businessmen prefer to think of themselves as being socially responsible. Dissolution of monopoly and antitrust policies have not proved very successful, mainly because big business is more technologically advanced than small business.

business is best left alone—that its main social function is to strive after profit, not to "do good" (in fact, businesses should not be allowed to use their profits for philanthropy). Many corporate executives find this view too uncomfortable and seek to define their roles as "professional" managers who deliberately follow socially responsible policies.

5 The dissolution of monopoly is another approach to business power. So are antitrust measures, designed to break "combinations in restraint of trade," which have long been established policy. Yet both approaches have their limitations. Bigness is often the other side of the coin of technical efficiency and may also bring enlightened employee or social practices. And antitrust activity runs up against problems of cost and time, the efficiency of big companies, and the dubious rationale of antitrust policy itself.

Economic and social regulation are both on the decline.

6 Economic regulation of industries began to give way in the 1970s to restored competition in airlines, trucking, telecommunications, and other industries. There is wide agreement that the results have been generally good. Social regulation—over environment, safety, civil rights, and other policies of corporations—has been cut back sharply beginning with the Reagan administration. Here the verdict remains controversial.

Other options.

7 Various other policy options include expanded use of liability laws to enforce corporate responsibility and economic democracy, even to the point of worker ownership. In some extreme cases, the government may in the future find itself in control of large corporations.

ECONOMIC VOCABULARY

Consumer sovereignty   320
Producer sovereignty   321
Product differentiation   322

Economic regulation   327
Social regulation   327
Deregulation   328

QUESTIONS

1. Make a list of the main institutional changes you can think of that would be needed if we were to establish a system of perfect competition.

2. Go through a magazine and analyze a dozen ads to see (a) how much genuine information they convey, such as price, technical features, availability, etc.; and (b) how much they try to influence taste by suggesting the social or other

benefits of using the product, without giving any economic information. Do the same for a newspaper. Why do you think that "informational" ads are more common in newspapers than magazines?

3. How do you feel about Friedman's ideas on business responsibility? Do you think that Mobil has a right to support *Masterpiece Theatre* and other such public TV shows? How about Mobil's right to publish editorials in support of its views on oil? And how about the contributions of small-arms manufacturers to the National Rifle Association?

4. Do you think a businessman has any right to decide what the most socially responsible policy for his company should be? Take the case of moving a plant from one region to another. Should business management alone decide this? If not, who?

5. Would you support the nationalization of a big company such as USX (formerly United States Steel) if it were threatened with bankruptcy that would impose terrible economic hardship on its workers and communities?

6. By and large, which do you consider to be the most dangerous *economic* problem: big business, big labor, big government? Which is the most dangerous *political* problem? The most dangerous *social* problem? Whatever your own list, can you imagine a rational argument for a list in which the three groups were differently rank-ordered according to areas of danger? Do you think there is a "right" way of looking at this problem?

CHAPTER 19

The Distribution of Income—in Theory

A LOOK AHEAD

With this chapter we enter a new area of microeconomics—income distribution. Here we present a discussion of how wages, rents, and interest are determined in the marketplace—in theory. In Chapter 20 we will look at the real world and discuss why and where the theory doesn't work as well as we should expect.

One by one we will consider each factor of production, deriving the forces of supply and demand that establish its level of remuneration. Actually, however, there is a central theme you will soon catch sight of: the marginal productivity theory of income distribution. This theory claims that each factor in a competitive market earns as much as the net revenue it brings into the firm. Marginal productivity theory thereby becomes the main idea for you to bear in mind—and note especially the surprising conclusion to which it points: There is no such thing, in a truly competitive world, as exploitation.

Although we have explored in some detail the demand for goods, we have left unexamined a crucial area of the market system. This is the market for factors, where wages, rent, and interest are determined.

This area is crucial for two reasons. First, it allows us to complete the analysis of the circular flow that has provided the basic pattern of our analysis. When we have understood the factor market, we will have knit together the household and the firm in their second major interaction—this time with the household acting as supplier rather than demander, and with the firm providing demand rather than supply.

Second, our analysis is crucial because it leads us to the consideration of a problem of major political and social importance: the *distribution of income,* the main theme in this and Chapter 20. In this chapter we look into the matter in theory—that is, as incomes would be determined in a perfectly competitive world. In Chapter 20 we look at the matter in fact—that is, as incomes are set in the imperfectly competitive world of our economy.

Factors and Factor Services

We must begin with a simple but distinguishing fact that separates the market for factors from that for goods. When we buy or sell goods, we take possession of, or deliver, an actual commodity. **But when we speak of buying or selling factors, we mean only that we are buying or selling a stream of services a factor produces.** When we buy or sell "labor," we do not buy or sell the human being who produces that labor—only the value of the work efforts. When we buy or sell "capital," we are not purchasing or selling a sum of money or a capital asset. We are hiring or offering the use of that money or equipment. Land, too, enters the market for factors as an agency of production whose services we rent but need not actually purchase.

Obviously we can buy land as real estate, and we can buy capital goods and various forms of capital, such as stocks and bonds. (We cannot buy human labor as an entity because slavery is illegal. In former times, though, one *could* buy labor outright.) It stands to reason, then, that there should be a relationship between the price of factors considered as assets (actual capital goods or real estate) and the price of the stream of services that factors produce: the *interest* earned on capital, the *rent* of land. There is such a relationship, which we will study later under the heading of "capitalization." Here we must recognize that the market for factors is not a market in which the assets are sold, but one in which the productive services—the earnings—of these assets are priced.

As in every market, these prices will be determined by the interplay of supply and demand. Therefore to study the factor market, we must first look into the forces that determine the demand for factors, and then into the forces that determine their supply.

Direct Demand for Factors

Who buys factor services? Part of the answer is very simple. **A portion of the services of labor, land, and capital is demanded directly by consumers for**

their own personal enjoyment, exactly as with any good or service. This kind of demand for factors of production takes the guise of the demand for lawyers and barbers and servants or the demand for plots of land for personal dwellings or the demand for cars and washing machines or other personal capital goods or the demand for loans for consumption purposes. To the extent that factors are demanded directly for these purposes, there is nothing in analyzing the demand for them that differs from the demand curves we previously studied.

Derived Demand

Most factors of production do not earn their incomes by selling their services directly to final consumers. They sell them instead to firms. In turn, firms want the services of these factors not for personal enjoyment, but to put them to profitable use.

Thus we speak of the firm's demand for factors as derived demand. Its demand is derived from consumers' demand for the output the firm makes. Each firm will hire labor (or any other factor) until the marginal revenue from that factor just equals the marginal costs of hiring that factor.

The marginal output a factor produces multiplied by the selling price of the product is called its **marginal revenue product.** If a factor produces three extra units of output that are sold for $10 per unit, its marginal revenue product is $30. If the number of units of output falls as more and more of a factor is added to the production process, these diminishing returns cause the marginal revenue product curve or the derived demand curve to slope downward.

We see this in Figure 1, where the derived demand for a factor leads firm 1 to employ quantity *OA*. Derived demand of firm 2 results in the hire of *OB*, and the summed demand of both firms gives us a market demand of *OC*.

This, however, leaves us with the question of factor price only half explained. We understand the elements that enter into the demand curve for the factor. But we cannot understand how the price of the factor is established until we know something about the supply curves in the factor market. That is the missing element we need to complete the circular flow.

THE SUPPLY CURVE OF FACTORS

What do we know about the willingness and ability of the owners of labor, capital, and land to offer their services in the marketplace at varying prices for these services?

Labor

By far the most important supply curve in the factor market is that of labor— meaning labor of all grades, from the least skilled workman to the most highly trained scientist or the most effective entrepreneur.

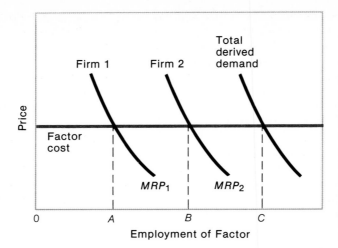

FIGURE 1
Derived Demand for Factors
The derived demand curve (or the marginal revenue product curve) slopes downward because each factor adds less and less to output as we add that factor. Multiply the falling marginal contribution of the factor times the selling price and you get the curves shown here.

As Figure 2 shows, the supply curve for the labor of most individuals has a curious shape. Up to wage level *OA,* we have no trouble explaining things. Economists assume that labor involves *disutility.* Moreover, just as we assume that increasing amounts of a utility-yielding good give us diminishing marginal utility, so we assume that increasing amounts of labor involve *increasing marginal disutility.* Therefore the curve rises up to level *OA* because we will not be willing to work longer hours (to offer a larger quantity of labor services within a given time period) unless we are paid more per hour.

The Backward-Bending Supply Curve. How, then, do we explain the backward-bending portion of the rising curve above wage level *OA?* The answer lies in adding to the rising marginal disutility of labor the falling marginal utility of *income* itself, on the assumption that an extra dollar of income to a person who is making $10,000 is worth less than the utility of an additional dollar when that person is making only $5,000. **Above a certain income level, leisure is preferable to more income.**

Together, these two forces explain very clearly why the supply curve of labor bends backward above a certain level. Take a designer who has been tempted to work 70 hours a week by wage raises that have finally reached $50 an hour. Now suppose that wages go up another 10 percent. It is possible, of course, that the marginal utility of the additional income may outweigh the marginal disutility of these long hours, so that the designer stays on the job or works even longer hours. If, however, her marginal utility of income has reached a low enough point and her marginal disutility of work a high enough point, the raise may bring a new possibility: The designer may work *fewer* hours and enjoy the same (or a somewhat higher) income as well as additional leisure. For example, as pay goes up 10 percent, the designer may reduce her workweek by 5 percent.

Backward-bending supply curves help explain the long trend toward reducing the workweek. Over the last century, weekly hours have decreased by about 40 percent. Although many factors have converged to bring about this result, one of them is certainly the desire of individual men and women to give up the marginal utility of potential income for that of increased leisure.

Individual vs. Collective Supply. A cautionary note is useful here. We can speak with some degree of confidence about the backward-bending supply curve of individual labor, especially when labor is paid by the hour or by the piece. But we must distinguish the supply curve of the individual from that of the labor force as a whole. As the price of labor rises, some persons will be tempted to enter the labor market because the opportunity cost of remaining "leisured" is now too great. This accounts for the entrance of many housewives into the market as the price for part-time office work has gone up.

This brings up the problem of the "participation rates" of the population that enters into the macroeconomic problem of employment. **Here it is useful to understand that the collective supply curve of labor is probably upward-sloping rather than backward-bending.** (It would be backward-bending if wages rose so high that married women, for example, dropped out of the labor force as their husbands' earnings rose, but that does not seem to be the case.)

Psychic Income. The supply curve of labor is further complicated because work brings not only disutilities, but positive enjoyments. Jobs occasion friendships, relieve boredom, and may lead to power or prestige. Many people derive deep satisfaction from their work and would not change jobs even if they could improve their incomes by doing so. Indeed, it is very likely that most individuals seek to maximize their "psychic incomes" rather than their money incomes, combining the utilities derived from their earnings and the quite separate utilities from their work, and balancing these gains against the disutilities work also involves.

The difficulty in speaking about psychic income is that it involves us in an unmeasurable concept—a tautology. Therefore when we talk about the supply curve of labor, we generally make the assumption that individuals behave roughly as money maximizers, an assumption that has prima facie evidence in the long-run exodus from low-paying to higher-paying occupations and from low-wage to high-wage regions.

Mobility of Labor. More than a million American families change addresses in a typical year, so that over a decade the normal mobility of the labor force may

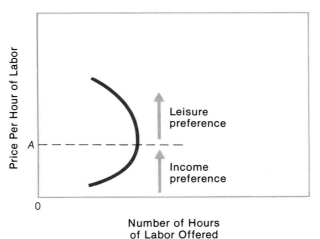

FIGURE 2
Backward-Bending Supply Curve of Labor
A typical labor supply curve for an individual bends backward because the balance between the utility of additional income and the disutility of earning it changes from "pro-work" to "pro-leisure."

transport 30 to 40 million people (including wives and children) from one part of the country to another. Without this potential influx of labor, we would expect wages to shoot up steeply whenever an industry in a particular locality expanded, with the result that further profitable expansion might then become impossible.

We also speak of mobility of labor in a vertical sense, referring to the movement from occupation to occupation. Here the barriers to mobility are not usually geographical but institutional (for instance, trade union restrictions on membership) or social (discrimination against the upward mobility of blacks) or economic (lack of sufficient income to acquire needed education). Despite these obstacles, occupational mobility is also very impressive from generation to generation, as the astounding changes in the structure of the U.S. labor force have demonstrated (see box page 343).

This is a force tending to reduce the differences between income extremes, since the mobility of labor will not only shift the supply curve to the right in the favored occupations (thereby exerting a downward pressure on incomes), but will also move the supply curve to the left in the disfavored industries, giving an upward impetus to incomes. Figure 3 shows how this process works.

Capital

What does the supply curve of capital look like? When we say "capital," we are not much interested in the supply of actual machines or equipment. Machines will be

FIGURE 3
Effect of Labor Mobility on Relative Wages
The diagram shows a low-wage employment paying OA wages, and a high one O'A'. The movement of labor out of the disfavored occupation or industry and into the favored one raises OA to OB, and reduces O'A' to O'B'. Note: The labor that goes into the high-wage employment is not necessarily the same labor that leaves the low-wage area. But as long as supply curves shift, the wage differential will change as shown.

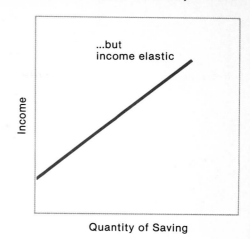

FIGURE 4
The Supply Curve of Savings
We do not greatly change our saving habits if interest changes, but do greatly change them as income changes. This last is a macroeconomic relationship of great importance.

produced, just like any other commodity, up to the point where the marginal cost of making them equals the marginal revenue from their sale.

When we speak of the supply of capital, therefore, we concern ourselves with the influx of new savings into the market, the source of the machines of the future. **How about the supply curve of savings? Economists have learned that savers change their habits of thrift much less in response to changes in the price of savings (interest) than in response to changes in the level of income. We can see this in Figure 4.**

Allocating Savings. Even though the price of savings may not greatly affect our thriftiness, it has a very important effect on what we do with our savings. As savers, we often reallocate the way we dispose of our savings, shifting our "portfolios" among checking accounts, savings accounts, insurance, and stocks and bonds, as the various returns offered by these assets change (or as our assessment of their risk changes). For example, high interest rates in the late 1970s resulted in a tremendous movement from non-interest-bearing checking accounts into interest-bearing savings accounts and then into money market mutual funds. Financial institutions also shift real investment funds in response to different rates of return.

Thus, when we picture the supply curve for saving, we should also bear in mind what this curve looks like to any particular demander. From the point of view of an enterprise in the market for capital, savings are highly price-elastic; that is, a firm can attract savings by offering a higher return than a competitive enterprise offers. As a result, savers will shift their capital from one enterprise to the other, as in Figure 5. This bears an obvious relation to the mobility of labor, and we can indeed speak of it as the *mobility of capital.*

FIGURE 5
Reallocation of Savings
The diagram shows us that capital moves, just as labor does, leaving low-remuneration employment for high-remuneration employment.

Land

Finally, let us consider the supply curve of land. At any moment, the total supply of land, like capital, is fixed. To a limited extent, there is a counterpart to saving that adds to capital. By applying capital and labor, we can slowly add to land by dredging, clearing forests, reclaiming swamps and deserts. Therefore the long-run supply curve for land is slightly price-elastic, as Figure 6 shows.

FIGURE 6
Supply Curve for Land
We can add only small amounts to usable land as its price rises. But as Figure 7 makes plain, we can add large amounts to usable space. What do you suppose the ratio of space to land is in New York City compared to a Great Plains town? Why is it worth building skyscrapers in New York but not in the rural Midwest?

As with capital, however, it is possible to speak of the *mobility of land*. This seems strange, since land is obviously not movable. Land can, however, be used for very different purposes, depending on the returns to be had. If we picture the supply curve of land for, say, shopping centers or orange groves or industrial sites, we can picture an upward-sloping curve, just like the supply curve of capital for any one use. Land can be—and constantly is—moved from use to use, as various enterprises bid for it. Thus the supply curve may be very elastic to any one user, even though the overall supply curve to society is very inelastic.

Land vs. Space. In addition, we must differentiate land from space. We can create space much more easily than we can create land. Space is essentially a function of the availability of capital and labor, not of land. Every time we put up a high-rise building where there was previously a low one, we have created more space on the same amount of land. As a result, the supply curve for space will be very price-elastic—a higher price for space (rent) bringing more onto the market, as Figure 7 shows. In the long run, space is available in indefinite amounts.

RENTS AND INCOMES

We are almost ready to tie together all our different supply curves, and to describe the overall working of the factor market. But the importance of time in bringing about increases in land or space alerts us to a very important reason for the existence of very large incomes (and very large disparities of incomes) in the short run. This is the phenomenon of **quasi rent** (also called *economic rent*).

Land Rent

First let us get rid of some confusing terminology by distinguishing quasi rents from the earnings of land as a factor of production, which is also rent. The distinction is

Long-run supply curve for space

FIGURE 7
Supply Curve for Space

clear in thought. It is muddied only because usage has chosen similar words for dissimilar things.

The rent earned by land as a factor of production is the payment we make to its owner for its services to the market. If we cease to pay land rent or pay less rent, the amount of land offered on the market will fall. If we pay more, it will rise. This rent is both a payment made to a factor of production to compensate its owner for its services and an element of cost that must enter into the calculation of selling prices. If a farmer must pay $100 rent to get an additional field, that $100 will clearly be part of the cost of producing a new crop.

Quasi or Economic Rent

Quasi rents differ in important ways from true land rent.

1. **Quasi rent is not a return "earned" by the factor, in that the payment has nothing to do with inducing the factor to enter the market.**
2. **Quasi rents are not a cost that helps to determine selling price. They are earnings determined by selling price.**
3. **Quasi rents apply to all factors, not just to land.**

An illustration may clarify the problem. Figure 8 shows the supply curve for "first-class" office space in New York City. Notice that over a considerable range there is an unchanging price for space. Up to amount *OX*, you can get all the space you want at rent *OA* (per square foot). This is real land rent, in the sense of being a necessary payment for a factor service. (it may be very low if space is plentiful, but here we assume a positive price.) If there were no rent paid, no space would be forthcoming.

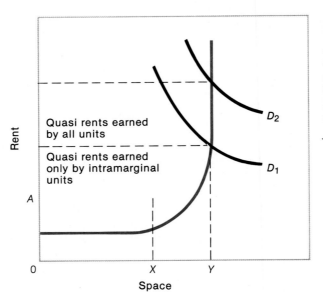

FIGURE 8
Rents and Quasi Rents
Are quasi rents scarcity returns? The diagram makes it clear they are. Are they monopoly returns? No, because they can be enjoyed by large numbers of intramarginal firms or individuals.

UNITED STATES' WORK PROFILE

What kinds of work do people do in the United States? Table 1 gives us a picture of the shifting occupational profile of the nation's work force over the last 80-odd years.

Note particularly the striking growth in professional and managerial work, together with the drift from blue- to white-collar jobs. This lies behind most discussion of "postindustrial" society as the direction in which we may be headed.

TABLE 1

	1900	1986		1900	1986
Managerial and professional			**Blue-collar**		
Professional and technical workers	4.1%	13.0%	Skilled workers and foremen	10.3%	12.2%
Managers, officials, and proprietors (nonfarm)	5.9	11.4	Semiskilled workers	12.8	11.4
			Unskilled workers	12.4	4.0
White-collar			Household and other service workers	8.9	18.0
Clerical workers	3.1	16.3	**Farm**		
Sales workers	4.8	12.1	Farmers and farm managers	20.0	3.0
			Farm laborers	17.6	

Source: Statistical Abstract of the United States, 1988.

Next, look at the situation after we have used up *OX* amount of space. We can rent additional space up to *OY,* but only at rising prices (rents). Perhaps expenditures are needed to induce landlords to upgrade "second-class" space. Each new area that is tempted onto the market at a higher price earns real rent, in that it would not appear on the market unless a higher price were being paid. But notice that all the offices previously offered at lower prices are now in a position to ask higher rentals because the price of the marginal unit has increased. Thus we have here a mixture of real rents and economic or quasi rents. **The marginal landlord is receiving real rent. All the other (intramarginal) landlords who can now get higher rentals are the beneficiaries of a scarcity price that gives them a bonus over the real rent they originally received. This bonus is economic or quasi rent.**

Finally we reach the point *OY,* at which there is no more space to be had at any price. Suppose the demand for space continues to rise from D_1 to D_2. The price of office space will rise as well, and *all* landlords will be receiving quasi rents on top of their real rents.

Rents and Prices

Here is where we make a clear distinction. True rent is a cost that must be paid to bring land into production. Quasi rent is not such a cost. It is wholly the result of scarcity and plays no role in determining the real cost to society of bringing a factor to market. If demand fell from D_2 to D_1, a great deal of quasi rent would disappear, although not a foot of office space would be withdrawn. There would merely be a transfer of wealth from landlords to renters.

Thus true rent helps determine price, whereas economic or quasi rent is determined by price. We can see that rent must be paid if office space OX is to appear, but that quasi rent is not a necessary cost of production for space thereafter.

This conclusion, however, applies only to our analysis of costs from a social point of view. From the point of view of the individual producer, the distinction disappears. A renter must pay the landlord whatever it costs to rent space, be it rent or quasi rent. Thus quasi rents enter into the renter's costs and help determine the price that must be asked for his or her goods.

Economic Rents and Allocation

From the social point of view, quasi rent (or, by its other name, economic rent) is a waste. If we could eliminate it—say, by taxing it away—it would not diminish production at all, only the incomes of the owners of scarce resources.

Quasi rents are therefore wholly "unearned" incomes. Nonetheless, they serve a useful function for society. They allocate a scarce commodity, in this case office space, among various claimants.

The fact that quasi rents are a monopoly return is neither here nor there so far as their rationing function is concerned. If there were no quasi rents, office space would be leased at prices that failed to equate quantities demanded and supplied. There would be a "shortage" of space and rationing would take place on some other basis—first come, first served or political influence or having an "in" with the landlord, instead of through the price mechanism.

Economic Rents and Incomes

Finally, we must take careful note of the fact that quasi rents are not returns limited to land. Take car rentals. Suppose we can rent all the car transportation we need at the going price. Suddenly there is a jump in demand and the rentable fleet is too small. Rentals will rise. Until additional cars come onto the market, the fleet owners will simply enjoy economic rents (quasi rents) on their cars.

In the same way, the earnings of actors or authors or of anyone possessing scarce talent or skills are likely to be partly economic rents. An actress might be perfectly happy to offer her services for a good movie role at $50,000, but she may be able to get $100,000 because of her name. The first $50,000, without which she would not work, is her wage. The rest is a quasi or economic rent. A plumber who would be willing to work for standard wages, but who gets double because he is the only plumber in town, earns economic rents. And as we have already seen, these rents explain a part of business profits, as returns going to inframarginal firms.

Capitalization

Economic rents lead us to the process called *capitalization.* As we have mentioned, buyers of land and capital often have the option of buying the actual real estate or machinery they use instead of just paying for its services. Capitalization is the means by which we place a value on a factor as an asset.

Suppose an office building makes $100,000 a year in rentals and we decide to buy the building. How much would it be worth? The answer depends, of course, on the riskiness of the investment. Some buildings, like some machines or bonds or businesses, are safer buys than others. For each class of risk there is a rate of return established by other buyers and sellers of similar assets. Suppose the rate of return applicable to our building is 10 percent. Then we will capitalize it at $1 million. This is because $1 million at 10 percent gives us a return of $100,000.

We can capitalize any factor (or any business) by dividing its current earnings by the appropriate interest rate. The appropriate interest rate tells us the opportunity cost of our money: how much we could get for it if we bought some other factor or asset of similar risk. Notice that as the interest rate falls, so does the opportunity cost. We have to be content with a smaller return of our money. Thus if we are buying land that rents for $2,000, and the appropriate interest rate is 10 percent, the land will sell for $20,000 ($20,000 × .10 = $2,000). If the interest rate *falls* to 5 percent, the value of the land will *rise* to $40,000.

Capitalization and Economic Rents

Capitalization is important in determining the asset prices of factors. It is also important because it gets rid of economic rents! Suppose the $100,000 rental income were virtually all quasi rent and that the building were sold for $1 million. The new owners of the building will still be making $100,000 a year, *but it will no longer be an economic rent.* It will be a normal market return on the capital they expended. They will have paid for their quasi rents in the opportunity cost of their capital.

The gainer in the transaction will be the original owner of the building. Perhaps the building cost him very little and the $1 million sale price came as a great capital gain. He will have capitalized his quasi rents into a large sum of capital; but on that sum, in the future, he can expect to make no more than the normal rate of interest.

Market Price for Factors*

We are finally in a position to assemble the pieces of the puzzle. We have traced the forces that give rise to the supply curves of the different factors, and we understand the explanation for the demand curves as well. Hence we understand how factors are priced in the market, which is to say we understand the mechanism for determining *factor incomes*.

Can we generalize about the result? One would think, in light of the variety of supply curves we have discussed, that this would be impossible. If we think about the nature of the demand curve for factors, however, we see it is not. The shape and position of the supply curve for any factor will determine how much of it appears on the market at any given price. **But whatever the amount of the factor, it will be paid a return equal to the marginal revenue product of that factor.** Remember, the entrepreneur will go on hiring all factors as long as their marginal revenue products are greater than their marginal costs. Thus, whatever the shape or position of the supply curve, the earnings of the factor will always be equal to the marginal revenue it brings to the buyer, as Figure 9 shows.

We could draw other curves showing the collective supply of labor, the supply of savings to a given user, or the total quantity of land, but the conclusion would be the same. In each case, the market rate of wages, interest, and rent would be equal to the marginal revenue product of that factor.

The Marginal Productivity Theory of Distribution

We call this generalization about factor prices the *marginal productivity theory of distribution*. **What it tells us is very simple. The income of any factor will be determined by the contribution each factor makes to the revenue of the enterprise. Its income will be higher or lower, depending on the willingness and ability of suppliers of factor services to enter the market at different prices; but at all prices, factors will earn amounts equal to the marginal revenue they produce.**

---

*In the 1960s there was a spirited controversy about the nature of capital, led by the late English economist Joan Robinson. Robinson challenged the concept of capital as a factor of production. Of course there were *capital goods* of all kinds, but what of capital itself? Labor could be measured in hours, but in what units should capital be measured? What, indeed, *is* a "unit" of capital? How could one add up all the various capital goods—shovels and machine tools and inventories—to arrive at a factor of production called *capital*?

Robinson argued on this point that conventional theory was inherently circular. Capital, unlike labor, is measured not in physical units, but by its *value*. But its value depends on its rate of return, which theory describes as the "marginal product" of capital. Now here is the problem. To know the value of capital you have to *know* its marginal product. In that case, how can one use the value of capital to *derive* its marginal product? Such considerations have shaken the foundations of the theory of capital, but they have not led to much change in the ordinary treatment of capital by businesspeople and economists. Both continue to speak of it as if no conceptual difficulties obscured its meaning—as if you could add up the stream of past investments, less depreciation, and arrive at a meaningful "value of capital" to put into a "production function." We will not probe more deeply into this complex question here, but the student ought to be aware that there are unresolved problems surrounding these basic ideas.

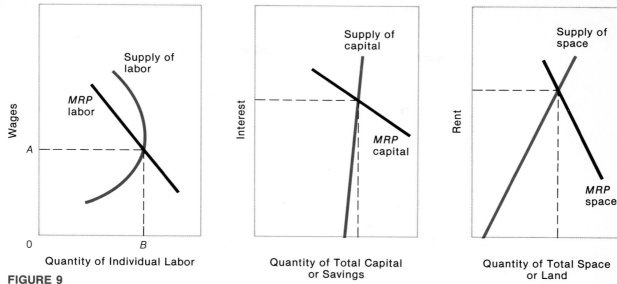

FIGURE 9
Marginal Revenue Products and Earnings
Despite their different shapes and locations, the various supply curves of the factors always help determine the quantity of the factor that will be hired and the remuneration it will receive. In each case, the demand curve is the marginal revenue product curve—the amount of income the entrepreneur will gain from hiring the factor in question. As our graph shows, these derived demand curves may also have differing shapes or locations, but in all cases the intersection of the two curves gives us the information we want. Notice the important fact that the earnings of each factor will be equal to the marginal revenue it earns for its employer. At quantity OB of labor, labor's MRP is OA. This is its wage. The equality of earnings and MRPs is the basis for the claim that in a market of perfect competition there can be no exploitation.

Two conclusions follow from this theory. **The first is that in a perfect market there can be no exploitation of any factor.** That is, each factor will receive an amount exactly equal to the revenue it produces for the firm.* There can be no unpaid labor or unrewarded land or capital. A worker or capitalist or landlord may not be willing to offer his services at going rates of pay, but none can claim that his earnings are less than the revenues he brings into the firm. For as we have seen, every profit-maximizing entrepreneur must keep on hiring factors until their marginal revenue products equal their marginal cost.

Moreover, no factor can claim that some other factor is paid too much. To be sure, some factors will earn quasi rents—a waste from society's point of view, as we have seen. But we have also seen that quasi rents are a temporary phenomenon, slowly eliminated by mobility of the factor in question into an area of scarcity. **In the long run, the return to land, capital, and labor will reflect the actual dollar contribution each makes to output.**

*When a factor is bought directly by a consumer, the factor will receive the money value of the marginal utility it produces for the consumer.

Price and Productivity

The second conclusion follows from the first: **It is that all factors will be paid in proportion to their productivity.**

Suppose an entrepreneur can hire a unit of factor A—say an acre of land that will produce a marginal revenue product of $20, or an extra worker whose marginal revenue product will be $40. We know that the entrepreneur will have to pay $20 to hire the acre of land and cannot pay more than that, and that he or she will have to pay $40 for the worker and cannot pay less than that.

What accounts for the difference between the earnings of a unit of land and a unit of labor? Their marginal revenue products. But these marginal revenue products, we recall, are only the *physical* marginal products of the factors multiplied by the market value of the output to which they contribute. The value of the output must be the same, since land and labor will both be adding to the output of the same commodity. The difference in their marginal *revenue* products is therefore solely the result of the fact that (in this example) a unit of land creates fewer units of output than a unit of labor does.

It follows, therefore, that relative factor prices must be proportional to relative physical productivities, or that

$$\frac{\text{price of factor A}}{\text{price of factor B}} = \frac{\text{marginal productivity of factor A}}{\text{marginal productivity of factor B}}$$

Marginal Productivity and "Justice"

This is a very remarkable solution to the problem of distribution. It says that in truly competitive systems, all factors will be rewarded in proportion to their contribution to output. If an acre of land is only half as productive as a unit of labor, it will be paid only half as much. If it is twice as productive, it will be paid double. If skilled labor produces three times as much as unskilled, its wage rate will be three times that of unskilled, and so on. **The resulting pattern of income distribution thus seems both just and efficient. It seems just because everyone is getting all the income he or she produces, and because no one is getting any income he or she has not produced. It seems efficient because entrepreneurs will use factors in a way that maximizes their contribution to output, thereby not only giving the factors their largest possible reward, but also giving society the greatest overall output to be had from them.**

Is this conclusion valid? Do the earnings of land, labor, and capital reflect their contributions to output? The question takes us from a consideration of how the factor market works in theory—that is, under conditions of perfect competition—to a consideration of how it works in fact. It leads us also to look carefully into the question of whether or not marginal productivity establishes a pattern of rewards that can rest its case on some definition of justice. We inquire into these extremely important questions in our next chapter.

LOOKING BACK

KEY CONCEPTS

Factor services

Direct and derived demand; derived demand is the marginal revenue product of the factor

Supply curve of individual labor is backward-bending.

Supply curve of savings is price-inelastic, except for allocation.

Supply curve of land vs. space

Quasi rents, or economic rents, are scarcity returns. They are price-determined, not price-determining.

Quasi rents are socially wasteful, but useful in allocation.

Capitalization determines factor values by dividing their earnings by the appropriate interest rate.

Ideally, all factors earn their MRPs.

1 The income of the factors of production is derived from the sale of their services—the energy and intelligence of labor, the use of land and capital.

2 The demand for these services sometimes arises directly from their purchaser, as in the case of land bought for a home, but generally it is derived demand—the demand of a firm for the revenues the services will bring. These revenues are called the marginal revenue products of the factor. They are the marginal physical increments to production the factor will create, times the selling price of that output.

3 The supply side of the factor market varies with each factor. Typically, the willingness of individuals to offer their labor increases as earnings rise, and then decreases, giving us a backward-bending supply curve of labor. This is because above a certain income level, individuals prefer to sacrifice some potential money income for leisure.

4 The supply curve of capital that most interests us is the supply of savings. The flow of savings is very responsive to income changes, much less so to price changes. But the allocation of savings among users is highly price-elastic.

5 The supply curve of land is highly price-inelastic; but the supply curve for space is very price-elastic.

6 Quasi rent, or economic rent, is the name for scarcity returns that accrue to factors (land, labor, or capital) by virtue of their scarcity. Unlike true rent, a quasi rent does not tempt additional factors onto the market. A quasi rent is therefore price-determined, not price-determining; it results from a high price for the factor at the margin, and does not constitute an explanation of why the marginal factor is high-priced. (From the viewpoint of the person who pays a quasi rent, it is, of course, a cost and enters into his costs.)

7 Quasi rents are a social waste because they do not induce additional production. But they play a useful role in the allocation of scarce resources.

8 Capitalization is the process by which we use factor earnings (including their quasi rents) to determine the value of the factors themselves. We capitalize a factor by dividing its earnings by the appropriate interest rate for its class of risk. Thus as interest rates decline, capitalized values rise. After a capitalized factor is sold, it no longer earns a quasi rent for its purchaser, but simply a normal return for its degree of risk.

9 We can generalize about factor incomes as ideally determined by the

interplay of their supply curves with their respective demand curves. The demand curves are their marginal revenue product curves or the curve of the marginal revenues they will earn for their buyer. This is called the marginal productivity theory of distribution. Under marginal productivity theory, each factor receives its full contribution to revenues as its reward. There is no possible exploitation.

$$\frac{P_x}{P_y} = \frac{MP_x}{MP_y}$$

10 All factors will also be paid proportionally to their contributions to revenues. Therefore we can write:

$$\frac{\text{price of factor X}}{\text{price of factor Y}} = \frac{\text{marginal product of factor X}}{\text{marginal product of factor Y}}$$

ECONOMIC VOCABULARY

Direct vs. derived demand 334–35
Marginal revenue product 335
Backward-bending supply curve 336
Psychic income 337
Quasi rent 341

Economic rent 342
Capitalization 345
Marginal productivity theory of
    distribution 346
Exploitation 347

QUESTIONS

1. When suburban homeowners buy real estate, what services are they actually buying? When they hire domestic help, what services are they buying? When they borrow money from a bank?

2. What is meant by the *derived* demand for labor? What is its relationship to the marginal revenue product of labor? To clarify your understanding, do the following: (a) Run over in your mind the law of diminishing returns; (b) Be sure you understand how this law affects marginal *physical* productivity; (c) explain how we go from marginal physical product to marginal *revenue* product; and (d) explain how marginal revenue product influences the willingness of the employer to hire a factor.

3. If the rent of a piece of land is $500 and the rate of interest is 5 percent, what is the value of the land? Suppose the rate rises to 10 percent; does the value of the land rise or fall? If the rental increases to $1,000 and interest is unchanged, what happens to the value of the land?

4. What do you think the supply curve of executive labor looks like? Is it backward-bending? Would you expect it to be more or less backward-bending than the supply curve of common labor? Why?

5. Exactly what is rent? How does it differ from quasi rent? Is there any similarity between rent and interest, or rent and wages? What is the role of ownership in rent, profits, *and wages?*

6. What is meant by saying that rent is price-determining? What does it mean to say that economic rent is price-determined? Show this on a diagram.

7. Explain carefully how factor returns are proportional to their marginal productivities. What conditions would be necessary to make this theoretical conclusion true in the real world?

AN EXTRA WORD ABOUT

Economic Justice

Most people in the modern world would admit to an underlying bias in favor of equality in their social values. We hear of policies in every nation that seek to diminish the differences between rich and poor. We hear of very few policies that openly advocate greater inequality. Even policies that support greater inequality—for example, tax loopholes for millionaires—are justified in terms of their ultimate effect in raising the incomes of *all,* which presumably lessens poverty.*

Starting with this bias in favor of equality, we need some understanding of the kind of exceptions we may make to the general rule. That is, we need to know and to look carefully into the arguments in favor of inequality. There are four of them.

1. We agree that inequality is justified if everyone has a fair chance to get ahead. Most of us do not object to inequality of outcome—in fact, we generally favor it—if we are convinced that the race is being run under fair conditions with no one handicapped at the start.

What are fair conditions? That is where the argument becomes complex. Are large inheritances fair? Most Americans agree that *some* inheritance is fair but that taxes should prevent the full passage of wealth from generation to generation. What about inheritances of talent? No one is much concerned about this. Inheritances of culture?

---

*In a very influential book, *A Theory of Justice,* published in 1971, philosopher John Rawls has added an argument in favor of equality as the norm. Suppose, says Rawls, that we were each to step through a "veil of ignorance" into a new society in which we knew nothing whatsoever as to the position we would occupy—neither our gender nor our occupation nor our personal talents. What general distribution of income would we probably wish such a society to have?

The answer, says Rawls, is an *equal distribution.* We might prefer an unequal one if we knew that the basis for inequality favored the particular characteristics we had on the other side of the veil, but not knowing, we would probably choose to take our chances as completely equal income recipients. Rawls's case is sophisticated and contains reasons for making certain exceptions to the rule of equality—exceptions that we follow in our own argument above. But his "justice as fairness" argument has become a powerful basis for making the *general* case for equality as the starting point for a just economic distribution.

For some time we have been getting exercised over the handicaps that are inherited by persons born in the slum or to nonwhite parents.

2. We agree to inequality when it is the outcome of individual preferences. If the outcome of the economic game results in unequal incomes, we justify these inequalities when they accord with different personal desires. One man works harder than another, so he deserves a larger income. One woman chooses to enter the law and make a fortune; another chooses to enter the ministry and make do with a small income. We acquiesce in these inequalities to the degree that they appear to mirror individual preferences.

3. We abide by inequality when it reflects merit. Merit is not quite the same as fairness or personal preference. It has to do with our belief in the propriety of higher rewards when they are justified by a larger contribution to output. Here is the belief which underpins the idea that factors should be paid their marginal revenue product. We do not object to factors receiving different remunerations in the market because we can show that each factor contributes a different amount to total output.

That is, of course, a value judgment. Suppose there are two workers, side by side, on the assembly line. One is young, strong, unmarried, and very productive. The other is older, married, has a large family and many expenses—and is less productive. Should the first be compensated more highly than the second? We find ourselves in a conflict of values here. Our bias toward equality tells us no. Our exception for merit tells us yes. There is no correct solution for this or any other problem involving value judgments. Once again, social values prevail, sometimes paying the younger person more than the older, sometimes both the same, sometimes the older worker more.

4. Finally, we agree in violating the spirit of equality when we are convinced that inequality is for the common good. The common good is often translated into practical terms of gross national product. Thus we may agree to allow unequal rewards because we are convinced (or persuaded) that this inequality will ultimately benefit us all by raising all incomes as well as the incomes of those who are favored.

The difficult question here is to define the common good. There are many conceptions of what such an objective should be. All incorporate value judgments. Even the common good of survival, which might justify giving a larger reward to those who must be entrusted with our survival, is a value judgment.

THE UNAVOIDABLE PROBLEM

Economic justice is a complex, confusing, and often disconcerting idea. It makes us uneasy, not only because it confronts us with the often shaky presumptions we make about it, but also because we recognize that no solution will ever be found that can be demonstrated to be superior to all others.

Yet there is no escape from trying to specify what is meant by economic justice. If we fail to make such an effort, we only end up with a hodgepodge of feelings, many of them contradictory or unsatisfying. This does not mean we can work out a scheme of economic justice free of contradictions or uncertainties. But at least we will have understood why certain contradictions are inherent in the problem, and will be in a position to act with both intelligence and purpose when forced—as are we all—to decide which economic policies are better and which are worse.

CHAPTER 20

How Incomes Are Distributed— in Fact

A LOOK AHEAD

Here is a chapter in which we examine two matters of great importance:

1 The way in which income is actually distributed among individuals or families.
2 The various ways in which we have tried to achieve a fairer income distribution than the existing one.

Once again, it is important not to get bogged down in facts, although the basic realities are important to know. The question to think about is *why* income distribution does not seem to bear much relation to marginal productivity theory, and *why* various efforts to change income distribution have had very different impacts. Thus we are still interested in theory, even though we zero in on the distribution of income in fact.

I n our last chapter we reached the conclusion that factor prices could be explained by their marginal productivities. Does this mean that we now have the key to understanding the actual distribution of income in our society? Can we explain riches and poverty, high-paid professions and low-paid ones, in terms of marginal productivity?

The quick answer to that question is no. Marginal productivity does not explain the basic facts of income distribution as we find it in the United States. Nonetheless, there is a valuable use for the theory. At the end of the chapter we will come back to the question of how we can use marginal productivity. First, however, let us discuss why it fails to explain income distribution as we find it in reality.

RICH AND POOR

Chapter 4 made us familiar with the contours of income distribution. Perhaps you recall our discussion of classes or of the income parade in the box on page 61. How much of this panorama can marginal productivity help us understand? By and large, we can eliminate two ends of the income parade. Marginal productivity theory does not explain the existence or persistence of most poverty, and it does not adequately account for the presence of most very high incomes. Let us begin by seeing why this is the case.

Poverty

Quickly let us review a few major characteristics of Americans who were in poverty in 1987:

- □ About 30 percent of them are black.
- □ About one-half are families headed by a female.
- □ One-tenth of them are over 65 years of age.
- □ Forty percent are juveniles.
- □ Fifty-three percent of the family heads are unemployed.

These are not, of course, the only "reasons" for being poor. **Note, however, that these characteristics of poverty have very little to do with productivity.** Instead, they seem to have much more to do with access to work, and with the incomes society makes available to those who do not labor in the market. Black unemployment rates are twice those of whites. Single mothers often face insuperable difficulties in finding adequate child care. And the elderly poor, often impoverished by medical expenses, are subsisting on meager pensions or relatively low social security benefits.

Low Wages

Marginal productivity theory therefore gives us very little insight into the reasons for the low income of the bottom fifth of the nation. It sheds light on this bottom bracket only to the extent that its members are employed in very-low-wage (presumably low-productivity) jobs. A considerable number of those in poverty do hold low-wage jobs: Two-thirds of poor adults work. But often their low pay is better explained by market imperfections than by attributing low productivity to them.

Thus poverty is a question that we must examine from perspectives other than that of marginal productivity. Why does the economy not produce full employment? Why does it have regional differences in productivity? Why does discrimination exist? Why is there a culture of poverty in the slums, from which it is difficult to break away?

Some of these questions are dealt with in this text. Others go beyond the scope or knowledge of economists. Clearly, when we want to explain most poverty, marginal productivity theory will serve us poorly.

Riches

What about the upper end of the income scale, the top 5 percent of families enjoying incomes over $82,273 or the topmost echelon of millionaires? Can marginal productivity help us explain high incomes?

To some extent perhaps it can. The marginal revenue product—that is, the salable output—of many skilled professions helps to explain why airplane pilots, surgeons, lawyers, skilled artisans, and TV newscasters have high incomes; but even here there is a problem. Some of these high incomes are quasi rents. Pay is high partly because there are many hurdles placed in the way of learning some highly paid skills. Thus, just as in the case of low-wage earners, market imperfections must be taken into account in explaining these extremes of income.

In addition, different ranges of income appear to be accepted in different nations. In the United States, for example, the range between the lowest prevailing wage in a large business establishment and the income of its top management is often greater than 50 to 1: $10,000 to $15,000 being an entry wage for an unskilled office or factory worker and $500,000 to $1 million the remuneration of topmost management. In Japan or Norway much smaller differentials are the rule. Japanese managers typically make less than ten times the salaries or wages of lower-income employees. In Norway the differential is smaller yet—perhaps as low as four to one. In addition, the tax bite on upper-income salaries, at least in Norway, is proportionally much more severe than it is in the United States. The moral seems to be that the ''rules of the game,'' as J. M. Keynes called them, are capable of considerable variation without dulling the incentive that presumably justifies the differentials in the first place.

Property

More important, the topmost echelons of income reflect the unequal ownership of property. As we have seen, wealth is very unevenly distributed. Almost half of all property income is channeled into the hands of the top 2 percent of households. In 1986 interests, dividends, and rents amounted to $595 billion, or 17 percent of all income.

Can marginal productivity explain this concentration of property incomes? Not very well. Conventional economic theory explains the accumulation of wealth by

PERPETUATION OF INCOME DIFFERENCES

Possession of wealth has the added advantage of making it easier for the wealthy, or their children, to go to college or professional school. Recall our anecdote on how poverty causes poverty in the box on page 85. Conversely, high incomes cause high incomes.

Table 1 shows the advantage accruing to children of upper-income families in acquiring the college education that is a steppingstone toward higher incomes for themselves.

TABLE 1

Family Income (1983)	% 1983 High School Graduates Enrolled in College
Under $10,000	25.7%
10,000–14,999	32.3
15,000–19,999	35.9
20,000–24,999	37.2
25,000–34,999	42.7
Over 35,000	58.2

Source: *Statistical Abstract of the United States*, 1985, p. 152.

saving. Undoubtedly some people do accumulate modest sums by refraining from consumption, but they do not accumulate fortunes. If you start with $100,000—a sum possessed by only a very small fraction of all families—and if you invest the sum at 10 percent, paying a 35 percent tax on your interest, it would take a long, long time (actually 37 years) to pile up $1 million.

Very few millions are put together this way. The goal of riches seems to have two approaches. One is via the road of inheritance, the source of approximately half of today's fortunes. The other is via the road of instant riches, the main source of new fortunes, and in most cases the original source of the old fortunes as well.

Instant Wealth

How does someone become rich overnight? Luck is helpful—once, anyway. People who make a fortune in one endeavor rarely go on to make as great a gain in another. Financial institutions, which employ the best expertise available, actually do not fare any better with their investments than the average performance of the stock market.

If luck seems to play a crucial role in selecting the winner, another element establishes the size of the winnings. Suppose an inventor figures it will cost $1

Another example of the tendency of the different income and social levels to reproduce themselves can be seen in the Table 2, which compares the occupations of sons with those of their fathers, for 1973. The figures are not up-to-date because more recent data do not exist; but there is no reason to believe the relationships have changed much, if at all.

TABLE 2

Father's Occupation When Son Was 16	*Son's Occupation in March 1973*		
	White-Collar	*Blue-Collar*	*Farm*
White-collar	60.8%	37.4%	1.8%
Blue-collar	31.6	65.1	3.3
Farm	16.5	44.1	39.4

Source: David L. Featherman and Robert M. Hauser, *Opportunity and Change* (New York: Academic Press, 1978), p. 66.

Although Table 2 shows considerable movement out of one's parent's group into other groups, it also shows that the great majority of white-collar families produce white-collar sons, the preponderance of blue-collar families produce blue-collar sons, and most young farmers come from farming families.

million to build and equip a plant to make a newly patented product. The product should sell at a price that will bring a profit of $300,000. A bank puts up the money.

The plant is built and the expected $300,000 profit is realized. Now comes the instant fortune. To the nation's capital markets, the actual cost of the plant is of no consequence. *What counts is its return and the going rate of return on similar kinds of investments.* If that rate is 10 percent, the inventor's plant is suddenly worth $3 million, for this is the sum that will yield $300,000 at a 10 percent return. The inventor is now worth $2 million over and above what he owes to the bank. He will have risen to the status of instant millionaire because the financial markets will have capitalized his earnings into capital gains, not because his marginal productivity—or his saving—has made him rich.

THE MIDDLE STRATA

Thus we do not look to marginal productivity theory—although we may use other elements of economic analysis—when we seek to explain the presence of very high incomes. Then what about the middle strata, the 75 percent of families who are

TABLE 3
Median Earnings of Males, 1984*
Is marginal productivity the reason for these differences? See text.

Professionals	$32,510
Sales workers	24,053
Managers	23,218
Clerical workers	22,140
Manufacturing operatives	19,217
Service workers	15,537
Laborers, nonfarm	15,023

*Full-time, year-round.
Source: Census Bureau, *Current Population Reports,* p. 60, No. 149, p. 13.

above the status of low income and below that of the top 5 percent? Can marginal productivity help us here?

Some Basic Problems

Consider Table 3. Can we say, on the basis of marginal productivity theory, that a salaried draftsman who earns $20,000 is twice as productive as a laborer who earns $10,000? Or should we say that the draftsman is *only* twice as productive as a laborer because the former makes only twice as much? It is hard to make sense of the question because it is very difficult to figure the marginal revenue products of engineers or laborers. Even if we knew their productivities, it would be difficult to state that earnings in different occupations reflected productivities because of the many barriers to mobility. We will soon discuss this further.

Meanwhile consider a second problem. If we examine the earnings of supposedly homogeneous groups such as female secretaries or male laborers or doctors or professors, we find that some members of the occupation may earn four or five times as much as other members. Few people would claim that a highly paid secretary is as productive as *five* low-paid secretaries or that similar productivity differences could be found in other occupations. Results such as these would be farfetched in the world of pure competition that marginal productivity theory describes.

MARKET IMPERFECTIONS

This last sentence gives us a clue, for it brings us to problems that prevent the market from bringing about the results that theory predicts. **Marginal productivity theory only applies under conditions of pure competition. Market imperfections play the same role in the factor market that noncompetitive market structures play in the market for goods and services. They result in prices higher or lower than the long-run equilibrium prices that a competitive supply and demand setting would produce.** Let us look into some of these imperfections.

Ignorance and Luck

Markets often fail to bring about a level of earnings corresponding to relative marginal productivities because marketers do not have all the relevant information. A skilled mason in Connecticut may not know that there is a brisk demand for masons in Arizona—or even Rhode Island. A high school graduate looking for her first job may not know that the possibilities for high wages are much greater in printing than in retailing. This is one reason why earnings depart from levels that can be explained by a theory based on rational, informed behavior. Luck and chance play roles in determining the spread of ordinary earnings, just as in the attainment of wealth.

Monopolies

Ignorance and luck are involuntary market imperfections. More striking are market imperfections introduced by institutions that deliberately seek to set factor prices above or below equilibrium prices. This is the case whenever there is an element of monopolization in the factor market; for instance, in a small town where one landowner controls virtually all the real estate or where a single bank controls the availability of local capital. In these cases, we would expect the level of rents or interest to be higher than the equilibrium level. In the same way, if one company dominates the labor market, we may find that wages are *below* their equilibrium levels—that labor is paid less than its marginal revenue product because it has nowhere else to look for work.

One of the most important institutions creating factor monopolies is the labor union. Essentially, a union tries to establish a floor for wages above the equilibrium rate that the market would establish. In this way, the economic effect of a union is exactly like that of a minimum wage law.

In dealing with monopolies of all kinds in the factor market, we have to distinguish between two questions. The first has to do with the earnings of the factors. No one doubts that factor earnings can be depressed below their competitive equilibrium levels in a one-company town or can be raised above their competitive levels by a powerful union. The more interesting question is the effect of such changes on the total earnings of the factor. Can a union, by raising wages, increase total payrolls? Or will the effect of higher wages be to shrink payrolls?

Rents and High Incomes

Anything that inhibits the mobility of factors—anything that impedes their movement from lower-paid to higher-paid occupations—creates or perpetuates economic or quasi rents and enters into the explanation of income differences. Barriers of race and wealth, of patents and initiation fees, of geography and social custom—all give rise to shelters behind which such rents flourish. If blacks, for instance, are systematically excluded from managerial positions, the supply of managers will be smaller than otherwise. Existing (white) managers will therefore enjoy economic rents.

Discrimination

The other side of this story is that barriers can constitute sources of discrimination that lower the earnings of those who are discriminated against.

To what extent does discrimination enter into income distribution in the United States? The most obvious instance has to do with blacks. Black families in all categories have incomes well below the corresponding type of white family, as Table 4 shows. The table does not show 1986 Census Bureau findings that the median white household has twelve times the assets of the median black household.

In itself these facts do not establish that wage discrimination exists. An apologist for differentials in wages could claim that there is a real difference in the marginal productivity of whites and blacks. In that case, the question is whether there has been discrimination at a more basic level; for instance, in the access to human capital.

Only a few years ago, it would have been simple to demonstrate that blacks were systematically prevented from acquiring equal skills or gaining access to jobs on equal terms. Their marginal productivity was lower because they were forced into the bottom jobs of society, unable to gain admission into many colleges, kept out of high-wage trades, and simply condemned by their own past poverty from accumulating the money needed to buy an education that would allow them to compete.

This picture is now changing in some important respects, as Table 5 shows. Mean earnings of blacks are closer to those of whites than in the past, especially among younger workers. Among black women aged 35 to 44, they are even higher. This change is the result of a substantial lowering of barriers against blacks entering many professions and occupations.

Discrimination against Women

A second major area of discrimination militates against women. Table 6 compares women's pay (on a full-time, year-round basis) to that of men. As the table shows,

TABLE 4
Median Annual Income by Family Type, 1986*
Black incomes fall below white incomes for every type of household.

Family Type	Black		White		Black/White Ratio
Married-couple families	26,583	(53%)	33,426	(83%)	.79
Wife in labor force	31,949	(34%)	38,972	(45%)	.82
Wife not in labor force	16,766	(19%)	26,421	(38%)	.63
Families maintained by men alone	18,731	(5%)	26,427	(3%)	.71
Families maintained by women alone	9,300	(42%)	16,716	(13%)	.59
All families	17,604	(100%)	30,809	(100%)	.57

Source: Census Bureau, *Current Population Report,* Series *P-60,* No. 157.
*The distribution of families by type is shown in parentheses.

TABLE 5
Mean Earnings of Black As A % of Mean Earnings of Whites, 1985
This table does not show an even more dramatic fact: Recent census studies reveal that whites have almost 12 times as much wealth (assets) as blacks.

Age	Black Workers
15–14	60%
25–34	65
35–44	64
45–54	61
55–64	59
65 and over	60
Total	64

Source: Census Bureau, *P-60*, No. 156.

women typically earn substantially less than men in all occupations. A portion of this differential may stem from women withdrawing from the labor force to have children and to nurture them in their early years, but there is no doubt that these "economic" reasons for pay differentials do not begin to account for the full differences we observe.

In recent years we have seen a good deal of stirring for equal rights for women, and we get the impression that discrimination against women is disappearing. The statistics do not support this. The proportional gap between male and female earnings of full-time workers has not changed substantially since the 1930s!

Will it change? The women's movement has won court battles to establish the right of equal pay for equal work, as well as equal rights to jobs, regardless of sex. Perhaps this will begin to alter our prevailing sexist patterns.

The United States has been very slow to admit women to a full range of professional and occupational opportunities. Only about 15 percent of our doctors are women, for example, whereas in West Germany 20 percent, and in the USSR 70 percent, are women. These surprising percentages leave little doubt that women *could* earn a great deal more than they do, if the barriers of discrimination were removed.

Reference Groups

Another distributional problem arises because people have strong feelings about how much they are entitled to. In our competitive model, each person is a rational income maximizer, out for himself. At no time does any supplier of labor look at the wages of *other* laborers, except to determine whether or not he is being paid the competitive rate of return.

Yet real people do not focus narrowly on their own wages, but look around them at the entire wage structure. A police officer looks at firefighters' wages, at truckers', perhaps even at schoolteachers' incomes. This interest in other incomes has different labels. Sociologists would call it an interest in *reference groups*.

Reference groups seem to be both stable and restricted—people look at groups that are economically close to themselves. This helps explain why very large inequalities in the distribution of economic rewards seem to cause relatively little dissatisfaction, whereas small inequalities can raise a great commotion. A police officer does not expect to make as much as a movie actress—Hollywood is not the reference point. She does expect to make as much as, or more than, a sanitation

TABLE 6
Male and Female Earning Differentials, Full-Time, Full-Year Workers

There is a striking male-female pay differential. Do you think this reflects differences in marginal productivity?

Occupation	Women	Men	Women's Earnings as a % of Men's
Professional	$20,899	$31,534	.66
Technical	17,566	26,336	.67
Sales workers	11,997	24,053	.50
Craft	13,777	22,580	.61
Clerical	14,417	22,140	.65
Operatives	11,817	19,217	.61
Service workers	9,506	15,537	.61
Nonfarm laborers	11,970	15,023	.80
Laborers, farm	5,089	9,564	.53

Source: Census Bureau, *P-60,* No. 149, p. 13. Data are for 1984.

worker, perhaps as much as a teacher. Changes in the pay of her reference groups therefore bring immediate changes in her estimation of the fairness of her own pay.

As a result of these comparisons, groups strongly resist changes in relative wage rates. Sometimes even the person benefiting from a change in relative wages may feel that it is unfair that he or she receive more than someone else. Consequently, labor economists have discovered that wage rates among many groups move together, almost independently of movements in the supply and demand curves in each occupation.

Uses of Marginal Productivity Theory

All these and still other difficulties explain why the distribution of income, even in the middle range, cannot be fully explained by marginal productivity theory, and why we must be very careful in assuming that the theory adequately accounts for variations in earnings—riches and poverty aside.

Should we then forget about the theory? Not quite. For just as the pure theory of competition helped to explain movements and tendencies in the real market, even if not real market prices, so marginal productivity can enlighten us with respect to economic reality. **It tells us how entrepreneurs behave in hiring factors. It explains the simple but crucial fact that entrepreneurs will not knowingly hire a factor (or a team of factors) that does not "pay its way." Thus the theory of marginal productivity serves as a first approximation to a theory of employment for the firm, even if it does not explain very much about factor incomes.** However incomes are determined—by law, power, custom, or the marketplace—entrepreneurs will be guided in hiring factors by their relative profitability, which is to say, by comparing their cost with the marginal revenue product that can be obtained from them. As its marginal productivities rise, more of a factor will be hired. As they fall, less of it will be used.

Thus the theory helps elucidate one aspect of economic life. We simply must be careful not to claim that it explains income distribution or that different levels of earnings are justified by marginal productivity.

PUERTO RICANS, CHICANOS, INDIANS, OTHERS

Blacks are by no means the only racial group that suffers from discrimination. Table 7 shows the family income of Hispanics relative to white families:

TABLE 7

	Income as % of White Family Income 1969	1986
Hispanic	54%	65%

There is a shocking absence of data on the poorest and smallest group of all: American Indians. Based on reports from about half of U.S. reservations, the median income of American Indians is on the order of *one-third* that of white families.

Now, a more cheerful word. If we look at income data of all ethnic groups, we find only three major groups with incomes below the national average: blacks, those of Spanish heritage, and Indians. Of 100 million Americans who claim ethnic backgrounds, 80 million have incomes *higher* than those of Americans who consider themselves to be ethnically native. In 1977 the ethnic groups with the highest average family income were Russians, then Poles, then Italians.

CHANGING INCOME DISTRIBUTION

Can we change the distribution of income? Of course we can. Should we? That is a more difficult question. When we speak of deliberately trying to change the distribution of income, our purpose is usually to make it fairer. By *fairer,* we generally mean more equal, although not always. Sometimes we say it is not fair that certain groups, such as schoolteachers, do not get higher incomes, even though they are already receiving incomes that are above the median for the society. In the discussion that follows, we will largely be concerned with ways of making income distribution fairer by making it more equal.*

If you want to change income distribution, you must choose among four basic ways of going about your task.

*See the extra word on economic justice at the end of Chapter 33.

1. You may try to change the marginal productivities of individuals and then let them fend for themselves on the market.
2. You may try to limit, or perhaps improve on, the workings of the market so that certain people will receive larger or smaller incomes even if their marginal productivities remain the same.
3. You may let marginal productivities and markets alone and intervene by the mechanism of taxes and transfers, rearranging the rewards of society according to some principle of equity.
4. Finally, you can introduce some system of rewards wholly different from market-determined rewards.

This last is the boldest and most far-reaching method, but it is one about which economists have very little to say. Accordingly, we will confine ourselves to the first three methods.

Changing Productivities

Assuming that low marginal productivity is a basic reason—if not the only reason—for low incomes, someone who wants to change income distribution would do well to begin by boosting the marginal productivity of the least skilled and trained.

How can **human capital** be improved? By and large, by giving *education,* a generalized skill, or *training,* a specialized skill, to those who lack them.

Education and Income. A glance at Table 8 makes it clear that there is a strong functional relationship between education and lifetime earnings. We must be careful not to jump to the conclusion that education is the direct cause of these earnings, however. For example, 30 percent of white high school graduates will end up making more money than the average college graduate, and 20 percent of college graduates will make less than the average high school graduate. Clearly there is no guarantee that education will pay off for everyone.

There is also a problem of scale. The table shows us that college graduates as a group have higher incomes. This may be because there are fewer of them and they earn scarcity rents. If everyone went to college, the supply and demand situation would be radically different, and the extra earnings of the college group much smaller.

TABLE 8
Male Education and Average Lifetime Earnings
Education and incomes are obviously correlated. This does not mean that education causes the whole difference. The payoff on educational investment is about 7 to 10 percent.

	Lifetime Earnings (1979)
Elementary school	
0–12 years	$ 845,000
High school	
4 years	1,041,000
College	
1–3 years	1,155,000
4 years	1,392,000

Last there is the problem of circular causation that we encountered earlier in this chapter (see the box, "Perpetuation of Income Differences," on page 000). Education may indeed be a factor in increasing lifetime earnings. It is also true that someone coming from a high-income family will receive more education and will probably earn a high income *because of his or her social station in life*. When we correct for the starting point on the income scale, education still yields a return, but a much smaller one than the figures in Table 8 indicate. **Probably the cost of a college education gives its recipient a lifetime return of about 7 to 10 percent on that investment, hardly a bonanza.**

Investment in Human Capital. Even if the advantages of education are frequently exaggerated in terms of their strictly economic results, there is no doubt that education is a help toward higher income. For one thing, it teaches general skills such as reading, writing, and math, as well as special skills. These are the attributes we speak of as *human capital.*

Equally valuable is its teaching of behavior expected in high-level occupations: how to speak politely, how to be punctual, how to relate to authority, and other often overlooked attributes of classroom discipline that prepare us for jobs, especially managerial jobs.

Intervening on the Demand Side of the Market: Minimum Wages

A quite different way of going about the task of changing the income distribution is to intervene on the demand side of the market. The most widespread current intervention is that of minimum wages—whether imposed by law or unions. Can unions raise wages? Can the government raise the wages of the poor by imposed minimum wages? Few questions in economics generate such heat.

Minimum wages enforced by law and minimum wages enforced by union contract have very similar attributes. Both are equivalent to price supports for agricultural products, in that they establish a price higher than that which the market would establish by itself. If they did not, they would not serve any purpose. Thus in Figure 1 we can view the wage line *AB* as established by union or government, for in both cases its effect is to establish a wage floor above that set by the intersection of supply and demand.

Three effects follow. Some workers will lose their jobs because the new higher minimum wage is above their marginal revenue product (or above what the employer estimates their *MRP* to be). In the diagram, this amount of lost employment is represented by $Q_1 - Q_3$. Here are the delivery boys who are let go when the minimum wage is raised and small grocery stores decide to cut down their help. Here are the elevator operators who are replaced by automatic elevators when a union wage contract finally tips the balance in favor of automation.

Second, some workers—those between O and Q_3—will find their incomes raised. Here are the grocery boys who are kept on at higher pay; the elevator operators who are not fired but have fatter pay envelopes.

Third, there will be a larger number of workers than formerly—those between Q_1 and Q_2—looking for work. Their condition will be neither better nor

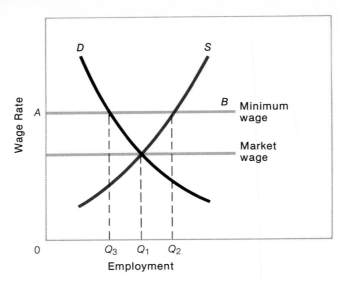

FIGURE 1
Effect of Minimum Wage Laws
The volume of employment would be O_1 if there were no union or minimum wage. This is also the amount of labor that workers would offer at that wage. At the new higher wage level OA employers want to hire only Q_3 worth of labor, while workers are interested in supplying Q_2 worth. As we can see, there must be a labor surplus, just as there is an agricultural surplus when farm prices are set above the market equilibrium.

worse than before the union floor or the minimum wage, for at the previous wage rate these people were not seeking work, nor did they have any income. Nonetheless, their presence in the labor market will be noted in the statistics of unemployment, and it may have social and political consequences.

Net Gain or Loss?

Is there a net gain or loss in the situation? As you can see, the increase in earnings of the group that is retained can be compared with the loss in income of the group that is fired. There are, however, problems in such a comparison. It is much easier to calculate gains and losses on a diagram than to compute them in real life. This is because everything hinges on the slopes of the two curves. Suppose, for example, we think that the demand for labor is extremely inelastic. Then, even though unemployment rises, no one will lose his or her job. All will remain employed with higher earnings. To make the point clear, we show this case in Figure 2, with a totally inelastic demand curve.

On the other hand, suppose the demand for labor is highly price-elastic. Then many workers could lose their jobs, as you can easily see if you draw a diagram with an elastic curve.

The Demand for Labor. What is the shape of the actual demand curve for labor? Studies indicate that it is probably quite steep, so that minimum wage laws do not have a severe adverse effect on total employment. Rather, their effect is likely to be heavily concentrated on certain groups, such as teenagers. The illustration of delivery boys is not an idle one. A high minimum wage may well result in substantial teenage unemployment in menial jobs. This has led to suggestions that there should be lower minimum wages for adolescents than for adults, a scheme that has been used in Europe but that has so far been opposed by labor unions in this

AFFIRMATIVE ACTION PROGRAMS

No government program to alter the distribution of earnings has been more controversial than the affirmative action requirements, for affirmative action offends people in a way that antidiscrimination laws do not. People may object violently to the results of antidiscrimination laws or to techniques of compliance, such as busing; but almost no one is willing to argue that an unequal start is a good thing. People may call training programs for the poor inefficient, but no one calls them un-American.

Affirmative action laws make people angry because they seem to be unfair. In order to find qualified members of minority groups, firms or agencies or universities have to pass over fully qualified members of majority groups. Is it fair not to hire a qualified white electrician because affirmative action gives a preference to a black one, or not to hire a young male graduate student as a teacher because a college is short of women instructors?

The fairness issue really comes down to the obligations of one generation to redress the grievances of another. Suppose that discrimination disappeared magically tomorrow. Blacks would still be holding the jobs that were open to them in the discrimination-filled past. If nothing further were done, it would take about 45 years—the time it takes for a generation to pass through the labor market—for the effects of past discrimination to be eliminated. Affirmative action can thus be viewed as an attempt to offset the impact of past injustice.

Does it also create present injustice? Is the white electrician, passed over because of affirmative action, fairly treated? Many people say no. At the same time, we must try to see the problem from the viewpoint of the whole society as well as from that of the offended person. Is it not possible that a society is becoming more fair, even though some individuals are being treated less fairly? Those persons who suffer from affirmative action today are the victims of our efforts to overcome the unfairness of the past. The problem is therefore whether we can remedy the failures of the past generations without inflicting injuries on some members of the present generation.

Ideally, there is no reason why not. To raise up a previously disprivileged person does not require that someone else be put down. But the ideal solution requires an expansive economy where the demand for talent outstrips the supply. In a sluggish environment, the fight for advancement becomes a zero-sum game, and my gain becomes possible only at the expense of your loss. This has been the situation during the past ten years of inadequate growth. In such a situation there are bound to be losers. The question is: Who will they be?

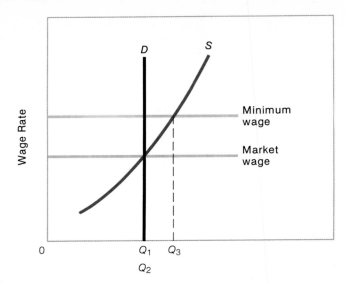

FIGURE 2
Elasticity and Income
The gain to those employed at a higher wage will reflect the elasticity of demand.

country who argue, quite correctly, that it would lead to the hiring of more teenagers at the expense of better-paid older workers.

Union wage settlements also have their gains and losses. Once again, the critical factor is the elasticity of the demand for labor. But there is a difference with respect to the impact of union settlements. Minimum wage laws affect only the fringe of workers whose pay is *below* the minimum. Union settlements typically affect *all* workers in the industry. The incentive to substitute machines for people or simply to economize on labor is therefore much greater. The economic consequences of a union wage settlement are, accordingly, likely to be more substantial than those of a boost in minimum wages.

Taxes and Transfers

A third means of altering income distribution is to tax high incomes and to subsidize low ones. Taxes and subsidies—or *transfers,* as they are called—are used by all governments to redistribute incomes. **By and large, there seems little doubt that the overall effect of this system leaves income shares much as they were before taxes for most income receivers above the poverty line.** In all brackets, income receivers pay about 20 to 25 percent of their incomes to the government, taking federal, state, and local taxes into account.

There is one exception. In recent years revolutionary changes have swept our tax system. Income tax rates, inheritance taxes, and capital gains taxes have been slashed, and income tax brackets indexed to the rate of inflation. At the same time, taxes to finance the social security system have been repeatedly raised. The net effect of these changes has been to shift the total burden of taxation away from the very wealthy. Whereas before the 1980s those with very high incomes tended to pay a somewhat higher share to the government than income receivers in the middle echelons, now that element of progressivity has been sharply reduced, if not eliminated.

Transfer payments, targeted to the poor, the elderly, and the infirm, make a much greater impact on the distribution of income than the tax system does. Without transfer payments, the share of the lowest 20 percent of families in the total income pie would be less than half of what it actually is. Lately, some critics have questioned whether transfer payments are truly an effective remedy for a maldistributed national income. They claim that such payments substitute for income that would otherwise be earned through labor, and that therefore the apparent gains from transfers are a statistical illusion. We examine these contentions in detail in the next chapter.

In Review

Can we change income distribution? Yes, of course. But not all ways of doing so are equally effective. Efforts to change marginal productivities have not shown marked results, although this does not detract from their worthwhileness on other grounds.

Interventions through minimum wages, unions, and government requirements have assuredly redistributed incomes among persons, but they cannot be shown to have altered the national pattern of the distribution of income. **Only income transfers—social security, unemployment insurance, and welfare—have made a substantial and dramatic difference.** We will examine these programs in detail shortly. But first we must acquire some further understanding of the great social problem to which they are addressed.

LOOKING BACK

KEY CONCEPTS

Poverty and riches are not explained by marginal productivity theory.

Middle strata display large intra-occupational variations.

Market imperfections lessen the applicability of marginal productivity theory.

The theory is a useful way of explaining how factor employment is determined.

1 Marginal productivity theory does not explain the two ends of the spectrum of income distribution. Most poverty arises from reasons other than low productivity or from reasons that lie behind low productivity. Very high incomes stem from property, rents, capitalization, and luck rather than from measurable high *MRP*s.

2 The middle strata of income are those most nearly explicable by marginal productivity. But here, too, there are inexplicable differences such as the very large variations we find in a given occupation.

3 The disturbing elements of the real world are many. One is the presence of monopoly elements in income determination. A second is the influence of discrimination. A third is the role of reference groups. All these and other elements lessen the applicability of marginal productivity theory, which assumes a world of pure competition.

4 Nonetheless, marginal productivity theory is useful as a means of explaining how employment is determined. Given the income of factors, however determined, employers will be guided by *MRP*s when they consider how much of a factor to hire.

Three strategies for income redistribution	5 There are three basic strategies for changing income distribution: changing the productivity of factors, changing the demand for factors, and directly changing incomes by taxes or transfers.
It is difficult to assess the effect of education on income and productivity.	6 Efforts to change factor productivity by education—building up human capital—are difficult to measure with precision. Undoubtedly education helps individuals toward higher incomes, but the effect is not clear-cut and may not obtain if everyone is equally educated.
Intervening to offset discrimination has only limited effectiveness.	7 Intervening on the demand side by affirmative action and other programs to remedy discrimination has helped professional blacks and women, but has not much affected the general earnings of disadvantaged groups.
Taxes do not redistribute incomes in the main strata of recipients. Transfers are very important for low-income receivers.	8 Taxes and transfers have different impacts. The effect of taxes is small in changing the shares of income enjoyed by most groups, with the possible exception of the bottom and very top. The most effective method of redistributing income seems to be transfer payments, which amount to 60 percent of the income of the lowest fifth of income receivers.

ECONOMIC VOCABULARY

QUESTIONS

1. How much of the differences in occupational earnings shown in Table 3 do you think can be ascribed to marginal productivity? Can you devise a research program that would enable you to study this with allowance for all market imperfections?

2. Which of the following do you consider to be market imperfections that result in earnings higher than those that would be produced by a free market: (a) certification by state boards before anyone can practice medicine; (b) limiting admission to medical school by aptitude examinations; (c) the costs of education, if these can be covered by a long-term loan.

3. Suppose it could be shown that the marginal productivity of blacks in a given occupation is less than that of whites. Would that explain their lower rates of pay? Justify them?

4. A woman patents a gadget that brings her an annual net income of $100,000. The market return for her category of risky products is 20 percent. What is her

patent worth? Can you show that the higher the degree of risk, the *less* will be her capitalized gain?

5. Do you think the present educational system works to reduce or to maintain the structure of inequality in rewards? How would you suggest changing it if you wanted less inequality? If you wanted more?

CHAPTER 21

Unemployment and Poverty

A LOOK AHEAD

This chapter confronts some of the theory we have learned with some unpleasant facts. It asks:

1 What are the different types of unemployment? How serious are they? And what are the causes of each?

2 What are the causes of poverty, and what has been the record of past antipoverty efforts by government?

Finally, we will ask whether the facts of unemployment and poverty correspond well or poorly to the theories articulated by recent critics of social welfare policy.

*U*nemployment and poverty remain today the most serious social problems of our times. They are not as serious *economic* problems as they were, say, 50 years ago, because unemployment insurance, the welfare system, and social security all help to remove some of the privation associated with a low income. Even without these programs, the general standard of living of the whole nation is higher, and wealth is more widely distributed through the population, so that more of the unemployed have family assets to fall back on than would have been the case back then. But as *social* problems unemployment and poverty are perhaps even more serious than they were. Since the 1930s, the rural country life into which the urban poor and the unemployed could (and did) retreat has for the most part disappeared. For most people today, being without work means having no purpose in life; to be without income is to feel without worth.

UNEMPLOYMENT

All unemployment is not the same. There is a world of difference, for example, between the millworker whose plant has closed down for good and the journeyman carpenter temporarily laid over between jobs. Equally, though for less obvious reasons, we must distinguish between the secretary minding her children at home while seeking employment in a downtown office building, and the housewife who may be doing exactly the same sort of housework each day, but who is not actively seeking some other employment.

Kinds of Unemployment

Economists distinguish among several types of unemployment. The journeyman carpenter mentioned above, along with agricultural laborers migrating from one harvest to another, this year's pool of college graduates interviewing for their first jobs, and many others, are described as **frictionally unemployed.** That is, their movement between jobs is part of their normal life style or a normal feature of the particular stage of their careers. It may not be pleasant, but it is temporary; it helps the economy to function efficiently; and it is not a major source of policy concern.

The secretary and the housewife are both "unemployed," if you like, and may spend their days in exactly the same way, but economists treat them as quite different cases. The secretary is counted as officially unemployed, the housewife as not. That is because the housewife is not *actively seeking work outside the home.* Her labor is not part of the market economy, and in technical terms she is said to be a nonparticipant in the labor force. (If she would like to work outside the home but is not actively looking because she has heard that no jobs are available, we would have still another term for her: *discouraged worker*). The secretary, on the other hand, is actively seeking paid employment, and therefore she is counted as unemployed. Is her unemployment frictional? That depends on how long it lasts and how often it recurs. If our secretary is a temp who regularly works only one- or two-week stints before seeking a new employer, then we would class her unemployment experiences as frictional.

Our concern for the unemployed must focus on the nonfrictional cases, on the millworker whose mill closes because of technological change or international competition, on the auto worker who receives a "pink slip" because of recession, on the teacher "RIF'ed" in a budget cutback, on the teenager who has never held a job because she could never find one. These are the people on whom the burden of unemployment falls. We will refer to them as the *involuntarily unemployed.*

Involuntary Unemployment

Microeconomic theory, as we learned in Chapters 14 and 15, tells us that employers will hire labor as long as the revenue produced by each successive person exceeds his or her cost. The same theory also tells us that workers will seek employment as long as the (marginal) utility of their income is greater than the (marginal) disutility of their work.

This makes perfect sense from the microeconomic point of view, in which we trace the reasons for, and the consequences of, the actions of individuals or firms. But this analysis of unemployment has a curious implication. According to this theory, no one can be involuntarily unemployed! A worker may dislike a job more than he or she likes its pay and may therefore decline the job—but that can hardly be called *involuntary* unemployment. And a worker who likes or wants a job has only to offer his or her services for slightly less than the going wage. In this view, only market imperfections (such as the minimum wage), can prevent workers from bidding down wages by enough to secure employment.

Keynes's Objection

That was the view of almost all economists in the 1930s, despite the fact that unemployment rates were climbing toward a quarter of the work force. It was Keynes who pointed to the flaw in the reasoning. He observed that there were circumstances which would induce employers to hire more workers even if they did not cut their wage demands. This occurred when prices rose, but money wages did not—for instance, if there was a flurry of speculative buying in the midst of a depression. Then business picked up, even if momentarily, and employers took on more workers.

Now here is the point. Because there was a great deal of unemployment, these workers were easy to find. Yet the fact that they were accepting the going wage even *though prices were rising* meant that actually they were taking a cut in real wages. If they were willing to work at these reduced real wages, they certainly would have been even *more* willing to work at the wage levels that prevailed before the price rise. Yet employers did not seek to hire them at those previous real wages, nor, absent the price rise, did real wages fall enough to induce employers to hire them. It followed, then, that unemployment in these circumstances had nothing to do with voluntary decisions taken by individual workers. Unemployment was forced on workers because employers were not concerned with microeconomic decisions about marginal revenue and marginal product, but about *expected longer-term results* of enlarging their output. They could not see, in the prevailing general business climate, how they could possibly sell an increased level of output. They feared that the longer-term results would simply be larger losses.

Micro vs. Macro

Involuntary unemployment therefore takes us to a different plane of analysis from voluntary employment. It involves such elements as expectations about the movements of large aggregates, like gross national product, over which employers have no control whatsoever. That is one of the fundamental differences between micro- and macroeconomics. As microeconomists, we cannot say a great deal about the unemployment that comes about because of *sectoral* movements. To understand the roots of mass unemployment, we must be macroeconomists. But to understand the nature of—and the remedies for—other kinds of unemployment, we need the kind of cost-revenue analysis for which microeconomics provides the necessary tools.

Unemployment and Social Insurance

While the unemployment insurance system is a social safety net for some, it misses a surprisingly large fraction of the unemployed. In 1987 only 37 percent of those unemployed were receiving any unemployment insurance checks at all. The rest had to rely on whatever savings they had, on their family, or on private charity—or simply went on relief. These large holes exist in the safety net because individuals lose their unemployment checks after they have been unemployed for more than two quarters, or because they have not worked long enough to be eligible for unemployment checks when they become unemployed. Even those lucky enough to get unemployment checks find that they replace less than half of their previous earnings. By contrast, the replacement rate is much higher in Europe and a much larger fraction of the unemployed are eligible for benefits. In Britain the unemployed are eligible for benefits even if they have never worked before!

POVERTY

We discuss poverty together with unemployment for a very good reason: **Changes in unemployment are the single largest cause of changes in poverty.** In recessions, when previously middle- or working-class citizens lose their jobs, the poverty rate rises. In recoveries, new opportunities open up and poverty declines as economic conditions improve. Thus the poverty rate rose steadily from 13 percent in 1980 to 15.3 percent in 1983 before declining by nine-tenths of a percentage point—nearly 1.8 million people—in the strong growth year of 1984. Moreover, where you find a particular demographic grouping that is prone to high rates of

UNEMPLOYMENT PROFILE

We need to pay heed to the extraordinarily wide variation of unemployment rates among different segments of the population. Just as an instance, unemployment rates for black teenagers, corrected for those who have dropped out of the labor force—not at school, not at work, not trying to get work—reach levels of up to 90 percent in central city slums!

Table 1 shows us the tremendous spread in the incidence of unemployment, disregarding the pathology of the slum. Notice that black males bear twice the impact of unemployment that white males do, black females double the impact of white females. The table bears study and thought.

Structure of Unemployment

TABLE 1

In July 1988 the national unemployment rate was 5.4 percent. This table shows how that average figure conceals very much higher rates among certain groups.

July 1988		*July 1988*	
Males	6.2%	Females	6.2%
White males	5.4	White females	5.2
16–19	15.5	16–19	13.4
20–24	6.6	20–24	7.1
25–54	3.3	25–54	4.2
55–64	2.6	55–64	2.8
65 & up	2.7	65 & up	5.2
Black males	12.7	Black females	13.2
16–19	34.4	16–19	34.9
20–24	18.4	20–24	22.3
25–54	8.8	25–54	9.2
55–64	3.6	55–64	3.1
65 & up	.7	65 & up	7.4

Source: Bureau of Labor Statistics, *Employment and Earnings,* August 1988, p. 10.

unemployment—such as blacks, Hispanics, or teenagers—you are likely to find a high incidence of poverty in that population. We can see the picture in Figure 2.

Nevertheless, the problem of poverty goes well beyond the problem of unemployment: to single and separated women with small children, to the elderly whose

IS THERE A NATURAL RATE OF UNEMPLOYMENT?

The collapse after 1969 of the short-run Phillips curve led many economists to the view that the "true" Phillips curve was not a curve, but a vertical line (see Figure 1). Such a line implies that there exists in the economy a single unemployment rate, dubbed the **natural rate of unemployment,** which is the only unemployment rate consistent with a stable, unchanging rate of inflation.

FIGURE 1

The natural rate hypothesis has radical implications for economic policy, undermining the prescriptions of Keynesian economics. For example, if

working years are behind them, to the disabled, the handicapped, and the educationally disadvantaged, and to those who live in parts of the country that have not enjoyed a full measure of growth and economic development.

Measuring Poverty

How do we know that a family is poor? This is not so simple a question as it seems. Moreover, much in our attitude toward poverty and toward the poor themselves can be shown to rest on the way in which we define it.

For the purpose of counting the poor, the government establishes a *poverty line*—an income level below which a family is considered to be poor. The poverty government policy attempts to reduce unemployment below the natural rate, the consequence would be not merely a higher, but steady rate of inflation as the stable, upward-sloping Phillips curve had seemed to show. Rather there would be *accelerating inflation,* worsening as time went on. If government persisted in this policy, *hyperinflation* and economic collapse would result.

The existence of a natural rate—that is, a rate above which inflation begins to move steadily upward—has become widely accepted among American economists. It has had much less influence elsewhere in the world, and virtually none on policymakers. It accords particularly well with the theory that says if economic actors can accurately anticipate events, it is likely that they will behave in inflationary ways, after unemployment reaches a perceived danger point. In that case, the economy would have a natural rate of unemployment.

But in recent years this hypothesis has come under increasing criticism. Two reasons account for the newly critical views. First, empirical estimates of the "natural" rate have shown it to be unstable: It appears to rise in recessions and decline in booms. This means that there is no simple, reliable way to predict just when a declining unemployment rate will lead to quickening inflation—something that one would hope the natural rate would allow us to do.

Second, there is increasing skepticism about the applicability of the rational expectations idea to the real economy. In a labor market where contracts prevail, rather than untrammeled perfect competition, and where reliable information about the economy is very costly and difficult for ordinary people to obtain, it may be impossible to form accurate predictions, so that the rational expectations theory does not apply. In that case, a natural rate of unemployment will not exist at all.

line is based on calculations of the cost of a minimal standard of living in different regions of the country for families of differing sizes. As part of this process, the Agriculture Department computes the cost of maintaining a basic family diet (the "Thrifty Food Plan"). In 1986 the official poverty line was $11,203 for a family of four.

Naturally, the poverty line changes from year to year with inflation, changes in the relative prices of foods and other commodities, and to some extent with changes in the standards of the community. Thus, while 50 years ago a rural family without electricity or plumbing might not be considered poor, today the costs of such necessities are incorporated in the poverty line. Still, the poverty line concept is known as an *absolute standard* for poverty, since it attempts to measure poverty by measuring purchasing power over a specific basket of consumer goods. *Such absolute measures tend to show that the incidence of poverty has declined over the past several decades,* although by all measures poverty rose in the late 1970s and early 1980s.

Absolute vs. Relative Poverty

A quite different conception holds that poverty should be thought of in *relative* terms, by comparing the income levels of the poor with those of society as a whole. The idea here is that poverty is *subjective* and *comparative* rather than absolute: People feel poor because they cannot have what others take for granted rather than because they cannot afford to purchase a specific item or items. Thus a family might be considered poor if its income were less than (say) half the median income for families of the same size—a result which for a family of four would have given a poverty line of $14,729 in 1986. **Measures of relative poverty, which are really measures of income distribution, show that there has been little change in such poverty over the years.** While living standards for the whole population have improved, the poor remain as far behind the average household as they ever were.

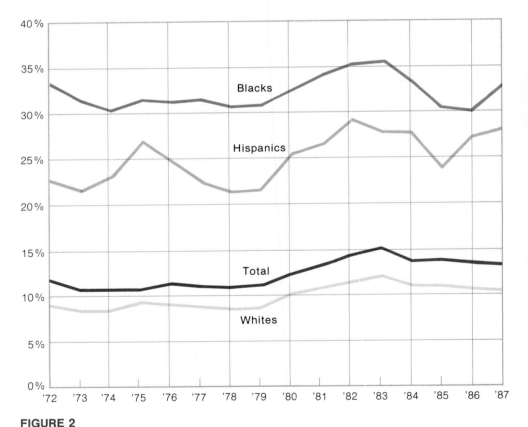

FIGURE 2
People Living in Poverty
Percentage of the total population and selected groups living below the poverty line for each year.
Source: *Census Bureau, P-60, No. 149.*

WELFARE PROFILE

What racial characteristics do welfare recipients have? The answer depends very much on whether we are examining short-term welfare recipients, who are on welfare for one or two years out of ten, or long-term recipients, who are on welfare for eight or more years out of ten.

TABLE 2

	Percent of Entire Population	*Percent of Short-Term Recipients*	*Percent of Long-Term Recipients*
All individuals	100.0%	12.3%	4.4%
White	88.3	84.5	44.7
Black	11.7	15.5	55.5

Source: Richard D. Coe, "Welfare Dependency: Fact or Myth?" *Challenge,* Sept.–Oct. 1982, p. 49. Reprinted with permission of publisher, M. E. Sharpe Inc., 80 Business Park Drive, Armonk, New York.

Table 2 shows that from 1969 to 1978 short-term recipients closely mirrored the racial proportions of the entire population, whereas long-term recipients were disproportionately black. The lesson seems to be that bad luck, which forces most individuals onto welfare, is color-blind, whereas the escape from bad luck is heavily weighted against blacks. This is largely the case because 40 percent of long-term black individuals on welfare were women with young children, who have a particularly hard time in finding or holding jobs. Even in this most disadvantaged group, however, approximately 60 percent were on welfare for five years or less out of ten.

CURING POVERTY

What can be done about poverty? One large answer brings us back to the issues of macroeconomics. Anything that will raise the rate of growth of GNP will, *ceteris paribus,* reduce the level of poverty. But there is also a second category of response, closer to the analytic viewpoint of microeconomics. Let us look into the problem from this vantage point.

Welfare

Few issues are more controversial these days than such transfer programs, known as *welfare.* Defenders of welfare programs declare them to be an essential part of the "safety net" of a fair-minded society. Opponents declare that welfare may be well-intentioned, but that it spreads the deadly virus of welfare dependency—a loss of incentive that eventually condemns the poor to a lifetime of passivity and helplessness.

Recently, the critics' case has been laid out at length by Charles Murray,* who argues for the abolition of most welfare programs on the ground that while spending for those programs has risen dramatically since 1950, poverty has not declined at all. Murray asserts that there is cause and effect here: Rising expenditures on social welfare have produced rising welfare dependency, destroying the structure of individual and family responsibility on which the work ethic itself is based.

Murray's arguments have generated much attention, but like the supply-side theories of a few years earlier, they have come under heavy criticism. Close students of the relationship between welfare programs and poverty come to just the opposite conclusion from Murray: that variations in poverty have stemmed primarily from changes in economic conditions, and not at all from a perverse effect of changes in welfare spending. They point out that welfare payments grew by the same amount from 1965 through 1969 as from 1969 through 1974, yet poverty declined in the former period and increased in the latter. The reason: declining economic performance, not a change in welfare policy.†

The Extent of Welfare

Other studies have approached this question on a case-by-case basis, to see what kind of families go on welfare and what happens to them when they do. These studies have tended to show some surprising results. One, for example, dealing with welfare recipients for the period 1969–1978, came up with the following conclusions:

1. In any single year, about 10 percent of the entire population received some welfare.
2. Over the entire ten years, about one-quarter of all individuals received some welfare.
3. About one-half of all families who received welfare were recipients for only one or two years in ten.
4. Less than one family in ten who received welfare continued to receive it for eight or more years out of ten.

Summing up an extended study into the characteristics of welfare studies, Richard D. Coe writes:

> It is difficult to conclude . . . that there is something inherently pernicious about the welfare system—that it poisons those who touch it with a debilitating dose of dependency. Quite the contrary. The welfare system would seem to be more accurately portrayed as a temporary fallback position for those individuals who suffer

*Charles Murray, *Losing Ground* (New York: Basic Books, 1984).
†Sheldon Danziger and Peter Gottschalk, "The Poverty of Losing Ground," *Challenge,* May–June 1985, p. 490.

TABLE 3
Female-Headed Households and AFDC Aid
Despite a rising percentage of female-headed households,
the real value of Aid for families with dependent
Children has fallen.

Year	Percentage of Nonaged Families with Children Headed by Women (%)	Real AFDC Plus Food Stamp Guarantee (Dollars)
1960	n.a.	$6,715
1964	n.a.	6,604
1968	10.7%	7,129
1972	13.8	8,894
1976	16.7	8,743
1980	19.8	7,486
1984	20.8	6,955
1985	19.3	5,624

unexpected shocks to their more normal style of life. For nonelderly men, these shocks would most likely be an involuntary job loss; for married women, a divorce or separation; for an unmarried woman, the birth of a child. For the vast majority of these people, the welfare system serves as a stepping stone back to a more normal standard of living.*

Finally, we should note that the real value of payments under the Aid for Families with Dependent Children (AFDC) and food stamps programs—the main welfare programs for poor families—has been declining consistently since 1972. Table 3 shows that the purchasing power of such assistance is now over 30 percent less than it was a decade and a half ago, despite the fact that the eligible population, measured by such indicators as the proportion of female-headed households, has been rising. In other words, smaller per person benefits are being spread out to meet an increasingly needy population.

Helping Poor Families

Can poverty be helped? Or should we accept whatever levels exist as the best results of the market system? This is a difficult question on which to arrive at a balanced view.

In the 1960s, under the leadership of President Johnson, the United States declared a War on Poverty. Everyone "knows" that it failed. But did it? If one looks at the incidence of poverty *after taking account of transfer payments* in various groups in 1967 and again in 1980, one comes to some surprising conclusions. Particularly, the incidence for nonwhite men fell sharply—by 40.5 percent!—while that for nonwhite women fell by nearly 15 percent. But the greatest progress of all came among the aged, whose poverty rates were cut in half for whites and by a third for nonwhites.

So it is clear that transfers can reduce poverty. But we must recognize that this

*Coe, "Welfare Dependency," *Challenge*, p. 49.
*James T. Patterson, *America's Struggle Against Poverty 1900–1980* (Cambridge: Harvard University Press, 1981).

was not entirely the result of the War on Poverty itself. James Patterson's study* identifies two different factors that were operating at the same time. The first and most important was the increase in the real value of social security payments beginning in 1972. Social security is not a welfare program—its payments flow to the poor and the nonpoor alike—but it is nevertheless America's most effective bulwark against poverty among the aged.

The second factor was a "welfare explosion" that occurred in the early 1970s. This consisted primarily of poor people taking advantage, as they had not previously, of all of the benefits Congress had made available to them in theory under the law. As a result of these two forces, poverty declined substantially, until recession and budget cuts pushed rates back up in the 1980s.

Can poverty be *eliminated*? Probably not, especially if one views poverty in relative rather than absolute terms. Still, there is no reason to think that the *level* of poverty is beyond influence or control. Indeed, the most careful studies confirm what common sense suggests: Within the modest limits of our existing assistance programs, people are better off with more money—as well as food, housing, and other essentials—than with less.

LOOKING BACK

KEY CONCEPTS

Frictional unemployment is a normal feature of an efficient economy.

1 Some workers will always be in transition from one job to another, and some types of work necessarily involve periods of unemployment. These are not matters of immediate policy concern.

Involuntary unemployment

2 Involuntary unemployment occurs when workers cannot find work at any reasonable wage. The level of involuntary unemployment rises and falls with the level of aggregate demand.

Unemployment has a highly differential impact.

3 Certain categories of workers, especially minorities and the young, experience more frequent and longer spells of unemployment than prime-aged white males.

Absolute vs. relative poverty

4 Official measures of unemployment are based on calculations of the cost of a minimally decent standard of living. These tend to show progress over time. Some scholars argue that poverty is inherently relative and subjective; measures of poverty based on the income distribution tend to show little change over time.

Unemployment causes poverty.

5 The most important determinant of changes in the rate of poverty is changes in the rate of unemployment. The rise in poverty in the 1980s is almost entirely due to the poor economic performance in the early part of the decade.

Transfer payments relieve poverty.

6 The growth in transfer payments in the 1970s has reduced the burden of poverty, especially on the elderly. Some critics suggest that they have also removed the incentive for poor people to work, but the evidence indicates that it is changes in unemployment, not changes in transfer programs, that are responsible for the rise in pretransfer poverty rates.

ECONOMIC VOCABULARY

Frictional unemployment 374	Absolute poverty 380
Involuntary unemployment 375	Relative poverty 380

QUESTIONS

1. The Bible tells us that the poor shall always be with us. Is this true if we define poverty in absolute terms? In relative terms? Suppose we had an egalitarian society, such as the early *kibbutzim* in Israel? Was there poverty on the *kibbutzim?* Were they "affluent"?

2. How are we to interpret the idea of involuntary unemployment? When 10 million people cannot find work, does that suggest forces beyond the control of individuals? And yet, would not work be available for many of these individuals if they offered their services at sufficiently low rates of pay? Is there an implicit social standard of wages that plays a role in the distinction between voluntary and involuntary unemployment?

3. Do you remember the story about poverty and its causes in Chapter 5? How would you interpret that story in terms of what you now know about poverty?

4. Do you think there is something to the idea of "welfare dependency"? If so, what changes in social institutions might reduce it? Sink-or-swim policies? Retraining? Relocation? How would you argue as an economist for these policies—or against them? How would you decide how much it would make sense to spend on policies such as job retraining?

PART IV

THE REST OF THE WORLD

The Gains and Strains of Trade

A LOOK AHEAD

In these last chapters we look again at America in the world economy: first, in terms of our economic relationships; at the end, in a broader, historic perspective.

Chapter 22 takes another look at the economics of international exchange. This will introduce us to one of the most useful ideas in all of economics—that exchange can yield gains in productivity. In order to understand this, we will have to master the principle of comparative advantage—the way in which trade can benefit two nations (or regions or individuals), even though one of the two is more productive than the other in everything it does! The answer to this seeming paradox, we shall see, lies in the efficiency of specializing productive effort. After we have learned about the gains from trade, we review the pros and cons of free trade.

*B*y now we are certainly aware of the importance of the world economy for American economic prospects. Nevertheless, we have not yet analyzed the central problem of international economic relations. That central problem is the gains from trade—and the strains of trade. Until we have understood these crucial issues, we cannot grasp the underlying issue of international economics: the bias of nationalism.

The Bias of Nationalism

The bias of nationalism is the curious fact that relationships and propositions that are perfectly self-evident in the context of "ordinary" economics suddenly appear suspect, not to say downright wrong, in the context of international economics.

Suppose that the governor of an eastern state—let us say New Jersey—wanted to raise the incomes of his constituents and decided that the best way to do so was to encourage some new industry to move there. Suppose furthermore that his son was very fond of grapefruit and suggested to him one morning that grapefruit would be an excellent addition to New Jersey's products. The governor might object that grapefruit needed a milder climate than New Jersey had to offer. "That's no problem," his son might answer. "We could protect our grapefruit by growing them in hothouses. That way, in addition to the income from the crop, we would benefit the state from the incomes earned by the glaziers and electricians who would be needed."

The governor might murmur something about hothouse grapefruit costing more than ordinary grapefruit, so that New Jersey could not sell its crop on the competitive market. "Nonsense," his son would reply. "We can subsidize the grapefruit growers out of the proceeds of a general sales tax. Or we could pass a law requiring restaurants in this state to serve state grapefruit only. Or you could bar out-of-state grapefruit from New Jersey entirely."

"Now, my boy," the governor would return, "in the first place, that's unconstitutional. Second, even if it weren't, we would be making people in this state give up part of their incomes through the sales tax to benefit farmers, and that would never be politically acceptable. And third, the whole scheme is so inefficient it's just downright ridiculous."

But if we now shift our attention to a similar scene played between the prime minister of the small nation Nova Jersia and his son, we find some interesting differences. Like his counterpart in New Jersey, the son of the prime minister recommends the growing of hothouse grapefruit in Nova Jersia's chilly climate. Admittedly, that would make the crop considerably dearer than that for sale on the international markets. "But that's all right," he tells his father. "We can put a tariff on foreign grapefruit, so none of the cheap fruit from abroad will undersell ours."

"My boy," says the prime minister after carefully considering the matter, "I think you are right. It is true that grapefruit in Nova Jersia will be more expensive as a result of the tariff, but there is no doubt that a tariff looks like a tax on them and not on us, and therefore no one will object to it. It is also true that our hothouse grapefruit may not taste as good as theirs, but we will have the immense satisfaction of eating our *own* grapefruit, which will make it taste better. Finally, there may be a few economists who will tell us that this is not the most efficient use of our resources, but I can tell them that the money we pay for hothouse grapefruit—even if it is a little more than it would be otherwise—stays in our own pockets and doesn't go to enrich foreigners. In addition to which, I would point out in my television appearances that the reason foreign grapefruit are so cheap is that foreign labor is so badly paid. We certainly don't want to drag down the price of our labor by making it compete with the cheap labor of other nations. All in all, hothouse grapefruit seems to me an eminently sensible proposal, and one that is certain to be politically popular."

Source of the Difficulty

Is it a sensible proposal? Of course not, although it will take some careful thinking to expose all its fallacies. Will it be politically popular? It may very well be, for economic policies that would be laughed out of court at home get a serious hearing when they crop up in the international arena. Here are some of the things that many of us tend to believe.

Trade between two nations usually harms one side or the other.

Rich countries can't compete with poor countries.

There is always the danger that a country may sell but refuse to buy.

Are these fears true? One way of testing their validity is to see how they ring in our ears when we rid them of our unconscious national bias by recasting them as propositions in ordinary economics.

Is it true that trade between businesses or persons usually harms one side or the other?

Is it true that rich companies can't compete with poor ones?

Is it true that one company might only sell but never buy—not even materials or the services of factors of production?

What is the source of this curious prejudice against international trade? It is not, as we might think, an excess of patriotism that leads us to recommend courses of action that will help our own country, regardless of the effect on others. For, curiously, the policies of the economic superpatriot, if put into practice, would demonstrably injure the economic interests of his own land. The trouble, then, springs from a root deeper than mere national interest. It lies in the peculiarly deceptive problems posed by international trade. What is deceptive about them, however, is not that they involve principles that apply only to relations between nations. All the economic arguments that elucidate international trade apply equally well to domestic trade. The deception arises, rather, for two other reasons.

1. **International trade requires an understanding of how two countries, each dealing in its own currency, manage to buy and sell from each other in a world where there is no such thing as international money.**
2. **International trade requires a very thorough understanding of the advantages of, and arguments for, trade itself.**

Gains from Trade

In a general way, of course, we are all aware of the importance of trade. *It is trade that makes possible the division and specialization of labor on which our productivity is so*

TABLE 1

Unspecialized Production: Case 1

Wooltown and Cottontown each put half their populations to work at wool and cotton, with these results.

Production	Wooltown	Cottontown
Wool (lbs)	5,000	2,000
Cotton (lbs)	10,000	20,000

largely based. **If we could not exchange the products of our specialized labor, each of us would have to be wholly self-supporting, and our standard of living would thereupon fall to that of subsistence farmers. Thus trade (international or domestic) is actually a means of *increasing productivity*, quite as much as investment or technological progress.**

The importance of trade in making possible specialization is so great that we should take a moment to make it crystal clear. Let us consider two towns. Each produces two goods: wool and cotton; but Wooltown has good grazing lands and poor growing lands, while Cottontown's grazing is poor, but growing is good. Suppose, moreover, that the two towns had equal populations and that each town employed half its people in cotton and half in wool. The results might look like Table 1.

As we can see, the same number of grazers in Wooltown turn out two and one-half times as much wool as they do in Cottontown, whereas the same number of cotton farmers in Cottontown produce double the amount of cotton that they do in Wooltown. One does not have to be an economist to see that both towns are losing by this arrangement. If Cottontown would shift its woolworkers into cotton, and Wooltown would shift its cotton farmers into wool, the output of the two towns would look like Table 2 (assuming constant returns to scale).

Now, if we compare total production of the two towns (see Table 3), we can see the gains from specialization.

In other words, specialization followed by trade makes it possible for both towns to have more of both commodities than they had before. No matter how the gains from trade are distributed—and this will depend on many factors, such as the relative elasticities of demand for the two products—both towns can gain, even if one gains more than the other.

Unequal Advantages

If all the world were divided into nations, like Wooltown and Cottontown, each producing for trade only a single item in which it has a clear advantage over all others, international trade would be a simple matter to understand. It would still present problems of international payment, and it might still inspire its prime ministers of Nova Jersia to forgo the gains from trade for political reasons that we will examine at the end of this chapter. But the essential rationale of trade would be simple to understand.

TABLE 2

Specialized Production

They move all their labor force to the more productive task, with these results.

Output	Wooltown	Cottontown
Wool	10,000	0
Cotton	0	40,000

TABLE 3
The Gain From Specialization
Comparing the output of the two towns together, before and after, shows the gains from specialization.

Output	Mixed	Specialized	Gain from Specialization
Wool	7,000	10,000	3,000
Cotton	30,000	40,000	10,000

It is unfortunate for the economics student as well as for the world that this is not the way international resources are distributed. Instead of giving each nation at least one commodity in which it has a clear advantage, many nations do not have such an advantage in a single product. How can trade possibly take place under such inauspicious circumstances?

To unravel the mystery, let us turn again to Cottontown and Wooltown, but this time call them Supraville and Infraville, to designate an important change in their respective abilities. Although both towns still enjoy equal populations, which are again divided equally between cotton and wool production, in this example Supraville is a more efficient producer than Infraville in *both* cotton and wool, as Table 4 shows.

Is it possible for trade to benefit these two towns when one of them is so manifestly superior to the other in every product? That seems out of the question. But let us nonetheless test the case by supposing that each town began to specialize.

Trade-off Relationships

But how to decide which trade each town should follow? A look at Figure 1 may give us a clue. Production possibility diagrams are familiar to us. Here we put them to use to let us see the results of trade.

What do the diagrams show? First, they establish maximums that each town could produce if it devoted all its efforts to one product. Since we have assumed that the labor force is divided, this means that each town could double the amount of cotton or wool it enjoys when it divides its workers 50-50. Next, a line between these points shows the production frontier that both towns face.* We see that Supraville is located at point *A,* where it has 5,000 pounds of wool and 20,000 pounds of cotton, and that Infraville is at *B,* where it has 3,000 pounds of wool and 10,000 pounds of cotton.

But the diagrams (and the figures in the preceding table, on which they are based) also show us something else. It is that each town has a different "trade-off" relationship between its two branches of production. When either town specializes in one branch, it must, of course, give up the output of the other. **But each town**

---

*Why are these lines drawn straight and not bowed, as in Chapter 7? As we know, the bowing reflects the law of increasing cost, which makes the gains from a shift in resource allocation less and less favorable as we move from one extreme of allocation to another. Here we ignore this complication for simplicity of exposition. We have also ignored the problem of variable returns when we assumed that each town could double its output of cotton or wool by doubling its labor force.

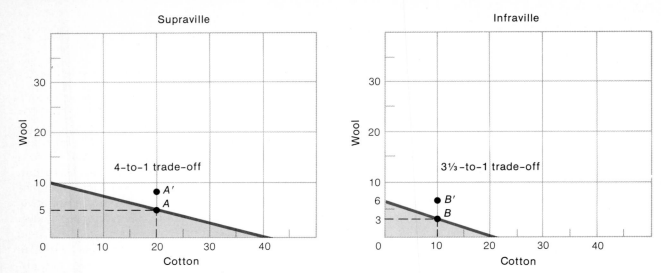

FIGURE 1
Production Possibilities in Two Towns Before Trade
Production possibility curves are graphic depictions of tradeoffs or (same thing) of opportunity costs. Supraville enjoys a wool cotton income at point A, Infraville at point B. Note that points A′ and B′ are out of reach for the two towns.

swaps one kind of output for the other in different proportions, as the differing slopes of the two $p - p$ curves show. Supraville, for example, can make only an extra pound of wool by giving up 4 pounds of cotton. That is, it gets its maximum potential output of 10,000 pounds of wool by surrendering 40,000 pounds of cotton. Infraville can reach its production maximum of 6,000 pounds of wool at a loss of 20,000 pounds of cotton. Thus, rather than having to give up 4 pounds of cotton to get one of wool, it gives up only 3.3 pounds. Therefore, in terms of opportunity cost—how much cotton has to be given up to get a pound of wool—wool actually costs less in Infraville than in Supraville!

Not so the other way round, of course. As we would expect, cotton costs Supraville less in terms of wool than it costs Infraville. In Supraville we get 40,000 pounds of cotton by relinquishing only 10,000 pounds of wool—a loss of a quarter of a pound of wool for a pound of cotton. In Infraville we can get the maximum output of 20,000 pounds of cotton only by a surrender of 6,000 pounds of wool—a loss of approximately ⅓ pound of wool rather than ¼ pound of wool for each unit of cotton.*

Comparative Advantage

Perhaps the light is beginning to dawn. Despite the fact that Supraville is more productive than Infraville in terms of output per man in both cotton and wool, it is *relatively* more productive in cotton than in wool. And despite the fact that

*It takes long practice to master the arithmetic of gains from trade. It is important, first, to get the idea; the calculations can be mastered later.

TABLE 4
Unspecialized Production:
Case II

In this case, one country is better than the other not just in one activity, but in both.

	Supraville	Infraville
Wool output	5,000	3,000
Cotton production	20,000	10,000

Infraville is absolutely less productive than Supraville, man for man, in both cotton and wool, it is *relatively* more productive in wool. To repeat, it requires a bigger sacrifice of wool to get another pound of cotton in Infraville than in Supraville.

We call this kind of relative superiority *comparative advantage.* **It is a concept that is often difficult to grasp at first, but that is central to the reason for trade itself. When we speak of** *comparative* **advantage, we mean, as in the case of Supraville, that among** *various* **advantages of one producer or locale over another, there is one that is better than any other.** *Comparatively* **speaking, this is where its optimal returns lie. But just because it must abandon** some lesser opportunity, its trading partner can now advantageously devote itself in the direction where *it* has a comparative advantage.

This is a relationship of logic, not economics. Take the example of the banker who is also the best carpenter in town. Will it pay him to build his own house? Clearly it will not, for he will make more money by devoting all his hours to banking, even though he then has to employ and pay for a carpenter less skillful than himself. True, he could save that expense by building his own house. But he would then have to give up the much more lucrative hours he could be spending at the bank!

Now let us return to the matter of trade. We have seen that wool is *relatively* cheaper in Infraville, where each additional pound costs only 3.3 pounds of cotton, rather than 4 pounds, as in Supraville; and that cotton is *relatively* cheaper in Supraville, where an additional pound costs but ¼ pound of wool, instead of ⅓ pound across the way in Infraville. Now let us suppose that each side begins to specialize in the trade in which it has the comparative advantage. Suppose that Supraville took half its labor force now in wool and put it into cotton. Its output would change as in Table 5.

Supraville has lost 2,500 pounds of wool but gained 10,000 pounds of cotton. Now let us see if it can trade its cotton for Infraville's wool. In Infraville, where productivity is so much less, the entire labor force has shifted to wool output, where its greatly inferior productivity can be put to best use. Hence its production pattern now looks like Table 6.

Infraville finds itself lacking 10,000 pounds of cotton, but it has 3,000 *additional* pounds of wool. Clearly, it can acquire the 10,000 pounds of cotton it needs from Supraville by giving Supraville *more* than the 2,500 pounds of wool it seeks. As a result, both Infraville and Supraville will have the same cotton consumption as

TABLE 5

Supraville uses specialization to boost cotton production at the expense of wool.

	Before the Shift	After the Shift
Wool production	5,000	2,500
Cotton production	20,000	30,000

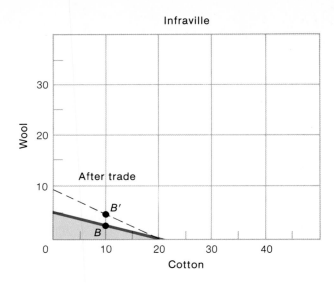

FIGURE 2
Production Possibilities in Two Towns After Trade
*Specialization has made more wool available. This is like moving the PP curve outward
along the wool axis. Points A' and B', formerly out of reach, are now accessible to the two
towns. (For clarity's sake, the graph shows a gain much larger than the 500 pounds
described in the text.)*

before, but there will be a surplus of 500 pounds of wool to be shared between
them. As Figure 2 shows, both towns will have gained by the exchange, for both
will have moved beyond their former production frontiers (from *A* to *A'* and from
B to *B'*).

This last point is the crucial one. The nature of production possibility curves is
such that any point lying outside the production frontier is simply unattainable by
that society. In Figure 2, points *A'* and *B'* lie beyond the pretrade *PP* curves of the
two towns, but trade has made it possible for both communities to enjoy what was
formerly impossible.

Opportunity Cost

**Comparative advantage gives us an important insight into all exchange
relationships, for it reveals again a fundamental economic truth we have
mentioned more than once before. It is that *cost, in economics, means***

TABLE 6
*Specialization is concentrated in wool in Infraville's
case.*

	Before the Shift	After the Shift
Wool	3,000	6,000
Cotton	10,000	—

opportunities that must be foregone. The real cost of wool in Supraville is the cotton that cannot be grown because workers are engaged in wool production, just as the real cost of cotton is the wool that must be gone without. In fact, we can see that the basic reason for comparative advantage lies in the fact that opportunity costs vary, so that it "pays" (it costs less) for different parties to engage in different activities.

If opportunity costs for two producers are the same, then it follows that there cannot be any comparative advantage for either; and if there is no comparative advantage, there is nothing to be gained by specializing or trading. Suppose Supraville has a two-to-one edge over Infraville in *both* cotton and wool. Then, if either town specializes, neither will gain. Supraville may still gain 10,000 pounds of cotton for 2,500 pounds of wool, as before, but Infraville will gain only 2,500 pounds of wool (not 3,000) from its shift away from cotton. Thus the key to trade lies in the existence of *different* opportunity costs.

Are opportunity costs usually different from country to country or from region to region? For most commodities they are. As we move from one part of the world to another—sometimes even short distances—climate, resources, skills, transportation costs, capital scarcity, and abundance all change; and as they change, so do opportunity costs. There is every possibility for rich countries to trade with poor ones precisely because their opportunity costs are certain to differ.

Exchange Ratios

But we have not yet fully understood one last important aspect of trade—the *prices* at which goods will exchange. Suppose that Supraville and Infraville do specialize, each in the product in which it enjoys a comparative advantage. Does that mean they can swap their goods at any price?

A quick series of calculations reveals otherwise. We remember that Supraville needed at least 2,500 pounds of wool for which it was going to offer some of its extra production of cotton in exchange. But how much? What price should it offer for its needed wool, in terms of cotton?

Suppose it offered 7,500 pounds of cotton. Would Infraville sell the wool? No, it would not. At home it can grow its own 7,500 pounds of cotton at a "cost" of only 2,273 pounds of wool, for we recall that Infraville traded off 1 pound of wool for 3.3 pounds of cotton (7,500 ÷ 3.3 = 2,273).

Suppose, then, that Infraville counteroffered to sell Supraville 2,500 pounds of wool for a price of 12,000 pounds of cotton. Would Supraville accept? Of course not. This would mean the equivalent of 4.8 pounds of cotton for a pound of wool. Supraville can do better than that by growing its own wool at its own trade-off ratio of only 4 pounds to 1.

We begin to see, in other words, that the price of wool must lie between the trade-off ratios of Infraville and Supraville. Infraville wants to import cotton. If it did not trade with Supraville, it could grow its own cotton at the cost of one pound of wool for every 3.3 pounds of cotton. Hence, for trade to be advantageous, Infraville seeks to get *more* cotton than that, per pound of wool.

Supraville is in the opposite situation. It seeks to export cotton and to import wool. It could make its own wool at the sacrifice of 4 pounds of cotton per pound of wool. Thus it seeks to gain wool for a *lower* price than that, in terms of cotton. Clearly, any ratio between 3.3 and 4 pounds of cotton per pound of wool will profit both sides.

The Role of Prices

Let us put this into ordinary price terms. Suppose that cotton sells for 30 cents per pound. Then wool would have to sell between 99 cents and $1.20 (30 cents × 3.3 and × 4) to make trade worthwhile.* Let us say that supply and demand established a price of $1.10 for wool. Supraville can then sell its 10,000 pounds of extra cotton production at 30 cents, which will net it $3,000. How much wool can it buy for this sum? At the going price of $1.10 per pound, 2,727 pounds. Therefore Supraville will end up with the same amount of cotton (20,000 pounds) as it had before specialization and trade, and with 227 *more* pounds of wool than before (2,500 pounds produced at home plus 2,727 pounds imported from Infraville—a total of 5,227 pounds). It has gained by trade an amount equal to the price of this extra wool, or $249.70.

How has Infraville fared? It has 3,273 pounds of wool left after exporting 2,727 pounds to Supraville from its production of 6,000 pounds, and it also has 10,000 pounds of cotton imported from Supraville in exchange for its wool exports. Thus it, too, has a gain from trade—the 273 pounds of wool (worth $300.30) over the amount of 3,000 pounds that it would have produced without specialization and trade. In brief, *both* sides have profited from the exchange. To be sure, gains need not be distributed so evenly between the trading partners. If the price of wool had been $1, trade still would have been worthwhile, but Supraville would have gained almost all of it. Had the price of wool been $1.19, both sides again would have come out ahead, but now Infraville would have been the larger beneficiary by far. The actual price at which wool would sell would be determined by the supply and demand schedules for it in both communities.

THE CASE FOR FREE TRADE

Would the prime minister of Nova Jersia be convinced by these arguments? Would his son? They might be weakened in their support for hothouse grapefruit, but some arguments would still linger in their minds. Let us consider them.

1. "OUR WORKERS CANNOT COMPETE WITH LOW-WAGE WORKERS OVERSEAS." This is an argument one hears not only in Nova Jersia, but in every nation in the world, save only those with the very lowest wage rates. Swedish workers complain about "cheap" American labor; American workers complain about sweatshop labor in Hong Kong. And indeed it is true that American labor is

---

*Obviously, these prices are used for illustrative purposes only. And once again, let us reassure you: These calculations are easy to follow, but not easy to do by yourself. Familiarity will come only with practice.

paid less than Swedish and that Hong Kong labor is paid a great deal less than American. Does that not mean that American labor will be seriously injured if we import goods made under "sweatshop" conditions, or that Swedish labor is right in complaining that its standard of living is undermined by importing goods from "exploited" American workers?

Like the answers to so many questions in economics, this one is not a simple yes or no. The American textile worker who loses his job because of low-priced textile imports *is* hurt; and so is the Swedish worker in an electronics company who loses his job because of American competition. We will come back to their legitimate grievances later. But we must note that both workers would also be injured if they lost their jobs as a result of domestic competition. Why do we feel so threatened when the competition comes from abroad?

Because, the answer goes, foreign competition isn't based on American efficiency. It is based on exploited labor. Hence it pulls down the standards of American labor to its own low level.

There is an easy reply to this argument. The reason Hong Kong textile labor is paid so much less than American textile labor is that *average* productivity in Hong Kong is so much lower than *average* productivity in America. **To put it differently, the reason that American wages are high is that we use our workers in industries where their productivity is very high. If Hong Kong, with its very low productivity, can undersell us in textiles, then this is a clear signal that we must move our factors of production out of textiles into other areas where their contribution will be greater; for example, in the production of aircraft.** It is no coincidence that aircraft—one of the highest-wage industries in America— is one of our leading exports, or indeed that more than 75 percent of our manufactured exports are produced by industries paying hourly wage rates above the national average for all manufacturing industries. In fact, all nations tend to export the goods that are produced at the highest, not lowest, local wages! Why? Because those industries employ their labor most effectively.

But suppose Hong Kong accumulated large amounts of capital and became a center for the manufacture of heavy equipment, so that it sold *both* garments and electrical generators more cheaply than we sold them. We are back to Supraville and Infraville. There would still be a *comparative* advantage in one or more of these products in which we would be wise to specialize, afterward trading with Hong Kong for our supplies of the other good. *

Many readers may say, "That is exactly the situation that faces us today! Are you telling us there is no problem in facing low-wage competition from Asia?" No, we are not saying that. But the problem involves helping displaced workers and businesses find alternative employments. The idea of comparative advantage tells us only that there is *some form* of employment in which our *comparative* productivity will be greater than that of Hong Kong, simply because our resources and opportunity costs are different. Perhaps it lies in developing new technologies. But just suppose that there were no such opportunities. Could Hong Kong then wipe out all American industry? Doubtful. What would they get paid with? How would

---

*Newspapers in Southeast Asia carry editorials seeking protection from American imports because, they say, we do not use labor in our production, and it is unfair to ask their citizens to compete with our machines that do not have to be paid wages.

we earn Hong Kong dollars to buy their goods unless we sold goods to the East for American dollars?

2. "TARIFFS ARE PAINLESS TAXES BECAUSE THEY ARE BORNE BY FOREIGNERS." This is a convincing-sounding argument advanced by the prime minister of Nova Jersia (and by some other prime ministers in their time). But is it true? Let us take the case of hothouse grapefruit, which can be produced in Nova Jersia only at a cost of 50 cents each, whereas foreign grapefruit (no doubt produced by sweated labor) can be unloaded at its ports at 25 cents. To prevent his home industry from being destroyed, the prime minister imposes a tariff of 25 cents on foreign grapefruit—which, he tells the newspapers, will be entirely paid by foreigners.

This is not, however, the way his political opponent (who has had a course in economics) sees it. "Without the tariff," she tells her constituency, "you could buy grapefruit for 25 cents. Now you have to pay 50 cents for it. Who is paying the extra 25 cents—the foreign grower or you? Even if not a single grapefruit entered the country, you would still be paying 25 cents more than you have to. **In fact, you are being asked to subsidize an inefficient domestic industry.** Not only that, but the tariff wall means they won't ever become efficient because there is no pressure of competition on them."

Whether or not our economic candidate will win the electoral battle, she surely has the better of the argument. Or does she? For the prime minister, stung by these unkind remarks, replies:

3. "BUT AT LEAST THE TARIFF KEEPS SPENDING POWER AT HOME. OUR OWN GRAPEFRUIT GROWERS, NOT FOREIGNERS, HAVE OUR MONEY." There are

HIGH WAGES?

How do you tell whether a country is a high-wage country or a low-wage country? If German workers are paid 8 marks per hour, are their wages high or low compared to ours? Clearly, you cannot tell without knowing the exchange rate. If 8 marks can be traded for $1, then German workers are paid the equivalent of $1 per hour. We can then compare the German rates relative to the American. If the average American wage is $4 per hour, we would conclude that German wages are low. If, however, 1 mark can be traded for $1, then German workers earn the equivalent of $8 per hour. In this case, German workers are highly paid *relative* to American workers.

We cannot really tell whether a country is high-wage or low-wage until we understand exchange rates and what determines them.

two answers to this argument. First, the purchasing power acquired by foreigners can be used to buy goods from efficient Nova Jersia producers and will thus return to Nova Jersia's economy. Second, if productive resources are used in inefficient, low-productivity industries, then the resources available for use in efficient, high-productivity industries are less than they otherwise would be, and the total output

of the country falls. To keep out foreign grapefruit is to lower the country's real standard of living. The people of Nova Jersia waste time and resources doing something they do not do very well.

4. "BUT TARIFFS ARE NECESSARY TO KEEP THE WORK FORCE OF NOVA JERSIA EMPLOYED." This is the time to remember our investigation of macroeconomic policies. As we learned in macroeconomics, the governments of Nova Jersia and every other country can use fiscal and monetary policies to keep their resources fully employed. If grapefruit workers become unemployed, governments can expand aggregate demand and generate domestic job opportunities in other areas.

THE CASE FOR TARIFFS

Are *all* arguments against tariffs? No. But it is essential to recognize that these arguments take full cognizance of the inescapable costs of restricting trade. They do not contest the validity of the theory of free trade, but the difficulties of its application. Let us familiarize ourselves with them.

Mobility

The first difficulty concerns the problem of mobility. When Hong Kong textiles press hard against the garment worker in New York, higher wages in the high-tech plants in California are scant comfort. The garment worker has a lifetime of skills and a home in New York, and she does not want to move to another state, where she would be a stranger, and to a new trade, in which she would be only an unskilled beginner. She certainly does not want to move to Hong Kong! Hence the impact of foreign trade often brings serious dislocations that result in persistent local unemployment, rather than in a flow of resources from a relatively disadvantaged to a relatively advantaged industry.

Transition Costs

Second, even if free trade increases the incomes and real living standards of each country participating in trade, **this does not mean that it increases the income and real living standards of each individual in each country.** The laid-off Michigan auto worker may find himself with a substantial reduction in income for the rest of his life. He is being economically rational when he resists "cheap" foreign imports and attempts to get his congressman to impose tariffs or quotas.

There is, it should be noted, an answer to this argument—an answer, at any rate, that applies to industrial nations. Since the gains from trade are generally spread across the nation, the real transition costs of moving from one industry, skill, or region to another should also be generally spread across the nation. This means that government (the taxpayers), rather than the worker or business, should bear the costs of relocation and retraining. In this way we spread the costs in such a manner that a few need not suffer disproportionately to win the benefits of international trade that are shared by many.

We should also be aware of the possibility that transition costs may actually exceed the short-term benefits to be derived from international trade. Transition costs thus place a new element in the system, since the standard analysis of competitive systems—national or international—ignores them. A country may be wise to limit its international trade if it calculates that the cost of reallocating its own factors is greater than the gains to be had in higher real income. Remember, however, that transition costs tend to be short-lived and that the gains from trade tend to last. Thus it is easy to exaggerate the costs of transition and to balk at making changes that would ultimately improve conditions.

Full Employment

Third, the argument for free trade rests on the very important assumption that there will be substantially full employment.

In the mid-nineteenth century when the free trade argument was first fully formulated, the idea of an underemployment equilibrium would have been considered absurd. In an economy of large enterprises and "sticky" wages and prices, we know that unemployment is a real and continuous object of concern for national policy.

Thus it makes little sense to advocate policies to expand production via trade unless we are certain that the level of aggregate demand will be large enough to absorb that production. **Full employment policy therefore becomes an indispensable arm of a free trade policy.** Trade gives us the potential for maximizing production, but there is no point in laying the groundwork for the highest possible output unless fiscal and monetary policy are also geared to bringing about a level of aggregate demand large enough to support that output.

National Self-Sufficiency

Fourth, there is the argument of nationalism pure and simple. This argument does not impute spurious economic gains to tariffs. Rather, it says that free trade undoubtedly encourages production, but it does so at a certain cost. This is the cost of the vulnerability that comes from extensive and extreme specialization. This vulnerability is all very well within a nation where we assume that law and order will prevail, but it cannot be so easily justified among nations where the realistic assumption is just the other way. Tariffs, in other words, are defensible because they enable nations to attain a certain *self-sufficiency*—admittedly at some economic cost. Project Independence, the United States effort to gain self-sufficiency in energy, was exactly such an undertaking.

In a world always threatened by war, self-sufficiency has a value that may properly override considerations of ideal economic efficiency. The problem is to hold the arguments for national defense down to proper proportions. When tariffs are periodically adjusted in international conferences, an astonishing variety of industries (in all countries) find it possible to claim protection from foreign competition in the name of national "indispensability."

Infant Industries

Equally interesting is the nationalist argument for tariffs advanced by so-called infant industries, particularly in developing nations. These newly formed or prospective enterprises claim that they cannot possibly compete with the giants in developed countries while they are small; but that if they are protected by a tariff, they will in time become large and efficient enough no longer to need a tariff. In addition, they claim, they will provide a more diversified spectrum of employments for their own people, as well as aiding in the national transition toward a more modern economy.

The argument is a valid one if it is applied to industries that have a fair chance of achieving a comparative advantage once grown up (otherwise one will be supporting them in infancy, maturity, and senility). Certainly it is an argument that was propounded by the youthful industries of the United States in the early nineteenth century and was sufficiently persuasive to bring them a moderate degree of protection (although it is inconclusive as to how much their growth was ultimately dependent on tariff help). And it is being listened to today by some underdeveloped nations who feel that their only chance of escaping from poverty is to develop a nucleus of industrial employment at almost any cost in the short run.

Producer vs. Consumer Welfare

The policy of free trade versus the policy of protectionism ultimately resolves into a choice between the well-being of two groups. **Free trade favors the welfare of consumers. Protectionism favors the welfare of producers.**

To be sure, consumers are producers and producers are consumers, so that in a frictionless, perfect world there would be little to choose between the two. But in a world where frictions are an important part of economic life, it matters very greatly whether we favor policies that benefit almost everyone to some degree, or policies that help or hurt a few people to a considerable degree. That is, in fact, the trade-off when we weigh the gains from trade that accrue as lower prices for textiles or shoes or cars against the impact of protectionism on the jobs of textile workers or shoemakers or auto workers.

In a way, the difficult choice that we face reminds us of the cost of inflation, felt by all, versus the cost of unemployment, borne by a few. The difference is that the political voice aroused by inflation drowns out the voice aroused by unemployment, whereas the injuries of those affected by foreign competition tend to override the murmur of consumers who would benefit from lower prices.

PROTECTIONISM

It is clear that when we add up the costs of a free trade policy, pursued in a world that is *not* prepared to undertake a full employment policy because of inflation fears, that is *not* much concerned about the costs of unemployment, and that *is* deeply interested in securing its national self-sufficiency, the classical arguments in favor of free trade lose a good deal of their force. The limitation of trade through tariffs or quotas or any other form of protectionism may indeed cut down the level of production, but that loss seems much less serious in the circumstances of modern industrial competition.

Is protectionism therefore justifiable as a policy? The question is an academic one, for in fact protection is to some degree the policy in all nations. The United States, for example, limits by agreement the number of cars the Japanese ship to us; has enacted a "trigger" pricing mechanism that automatically puts on a tariff when steel imports exceed a certain level; allows industries to appeal if they can establish "unfair" competition (usually export subsidies from foreign governments); and has other protective institutions. Indeed, protection in the 1980s grew more rapidly in the United States than in any other industrial nation, so that the proportion of imports restricted by one device or another rose from 9 to 15 percent, according to the World Bank.

The Special Case of the Underdeveloped World

One immediate need is to find a way of improving economic relations between the advanced, industrialized world and the backward underdeveloped regions. Free trade has long been preached as a doctrine that would shed its benefits on all alike. In fact, however, it has not worked that way so far as the underdeveloped nations have been concerned. Many of these nations have been until fairly recently colonial possessions of the developed countries. As such, their economic structures were originally shaped to serve as useful adjuncts to the economy of their "home" countries. The result, a typical attribute of underdeveloped economies, was an extreme tilting toward monoculture—one crop such as bananas or coffee, or one product such as tin or copper—and the systematic discouragement of industrial sectors that might have offered competition with their colonial masters.

This has placed the underdeveloped world in a difficult economic situation for which free trade has given no remedy. As sellers of raw commodities, they face a highly inelastic demand for their goods. Like the American farmer, when they produce a bumper crop, prices tend to fall precipitously and demand does not rise

TRANSPORTATION COSTS

If every industry must have a comparative advantage in one country or another, how can there be steel industries (or any other) in more than one country? The answer, quite aside from considerations of nationalism, lies in *transportation costs*, which compensate for lower production costs in many products and thereby allow a relatively inefficient industry to supply a home market.

Transportation costs also explain why some industries, such as brick-making, are spread out in many localities, whereas others, such as diamond cutting, are concentrated in one place. If diamonds were very bulky or bricks very light, the first industry would become more dispersed, and the second less so.

proportionately. At the same time, the prices of the industrial materials they buy in exchange tend to be firm or to rise over the years.

Terms of Trade. Thus the terms of trade—the actual *quid pro quo* of goods received against goods offered—have tended to move against the poorer nations, who have given more and more coffee for the same amount of machinery. In some years, when commodity prices have taken a particularly bad tumble, the poor nations have actually lost more in purchasing power than the total amount of all foreign aid they received. In effect, they subsidized the advanced nations! As an example, it has been estimated that falling prices cost the African nations more, in the first two decades after World War II, than all foreign funds given, loaned, or invested there.

It is possible—we do not yet know—that the internationalization of finance and production may create more new industrialized countries (called NICs), such as Hong Kong, Korea, Singapore, and Taiwan, the four great success stories of development in the 1980s. Already the value of U.S. trans-Pacific trade exceeds that of the trans-Atlantic: The United States economy today faces to the West, not to the East. It is imaginable that the center of industrial life will move away from its historic European-American center into an Asian or Latin American base.

At best, however, that is a distant prospect. Today the underdeveloped world is burdened with debts, and struggling to meet—much less raise—the needs of its vast populations. With 70 percent of the world's peoples, the poorest regions of the world still mount only 10 percent of its total output. In this situation of vastly unequal power, an insistence on free trade is more likely to reproduce the existing tension-ridden relationships of inequality than to lead to a more equitable and mutually rewarding division of the world's production and distribution.

As a consequence, most of the underdeveloped countries have sought to arrange commodity agreements—the international counterparts of the arrangements that support agricultural (and sometimes mining) prices and that regularize marketing in the developed, capitalist world. The developed world has not, however, been quick to respond to the plight of the poorer world. Here lies a source of serious economic and political friction in the present and for the future.

LOOKING BACK

KEY CONCEPTS

Bias of nationalism

1   The bias of nationalism is deep and pervasive. It leads us to assume that gains from trade, which we take for granted within a country, do not apply between countries.

Gains from trade stem from the specialization of labor.

2   The gains from trade essentially stem from the improvement in productivity that results from specialization or a better division of labor. Trade is an indirect means of enhancing productivity.

Principle of comparative advantage gives gains to trading partners even when one is more productive in all activities.

3   The principle of comparative advantage shows that trade is profitable even when one trading partner is more productive in all lines of endeavor than another. This is because it is possible for the superior partner to increase production in the activity that is comparatively best for itself, thus more than making up any loss from shifting resources out of the activity that is comparatively less advantageous.

Specialization allows countries to go beyond their former *PP* curves.

4   By specializing production, the two trading partners gain a combined output that is larger than they could get by producing without specialization and trade. This is true as long as opportunity costs are not the same in both countries, which is almost always the case. Then specialization allows both countries to go beyond their former *PP* curves.

Prices, or exchange ratios, must lie within the ratios of trade-off.

5   Exchange ratios, or prices, must lie within the trade-off ratios of actual output. Otherwise the comparative advantages of the two nations would be lost.

The case for free trade is a case for maximizing productivity and consumer well-being.

6   The case for free trade stresses the gains for the entire society that come from maximizing production. By allowing ''cheap'' imports to come in without tariffs, we force labor to move away from low-productivity to high-productivity industry, and we benefit consumers.

Free trade also imposes costs.

7   The case for free trade hinges on a willingness to pursue full employment and to compensate the damages of competition. This seems unlikely to be realized.

Protectionism, in some degree, appears in all industrial nations exposed to modern intensified international competition.

8   Some degree of protectionism appears inescapable in a world of greatly intensified international production and competition. All industrial nations practice some degree of protectionism policy. The goal is to steer between the division of labor and the disruptions of unmanageable competition.

Free trade does not shed its benefits equitably when the structure of trade is distorted, as is the case with the underdeveloped world.

9 The arguments for free trade do not take into account the historical circumstances under which the underdeveloped nations' economies were formed. These tend to be monocultures of agriculture or mining, selling products that are highly price inelastic. Most of these nations seek commodity agreements that are the international counterpart of U.S. (or European) farm subsidies or marketing arrangements.

ECONOMIC VOCABULARY

Trade-off relationships   393
Comparative advantage   394
Opportunity cost   396
Mobility   401
Transition costs   401

Self-sufficiency   402
Infant industries   403
Producer vs. consumer welfare   403
Protectionism   404
Terms of trade   405

QUESTIONS

1. What do we mean when we say that trade is "indirect production"?

2. Suppose that two towns, Coaltown and Irontown, have equal populations but differing resources. If Coaltown applies its whole population to coal production, it will produce 10,000 tons of coal; if it applies them to iron production, it will produce 5,000 tons of iron. If Irontown concentrates on iron, it will turn out 18,000 tons of iron; if it shifts to coal, it will produce 12,000 tons of coal. Is trade possible between these towns?

3. In which product does Coaltown have a comparative advantage? How many tons of iron does a ton of coal cost her? How many does it cost Irontown? What is the cost of iron in Coaltown and Irontown? Draw a production possibility diagram for each town. Show where the frontier lies before and after trade.

4. If iron sells for $10 a ton, what must be the price range of coal? Show that trade cannot be profitable if coal sells on either side of this range. What is the opportunity cost of coal to Irontown? Of iron to Irontown?

5. Is it possible that American watchmakers face unfair competition from Swiss watchmakers because wages are lower in Switzerland? If American watch workers are rendered unemployed by the low-paid Swiss, what might be done to help them—impose a tariff?

6. Is it possible that mass-produced, low-cost American watches are a source of unfair competition for Switzerland? If Swiss watchmakers are unemployed as a result, what could be done to help them—impose a tariff? Is it possible that a mutually profitable trade in watches might take place between the two countries? What kinds of watches would each probably produce?

7. Are the duties on French wines borne by foreigners or by domestic consumers? Both? What, if any, is the rationale for these duties? How would you go about estimating the transition costs if we were to abolish the tariff on all wines and spirits? Who would be affected? What alternative employment would you suggest for the displaced labor? The displaced land?

8. Let us suppose that the Japanese perfect a new model of car that will do a hundred miles on the gallon. The car threatens to wipe out General Motors and to deprive 500,000 auto workers of their jobs. What measures, if any, would you advocate with respect to importing the new vehicle? Suppose the Japanese agreed to buy GM's main plants and produce it here. Would you object to that?

CHAPTER 23

Buying and Selling Abroad

A LOOK AHEAD

Our focus shifts from problems at home to problems in the international arena. This chapter:

1 Clarifies what we mean when we say that the dollar is falling or rising.
2 Teaches us the basic elements of international exchange.
3 Introduces us to the problems of fixed and flexible exchange rates.

W e have already come to grips with some of the problems of international trade and finance. We have not yet, however, systematically investigated the mechanisms by which foreign trade is carried out in a world of many currencies. That is what we will do in this chapter.

The Foreign Value of the Dollar

When the dollar rises or falls in the international money markets, it does not mean that a dollar will buy more or less American goods. That is a very important point to bear in mind. **When we speak of the dollar in foreign trade, it means only one thing: A dollar will buy more or less foreign money**—German marks, French or Swiss francs, Swedish krona, or whatever. As a result, it becomes cheaper or dearer for us to buy foreign goods and services.

The Rate of Exchange

Let us review what we mean by this. Suppose you enjoy French wine. French wine is sold by its producers for francs, the currency in which French producers pay their bills and want their receipts. Let us suppose they price their wine at 20 francs the bottle.

How much would 20 franc wine cost in America? The answer depends on the rate at which we can exchange dollars for francs—that is, it depends on the price of francs. We discover this price by going to banks, who are the main dealers in foreign currencies of all kinds, and inquiring what the dollar-franc *exchange rate* is. Let us say we are told it is 5 francs to the dollar. To buy a bottle of French wine, then (ignoring transportation, insurance, and other costs), will cost us $4.00 (20 francs ÷ 5 = $4.00).

Now suppose that the dollar rises. This means that the dollar becomes dearer on the market for foreign money. It follows, of course, that francs will become cheaper in terms of dollars. Instead of getting 5 francs for a dollar, we now get 10. Meanwhile, the price of wine hasn't changed—it still costs 20 francs. But it now costs us $2, not $4, to purchase 20 francs. **A rising dollar therefore lowers the price of foreign goods in terms of American money.**

Conversely, a falling exchange rate would raise it. Imagine we were contemplating a trip to Germany. We inquire into the prices of German hotels, German meals, and the like, and we are told that we can do it comfortably for (let us say) 100 marks per day. "How much is that in American money?" we ask. The answer depends, of course, on the exchange rate. Suppose the rate is 3 marks to the dollar. Then 100 marks would be the equivalent of $33 a day. But if the dollar happened to be falling, we could be in for an unpleasant surprise. Perhaps by the time we were ready to leave, it would have fallen to 2 marks to the dollar. It still costs 100 marks a day to travel in Germany, but it now costs $50 to buy 100 marks, not $33.

We must remember, however, that international economics must always be viewed from both sides of the ocean. When the dollar rises, foreign goods or services become less expensive for us. But for a German, just the opposite is true. A

German tourist coming to America might be told that he should allow $50 a day for expenses. "How much will that cost me in marks?" he asks his bank. The answer, again, hangs on the exchange rate. If it costs only 2 marks to buy a dollar, it will obviously be cheaper for the German tourist than if it costs 3 marks. Notice that this is exactly the opposite of the American tourist's position.

THE MARKET FOR DOLLARS

International economics asserted its importance in the early 1980s, when the dollar was very high. We know now that this means that the price of dollars, on the market for foreign currencies, must have been rising. Why did the dollar rise? As with all price changes, our first task is to look at the supply and demand situation. And that requires us to investigate the nature of the market for dollars and other currencies.

Here we can best begin by mentally grouping all the kinds of dealings in which dollars and other currencies change hands into two basic markets. **One is the market for currencies to carry on current transactions. The other is the market for currencies to carry on capital transactions.** You will have no trouble following the story if you bear these two markets in mind.

Current Transactions

The first market in which currencies are bought and sold is that in which the current transactions between firms, individuals, or governments are carried out. Here *the demand for dollars* comes from such groups as foreigners who want to import U.S. goods and services, and who must acquire dollars to purchase them; foreign tourists who need dollars to travel in the United States; foreign governments who must buy dollars to maintain embassies or consulates in America; and firms abroad (American or foreign) that want to send dividends or profits to the United States in dollars. All these kinds of transactions require that holders of marks or francs or yen offer their currencies on the foreign exchange market in order to buy U.S. dollars.

And, of course, there are similar groups of Americans who *supply dollars* to the foreign exchange market for exactly the opposite reasons. Here we find American importers who want to bring in Japanese cameras and must offer dollars in order to acquire the yen to make their purchases; American or foreign firms that are sending dividends or profits earned in the United States to a foreign branch or headquarters; Americans or foreign residents who sell dollars in order to buy lire or drachmas or kronor to send money to friends or relatives abroad; and the American government, which uses dollars to buy foreign currencies to pay diplomatic living expenses or to make military expenditures abroad.

Taken all together, these supplies and demands for dollars establish what we call our balance on current account. As Figure 1 shows, this balance took a tremendous fall after 1982.

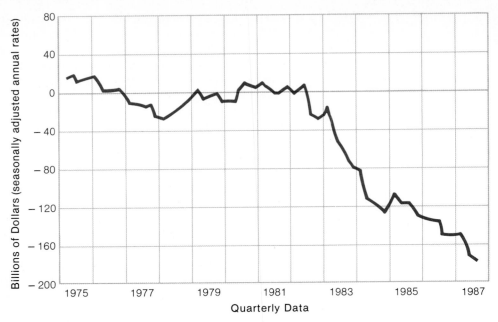

FIGURE 1
Balance on Current Account, 1987
The balance on current account sums up all the supplies and demands for dollars needed for trade, travel, remittances of profits, government expenses, and the like. Until recent years, the market for current account almost always showed a favorable balance. This is no longer the case.
Source: *Department of Commerce.*

Behind the Trade Deficit

What happened to turn the balance from black to red? The answer, as we know from Chapter 6, involves two quite separate reasons. The first is that the dollar rose very sharply on the international money markets, beginning in the early 1980s. We will look very shortly into the causes for this rise, but for the moment we can simply take the rise itself as an important element behind our falling balance of trade.

We have just seen what happens to trade when a currency rises: The high-currency country finds it cheap to buy abroad and low-currency countries find it expensive to buy in the high-currency nation. This is exactly what happened to the United States. Between 1979 and 1985, the French franc fell from 4 francs to a dollar to 10; the German mark from 1.8 to a dollar to 3.3; the British pound from $2.08 to $1.09. Tourists went on specially arranged charter flights to London to pick up tweeds and woollens at half their normal prices. Our imports began to rise sharply—from a level of over $300 billion in the early 1980s to a level of nearly $450 billion in 1985. (The exact figures are in Table 2 in Chapter 6). Imports also rose because our domestic recovery provided U.S. citizens with more dollar incomes, a considerable portion of which they devoted to buying foreign goods—the propensity to import at work.

THE MARKET FOR CAPITAL

If we think about it, we have now deepened the mystery. Americans were eagerly buying foreign currencies (and selling dollars to get them) to finance the great import boom. Foreigners were unwilling or unable to buy American exports because they were so expensive. One would think that the large supply of dollars offered by Americans and the small demand for dollars stemming from foreigners would lead the dollar to *fall* in price, not rise.

And that is, in fact, exactly what *would* have happened if the only source of supply and demand in the exchange market were the needs of traders of commodities, tourists, and the like. But there is another source of supply and demand that arises to fulfill a set of needs different from those of current transactions. This is the supply and demand for dollars that arises for *capital purposes*—building or buying plants and equipment in another country, or buying stocks and bonds denominated in another country's currency.

The first of these capital flows is called **direct investment.** It arises from the efforts of American firms (mainly multinationals) to expand their ownership of plants and equipment abroad, and from the corresponding efforts of foreign companies to do the same thing here.

The second part of the capital market is made up of American or foreign individuals or firms who want to add to their overseas **portfolio investments** of stocks and bonds. Here we have Americans who buy stock in a Swedish firm or who buy German government bonds, and foreign investors who buy General Motors stock or U.S. Treasury bonds.

The Capital Inflow

If the dollar in the early 1980s was high despite the excess of imports over exports, the net demand for dollars on capital account must have been larger than the net supply of dollars on current account. Why should that demand have been so large? The answer lies in the relatively high rate of real return offered by United States financial assets—such as Treasury bonds—compared with their equivalents abroad.

In 1985 American nominal interest rates, although well beneath their 1980 peaks, were still very high by historical standards: One could buy 10-year Treasury bonds that paid 10 percent interest (in 1960 they paid only 4 percent!). From this yield, an investor would mentally subtract the inflation rate in 1985 of roughly 3.5 percent. The result was a real return of over 6 percent—perhaps half again as much as that obtainable in comparable bonds abroad. As a consequence, foreign capital poured into the United States in such vast quantities that the dollar—despite the worsening trade balance—rose by 47 percent from 1980 to 1985.*

This inflow of dollars could not go on indefinitely. At some point investors would

---

*The inflow of foreign funds helped finance our domestic budgetary deficit by buying 13 percent of Treasury bonds issued that year. We have seen that this helped us to finance the deficit without the "crowding out" that had been anticipated and feared. It also saddled us with a substantial external debt for the first time in a century.

hesitate before putting their funds in a nation whose ability to earn foreign exchange was in question. And even before that point, the damage caused by the high rates to our trade balance was a powerful incentive for the United States government to act. Act it did, in September 1985, by convening the major economic powers in a five-nation conference. There it was announced that measures would be taken by *all* the central banks to bring the dollar into a more sustainable relation to other currencies. This meant that the Federal Reserve would add to its reserves of foreign currencies and that other central banks would sell dollars to reduce their reserves.

From 1985 through 1987, the dollar's value declined sharply in relation to the yen, the deutschemark, and the other major currencies, until by early 1987 it was only a little above its value in 1980. And, within a year, U.S. exports began to recover. In 1987 and 1988 the real volume of U.S. exports rose over 15 percent, and some of our exporting industries moved close to their full capacity to produce.

Did the dollar's decline solve the U.S. trade problem? Sadly, it did not. For during the period of the high dollar, U.S. consumers had developed an insatiable appetite for imported manufactured goods. And so imports continued to rise as the dollar fell, even though they were becoming increasingly expensive. As we go to press, the pressure on the dollar continues, and we expect that this pressure will not let up until a full adjustment has occurred.

Finding a Balancing Rate

What does this imply for American policy with respect to the exchange rate? The main objective of that policy is not difficult to explain. Essentially the United States—like all other nations—must try to find a rate of exchange that will balance out the supplies and demands for its currency. The aim of our foreign economic policy can therefore be very simply stated. It is to establish a price for American dollars that will result in an "equilibrium" between America's needs for foreign currencies and foreigners' needs for our own.

Consider what happens if a country does not have such an equilibrium relationship. If the rate is too high, there will be a stimulus for the country to buy imports and a deterrent for its exports. The result will be unemployment in its export industries and, as a consequence of the multiplier, unemployment elsewhere. That was the American problem in the early 1980s, when our overvalued dollar was a major cause of a loss of 1.6 million jobs in exporting industries.

But an undervalued exchange rate also brings problems. Now there is an incentive for foreigners to buy the cheap exports or assets of country A. Foreign money will flow into A's banks, raising the money supply. (Foreign deposits increase *M* because the new deposits do not come from another domestic bank.) As the money supply increases, inflationary pressures also increase. The country will suffer from rising prices.

Thus we can present the problem of exchange rates that are too high or too low in this fashion:

Undervalued (too low) exchange rates lead to inflation.
Overvalued (too high) exchange rates lead to unemployment.

WHAT CAN BE DONE?

What can we do to bring about a better balance between the supply of and the demand for dollars? What can any nation that finds itself in a balance of payments squeeze do to right the balance?

Flexible Rates

Here we must first ask whether a nation in balance of payments difficulties need do anything. For let us not forget that a powerful force exists to right the imbalance by itself. This is the force of the marketplace—the pressure of buying and selling that arises spontaneously from the advantages and disadvantages open to traders on the international marketplace.

Imagine for a moment that we did not have a massive inflow of capital on portfolio account. In that case, as we have already noted, the excess of American demands for foreign currency (to finance imports) over the foreign demand for American dollars (to finance imports into *their* countries) would result in a fall in the price of dollars, exactly as if the dollar were a commodity such as shoes, for which the supply were greater than the demand. As the dollar fell, American goods would become cheaper for foreign buyers; conversely, foreign goods would become dearer. In this way, a system of "flexible" (changeable) exchange rates automatically tends to establish a balance in the supplies of and demands for currencies.

Speculative Flows

As we have seen, the difficulty arises from flows of portfolio capital that enter and leave countries for reasons quite unconnected with the prices of imports or exports. The treasurer of a multinational corporation is not interested in the foreign trade balance of a nation, but in the expected future price of its currency. If he thinks its price will appreciate (go up), it will be to his advantage to buy that nation's currency and wait for gain. If he expects it to fall, he will draw his funds out before the decline in exchange rates costs him money.

Two bad effects follow from this state of affairs. First, the flows of speculative capital prevent currencies from responding to market pressures and reaching prices that will "clear" the market. Second, the key importance of expectations makes capital flows highly unstable, and capable of reversing themselves overnight. Under conditions of a panicky flight, a currency can descend in a matter of weeks or days from "too high" to "too low." This is as disruptive for international trade as it would be if the value of domestic currency were arbitrarily changed from one city to the next, so that we never knew what the purchasing power of New York dollars was going to be in Chicago.

Exchange Controls

Is there not some way of preventing these speculative capital movements? One way that has been used many times is to institute an elaborate system of *exchange controls.* Under such a system, anyone who seeks to buy foreign currency must specify the reason for doing so. An importer of machinery is likely to get all the foreign exchange he or she wants, but an importer of luxury cars or a would-be tourist is not. Similarly, a foreign corporation seeking dollars to build or buy a plant abroad will have no trouble with the authorities, whereas a corporation seeking only to park excess funds may not get permission to do so.

Most economists regard exchange controls as a poor way to prevent speculative disruptions. By their nature, controls are cumbersome, bureaucratic, and arbitrary. They require decisions as to what kinds of imports are useful and what kinds are not—decisions in which private opinion takes priority over market preferences. They must differentiate between liquid capital that will be used in the receiving country for the financing of new investment and liquid balances that are here only for speculative purposes. These are difficult, perhaps impossible, decisions to make rationally. Thus exchange controls are always regarded as a last resort, never a first one. We mention them because many nations, hard pressed to achieve a healthy balance of payments, have been forced to institute such controls.

Fixed Exchange Rates

How else can we achieve the equilibrium rate of exchange we seek? Many economists have begun to ask whether there should not be a return to a different system of international currency exchange—*fixed,* rates rather than the flexible rates we now have.

We had such a system of fixed rates for many years after World War II under the Bretton Woods Agreement, signed in 1945 among the major powers. Under this agreement, all major countries announced the value of their currencies with respect to gold (or to other key currencies, such as the dollar.) The dollar, for example, was officially valued at one thirty-fifth of an ounce of gold, or $35 per ounce. These announced rates thereupon regulated the price at which all countries bought or sold foreign exchange. Under special circumstances a nation in international economic difficulties could alter its fixed rate with the permission of the International Monetary Fund (a branch of the United Nations established by the Bretton Woods Agreement to serve as a kind of world central banker), but this was the exception, not the rule.

The Trouble with Fixed Rates

Why did fixed rates not last? The reason must be apparent. Although flows of speculative capital were much less unsettling under the fixed rates system, because they did not affect exchange rates, **there was no automatic self-corrective market mechanism to help keep the balance of payments in equilibrium.**

In those days, the United States was still a major world exporter and ran a large surplus on its current account. As a result, the dollar should have risen, helping to bring the export surplus to an end. But since the dollar was fixed and could not rise, other countries were forced to devalue—lower their exchange rates—to achieve a viable balance with the United States. These devaluations were unsettling and demoralizing. Thus the system of fixed exchange rates became unpopular precisely because it was fixed and inflexible. Economists welcomed the eventual end of the fixed exchange system because very few of them foresaw the destabilizing effects that would follow from a system of flexible rates.

International Currency Reform

Is there some manner of having the best of both worlds—a system that permits market pressures to keep exchange rates in some sort of balance, while preventing disruptive capital flows? In the air today are many plans to attempt to do just that. Most of them envisage a new form of international agreement under which exchange rates will be fixed *within a reasonably wide band,* allowing them to respond to normal market pressures, but preventing the wild swings that have proved so destructive.

These plans are not easy to devise, for a new fixed-flexible system must allow the limits of the band to change if a nation's international situation changes—for example, if its productivity lags behind or races ahead of that of its competitors. With all its difficulties, however, some such general reform seems likely to come onto the agenda in the coming years. It is not only our own serious position of disequilibrium that must be put to rights, but the general economic stability of the world economy.

LOOKING BACK

KEY CONCEPTS

A rising or falling dollar means that dollars buy more or less foreign currency, not more or less U.S. goods.

1 A rising or falling dollar has a different meaning in international trade than in a domestic economy. Domestically, a rising or falling dollar means that prices have changed, so that a dollar can buy more or less goods. In international exchange, it means only that a dollar can buy more foreign currencies. From the international point of view, when the dollar rises, the exchange value of the currency it is traded against must fall.

Two markets for foreign exchange: current and capital

2 There are two separate markets for dollars (or any other currency). One is made up of the supplies and demands for current transactions—mainly imports and exports—and the other comprises supplies and demands for dollars (or other currencies) wanted for capital purposes, whether direct or portfolio investment.

The adverse balance on current account arises mainly from high exchange rates.

3 The U.S. trade deficit reflects an excess of supply over demand in the current market. This is the result of our import surplus. In turn, the import surplus can be traced to the effects of the high dollar and to the loss of international competitiveness.

The demand for portfolio investment has dominated the market, as foreign funds have sought high U.S. real interest rates.

4 The demand for dollars for capital purposes has been sufficiently large as to overbalance the trade deficit. This demand for foreign capital does not so much reflect an influx of direct investment as portfolio investment, taking advantage of very high U.S. real rates of interest.

Dangers of an exchange rate that is too low—or too high. The ideal rate balances total supplies and demands.	5 We can generalize the international exchange rate problem in this way: A rate that is too high (like the U.S. rate in the mid-1980s) brings an excess of imports and unemployment. A rate that is too low brings an excess of exports and an impetus toward inflation. The ideal of foreign economic policy is therefore to find a price for one's currency that equilibrates the demand for it for all purposes with its supply for all purposes.
Flexible rates balance current accounts but allow speculative inflows to interfere with equilibrium.	6 Under a flexible exchange rate system such as we now have, the excess of demand over supply (or vice versa) tends to bring about an equilibrium exchange rate in the balance on current account. But flexible rates are the source of much trouble from speculative capital flows. There is a strong temptation to control speculative flows with exchange controls—a bureaucratic and inefficient measure of last resort.
Fixed exchange rates avoid speculative problems but bring problems of their own.	7 Fixed exchange rates establish durable exchange rates that greatly reduce the damage from speculative inflows. These fixed rates are changeable downward (devaluation) or upward (revaluation) only through international agreement. Devaluations have also been disruptive of foreign trade.
International currency reform will probably try to gain the advantages of both systems.	8 Many economists today hope for a new currency system that will keep rates flexible within bounds but prevent wide swings as a consequence of capital movements.

ECONOMIC VOCABULARY

QUESTIONS

1. If the rate of exchange falls, does this make traveling abroad cheaper or more expensive? Does it make American exports more or less attractive to a foreign buyer? U.S. Treasury bonds more or less attractive to a German investor?

2. Explain why a fall in the exchange rate of the dollar against francs must be exactly the same as a rise in the exchange rate of francs against dollars.

3. If you were the treasurer of an international corporation, would you seek to find the place of highest return for your liquid capital? Why would the inflation rate enter into your calculations? Would you be concerned about the possible wider repercussions of your business decision? Do you think you could be—and still be an effective treasurer?

CHAPTER 24

Where Are We Headed?

A LOOK AHEAD

At the end of our book, we step back for a long historic overview.

1 This leads us first to consider the astonishing turnaround in expectations over the last 50 years. Half a century ago, capitalism was widely considered to be a dying economic system, socialism a rising one. Neither expectation has been fulfilled.

2 The reason for this turnabout lies partly in the issues we have covered in this book; namely, the evolution of both micro and macro policies within capitalism to ward off or contain its most self-destructive features. To an equal or even greater degree it lies in unforeseen difficulties within socialist economic planning.

3 The Soviet Union and China are today embarked on programs of deep restructuring that will bring back many elements of capitalism, especially the widespread use of a free market.

4 What does this mean for the prospects for capitalism? We hazard a risky look toward the future.

*I*n this last chapter we come back to the theme of the first—the trajectory of economic history. This time, however, we face toward the future rather than the past, to ask not where capitalism came from, but where it is going.

This is a question conventional economics does not generally address, and for good reason; the question goes far beyond the competence of economists as such. In the end, it will likely be considerations of political wisdom, of social morale, and of institutional adaptability that will determine the future of the United States, Japan, and the European nations that make up most of the capitalist world. The same is true for the future of the Soviet Union, China, and the East European countries that make up the socialisms of the world. And it is true once again for the Third World: the Brazils and Mexicos and Indias and Egypts that are struggling to find their place in the economic sun, some as capitalist economies, some as socialist ones, and some—we instance Iran—as neither.

All the knowledge of the historian, the political scientist, and the philosopher will not allow us to foretell this immense story in detail. Nevertheless, economics may teach us a few lessons that bear on—even if they do not allow us to predict—the shape of things to come.

A LOOK BACK OVER RECENT HISTORY

Yesterday's Outlook . . .

Let us start by reviewing an extraordinary turnabout in the way we perceive economic history itself. Here we must look back to the late 1930s—a mere blink of the eye as historic chronologies usually unfold. The direction of world economic change seemed very clear in those days: World capitalism appeared to be on the way out; world socialism on the way in. Without a single exception, the Western capitalist nations had gone through, or were still embroiled in, the most devastating economic depression in history. Ahead lay a world war whose outcome, most observers quite correctly foresaw, would be the destruction of capitalist colonial empires abroad and the emplacement of "socialistic" welfare schemes at home. Who could entertain optimistic expectations for capitalism in the face of such events and prospects?

Meanwhile, the fortunes of socialism were rising as dramatically as those of capitalism seemed to be fading. The Russian Revolution had seized the imagination of much of the world. In the old colonial regions, socialist parties and leaders were already preparing to reorganize the lands of Asia and Africa under the banner of national planning, whose galvanizing force had been made evident by the Soviet example. The coming war seemed to the Third World a great turning point, signaling the end of the old order and the beginning of the new. With such expectations, who would not have painted the socialist future in bright colors?

. . . And Today's

Need we say that things have not turned out that way? Capitalism is very much alive today, though not, as we know, in perfect health. More striking, socialism is in the midst of a transformation that is deliberately introducing into its midst many aspects of the capitalist system.

Perhaps most surprising of all, the Koreas and Mexicos and Third World countries generally have not left the fold of the capitalist system but have become even more enmeshed in it. Some of that entanglement is the result of their financial indebtedness to their former political and military opponents and masters. But perhaps more significant, the entanglement also proceeds from the emergence of new centers of industrial production in many countries that were certainly not capitalist 50 years ago—Hong Kong, Singapore, Taiwan, South Korea—and the strong signs of further capitalist development elsewhere—Brazil, Mexico, India. In the face of these events, who would today declare that capitalism is dying or that socialism is the wave of the future?

Why History Changed Course

Can we explain this astonishing change of historic course? Two generalizations will help us think about what has happened.

1. CAPITALISM HAS CHANGED. Capitalism is very much a vital economic force today, but it is not the same capitalism as that to which the gloomy predictions of the past applied. The nature of the change has been spelled out in the pages of this book and does not need to be reviewed here. At its core is the introduction into every advanced capitalist nation of measures to cushion the social (and political) effect of economic malfunction. We can summarize the change by saying that macroeconomic policies to improve and maintain economic growth, however imperfect, have effectively prevented the disaster of another Great Depression.

As every reader of this book must know, that certainly does not mean that capitalism is free of serious problems. Nonetheless, it helps explain the profound change that marks off capitalism's present self-assessment from that of the not-so-distant past. **The outlook for the future, at least in the major capitalist nations, no longer appears to be a choice between capitalism and socialism.** Rather, it concerns the *kind* of capitalism most likely to work well. The debates we have followed in our text—debates over Keynesian policies, welfare, government deficits, protectionism, industrial regulation—are taking place within a general consensus about the viability of capitalism very different from that of 50 years ago.

2. SOCIALISM HAS REVEALED UNEXPECTED ECONOMIC DIFFICULTIES. By and large, the early enthusiasts for socialism laid their bets on two aspects of a planned economic system. One was its capacity to move a backward, moribund economy off dead center. The other was its potential to eliminate the inefficiencies and wastefulness of capitalism. One of those bets paid off, at least in part. The other did not.

The bet that paid off was the ability of central planning to bring backward nations into the modern world. This was most dramatically evidenced in the Soviet Union (into whose history we shall shortly look) and in China. No one can compare the old Tsarist empire or the hopelessly inefficient Chinese landlord system with the societies created by the Soviets and the Chinese communists and not recognize that an unprecedented transformation has taken place, however horrendous the cost.

Getting a society off dead center is one thing; keeping it going is another. Here is the bet that socialism lost. **Without exception, the impressive socialist "take-offs" were followed by increasingly disappointing, and finally disastrous, economic performance.** Moreover, the reason for the failure was the same in every case—the vitality of the early stage of mobilization was followed by the inertia, then by the downright disorganization, of bureaucratization. The unexpected lesson of socialism was that planning was an easy word to spell, but a hard one to spell out. Planning was intended to be the remedy for the ills of capitalism; it became a remedy in many cases worse than the disease.

THE RUSSIAN EXPERIENCE

Let the reader be warned that this is not a final balance sheet on the outlook for either capitalism or socialism. Before we attempt that, we need to look a little more closely into the actual problems the two systems have confronted. From our preceding chapters we know something of the difficulties that capitalism has faced and the remedies it has devised and is still devising. But we have not yet had the chance to look at socialism, either as a historical success or as a failure. Hence let us follow its story in a thumbnail review of the single most important socialist state, the Soviet Union.

1. Planning under Lenin

Many of the problems of early Soviet history sprang from a total unawareness on the part of the original revolutionaries of the staggering difficulties of *actually running* an economy. In a famous passage in *State and Revolution,* Lenin wrote that the task of planning a socialist system would be mere child's play—no more than the "extraordinarily simple operations of watching, recording, and issuing receipts, within the reach of anybody who can read and who knows the first four rules of arithmetic."

Things quickly turned out to be considerably more difficult than that. As a result of disdain for "bourgeois" precepts about efficiency and because of the abolition of normal market relationships, industrial output declined precipitously. By 1920 it had fallen to *14 percent* of prewar levels. As manufactured goods became scarce, peasants became unwilling to part with their output for worthless money. The result was a wild inflation followed by degeneration into an economy of semibarter. For a while, toward the end of 1920, the socialist system was at the brink of complete collapse.

To forestall the impending disaster, Lenin instituted a New Economic Policy, the so-called NEP. This was, in effect, a partial reconstitution of capitalism. Retail trade was reopened to private ownership and small-scale private businesses were allowed to resume their undertakings. Most important, farm output was no longer requisitioned by the state for distribution to urban workers, but was sold at regular market prices. Only the "commanding heights" of large-scale industry and finance remained in government hands.

SOCIALISM AND COMMUNISM

What is the difference between *socialism* and *communism?* In the West, *socialism* implies an adherence to democratic political mechanisms, whereas *communism* does not. But within the socialist bloc there is another interesting difference of definition. Socialism there represents a stage of development in which it is still necessary to use "bourgeois" incentives in order to make the economy function; that is, people must be paid in proportion to the "value" of their work. Under communism, a new form of human society will presumably have been achieved in which these selfish incentives will no longer be needed. Then will come the time when society will be able to put into effect Karl Marx's famous description of communism: "From each according to his ability; to each according to his need." In a true communist economy—the final terminus of economic evolution envisioned by Marx—the necessary but humdrum tasks of production and distribution will be done through the voluntary cooperation of all citizens, and society will turn its serious attention to matters of cultural and humanistic importance.

2. Stalinist Collectivism

NEP recussitated the economy, but ushered in a period of intense debate. The debate was not over the basic aim of the Soviet government—that was still to replace private ownership in both industry and agriculture by state ownership and direction. The critical question was how fast to proceed. A slow pace of socialization meant that the institutions and psychology of private property and private enterprise would become more and more deeply embedded; a fast pace threatened to bring another spell of peasant resistance that might again throw the economy into turmoil. The question over which the debate raged was therefore the degree to which the peasant had to be "appeased" while the nation was inching toward socialism.

The argument was never truly resolved. In 1927 Stalin moved into command and cut the Gordian knot by forcibly collectivizing most peasant holdings—at gunpoint.

Forced collectivization solved in one swoop the question of how to get food from the country to the city, but it did so at frightful cost. Many peasants slaughtered their own livestock rather than have it commandeered by the government; others practiced sabotage to lower their crop yields. The Communist authorities reacted with brutal force. An estimated 5 million "kulaks" (rich peasants) were executed or put into labor camps, while in the cities an equally merciless discipline was used to secure industrial output. Workers were summarily ordered to the tasks required by the authorities; the right to strike was abolished; trade unions were reduced to impotence. Not surprisingly, living conditions fell to very low levels.

Nevertheless, in a very important sense, Stalinist policies "worked." Under Stalin's iron hand the Russian economy was transformed into a kind of war machine directed against the economic enemy of backwardness, as rail lines, electric power networks, steel complexes, and other essential elements of a modern economy were forcibly brought into being. Later this same war machine was used to sustain the Russian forces that finally turned the tide against Hitler's invading army.

A different way of putting it is that Stalinist planning was essentially directed at achieving "extensive" growth—growth through the addition of more manpower-hours of labor and capital inputs. Lacking was any interest in "intensive" growth—growth that emerged from higher productivity per worker, usually the consequence of new machinery or technological advance. Seweryn Bialer, a renowned expert on Russia, notes that 90 percent of the economic growth of the United States in the twentieth century was achieved through intensive growth, only 10 percent through extensive growth. In the Soviet Union, it was the other way around.*

3. The Postwar Period

Stalinism "worked" again in the years following World War II, when the ravaged Russian economy was rebuilt in a storm of energy resembling that of the early 1930s. Now, however, the problems of socialism began to change. For once the essential work of rebuilding had been accomplished, the main task of planning changed from construction to coordination. The challenge facing the planners was no longer to bring into being the basic framework of a modern industrial state but to make such a framework function effectively.

That proved to be much more difficult than the earlier effort. Under Stalin's successors, especially in the late years of Leonid Brezhnev, the system began to show alarming signs of failure. According to U.S. government estimates, real Soviet gross national product grew at an average annual rate of about 6.5 percent between 1965 and 1980, but from 1980 to 1985 it grew only by only 1.8 percent per year. In a few parts of the economy, where no expense was spared and where the bureaucracy was subordinated to the highly demanding requirement of special "consumers," the system had its triumphs—the Soviets launched the first space shot, built impressive military planes and tanks, and created whole new cities in strategic regions. But in other areas, where the special interests were not in a position to dominate the bureaucracy, very different results followed.

Bialer gives a few examples:

1. The Soviet Union produces twice as much steel as the United States, but there is a chronic shortage of steel. Why? Because Russia wastes steel in both capital and consumer goods, using much more than is employed in comparable items in the West.

2. The U.S.S.R. is the largest shoe producer in the world, but perhaps the worst—an average shoe may fall apart in a few weeks. Consequently, huge inventories of unwanted shoes rot in Soviet warehouses.

*Seweryn Bialer, "Gorbachev's Program of Change: Sources, Significance, Prospects," in Seweryn Bialer and Michael Mandelbaum, *Gorbachev's Russia and American Foreign Policy* (Westview Press, 1988), p 235.

3. Soviet educational facilities graduate three times as many engineers as American universities, but few of them qualify for U.S. jobs (if they emigrate here) because their training is so narrow.

4. The U.S.S.R. is the world's largest lumber producer, but it utilized only 30 percent of its timber by weight. In Canada, Sweden, and the United States, the utilization rate is 95 percent.*

These examples bear most sharply on the quality of consumer goods, and on the quality of consumer life. Civilian housing is so scarce that married couples often wait years for their own apartment. The level of civilian medical care has declined so sharply that life expectancy has actually declined in recent years. In 1985 only 23 percent of urban and only 7 percent of rural families had a telephone.

SOVIET PLANNING . . . AND PERESTROIKA

Why has Russian planning been an increasingly evident failure? Let us answer the question by learning how planning actually works—or at least how it worked until the present era of perestroika (restructuring), to which we will shortly turn.

The "Old" Soviet Planning System

Until recently, Soviet planning was carried out in successive stages. It began at the center, where the Gosplan, the official state planning agency, laid out the basic guidelines for a five-year effort. This five-year plan dictated such crucial matters as the rates at which consumption and investment would grow, the foreign trade balance with the Soviet Union's satellite states, and the priorities for basic research.

The five-year plan was then broken down into one-year plans. These one-year plans, specifying the output of major sectors of industry, were transmitted to various government ministries concerned with, for example, steel production, rail transportation, and lumbering. In turn, the ministries referred the one-year plans further down the line to the heads of large industrial plants, to experts and advisers, and so forth. Thus the overall design was unraveled into its constituent parts, until finally the threads were traced back as far as possible along the productive process—right to the officials in charge of factory operations.

Thus the factory manager of, say, a coking operation would be given a set of instructions to make his operations dovetail with those of the industries to which his output would flow and from which his inputs would arrive. The manager would then confer with his staff of production engineers and plant supervisors and would transmit up the line his requirements for meeting his "targets"—perhaps an authorization to hire more workers, or to order additional machines. In this way, "demand" requirements flowed down the chain of command and constraints of "supply" flowed back up, all coming together in a giant production blueprint (actually a vast series of computer printouts) in the Gosplan offices.

*Bialer, "Gorbachev's Program of Change," p. 242.

Success Indicators

As we can imagine, the coordination and integration of these plans was a fantastically complicated task. Even with the most sophisticated planning techniques, the process was slow, cumbersome, and mistake-prone. To get around the constant shortages that cropped up (bringing things to a grinding halt), factory managers were given strong financial incentives to *surpass* their planned output.

But this only introduced yet another problem. For the "success indicators" by which plan achievements were measured invariably produced their own bottlenecks and distortions. If the target for a textile mill were specified in yards of cloth, there was obviously a strong temptation to weave the cloth as loosely as possible to maximize the yardage from a given input of thread. If the success indicator was a measure of weight, the temptation was to skimp on quality or design. A cartoon in the satiric magazine *Krokodil* showed a nail factory proudly displaying its "record output"—one gigantic nail suspended by an immense gantry crane. The economic system was, in fact, soon heavily dependent on so-called *tolkatchi*—wheelers and dealers who arranged for shipments to be rerouted, shortages filled, and excess inventories disposed of—all behind the authorities' backs (but sometimes with their tacit permission).

Perestroika

It was to remove these suffocating inefficiencies that Mikhail Gorbachev began to speak of perestroika—the fundamental restructuring of the economic system—in 1985.

What is perestroika? We do not yet know because it still exists more in intention than in fact. Not until 1991 will we have the first five-year plan under the new arrangements about which Gorbachev has written and spoken. So we must content ourselves with a few central aims of the new system, some of which will surely be achieved in full, more of which will be achieved in part, and some of which will perhaps not be achieved at all.

1. There will still be five-year plans, but they will more closely resemble the general objectives of many European economies; specifying targets for GNP, for regional development, for levels and kinds of taxation, social policy, and the like. **With respect to the greater part of consumer output, virtually all planning will go.** Academician Nikolai Shmelev, an architect of perestroika, states that within a few years 70 percent of Soviet output will be subject to market disciplines and free prices. Old-style planning will remain only in strategic areas such as military production and perhaps for such important outputs as steel.

2. The Gosplan will continue, but the ministries of production that oversaw the production of nuts and bolts, shoes and sealing wax, will largely disappear or will play greatly reduced roles. **Production will be increasingly entrusted to the decisions of plant managers whose "success indicators" will be the profitability of their operations.**

3. So that they can earn profits, plant managers will be permitted to make their

own arrangements for delivery and for shipment. That is, instead of having inputs delivered to them as part of a plan, they will *buy* their inputs from whomever they please; and instead of shipping their outputs according to plan, they will have to *sell* their outputs as best they can. **This means that the economy will begin to be linked up by a market system instead of by a blueprint.**

4. **Managers will also be free to hire and to fire workers.** This will introduce the previously unknown element of labor discipline into the system. Today absenteeism is rife because workers know that they cannot be dismissed from their jobs for minor infringements.

5. **Many kinds of small businesses will be encouraged**—restaurants, small retail stores and wholesale establishments, automobile repair shops, and the like. More important, agricultural output will be increasingly (although not totally) provided by household plots or cooperatives (not collectives) selling their output on the market.

Can Perestroika Succeed?

Will perestroika attain its bold ends? The answer probably depends more on political than strictly economic factors. Perestroika will cost people jobs—not least the bureaucrats in the various production ministries whose work will be abolished and who will have to relocate themselves in the new economic structure. It will bring anxiety, perhaps some hardship, to workers who will not be able to count on assured employment. It will introduce the sweet taste of success for those who open profitable stores—and the sour taste of failure for those whose enterprises do not make the grade. It will require new attitudes that may bring down the charge of being "antisocialist" on the heads of those who hold them.

All this means that perestroika cannot possibly be an overnight success. The improvement in efficiency and consumer well-being is likely to come slowly; the pains of transition are likely to come more quickly. Seweryn Bialer reports that a major victory for perestroika would mean that 10 to 15 years from now the Soviet Union would cease *falling behind* the West!*

The new spirit of *glasnost* (openness) that is the political counterpart of restructuring means that those whose incomes or livelihoods or values are hurt will voice their protests freely and even vehemently.

So it would be foolhardy to assume that the economic (or the political) course of Russian socialism will abruptly change. But it would be even more foolish not to recognize perestroika as an epoch-making attempt to create a new and more efficient socialist economy, along with a new and more democratic socialist polity. It may be a decade before we will be able to evaluate the successes and failures of this historic experiment.

---

* Bialer, "Gorbachev's Program of Change," p. 272.

A MATTER OF NUMBERS

One gets a glimpse into the problems of perestroika in unexpected ways. A high-ranking Soviet economist called on one of the authors of this book, as we were writing this section, to talk about problems and prospects for "deplanning" the Soviet system. He was full of enthusiasm. "Do you realize," he asked, "that in three years we hope to reduce the number of planned prices from over *two million* to less than one thousand!"

The author was considerably impressed. But then he began to think. The two million prices included the price tag for each and every size of nail and screw, each and every cut of shirt and blouse, every item on the menus of the state's restaurants. This did indeed require a staggering number of price decisions, but the decisions did not profoundly affect the allocation of Soviet resources. The same could not be said about the "less than one thousand" prices that would remain under control, for they would doubtless include steel, coal, basic chemicals, and the like. Thus a number that signifies a free economy to someone who has lived in a controlled system still sounds like a planner's nightmare to someone accustomed to a market society.

MEANWHILE, IN CHINA

The Soviet Union is not the only socialist economy in which we find a turn toward the market. Equally stunning was the Chinese turnabout. Although far less industrialized than the Soviet Union, China has also suffered from bureaucratic sclerosis. Hence as early as 1956 Mao Zedong decided that China had to undertake a reform to decentralize the management of its economy.

The initial changes were not promising. Decision-making power shifted back and forth between Beijing and the provinces, bringing a cycle that the Chinese themselves described as "Relax control and get chaos; recentralize and get inertia." As with Gorbachev's perestroika, ending the impasse required the adoption of a bold new plan, proposed in 1979. Its nickname was DPRR, for "Delegate Power and Relinquish Revenues."

As its name suggests, DPRR aimed to release the Chinese economy from the paralytic effects of centralized planning. Hence it included a number of startling innovations to counterbalance the inertia of planned activity. The collective farm system was abandoned in favor of household production from land *rented* by peasant families! Small-scale private enterprise and cooperative undertakings were encouraged, and 80 million off-the-farm jobs were created in the agricultural sector. Local authorities were given autonomy over the expenditures of their share of tax revenues. And perhaps most significant, China opened its doors to foreign enterprise, taking the risk of becoming infected with the capitalist virus in exchange for the transfusion of Western technology. As with the Soviet system, key parts of the economy remained under state control, but here, too, an effort was made to encourage innovative and profit-seeking management.

Was DPRR a success? As a matter of economics, it is too soon to say. China did enjoy one of the highest growth rates in the world in the early 1980s. But economic liberalization sparked strong demands for political freedom, and this the regime was not prepared to grant. The brutal massacre of pro-democracy protesters in Tiananmen square in June of 1989 discredited China's government in the world community, and may have slowed or even stopped, for a time, progress toward a workable economic system.

Market Socialisms

Other departures from central planning can be found in the socialist world. In Yugoslavia much of the economy is today run in a "capitalistic," profit-seeking manner. At the same time, an effort has been made to bring socialist democracy "inside" these capitalist-like firms by establishing workers' councils that determine, together with the manager, how profits will be used, how wage scales will be set, and—at least in theory—whether the manager himself will be kept on! In Hungary more than 10,000 new small private enterprises were formed in 1980 with the approval of the authorities. During the next few years the entire growth of Hungarian national product came from these firms, not from the 1,000 large-scale state and cooperative enterprises. In Czechoslovakia, Bulgaria, and Poland similar kinds of experiments are under way, their successes or failures still to be determined.

What is important is that "market socialisms" of one kind or another have become the norm for socialist economies, taking the place of the centralized structures that were the norm only a decade ago. Market socialisms have not yet worked as their designers hoped. A sluggish core of central planning remains. Yet the political authorities are loathe to surrender central planning, lest the market mechanism become what many fear it will be—the nose of the capitalist camel under the socialist tent.

Thus, in all these new socialist systems we find a tension between the *economic* arguments of efficiency and the *political* arguments of social planning. In our view, this tension will not be easily resolved. The socialist governments will not permit a transition to a fully capitalist system. But neither do they want a return to the failed model of a centrally planned system. As a result, we are likely to see mixed socialist systems—generally free, capitalist-like consumer good sectors, with some kind of continuing government supervision of output and management in the central core of industrial production. Agreements will no doubt be concluded with foreign capitalist firms that will introduce new technologies and perhaps add the stimulus of competition, but it is doubtful that socialist economies will open themselves to world trade on a purely market basis. The rhetoric of socialism will surely persist—along with the siren songs of capitalism's life style. As far ahead as we can see—just to the horizon of the new edition we hope to produce three or four years hence—we picture socialism as a society with these conflicting tendencies.

PROSPECTS FOR CAPITALISM

The drift of planning toward markets in socialist countries raises a question of fundamental importance. Why plan at all? Why not let the market take over the task of coordination that has proved to be such a formidable hurdle for socialism, for is not the market itself a "planning" mechanism?

The question brings us back to the trajectory of history. If, as is surely the case today, the momentum of socialism is dampened, can we anticipate that the market system now has a clear field? Will capitalism continue, at least in the advanced Western societies, indefinitely?

Capitalism's Problems

That is the question with which the worldly philosophers wrestled, and as we recall from Chapter 3, they came to different conclusions. We cannot provide a resolution of their differences, and it is not within our abilities to answer the question itself more convincingly than they. Yet our economic studies, and now our brief survey of the problems of socialism, allow us to suggest a way of thinking about this all-important, but extraordinarily difficult, problem.

Let us begin by asking if there is one central difficulty that threatens capitalism in the same manner that the bureaucratic disease threatens socialism. The answer must surely spring to our minds from the topics we have covered in this book. As we would expect, it is the opposite of the problem of centralized planning: Planning's nemesis is its inability to break away from a plan. Capitalism's nemesis is its inability to formulate one. By "plan" we do not mean a blueprint for the entire economy. We mean the formulation of social objectives other than those that arise from the workings of the marketplace itself.

It is certainly easy to remind ourselves of the manner in which this difficulty appears. Perhaps the most egregious example is the tendency of market systems to tolerate poverty because they do not generate nonmarket mechanisms of distribution adequate to the needs of the poor. Another problem is the failure of capitalisms to pay sufficient attention to the quality of life, turning a blind eye to the deficiencies and excesses (urban blight side by side with conspicuous consumption) that emerge in a society following the guidance of the market. Yet a third are the malfunctions generated by the workings of capitalism itself—its succession of booms and busts, its persisting inability to provide employment for all who seek it, its tendency to generate huge enterprises that defy the very power of the nation-state itself.

The Rise of Capitalist Planning

These difficulties are as deeply rooted in the workings of the market system of capitalism as the difficulties of socialism are rooted in the workings of its system of central allocation. Moreover, just as the problems of socialism could be ignored during its early stages, when the full force of the planning operation was working its mobilizing miracles, so the drawbacks of the market mechanism could be ignored in the early phases of capitalism, while the system was availing itself of the tremendous capacity of the market to match output to market demand.

But as a market society becomes more advanced, its requirements change, just as do those of a socialist society. These latter, as we have seen, desperately need the flexibility and adaptability that central planning cannot give. And capitalisms begin to need the presence of public guidance that the market cannot provide. **The result is that just as we see socialisms turning toward the market, we have seen capitalisms turn toward the state.**

Central planning, to repeat, is not the answer. The planning mechanisms of capitalism comprise the whole range of measures by which it intervenes in, seeks to change the course of, and tries to overcome the problems that arise from the unhindered market. Planning in capitalism therefore embraces its taxes, its fiscal policy and monetary policies, its programs of public investment, its measures of income support and redistribution, its regulation of big business—in short, the gamut of public activities whose various forms and modes of application we have followed in the pages past. Now, however, we no longer view these policies piecemeal, but see them as a response of the system to its problems, similar, in mirror fashion, to the quite opposite response of socialism to its chief functional difficulty.

Politics vs. Economics

Will these measures guarantee the longevity of capitalism? That question can no more be answered with assurance than the same questions directed at socialism. We know from past experience that the malfunctions of capitalism can be very grave. We believe these malfunctions can be made socially tolerable, even if not removed. But here, too, we have no alternative but to await the verdict of history.

One last word must be said with respect to this verdict. We spoke in the opening paragraphs of this chapter about capitalisms and socialisms, not capitalism and socialism. It is wise to return to this careful phrasing as we reach the end of our book. It is likely that there will be successful capitalisms and unsuccessful ones, just as it is probable that some socialisms will flourish and some will not. "In the end," to repeat the words of our opening page, "it will likely be considerations of political wisdom, of social morale, and of institutional adaptability that will determine the futures of the . . . nations that make up most of the capitalist world. The same is true for the . . . countries that make up the socialist world."

Common Problems

That final emphasis brings us to one last generalization about the future. It is that we have spoken of the great differences between the two great world systems, but have ignored their equally great common concerns. Three in particular deserve our attention.

1. CONTROL OVER TECHNOLOGY. All modern societies tend to find that their technological capabilities are constantly increasing, while the social, political, and moral institutions by which those capabilities are controlled cannot

match the challenges with which they are faced. Television, for example, is an immense force for cultural homogenization; medical technology changes the composition of society by altering its age groups and life expectancy; rapid transportation vastly increases mobility and social horizons; and the obliterative power of nuclear arms casts a pervasive anxiety over all of life. All these technologically rooted developments fundamentally alter the conditions and problems of life, but we do not know what social, political, and moral responses are appropriate to them. As a result, all modern societies—socialist and capitalist— experience the feeling of being at the mercy of a technological and scientific impetus that shapes the lives of their citizens in ways that cannot be accurately foreseen nor adequately controlled.

2. THE PROBLEM OF DEMOCRACY. The second problem derives from the first. Because advanced societies are characterized by high levels of technology, they are necessarily marked by a high degree of organization. The technology of our era depends on the cooperation of vast masses of people, some at the levels of production, some at the levels of administration. The common undergirding of all advanced industrial societies lies not alone in their gigantic instrumentalities of production, but also in their equally essential and vast instrumentalities of administration, whether these be called corporations, production ministries, or government agencies.

The problem, then, is how the citizen is to find a place for his or her individuality in the midst of so much organization; how he or she is to express his or her voice in the direction of affairs, when so much bureaucratic management is inescapable; how he or she is to participate in a world whose technological structure calls for ever more order and coordination. This is a matter which, like the sweeping imperative of technology, affects both capitalism and socialism. In both kinds of societies, individuals feel overwhelmed by the impersonality of the
work process, impotent before the power of huge enterprises—above all, the state itself—and frustrated at an inability to participate in decisions that seem more and more beyond any possibility of personal influence.

No doubt much can be done to increase the feeling of individual participation in the making of the future, especially in those nations that still deny elementary political freedoms. But there remains a recalcitrant problem of how the quest for increased individual decision-making and participation can be reconciled with the organizational demands imposed by the technology on which all advanced societies depend. This is a problem that is likely to trouble societies—capitalist or social-ist—as long as technology itself rests on integrated processes of production and requires centralized organs of administration and control.

3. THE PROBLEM OF THE ENVIRONMENT. All industrial nations may be facing an era in which economic growth begins to absorb resources at rates faster than we are able to provide them with new technologies; **and all industrialized societies— indeed, the whole world—may soon enter a time in which environmental limitations come into conflict with expectations of growth.**

In this period industrial socialist and capitalist nations again seem likely to share common problems—not only in overcoming environmental limits to growth, but also in achieving social harmony under conditions of increasing resource diversion

A PERSONAL VIEW ABOUT PLANNING

For reasons that are strewn throughout these pages, we expect that the long-term trend in most capitalist nations will be toward some kind of "planning." There are many such kinds, and that which works in one capitalist nation, such as Japan, may be totally inapplicable to another, like Italy or Canada or ourselves. Each nation must find its own way of devising macro and micro policies.

Thus we do not predict any particular direction of kind of planning for the United States. What we do expect is that the problems and market forces and technological capabilities of our age will blur the present distinction between "public" and "private" spheres, moving us, together with other capitalisms, in a direction that will have more business-government integration, more labor-management coordination, perhaps more national insulation against international competition.

This is a view which is deplored by the Left and denounced by the Right. Beyond that, both declare that planning does not work. They are certainly correct that planning does not work very well. What clearer evidence could there be for that than the universal presence of a crisis in all capitalist nations, despite the drift into planning of various kinds? But this objection misses a key consideration. It is that no manner of guiding society, from the most centralized to the most laissez-faire, can be expected to produce a smoothly working system in the face of today's social, political, and technological forces. The very elements that underlie our contemporary troubles—the tensions that divide the rich and poor nations, the impact of technologies of awesome power, the narrowing of ecological tolerances, the disappearance of the public fatalism of the past—must trouble any kind of economic system and any kind of government. It is not capitalism alone that is in crisis, but all modern industrial society. **A realistic attitude toward planning is not that it should work well, but that it should work *well enough*.** That seems a goal within reach.

toward public rather than private goods. Here, too, similar social and political problems may override differences in economic institutions and ideologies.

Envoi

In a larger sense, then, we go beyond economics to the common human adventure in which economic systems are only alternate routes conducting humanity toward a common destination. Perhaps it is well that we end our survey of economics with the recognition that the long history of the market system does not project us onto a final stage in social history. Rather, we arrive at a state in which some kinds of problems,—the pitifully simple problems of producing and distributing goods— find resolution, only to reveal vastly larger problems springing from the very technology and organization that supplied the earlier answers.

LOOKING BACK

The end of a long book is a time for celebration, not homework. This is a chapter to think about, not to "learn." It does not lend itself to neat summaries and vocabulary items. We hope, rather, that it will bring the study of economics to a conclusion on a high note rather than a low one, and that it will leave you with the feeling that a subject of immense interest and importance awaits further exploration—by you.

Glossary

Allocation   The act of apportioning or distributing resources or incomes.

Antitrust legislation   Legislation designed to minimize or prevent monopolistic behavior or monopolistic market structures.

Appreciation of exchange   A rise in the ability of one nation's currency to buy the currency of another nation.

Average productivity   The contribution to output of the average unit of any input. This is obtained by dividing total output by the number of units of the input. It is not the same as the contribution of the last, or marginal unit.

Backward-bending supply curve   A supply curve of labor services that displays a preference for fewer hours of labor (more leisure) when the price of labor rises above a certain level.

Balance of payments   A set of accounts that records transactions between two countries. (See *Balance on capital* and *Current accounts.*)

Balance on capital account   The net sum of demands and supplies for foreign exchange for all items on capital account, mainly direct and portfolio investment.

Balance on current account   The net sum of demands for and supplies of foreign exchange for all items on current account, mainly merchandise exports and imports and similar transactions.

Bonds   Obligations issued by private or public institutions with fixed dates of repayment and stated interest rates or coupons. (See *Yields.*)

Budget   The amount of spending power possessed by an economic actor.

Capital   Wealth in an abstract form produced by capitalism. Also often used to refer to a financial sum of wealth.

Capital goods   Final output used for production, not consumption. (See *Investment.*)

Capitalism   An economic system oriented toward the accumulation of capital (or generalized, abstract wealth), coordinated by a market system in which land, labor, and capital have become "factors of production."

Capitalization   Calculation of a sum of wealth by dividing a flow of income by a rate of interest. A piece of land that yields an income of $100 is capitalized at $1,000 if interest rates are 10 percent ($1,000 ÷ 0.10 = $100) or at $500 if interest rates are 20 percent.

Capital/output ratio   Relationship between the values of the capital stock and the flow of output of a firm, industry, or nation. Marginal capital/output ratios relate increases in output to increases in the capital stock.

Ceteris paribus   Latin phrase meaning "other things being equal." The phrase refers to the need to allow for variations in the conditions that affect an experiment or an observation. For example, *ceteris paribus* requires us to make allowance for changes in income or taste when we are seeking to establish the relation of quantity demanded and price.

Clearing markets   A market condition in which quantities demanded just balance quantities supplied.

Cobwebs   Erratic jumps in prices that characterize markets which do not constantly adjust over time. Cobwebs may describe a sequence of prices that "explode" or oscillate or gradually converge to equilibrium.

Comparative advantage   The relative edge enjoyed by one nation (or region or economic actor) in producing one commodity compared to another. A country can have a comparative advantage in producing a commodity even if its absolute productivity in that commodity is less than that of its trading partner.

Competition   The vying of buyers and sellers in a marketplace. Competition has two aspects: (1) the contest of buyers against sellers, (2) the mutual rivalry of sellers against sellers and buyers against buyers.

Complement   The technical linkage of commodities, such as cars and gasoline. Increases in the demand for a commodity automatically raise the demand for its complement.

Concentration   The degree of market control enjoyed by the largest firms in an industry. Concentration ratios often measure the percentage of industry sales enjoyed by the largest four or eight firms.

Conglomerates   Large corporations, usually formed by merger, that operate in widely different markets.

Constraints   Barriers or boundaries to desired behavior.

Consumer sovereignty   The power exerted by consumer demand over the allocation of resources.

Cost   Cost in everyday speech refers to the expenses incurred in production. In economics it refers to missed opportunities—opportunities foregone because resources are committed to a given use. This is called opportunity cost. (See also *Sunk cost.*)

Cost-benefit analysis   The attempt to calculate the direct and indirect costs and benefits, whether paid or not, of any economic action.

Cost push   An explanation of inflation that stresses increases in factor prices such as higher real wages, or the increase in cost of resources or other inputs. (See *Demand pull.*)

Credit crunch   A severe restriction of bank credit, forcing the drastic curtailment of bank lending to businesses or consumers.

Deficit spending   Spending financed not by current tax receipts, but by borrowing or by drawing on past reserves.

Demand   Willingness and ability to buy. Demand is a schedule that relates the quantities demanded with differing prices. (See also *Quantity demanded.*)

Dependent variables   Quantities whose value is determined by the value of another "independent" variable, contained in the equation.

Depreciation   The decline in the value of capital goods over time. The term is also used to designate funds set aside to replace the worn-out capital.

Depreciation of exchange   A fall in the ability of one nation's currency to buy the currency of a foreign nation.

Derived demand   Demand for factors of production that results from the demand for goods and services.

Devaluation   A policy deliberately intended to cheapen the exchange value of a currency in order to encourage exports. (Technically, devaluation means cheapening a currency in terms of gold.)

Diminishing returns   The eventual tendency of outputs to rise more slowly than input as more and more of one factor is added to fixed amounts of other factors. Also known as the *law of variable proportions.*

Direct investment   Investment in plant and equipment, as contrasted with financial investment.

Direct taxes   Taxes levied by local, state, or federal governments on incomes.

Diseconomies of scale   Increases in unit cost resulting from inefficiencies of technology or organization at rising levels (scales) of output.

Distribution   The process of allocating output or income among the population. Also used to refer to the results of this process, for example when we say that "income distribution is very unequal."

Economic profit   Profit after the deduction of interest on capital. Profit is any residual after all factors have been paid their full values.

Economic rent   (See *Quasi rent.*)

Economies of scale   Reductions of cost resulting from improved technology or organization at rising levels (scales) of output.

Efficiency   Relation of output to input.

Elasticity   A measure of the relation between price and quantity, or between income and quantity. If the percentage change in quantity demanded is greater than the percent change in price or income, we speak of elastic demand; if it is less, of inelastic demand.

Endogenous   Influences internal to a system. The rise in income that results from the multiplier effect is endogenous to the determination of GNP.

Entrepreneur   The person whose economic task is to direct the enterprise. His or her main task is to choose the proper scale, to make the best combination of factors, and to establish the best level of output. The entrepreneur may or may not own the enterprise, and therefore may or may not receive profits.

Entry   The ability to move into a market or line of production.

Equations   Mathematical statements usually involving dependent and independent variables in a functional relationship.

Equilibrium   A self-correcting and self-perpetuating level of prices or economic activity. Equilibrium prices equate quantities demanded and supplied, and thereby "clear" markets. Equilibrium flows of output, such as GNP, balance opposing tendencies of savings and investment to create a self-perpetuating flow.

Equimarginal rule   The general guide to optimization through equalizing the marginal returns of all factors.

Equity   Ownership, usually stock ownership.

Eurodollars   Supplies of dollars held by foreign or American banks outside the U.S.

Ex ante   The view looking forward. Ex ante refers to economic activity that has not yet taken place. Ex ante quantities or values may therefore differ from ex post figures, after the event.

Excess capacity   A market situation in which the capacity to produce is larger than the output desired by the market. Excess capacity is typical of oligopolistic industries.

Exchange rate   The price of foreign currencies in terms of one's own currency.

Exogenous   Influences originating outside the system. An exogenous influence on GNP would be a change in the weather, or a war.

Exploitation   Payment to a factor of less than the value of the output it produces.

Ex post   The view looking backward. Ex post refers to economic activity that has already happened. (See *Ex ante.*)

Externalities   Effects (good or bad) imposed by the act of production, or consumption, for which no price is charged. A typical bad or negative externality is the pollution imposed on the public by smoke from a factory.

Factor market   The market in which the services of labor, land, or capital are sold. Factor markets regulate wages, rents, and interest rates.

Factor of production   The name given to the main kinds of inputs, land, labor, and capital, in a market society.

Federal Reserve banks   One of the 12 federally created central banks. Commercial banks may become members of the Federal Reserve System, but are not themselves Federal Reserve banks.

Fiscal policy   Government efforts to control the level of employment or prices by spending and taxing, rather than by monetary policy.

Fixed costs   Costs that do not change with the level of output. These are usually contractual costs such as rent, depreciation, etc.

Fixed exchange rates   Exchange relationships between currencies fixed by government agreement and maintained by the action of central banks.

Foreign exchange   Supplies of foreign currencies held by the banks or government of any nation.

Free riding   The ability of economic actors to enjoy the utilities of certain outputs without paying for them.

Full employment budgets   Calculation of the impact on GNP of government receipts and expenditure flows assuming that receipts and expenditures are at the levels corresponding to full employment.

Functional relationships   Relationships in which the value of one variable is determined by another.

Graphs   Visual representations of functional relationships or of the movements of variables through time.

Gross national income   The sum of factor incomes, tax receipts, and depreciation accruals. GNI is always identical with GNP.

Growth   Increase in output. (See *Nominal growth* and *Real growth.*)

Horizontal equity   A pattern of tax incidence that results in equal payments of tax among all members of the same income level.

Human capital   The money value of skills or education.

Identities   Mathematical statements of definition.

Imperialism   Domination by a highly developed, powerful nation. Specifically used to describe the penetration of capitalist nations into the underdeveloped world.

Incidence of taxation   The pattern of impact of taxation. The incidence of taxation attempts to discover where the burden of a tax ultimately falls.

Incomes policy   Anti-inflation measures that depend on voluntary acceptance of income limitations, such as moderated wage demands.

Increasing cost   The tendency of cost per unit to rise as the volume of output exceeds the point of greatest efficiency. (See *Law of increasing cost.*)

Increasing returns   The initial tendency of output to rise faster than input, as one factor is added to fixed amounts of other factors.

Independent variables   Quantities whose value is determined independently—that is, outside the equation.

Indexing   Adjustment of nominal payments in accordance with a price index.

Indirect taxes   Taxes levied by local, state, or federal government on the value of output. Cigarette or gas taxes are instances of indirect taxes.

Industrial policy   The use of government policies to encourage (or discourage) industries, especially in international trade.

Infant industries   Newly founded industries, especially in developing nations, that require tariff protection in order to achieve competitive scale.

Inflation   A process in which prices in nearly all markets display a chronic upward tendency.

Interest   The price of the factor capital.

Intermediate goods   Goods or services that enter into final goods. For example, wheat is an intermediate good entering into bread.

Intersectoral offsets   Spending by one sector, usually business or government, used to offset the insufficient spending of another sector.

Inventories   Goods on raw materials that have been produced but not yet sold to final purchasers. All increases in inventories are counted in the national accounts as net investment.

Investment   The act of building capital. (See *Real vs. financial investment.*)

Invisible hand   A famous phrase used by Adam Smith to indicate that individuals who followed their private self-interest would in fact fulfill a larger purpose, as if "led by an Invisible Hand."

Kondratieff cycle   A cyclical pattern of roughly 25 buoyant and 25 stagnant years that may describe capitalist history. Its mechanism and even its existence are uncertain.

Law of increasing cost   Eventual tendency of costs of a given output to rise as additional inputs of all factors (not just one) are used to produce it.

Law of variable proportions   The tendency of output first to rise more rapidly than input, then more slowly, as one factor is added to fixed amounts of other factors.

Liquidity preference   The differing proportions of one's wealth that one seeks to hold in liquid form at differing interest rates. High interest rates impose high opportunity costs on holding cash. Therefore, usually we prefer to be less liquid when we can use our cash to earn high interest. Conversely, we seek more liquidity when the opportunity cost is low. Risk also plays an important part in determining our willingness to be liquid or illiquid.

M1   (See *Money supply.*)

Marginal   Additional, incremental (plus or minus).

Marginal cost   The change in the cost of a firm resulting from a change in its output.

Marginal productivity   The change in output that can be ascribed to the addition or subtraction of any factor.

Marginal revenue   The change in the revenue of a firm resulting from a change in its output.

Market share   Proportion of an industry's sales enjoyed by a firm.

Market socialism   Socialist economies that continue to use markets as allocation mechanisms or as incentive systems, in addition to central planning of major elements such as investment.

Market system   The structure of exchange relations of buying and selling that sustains the economic process of capitalism.

Maximizing   The driving force of economic activity described as the pursuit of the largest possible amount of pleasurable wealth.

Mercantilism   The prevailing mode of economic organization in the period between late feudalism and early capitalism, characterized by a highly regulated domestic economy and an effort to achieve a surplus of exports over imports.

Microeconomics   That portion of economics concerned with the activity of individuals and firms, mainly with regard to the allocation of resources.

Mixed economies   Economies that combine attributes of capitalism, such as private property and market mechanisms, with elements of socialism, in particular welfare structures and some degree of government control over economic activity.

Mobility   The capacity to change economic location or function.

Monopolistic competition   Market structures in which there are large numbers of sellers of differentiated products.

Monopoly   A single seller who supplies the entire output of a given market.

Multinational corporations   Corporations that derive a substantial proportion of their income or sales from overseas production, as contrasted with exports.

National income   The total amount of factor incomes earned over a period of time. National income does not include transfer payments.

Nationalization   Purchase or seizure by the government of a privately owned firm.

Net national product   Gross national product minus depreciation. Net national product is also national income (factor earnings) plus the value of indirect taxes.

Nominal growth   Increase in output measured in current dollars, without allowance for changes in the purchasing power of dollars. If we compare the GNPs of two years, without deflating the dollar amounts, we are comparing nominal growth.

Nominal values   The values or prices of objects in current terms with no adjustment for changes in the value of the monetary unit.

Oligopoly   A market structure in which output is provided by a small enough number of sellers so that one seller can anticipate that others will react to changes in his strategy. In a competitive market there are so many participants that no firm can expect its own actions to disturb the workings of the market.

Opportunity cost   The wealth or enjoyments that cannot be obtained because resources or inputs are already committed to a given purpose. All economic activities entail opportunity cost. Every act of consumption or production rules out the possibility of some alternative action.

Optimization   The search for the most efficient allocation of wealth or resources.

Overhead cost   Costs associated with administration or sales, rather than with direct factory-floor production.

Per capita GNP   Gross national product divided by the population.

Perestroika   The restructuring of the Soviet economy by enlarging the sphere of private decision making.

Physiocracy   A school of economic thought developed by Francois Quesnay (1694–1774) that stressed the productive power of the land.

Portfolio investment   Financial investment, as opposed to real investment in plant and equipment.

Price index   A statistical measure of price levels in which one year is chosen as a base, and the other years expressed as a percentage of that base.

Price leadership   Role played by an industry leader that is the first to change prices in an oligopolistic market.

Production   The use of labor and resources to create wealth.

Productivity   A measure of output per unit of input over a given period of time, such as yearly or hourly output per worker or per machine.

Progressive incidence   A pattern of taxation that imposes proportionally heavier burdens on high income groups than on low income groups.

Proportional incidence   A pattern of taxation that imposes equal percentage burdens on all income levels.

Psychic income   The value of nonmonetary income in terms of utilities.

Public goods   Outputs provided by the public sector and not allocated by the price mechanism.

Purchasing power   The ability to buy.

Pure competition   A market structure characterized by large numbers of actors, easy entry and exit, undifferentiated products, and widespread information about market conditions.

Quantity demanded   The amount of a commodity or service that we are willing and able to buy at a given price. (See also *Demand.*)

Quantity supplied   The amount of a commodity or service that we are willing and able to supply at a given price. (See also *Supply.*)

Quasi rent   Returns to a factor that derive solely from its scarcity, above the returns needed to induce the factor into production. Also called economic rent.

Rationality   The assumption that people can intelligently adapt their actions (means) to their purposes (ends).

Rationing   The distribution of resources according to some allocation mechanism. The mechanism may be the price system, or it may be a nonmarket system, such as coupons.

Real growth   Increases in output corrected for changes in the purchasing power of the currency.

Regressive incidence   A pattern of taxation that imposes proportionally larger burdens on low income groups than on high ones.

Rent   Rent is the return paid to the owner of land or any resource for the use of his property. It is a payment necessary to bring that resource into production, and therefore differs from a quasi rent, which is a payment that results only from scarcity and is larger than that needed to bring the factor into use.

Reserve requirement   The proportion of deposits that must be kept in vault cash or at a Federal Reserve bank. Reserve requirements are set by the Board of Governors of the Federal Reserve System.

Reserves   Deposits that may not be loaned or invested. Reserves must be held in cash or at a Federal Reserve bank.

Scale   The size of operations, mainly of a plant. Scale is usually determined by the physical characteristics of the capital equipment used, although land or labor may be the determining elements.

Schedule   A list of different values of a variable, such as quantities or prices.

Sector   A division of the economy with common characteristics. Usually we speak of the public and the private sector; of the consumption, investment, and government sectors; or of the agricultural, industrial, and service sectors.

Shortage   The failure of a market to clear when the price is below equilibrium levels and there are unsatisfied buyers at the going price.

Sticky prices The tendency of many prices to remain unchanged despite changes in demand and supply. This may be the consequence of contracts (a wage or rent contract) or of institutional inertia.

Stocks Legal instruments of ownership in corporations.

Substitution The capacity of one commodity to provide the utilities of another. Increases in the price of a commodity result in increases in the demand for its substitutes.

Sunk cost The cost, either in money or in foregone opportunities, that has been incurred up to the present with respect to any economic act of production.

Supply Willingness and ability to sell. Supply is a schedule that relates the quantities offered with differing prices. (See also *Quantity supplied.*)

Supply-side economics Policies seeking to use taxes or deregulation to impart a strong momentum to the economy.

Surplus The failure of a market to clear when the price is above equilibrium levels and there are unsatisfied sellers at the going price.

Terms of trade A comparison of the quantities of goods that are required to gain a given amount of goods in return. For example, the Brazilian terms of trade could measure the number of sacks of coffee needed to "buy" a computer.

Tight money A condition, associated with restrictive monetary policy, that makes it difficult for borrowers to obtain bank loans.

Tradeoff An exchange relationship denoting how much of A is needed to obtain a unit of B.

Transactions demand The amount of cash we need to carry on normal economic transactions. At higher levels of economic activity there is normally a higher demand for transactions balances, for such purposes as meeting payrolls or financing ordinary expenditures.

Transfers Any payment from one person or institution to another made for purposes other than to remunerate work. Social security is a transfer payment; so is the payment of an allowance to a minor, or a charity payment.

Unemployment Inability to find acceptable work at the going wage level.

Utility Pleasure or well-being.

Variable costs Costs that change directly with output, such as wages, or materials costs.

Variable proportions See (*Law of variable proportions.*)

Wealth Production that yields utilities.

Index